Toronto
Public
Library

3 9100 00062 116 2

86702

D0847487

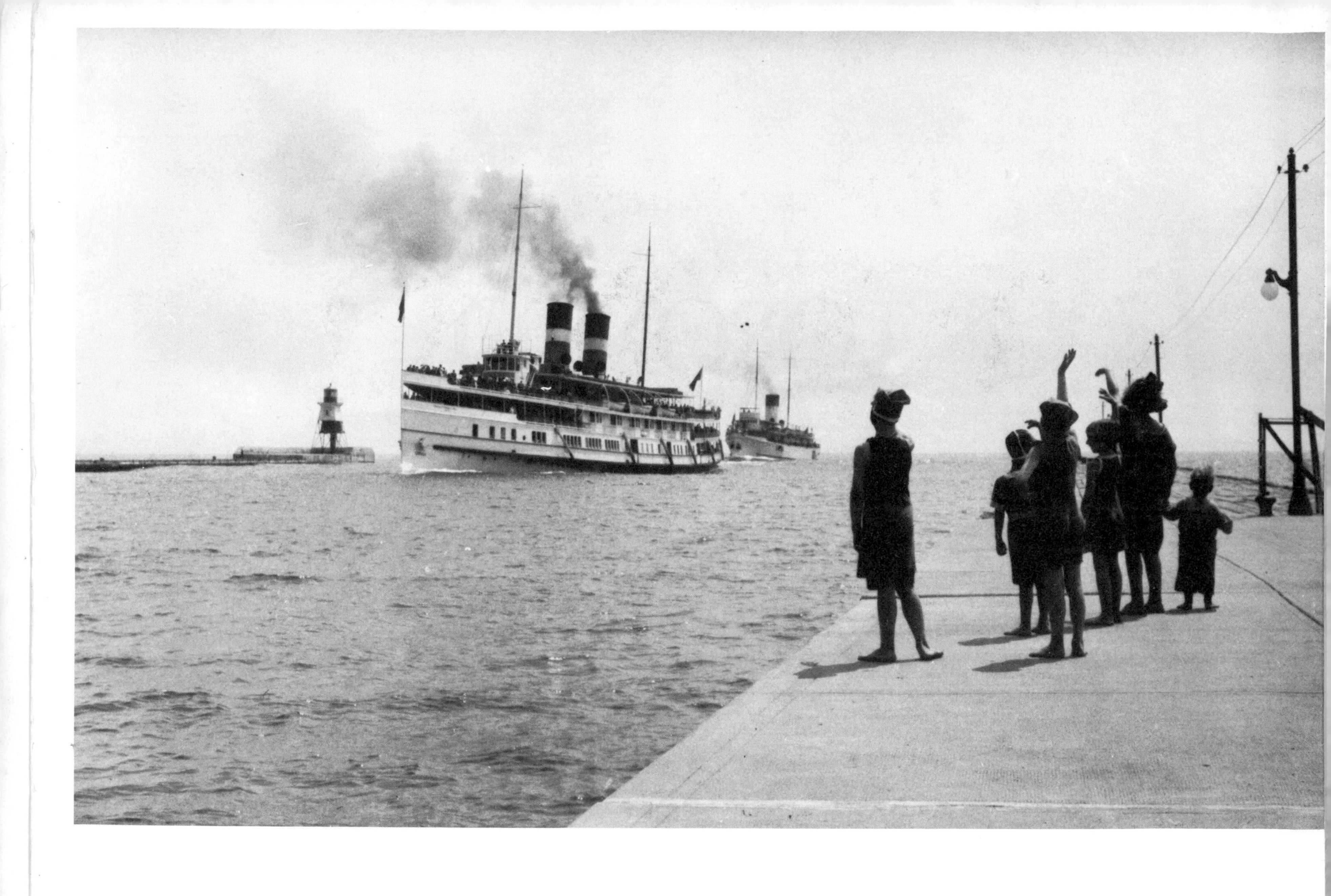

N 0-88862-738-6 cloth

r design: Don Fernley

raphy: Department of Geography, University of Toronto

Cataloguing in Publication Data

ames T.

nce 1918

y of Canadian cities)

by the National Museum of Man, National

anada.

218

History. 2. Toronto (Ont.) —

tional Museum of Man (Canada)

971.3′541 C84-099504-0

5

blishers

lding

85 86 87 88 89 90

This book has been published with the help of a grant from the Social Science Federation of Canada, using funds provided by the Social Sciences and Humanities Research Council of Canada.

Illustration Credits

Illustrations are reproduced courtesy of: *Toronto City Archives:* 10, 15 top, 16, 18, 24, 28, 29, 30, 32 left, 40 top, 44 bottom right, 46, 47, 49, 52 top left, 61, 66, 67, 69, 71 bottom, 72, 78 bottom, 97 top, 101 bottom, 103, 143, 179, 190, back cover top left and top right. *Canapress Photo Service:* 36, 58, 87 bottom, 88, 100, 121, 127 left, 131, 144, 148 left, 149, 155, 159, 161, 163, 165, 169, 171, 172, 180, 182, 185, 191, back cover bottom left. *York University Archives, Telegram Collection:* 63, 80, 89, 91, 95, 107, 117, 124 top, 127 right, 129 top, 132, 137, 141, 153 bottom right, 162, 188. *Public Archives of Canada:* 2, 15 bottom, 27 bottom, 39 right, 44 except bottom right, 49, 52 top right, 55, 78 top, 93, 97 bottom. *Globe and Mail:* 71, 83 left, 98, 112, 123, 124 bottom, 133, 139, 150, 153 top and bottom left, 156, 181, back cover bottom right. *Toronto Star Syndicate:* 22 left, 83 right, 148 right. *Metropolitan Toronto Library:* 27 top, 32 right, 40 bottom, 52 bottom. *Archives, Toronto Board of Education:* 20, 129 bottom, 175. *Commonwealth Microfilms:* 22 right, 75. *Archives, Eaton's of Canada:* 39 left, 146. *Mike Filey:* 48, 76. *United Church Archives:* 54, 56. *Multi-cultural History Society of Ontario/Ontario Archives:* 73. *Maclean's Magazine:* 86, 119. *Massey-Ferguson Limited:* 87 top. *Toronto Harbour Commission:* 101 top. *City of Toronto:* back flap. *Masterfile:* front cover.

The History of Canadian Cities

TORONTO

SINCE 1918

An Illustrated History

James Ler

James Lorimer & Comp
and
National Museum of M
National Museums of Cana
Toronto 1985

P
w
ISB
Cove
Cartog

Canadian
Lemon, J
Toronto s
(The Histor
Co-publishe
Museums of C
Includes index.
Bibliography: p.
1. Toronto (Ont.) —
Description. I. Na
II. Title. III. Series.
FC3097.4.L45 1985
F1059.5.T6857L45 198

James Lorimer & Company, P
Egerton Ryerson Memorial Bu
35 Britain Street
Toronto, Ontario M5A 1R7
Printed and bound in Canada
6 5 4 3 2 1

Table of Contents

List of Tables 6

List of Maps 6

Foreword: The History of Canadian Cities Series 7

Acknowledgements 8

Introduction: Essential Toronto 11

Chapter One: The Silver Age, 1918-1929 19

Chapter Two: The Dirty Thirties 59

Chapter Three: Planning for Growth, 1940-1953 81

Chapter Four: Toronto's Mosaic, 1954-1966 113

Chapter Five: Multicultural and Financial Metropolis, 1955-1984 151

Conclusion: Toronto Past and Future 189

Appendix: Statistical Tables 194

Notes 200

A Note on Sources 218

Index 219

List of Maps

1. City Wards and the Balkanization of the Suburbs in the 1920s 34
2. Land Use 1914 and Built-up Area, 1914 and 1931 42
3. City Planning Board's Neighbourhood Classifications, 1944 105
4. Metro Toronto in the 1953, and Built-up Area, 1966 135
5. Proposed Metropolitan Toronto Plan, 1959 140
6. Metropolitan Toronto and Municipal Wards, 1975 154
7. Toronto-centred Region Plan, 1970 167
8. Distribution of Jewish Population in Metro Toronto, 1981 176
9. Distribution of Italian Population in Metro Toronto, 1981 176
10. Distribution of Other Non-English Population in Metro Toronto, 1981 177
11. Average Household Income in Metro Toronto, 1980 177

Appendix
List of Tables

I Population Growth in Toronto and Region, 1911-1981
II Population Growth in Toronto and Suburbs, 1911-1981
III Urban Population Growth and Distribution in Ontario, 1911-1981
IV Age Composition of Toronto's Population, 1921-1981
V School Enrollments in City of Toronto, Selected Years
VI Birthplace of Toronto's Canadian-born Population, 1911-1961
VII Birthplace of Toronto's Foreign-born Population, 1911-1981
VIII Ethnic Origins of Toronto's Population, 1911-1981
IX Religious Affiliations of Toronto's Population, 1911-1981
X Toronto's Labour Force, 1911-1981
XI Growth and Decline of Manufacturing in Toronto, Metro and CMA, Selected Years
XII Economic Comparisons: Toronto vs Other Cities, Selected Years
XIII Value of Buildings Erected and Assessment, Selected Years
XIV Housing in Toronto and Montreal, 1921-1981
XV Public Transportation in Toronto, Selected Years
XVI Municipal Expenditure, Toronto and Metro, Selected Years

Foreword
The History of Canadian Cities Series

The History of Canadian Cities Series is a project of the History Division, National Museum of Man (National Museums of Canada). The project was begun in 1977 to respond to a growing demand for more popular publications to complement the already well-established scholarly publications programs of the Museum. The purpose of this series is to offer the general public a stimulating insight into Canada's urban past. Over the next several years, the Museum, in cooperation with James Lorimer and Company, plans to publish a number of volumes dealing with such varied communities as Montreal and Kingston, Halifax and Quebec City, Ottawa and Sherbrooke.

It is the hope of the National Museum of Man that the publication of these books will provide the public with information on Canadian cities in a visually attractive and highly readable form. At the same time, the plan of the series is to have authors follow a similar format, and the result, it is anticipated, will be a systematic, interpretative and comprehensive account of the urban experience in many Canadian communities. Eventually, as new volumes are completed, *The History of Canadian Cities Series* will be a major step along the path to a general and comparative study of Canada's urban development.

The form for this series — the individual urban biography — is based on a desire to examine all aspects of community development and to relate the parts to a larger context. The series is also based on the belief that, while each city has a distinct personality that deserves to be discovered, the volumes must also provide analysis that will lift the narrative of a city's experience to the level where it will elucidate questions that are of concern to Canadians generally. These questions include such issues as ethnic relationships, regionalism, provincial-municipal interaction, social mobility, labour-management relationships, urban planning and general economic development.

In this volume, James Lemon chronicles the story of Toronto in the years since the end of the Great War. During these six decades, the city has undergone a remarkable metamorphosis in terms of its society and politics, its urban landscape and its population and ethnic composition. In the process, the old Toronto — a city of 500,000 that was 80 per cent British and Protestant in 1918 — was transformed into a sprawling national metropolis of more than 3,000,000 people, less than half of them Anglo-Saxon. Yet, as Professor Lemon argues, Torontonians have maintained a sense of community which makes Toronto unique among large North American cities.

This volume was written by a well-known urban historical geographer. Professor Lemon teaches at the University of Toronto and has long been involved in the city's public life. He has served as a school trustee, a leading member of residents' groups, and as a director of Metro Toronto's Social Planning Council. James Lemon has also published widely on the topic of urban evolution and is able to put Toronto's particular characteristics in the context of North American trends. As well, Professor Lemon's volume can be best appreciated as a companion volume to *Toronto to 1918: An Illustrated History*, by J.M.S. Careless, which was published in 1984.

Professor Lemon's text is enhanced by a wide variety of photographs and specially prepared maps. This illustrative material is not only visually enjoyable, it also plays an essential part in re-creating the past. While illustrations and maps cannot by themselves replace the written word, they can be used as a primary source in a way equivalent to more traditional sources. The fine collection of illustrations in this volume captures images of a wide variety of situations in Toronto, allowing a later generation to better understand the forms, structures, fashions and group interactions of an earlier period.

Alan F.J. Artibise
General Editor

Acknowledgements

For a volume that reaches the present time and covers so many topics, one runs the risk of not remembering all those who have contributed generously of their time. Thus, first of all, I acknowledge collectively the great number of colleagues and friends with whom I have discussed issues and sources, formally or casually. Some are cited in footnotes.

More particularly, I am grateful to the staffs of various archives and libraries. Back in the summer of 1970, Stephen Speisman, now the archivist with the Canadian Jewish Congress, and I undertook a study of the Annex neighbourhood, then one of a few scholarly ventures using material in the City Archives. In that sparsely occupied place, we were helped greatly by archivists Robert Woadden and Scott James of the city clerk's office. More recently, Victor Russell, Linda Price, Karen Teeple, Glenda Williams and Elizabeth Cuthbertson have been unstinting in their aid. The many hours in the basement of City Hall, where much of the work was undertaken, have been enjoyable because of their interest and enthusiasm for the project.

I am also indebted to the staffs of the Planning and Development Department at City Hall, the Municipal Reference Library, Toronto Board of Education Library and Archives, the Baldwin Room at the Metropolitan Library, the Robarts and the Architecture Libraries at the University of Toronto, the Archives at the University of Toronto and at York University, the Ontario Archives, the Multicultural History Society, the Harbour Commissioners Archives, and the Public Archives of Canada. The statisticians at the Toronto Board of Education and the Metropolitan School Board provided data, as did the Metropolitan Toronto clerk's office, the Ontario Ministry of Citizenship and Statistics Canada. The Labour Council of Metropolitan Toronto and the Social Planning Council permitted me to look at manuscripts and reports. At the latter, discussions with Marvyn Novick and Jeffrey Patterson were crucial. Ian Drummond loaned manuscript material on Ontario's economic past. J.F. Brown loaned manuscript correspondence on planning in the 1940s.

A special word of thanks goes to Edith Firth, formerly of the Baldwin Room, who was willing to talk a number of years ago about Toronto to a raw neophyte just starting to study the place. John André too was encouraging when I explored York Township in the Borough (now City) of York offices. Keith Bell and Bob Clifton told me all about baseball in Toronto. The Reverend Elmer Stainton arranged a lecture at the St. Clair 60 Club.

The breadth of the study precluded doing many interviews. Informally, Hans Blumenfeld drew on his unparalleled experience in planning. I am grateful to A.L.S. Nash and to Matthew Lawson for discussing planning issues in the 1940s and 1950s. Norah Johnson not only arranged these latter two interviews, but provided material from her collection and also recalled her involvement in the heady days of planning in the 1940s.

In the production of this book, I owe the greatest debt to Ms Johnson. She frequently drew on her earlier experience in our innumerable discussions, and also undertook research (particularly on the theatre), read, edited and typed the final draft. My University of Toronto colleagues, James Simmons, Roger Riendeau and Lorne Tepperman, read critically all or parts of the manuscript, as did Frances Frisken of York University, series editor Alan Artibise and Ted Mumford of Lorimer and Company. Former Controller and Alderman William Archer read it thoroughly, catching a number of flaws. Since he and I do not interpret Toronto in altogether the same fashion, I cannot hold him, or indeed the other readers, responsible for what is said.

Charlotte Sykes, the first researcher to help on the project, was very supportive while assembling materials. Robert Lewis enthusiastically ran down much of the data for the tables and more — many of the numbers in the text were drawn from tables not found in the back of the book. Mary Augustine showed a great deal of interest in what was being said while patiently typing the first draft from a difficult handwritten manuscript. Dawna Henderson helped to find photographs. Mike Filey graciously provided several prints. Judith Kjellberg at the University of Toronto Centre for Urban and Community Studies energetically tracked down reports. Vivienne Young, who undertook earlier research for me on Toronto, made a valuable contribution. My wife, Carolyn, has been exceedingly supportive, specifically in helping to track down photos, as have my daughters, Margaret, Janet and Cathy.

This book is dedicated to my mother and in memory of my father, from whom I learned to involve myself in town affairs. My father's stint as reeve of West Lorne in the late 1930s sparked my interest in municipal questions. The sheer activity in his and my grandparents' store on the main street, in the church and on the baseball field left their mark. Although they did not know it, their concerns also led me to study early Pennsylvania as an antecedent to the settlement of Ontario. Their breadth and depth of interest in so many directions made the task of writing this book instinctively easier than it might have been without those earlier experiences.

The book relies so heavily on undergraduate and graduate papers from courses on Historical Toronto and Urban Historical Geography of North America that I am also dedicating the book to the several hundred students who struggled to write them. Without their efforts, putting together this book, particularly for the earlier years, would have been far more difficult and time-consuming. I hope they recognize that their effort was not in vain. For other researchers, their papers are deposited in the University of Toronto Archives.

James Lemon
February 1985

Spadina Avenue, looking north from Queen, in the mid-1920s. Laid out as a wide avenue in the early nineteenth century, Spadina remains one of Toronto's most interesting streets.

Introduction

Essential Toronto

In the 1970s, popular American magazines heaped praise on Toronto as "the city that works" and a "model of the alternative future." A scholarly journal publicizing a prestigious convention went so far as to say the city represented "civilization" to Americans. While Americans flock to Toronto for conventions and holidays, Torontonians may wonder why these visitors think the place so civilized.[1]

As the Americans invariably note, Toronto is clean and safe. They are impressed that the homicide rate is far lower than in U.S. metropolises. Perhaps, too, the streetcars remind them of something lost in the maelstrom of change south of the border. But more conspicuous is the contrast between inner cities. In their own cities, Americans confront many buildings that have been allowed to deteriorate, and others that have been abandoned. In Toronto, they see careful renewal (though not all residents would agree). Looking deeper, Americans might also see far fewer social differences between suburbs and inner city. Poverty is found in the suburbs as much as in central Toronto, and the middle class has not entirely fled to the suburbs. It is obvious that Toronto's stance on multiculturalism has not eliminated discrimination against visible minorities, but racial prejudice hardly constitutes an American-style threat to the way the city works or to the activities of Torontonians. More positively, Americans observe a strong commitment to the arts in Toronto. A closer study of the city's social fabric would reveal a public school system and an institutional framework for social and community services that are unrivalled in the metropolitan areas of the U.S.[2]

Toronto's public environment, which Americans find so refreshingly different, could be seen as the result of affluence arising from a diversified economy anchored in finance. If, in many respects, the Canadian economy is enclosed within the American, Toronto (and indeed other Canadian cities) has been able to take enough of the wealth to provide a relatively genial material and social environment. But many U.S. metropolises have plenty of wealth and some are richer than Toronto. The reasons for the contrast lie beyond affluence.

The differences cannot be explained by a rapid growth pattern hitting Toronto later than U.S. metropolises, nor by the consequent lag in solving urban problems. Certainly Toronto did not grow as quickly as late nineteenth-century New York and Chicago, and so it learned from their mistakes. But since the 1940s especially, innovations have originated more in Canada and Toronto, while the differences with U.S. cities have become magnified.

In the 1800s, Americans tended to let the "market mechanism" sort out the supposedly optimal solutions for cities, even to the point of letting tram lines compete on the same streets. Consequently those possessing a great deal of economic power wielded control over developing the urban environment. Many of the same elite then had to solve the problems this dominance raised.

In this century, especially since 1945, the U.S. federal government has accentuated this power by providing massive financial support to corporations building suburbs, especially through easy mortgaging. In the name of national defence, the federal government paid most of the cost of freeways between and within cities. It also contributed to central city redevelopment that saw more housing torn down than built. As a result, the condition of the older central cities markedly deteriorated. Office construction could not shore up a tax base weakened when the middle class was drawn to the new suburbs. Ethnic slums of the turn of the century gave way to even more extensive black ghettos. Although many middle-class Americans thought the federal government gave too much to the poor through public housing in the 1950s and 1960s, in actual fact this spending was modest compared to the outlay for suburbs and freeway expansion. By the 1970s, many cities were enduring fiscal crises. Ironically, more federal money was then needed just to keep local governments going.

In Canada, civic, provincial and federal administrations—with strong citizen support and criticism—have hedged in the urban sorting-out process and land speculation, so that distortions have been less marked. The result of a large federal presence in suburban development has not been the weakening or devastation of central cities. They have actually become stronger, most obviously in the affluent cities like Toronto. Business has operated within a framework of greater restraint and more regulation and with less financial support than in the U.S., where the defence and space industries receive massive subsidies. Municipalities, as much as higher levels of government, have created visible public enterprises. Toronto has fostered monopolies—in public transportation, for example, first with franchises and then under public ownership beginning in 1921.

All in all, Toronto and other Canadian cities have exhibited a far more careful management of resources than American cities. This care is embedded in a culture that is less wasteful, more cautious, more saving, that "makes do" much more than does the Yankee culture. In this sense, Toronto is still very British. In large measure, this difference is the result of living next to the country that exults in freedom, in enterprise, where the public sphere has been left behind in pursuit of property and individual well-being. Ironically, at the same time, Toronto's safe environment has allowed American corporations to invest with confidence.

Through this account of Toronto since 1918, public action will predominate. The central thesis is that Torontonians have sought to create and maintain a stable, orderly environment and to achieve a greater degree of social equality than has been pursued in the U.S. Torontonians often argued vehemently about the best ways to attain these goals. The strongest emphasis therefore is on the politics of modifying the landscape, improving social welfare and restructuring government. The planning of public transportation, education and housing also looms large. Since much of the analysis is based on the public record, major actors include officials, newspapers, ratepayer and resident groups, labour unions and business organizations—all of whom have played significant roles in shaping the city.

But there is more to a city than its politics. Toronto's economic, demographic, social and landscape dimensions are also lenses through which life in Toronto can be viewed. For example, we will see how Toronto's metropolitan reach over the hinterland expanded; how its citizens came to accept a multicultural city in place of a very British one; how social life was enriched; how the city grew physically, and so on.

In each chapter Toronto's metamorphosis is captured by looking in particular at a focal concern of the period. Chapter 1 focusses on the politics of restraint in education and in limiting municipal expansion in the 1920s. The woeful economy of the 1930s and the need for action on welfare, jobs and housing are stressed in Chapter 2. The politics of planning, resulting in substantial changes in running public affairs, is highlighted in Chapter 3. The massive change in Toronto's population as it grew rapidly from 1954 to 1966 led to a redefinition of its public ideology, as described in Chapter 4. In the last chapter, the major reform impetus of the late 1960s and Toronto's arrival as Canada's financial metropolis are the major considerations.

Over the course of these five periods, several impressive transformations occurred. Culturally and economically, Toronto extended its influence in the country, as its traditional industrial strength was superseded by expanded media and financial power. At the same time, the city became more economically subordinate to the U.S. The growth of Toronto's population was rapid, especially in the 1950s and 1960s, and its ethnic composition changed dramatically from British to a mix of many peoples. As in the rest of the country, affluent Torontonians came to accept the validity of the welfare net. The notion of housing as a social right for everyone developed, certainly slowly and haltingly, but more thoroughly than elsewhere. Social planning emerged as a foundation of the public sphere, with Torontonians sometimes leading the way in the country.

Even more marked has been the appearance of land-use planning to foster efficiency in public spending and, not least, to protect neighbourhoods. The city's landscape has been altered significantly since 1918. Then the waterfront was being industrialized; in the 1980s it is being turned over to recreation and housing. In 1918 there were only a few downtown skyscrapers; though they were joined by several more in the late 1920s, the creation of today's skyline really started about 1965. By 1920 the car was only beginning to make an impact on the face of the city. In the postwar era the car brought large suburban lots, freeways, shopping centres and low-density industrial and office parks.

Social and land-use planning were put in place through political reform. While an earlier reform thrust had been largely spent by 1918, determination to make social changes arose in the 1940s and again between 1965 and 1975. This was reflected in, and encouraged by, shifts in electoral politics. Dominantly Tory Toronto became more diverse after the 1920s as Liberals and members of the Cooperative Commonwealth Federation (later the New Democratic Party) came to challenge Tories at City Hall and to gain a greater share of Toronto seats provincially and federally. Government spending in social fields, and more directly in the economy, increased greatly in the wake of the Depression, profoundly affecting the life of Torontonians and weakening municipal autonomy.

As the city approaches its two-hundredth year of continuous settlement, Toronto is immersed in yet another period of slow growth, following the explosive expansion of the postwar period. Possibly now is the time Torontonians should accept American praise with a grain of salt: is Toronto indeed the "alternative" great city? But such a question cannot lead us to the quiddity of Toronto. Only living in it is of the essence.

TORONTO IN 1918

By 1918 Toronto had long since established itself as not only the capital of the province but also its economic and cultural centre. It vied with Montreal as the premier economic metropolis of the country and was easily ahead as the central focus of anglophone Canadian culture. The prewar era had been a golden one for Toronto's economy. Its wholesalers clearly dominated southern Ontario. The retailing giants, Eaton's and Simpsons, sent their mail order catalogues across the country. Railways brought the mining wealth of Northern Ontario and northwestern Quebec "under the dominance of Toronto." Toronto financed street railways and electricity in South America. The economic elite shared the boardrooms of business, hospitals, the university and so on through interlocking directorates.[3]

In 1906 the *Globe* claimed that Toronto was "now the chief banking centre of Canada." Certainly Toronto's banks had experienced, as it said, an "incredible increase" of assets through economic growth, the expansion of branches in the west and east and the *de facto* move of the Bank of Nova Scotia to Toronto. But the judgment was premature: the even more spectacular rise of the Royal Bank, also formerly Nova Scotian, gave Montreal an edge by 1918 as mergers concentrated banking in the two metropolises. Similarly, Canada Life, Toronto's largest insurance company, fell behind Sun Life. But the middle class sought more protection, so assets grew greatly. From a world perspective, Toronto was a regional satellite of New York, and would remain so.[4] (Table XII)

Ontario's manufacturing had expanded greatly in the late nineteenth century. By 1900 much was concentrated heavily in and around Toronto, as many smaller firms in small towns gave way to larger companies — partly through mergers, such as the one creating Canadian Cycle and Motor. Also, increasing direct American investment in branch plants, inspired by the National Policy and the availablity of Niagara hydro-electricity, favoured Toronto. For example, Canadian General Electric, a large U.S. company created through mergers, started plants in Toronto.

With more than 65,000 industrial employees in 1911, Toronto was well ahead of other places in Ontario. Toronto led in clothing, printing and publishing, metal fabricating, and several food processing sectors. But with this specialization Toronto was still much more diversified than industrial and mining cities like Hamilton and Sudbury, ensuring that Torontonians were far less vulnerable to business cycles.

Yet prosperous times did not benefit everyone equally. The enormous economic growth up to 1914 did not yield higher real wages for all workers in manufacturing and construction, though home ownership rose. One analysis suggests that only during the Great War did real wages rise, as union membership and the demand for labour shot up. Instability would mark the 1920s.[5] (Tables X, XI)

In 1918 the population of Toronto and its urbanizing outskirts had reached 500,000. Toronto was large enough to be considered a metropolis, though it still bore many of the signs of a small city. It had grown tremendously since 1900, when it housed only 200,000. Eighty per cent of the population could claim British ancestry. More than three in four were Protestant, primarily Anglican, Presbyterian and Methodist. Most of the dominant bankers, merchants and manufacturers and lawyers were British — but then so were most of the working and middle classes.

Up to 1913 migration from rural areas and small towns had increased. Immigration from Britain had been so high that a quarter of Torontonians claimed a British birthplace. Since so many were Protestants and fewer Irish arrived than earlier, Roman Catholics had fallen to 15 per cent of the population. Among the immigrants from overseas were Jews from Russia and some Italians whose "cheery" faces, noted English poet Rupert Brooke, "pop up at you out of excavations in the street." Unlike New York and other northern U.S. cities, Toronto hardly had to absorb masses of immigrants from eastern and southern Europe, nor blacks from the southern states. But a xenophobic apprehension was expressed about the immigrants who did arrive in Toronto. The glories of the white race—and particularly of the British Empire, as celebrated through textbooks, cadet corps, Empire Day observances and Orange Order propaganda—fostered jingoism and so prepared Torontonians for the trenches of France, where 13,000 of Toronto's young men died. That indecisive bloodbath did not quell racism; only Nazism pushed it under the surface in the mordant 1930s.[6] (Tables I–IX)

The landscape of Toronto had been dramatically changed between 1900 and 1913, when development largely stopped. After the extensive 1904 fire in the central area, wholesalers rebuilt their warehouses, though with less style than had the early great merchants. The Royal Bank and Canadian Pacific, with headquarters in Montreal, built skyscrapers reaching twenty storeys at King and Yonge close to Bay, the twentieth-century focus of finance. Prominent stock brokerage firms, such as A.E. Ames, clustered near the stock exchanges. A bit farther north, City Hall (opened in 1899) brooded over Bay Street. Simpsons and Eaton's anchored the main shopping district at Queen and Yonge. Around Holy Trinity Church were Eaton's factory lofts. Toward the west many more sweatshops of the needle trades had emerged. Warehouses and light manufacturing occupied much of the area in between, displacing much low-income housing. Heavier industries polluting the air with coal smoke were located on the east waterfront and to the west along rail lines, in Parkdale and around the Junction, where Massey Harris and Joseph Flavelle's predecessor of Canada Packers were prominent, and in Mount Dennis and Weston. Industrial districts along the Lakeshore beyond the Humber and in Leaside appeared. On the waterfront, industrial and recreational facilities were built following the 1912 Harbour Commissioners' plan, though the war slowed the process.[7]

The explosive growth of population resulted in a house construction boom between 1896 and 1913. Speculation was so rampant that Toronto pushed successfully for provincial planning legislation in 1912 to control indiscriminate subdividing on the fringes, and passed its own bylaw limiting the intrusion of apartment buildings into neighbourhoods, though politicians would often breach the rule. The boom ended about then: in the 1920s development would fill in some of these subdivisions but others were without houses until the next great expansion of the early 1950s. The new suburbs (which would later be part of the inner city) were served by streetcar shopping strips with stores on the ground floor and apartments or meeting places above. The spires and towers of churches built from the largesse attained through commerce, mining and industry still dominated the roofscapes of semi-detached neighbourhoods.[8]

A major response by the city to the enormous growth was the construction of civic streetcar lines on the Danforth, Gerrard, Coxwell and St. Clair, and agitation for public ownership of all transit lines (and of electricity). The Toronto Railway Company (TRC), enfranchised in 1891 for thirty years, refused to extend its lines beyond the 1891 boundaries. Like all time-bound franchises, the TRC did little improving in its last decade. By 1910 the public outcry was already shrill; by 1915 city bureaucrats were recommending municipal ownership of the trams (and also of electricity); in 1918 the people voted overwhelmingly to create the Toronto Transportation Commission. Meanwhile, cars were appearing in large numbers.[9]

Annexation was another response of the city politicians and bureaucrats to expansion. Like many North American cities, Toronto expanded by gobbling up incorporated villages and towns and unincorporated urbanizing areas. A first wave in the 1880s was followed by another between 1904 and 1912. After North Toronto and Moore Park in the affluent northern sector were taken in, the process largely stopped, leaving poorer working-class and even a few rich districts in York Township. City officials argued that funds for servicing were depleted. Not until 1953 was the suburban question partially resolved through the creation of Metro.[10]

The city expanded its concern for the health and welfare of its citizens, partly through the influence of the Christian "social gospel." In 1914 Mayor Horatio Hocken claimed that, especially since 1909, Toronto had developed "human services" just like "great American cities." In an Ottawa speech he listed in detail the "welfare work" undertaken. The city's abattoir kept small businesses going

In their leisure time, Torontonians could take the ferry to Hanlan's Point in summer; or, in winter, go tobogganning down well-used runs at High Park — provided it wasn't Sunday.

Eglinton west of Yonge had a distinctly pastoral appearance, as building on land long subdivided was slower and patchier than expected. Toronto stopped annexing urbanizing fringe areas after 1912, leading to the fragmentation of York Township and uneven services. One of the new municipalities was Swansea, where the fire brigade at left was photographed in 1924.

against "the great trust" of Flavelle and improved sanitation. In public health $750,000 was spent in 1914, compared to a pittance five years earlier. There were more visiting nurses for child welfare, better milk inspection and other improvements, producing a great reduction in communicable diseases and the death rate. In the wake of the Guild of Civic Art's 1909 city plan, nine supervised playgrounds and many playing fields appeared where there had been none, helping to reduce delinquency. Other signs of reform included a detention home for "lunatics;" children's and women's courts; an industrial farm for minor offenders; a minimum wage for municipal employees (thanks to Controller James Simpson of the labour movement); even a Municipal Loan fund for unemployed professionals; a city-appointed Social Service Commission to examine and advise non-profit charities which were just becoming professionalized; and a quasi-public housing company which had already built some garden apartments to replace slums. Mayor Hocken might have added that the Board of Education had started the construction of technical and commercial high schools, and that, under J.L. Hughes, Toronto had been a leader in progressive education. Unemployment forced the city to pay relief costs, however, for which Hocken felt public works were an inadequate solution. Obviously, most Torontonians would continue to believe that the economy was best left in the hands of bankers, industrialists and commercial leaders rather than in the government's.[11]

All of these public activities cost the municipality a great deal of money, and in relatively greater amounts as time went on, at least to 1914. The city budget climbed from under $6 million in 1900 to $35 million in 1920, an increase per capita from $30 to $70, gained through borrowing and higher taxes. Nonetheless, surpluses were managed each year. Toronto's budget still virtually matched the province's. All of these improvements were achieved without great reforms in government itself. In 1896 the creation of the Board of Control had centralized budgetary power, though not to the same degree as in many American cities where the mayor's office was often strengthened. In 1891 the ward map was redrawn from more or less square blocks to north-south strip wards in the centre, undoubtedly increasing the power and responsibility of the affluent who were shifting northward and weakening the influence of working-class homeowners south of Bloor Street. Even so, a high level of public participation remained. Ratepayer and Home and School associations in neighbourhoods had been active since 1900. The Bureau of Municipal Research was formed in 1914. The newspapers stressed local issues, with detailed reports and forthright editorials. Hocken's claim of "a new spirit of municipal government" would persist, though with somewhat less vigour. Although most of the gains were firmly in place, enthusiasm for human services weakened with his departure from city hall in 1915, when tighter-fisted Tommy Church replaced him. Indeed, not until the mid-1930s and especially the 1940s was there again a new spirit in social welfare, housing, land-use planning, and local government reform sufficient to redirect public spending.[12]

To Rupert Brooke, Toronto was the "soul" of Canada and not "hellish" like New York. "It is all right. The only depressing thing is that it will always be what it is, only larger...." So Toronto was expected to remain very much Toronto the Good. People trooped to church and preachers were as crucial as newspapers in forming opinion. Although the churches had lost the Sunday streetcar battle in the mid-1890s, politicians buckled before them in 1912 on the question of tobogganning in High Park on Sundays, at least temporarily. Sunday activities would remain a contentious issue, though the Lord's Day position gradually eroded. The dry forces succeeded as never before in 1916, when the Tory government surrendered to enormous pressure and virtually eliminated the sale of booze. This planned purification of society was shortlived, however. Male Toronto and higher levels of government also gave in to a related campaign: women's suffrage.[13]

All the while, ordinary Torontonians scuttled across the railway tracks dodging trains to catch the ferry boats to cottages on the islands or to the amusement park on Hanlan's Point and, if never on Sunday, to Maple Leaf ball games. Or they took the streetcar to Scarborough Beach park. More and more of the middle class joined the rich in Muskoka summers. And Henry Pellatt built Casa Loma as the great elite sought to display their wealth and power.[14]

Bay Street looking north to City Hall, 24 December 1924. The buildings on the immediate left would soon be replaced by the Sterling Tower, one of several skyscrapers built in the 1920s. Farther along towards City Hall is Toronto's earliest "skyscraper," the Temple Building, all of eleven stories. It too was to disappear, in the 1970s.

Chapter One

The Silver Age, 1918–1929

The end of the war marked the beginning of Toronto's silver age. Though there would be no return to the golden years of incredible growth that preceded the war, during the 1920s much was achieved to make the city a more liveable place. And no one was louder in his praise of the city and its accomplishments than Commissioner of Finance George Ross. In his 1927 report he wrote:

> The City is prosperous and there is a strong community feeling, which has manifested itself in the municipal ownership of transportation, light and power systems, waterworks and other public services. The citizens take pride in the splendid condition of their city, its clean, well lighted streets and boulevards and its fine parks and recreation centres.

As well, the high level of home ownership, according to the commissioner, implied "a settled population" and "a contented community."[1]

The 1920s, however, were not all that serene. Not far below the surface of city life were signs that Torontonians were somewhat less euphoric and comfortable than Commissioner Ross reported. Former Mayor Hocken's pride in having expanded human services up to 1914 was replaced by demands for restraint. Housing for the poor dropped off the agenda, and the voice of efficiency ruled out the annexation of suburbs, most of which had weak property bases. Stemming the tide of reform could not, however, check the development of education.

A shaky economy, on the downside of a long cycle of growth, did not recover its prewar pace even when superheated by speculation late in the decade. Affluent Toronto did not experience anything like the Winnipeg General Strike, nor the extent of grinding poverty found in Montreal, but unemployment and inadequate wages still haunted many lives. On the cityscape, a revived public transportation system improved commuting, while the weaker economy limited industrial growth on the waterfront and speculation eventually led to an excess of office buildings downtown.

Slowed population growth and immigration ensured that Toronto remained predominantly British. But the cultural sway of the British Empire was weakening. American influences seeped in, though Torontonians' diligent churchgoing reflected their tenacious pursuit of stability. A debate that dominated headlines at the start of the decade opens a window on civic life and the rhetoric of the principal actors during the period.[2]

SERVICES AND SOCIAL LIFE

How far Toronto had moved from its prewar expansionist and reformist stance was revealed in 1920 in a fierce controversy over the financing of public services, particularly education. In February the *Mail and Empire* and the *Globe* shot salvos at departmental and school board annual spending estimates. The *Mail*, singling out the Works and Parks commissioners' request for increases of 36 and 133 per cent, respectively, asserted that Toronto "must stem the tide of extravagance." The *Globe* attacked the Health Department, headed by the perennial expansionist Dr. Charles Hastings, as "notoriously the most reckless at City Hall." Although admitting that junior teachers deserved higher salaries, the paper rejected proposals for new school construction. Outgoing Finance Commissioner Thomas Bradshaw railed against the commissioners, school administrators and politicians who would spend more on programs and schools.

> I thought that Council was losing its head altogether and going ahead authorizing works and approving expenditures with an absolute disregard as to how the money was to be secured. It was simply repeating the follies of 1914 and pre-

Open-air reading class at Orde Street School, 1921. This technique for preventing tuberculosis was one of the Board of Education's special programs, considered "fads" or "frills" by tight spenders. This particular program faded after a few years — because of the effect on children's health.

According to the Board of Education's 1921 annual report, this is "A lesson in the dining room — Orde Street Housewifery Centre."

vious years and creating a situation that was becoming alarming.[3]

Soon after, the Board of Control announced its intention to reach the "safe haven of a 30-mill tax rate." Alderman Robert Cameron trotted out the powerful argument of fiscal conservatives: "We cannot drive people out of the city because of a high tax rate." Dr. Hastings spoke out for the other side, asserting that it would be cheaper to promote better health and declaring that "the city could not afford to take risks with human life, and that every cent taken off his figures simply means less efficiency."

But the strongest rhetoric was reserved for School Board proposals, and it was Mayor Church, "like a prophet of old," who led the attack. He accused city government of paying for fads and frills—"Why can't the people pay for their own work books?"—and proposed that the board dispense with manual training, all its supervisors and half its inspectors who "spend all their time in politics." Threatening to resign if the tax rate reached 37 or 40 mills, he continued his attacks on superannuation increases, declining class sizes and "dressing dolls." Not only that: Church asserted that "Toronto is becoming a dumping ground for education," as non-residents from the suburbs exploited the system. The mayor not only wanted the large capital budget for construction lowered but also moved a reduction in current expenditures, something City Council had not done in many years. Alderman Cameron proposed further cuts, arguing that not only domestic science and manual training should be ended, but also the Penny Bank—an ironic move considering that this project encouraged thrift among children. The executive of the Board of Trade backed Bradshaw "in his crusade against additions to the city debt charges." As a result, the Board of Control granted only $1 million of the $4 million requested for capital expenditures.

But "the barking serial" continued and, though the tone did not change, the argument shifted somewhat. The *Star* attacked the lack of longer term budgeting, and the *Mail and Empire* even criticized Church. The new School Board business manager, W.W. Pease, ably defended needs; the Bureau of Municipal Research argued for the Penny Bank; and the United Women Voters (predecessor of the Association of Women Electors) supported manual training and domestic science. Leaving cuts aside, Church began arguing for greater provincial input, claiming that Toronto got only 8 per cent of provincial funds while supplying 54 per cent of revenue. Since the obvious source of pressure was the Adolescent Attendance Act of 1919 (which raised the school leaving age from fourteen to sixteen as of 1921), he might well have focussed attention on the province in the first place. In June the government did, in fact, raise the grants to industrial schools by 25 per cent and, overall, doubled support to 5 per cent. But this was only a modest cushion.

So the pot continued to simmer through the summer of 1920. In September enrollment was up again, and in October the Board of Control granted another $450,000 for construction. It could hardly refuse after the Board of Trade and the Canadian Manufacturers' Association supported the expenditure. Nor could it buck the pressure of a public meeting of many groups, including the Local Council of Women, which noted that 115 classes were in portables and that the average class size was 45 pupils—not 30, as claimed by Church.

The debate intensified during the election campaign of November and December, leading up to the annual January 1st vote. The School Board's publicity bore slogans such as "Toronto's future citizens are Toronto's wealth," to which Church replied that the board could use Sunday schools, cut kindergarten and the like, and drastically alter its management. The chairman of the board then responded, "I'm not going to reply seriatim to Tommy's rot.... The Chief Magistrate, above all men, should stick to the truth." Making clear where it stood, the *Telegram* presented an outrageously biased series on school costs. Harkening back to the 1890s, when "the three R's ruled supreme," the series pointed to lower spending per pupil in Buffalo, Detroit and Chicago, and asked, "Is Toronto the goat educationally?" Indeed, "the very make up of the modern schools breathes forth a luxury of the 'school that Mother used to go to' could never boast." Even more, and without irony, "Nowadays tots... are sent to school to be out of their mother's way." Finally, the board, with its "swarm of officials," was "far too independent of all authority" in

> tossing law, advice and caution to the winds, installing swimming pools, tearing down old buildings which would have relieved congestion, tripling the clerical staff at the Administration building and creating positions for high salaried officials.

The reaction to Church and the *Telegram* was vigorous. Public meetings and an educational pageant, called "Fads and Frills," a pointed

Mayor Tommy Church's attempt to restrict school spending in 1920 divided Torontonians. The Star *saw him as stingy, titling this cartoon "Education à la Mayor Church."*

But the Telegram *deemed Church the saviour of the taxpayer for resisting the big spenders, including School Board Chairman Dr. John Noble, portrayed here. The caption had Noble asking for "More."*

rejoinder to Church, dramatized the School Board's plight and low teachers' salaries. Sam McBride, who was challenging Church for the mayor's chair, attacked the restraint measures of his opponent and the conservative bias of the *Telegram*. At least Church was forced to retreat from taking educational expenditures to the taxpayers through a referendum.

But none of this mattered: Church easily beat McBride. The chairman of the School Board and some expansionists on the board and council lost their seats. Of course, Church had again shown himself to be an astute politician; he appealed to the voters—in those days only property owners, many of whom had multiple votes if they owned property in more than one ward. Certainly there were reasons for voter caution: 1920 was a very inflationary year and the city was about to borrow heavily to upgrade the streetcar system. Church and the fiscal conservatives slowed down change with their appeal for restraint. Not until 1928, with the election of Sam McBride, did the growth impulse return. Even so, in the 1920s affluent Toronto spent and borrowed a good deal of money. And every year the mill rate reappeared as an election issue, although the rate was in fact held down close to 30.

Nonetheless, during the 1920s the educational system, taking a third of the tax dollar, continued to expand, though, as with all social services, at a slower pace than before the war. Elementary schools were added in the east and north ends of the city where the population continued to grow. Public daytime enrollments increased (as a ratio to city population they rose to 14.6 in 1922—the highest ever in this century—before declining slightly by 1929). It was clear that the public schools were becoming overcrowded, a fact that Church would not admit. Expansion of special education was apparent, as classes for the deaf, slow learners and physically handicapped were begun. Separate schools were growing, catering to 14 per cent of all elementary students in 1929, roughly in proportion to Roman Catholics in the city.[4] (Tables V, IX)

But it was in secondary education that the greatest gains were made. During the decade, enrollments tripled, the direct result of the legislation requiring attendance to age sixteen, and more basically because young people had become redundant to the economy. By 1930 several new high schools had been built. Evening classes served another 17,000, mostly in the new technical and commercial schools. Little wonder, then, that the School Board called upon the city to issue debentures for these large schools. By 1929 the cost per student had risen since 1919 from $63 to $89 for elementary education and $133 to $160 for secondary. In the face of a weaker economy and of an intransigent mayor, the reform impulse continued, if less markedly.[5] (Table V)

After the incredible gains in public health prior to 1918, Dr. Hastings's second decade saw far more modest increases in spending. Nevertheless, advances were made in several areas, such as district nursing staffs, industrial work conditions, check-ups for school children, education in personal hygiene, and control of contagious diseases. Hospitals were improved, sewers were added, and in 1925 electors voted to borrow $14 million for waterworks improvements. By 1931 typhoid fever had been virtually eliminated. The infant mortality rate continued to fall dramatically. Only the influenza epidemics in 1918 and 1920 raised the death rate briefly. If politicians were impatient with Hastings, outside experts were impressed: "Toronto has a marvellous organization and the finest health service in the world, . . . a model among municipal health institutions." Meanwhile, Nobel prize winners F.G. Banting and J.J.R. Macleod shared with C.H. Best and J.B. Collip the discovery of life-saving insulin.[6]

In 1918 other social services in the city were very limited by today's standards. In 1921 "the vast majority of adult blue-collar workers in Toronto could not support a family of five to an acceptable level of 'health and decency'." (By 1929 the word "vast" could have been deleted.) While fewer lived in poverty than in Montreal, many of Toronto's breadwinners still had to send out other family members to work, mostly at low wages, and many took in boarders. The very poor were forced to scavenge for winter fuel.[7]

From 1912 to 1921 the Social Service Commission, mandated by the city and composed of businessmen, advised City Council on welfare matters, allocated grants to voluntary agencies and administered relief funds. By the end of the war, it was cutting back on grants—"organized raids on the treasury," as one controller put it. But widespread dissatisfaction with the commission, particularly on the part of professional social workers, forced the council to end its operations. Despite fears that Hastings would overspend, from 1921 to 1929 the Health Department took over these roles. Only in 1932 was a Welfare Department set up. By 1930 about 7 per cent of the city's budget went to direct human help, mostly for relief. That this figure had doubled over the decade was in part the result of intransigence at the provincial and federal levels. The provincial

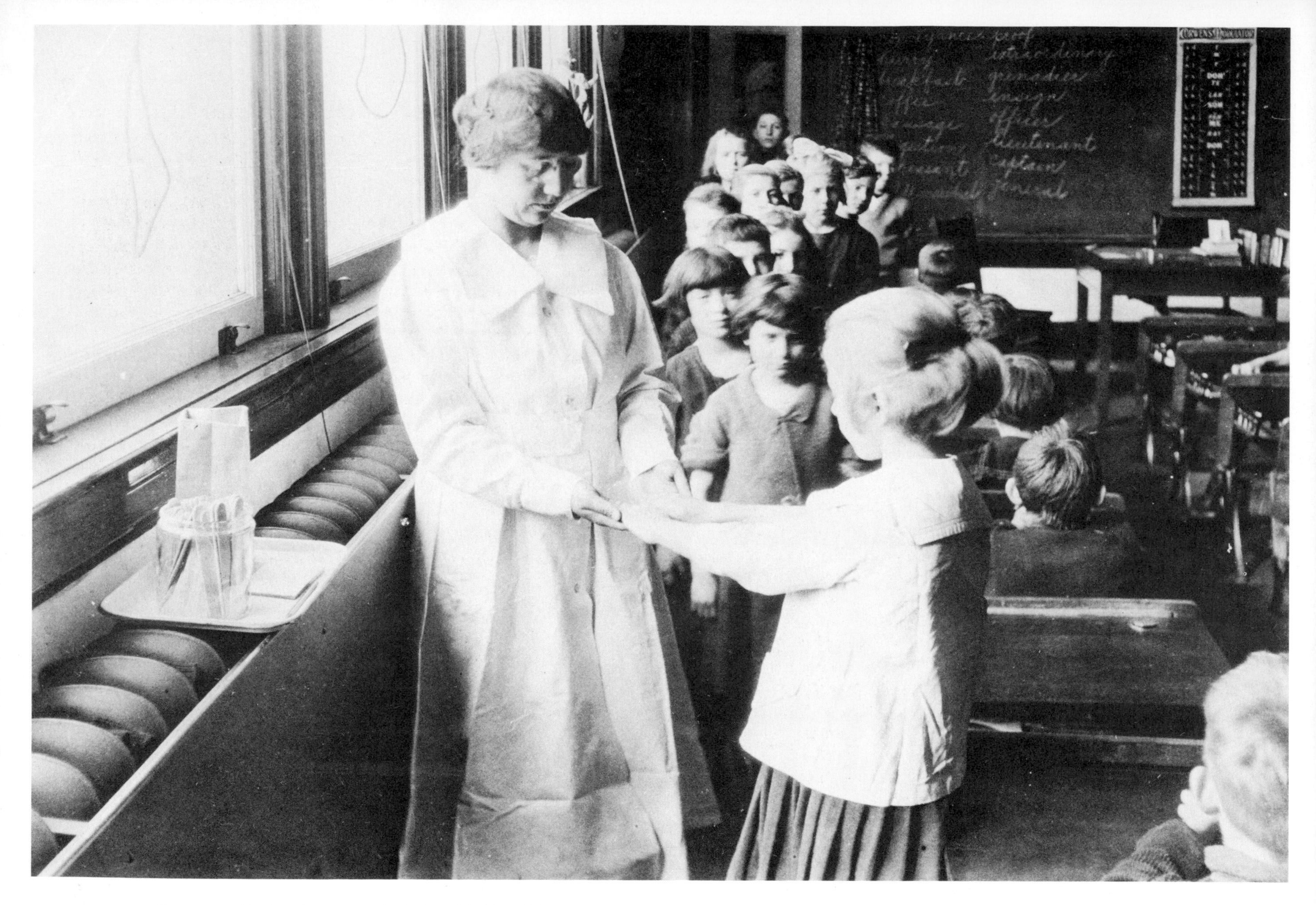

By 1914 public health programs had reduced death and disease rates greatly. In the 1920s preventive measures became routine.

farmer-union coalition, which lasted from 1919 to 1923, was sympathetic, but neither its successor, the Howard Ferguson Tory regime, nor Mackenzie King's federal government was willing to act on unemployment relief, and acted only marginally on old age pensions. Direct relief had to be shouldered by the city, and when unemployment rose, it had no choice but to respond, if only marginally.[8]

Volunteer charity organizations gradually achieved wider recognition, though in 1929 their efforts were still fragmented. In 1914 the Neighbourhood Workers Association (NWA) was organized for case work and to act as an umbrella organization for charities. In 1919 with the assistance of the Rotary Clubs, the NWA helped to set up the Federated Charities, the forerunner of the United Way. Catholic charities joined, but only temporarily.

This postwar effort toward comprehensiveness had been galvanized by the Bureau of Municipal Research's study "Toronto Gives," which advocated joint work and elimination of inefficiency, noting in the process that fourteen agencies received nearly half of their funds from clients. In 1919 the Child Welfare Council was founded to integrate and co-ordinate the efforts of fifty-seven agencies. Even so, in late 1920, the general secretary of the NWA had to admit that "welfare work is not a system — it is a disorderly heap." Soon after a prominent provincial official said that child welfare agencies were "working at random" and that Toronto was "the worst city of its size on the Continent in this respect...." Even though the settlement houses came together in 1924 to co-ordinate their efforts and social work became increasingly professionalized, a sense of fragmentation remained. In "Social Audit of Toronto Welfare Agencies," a U.S. welfare body recommended a community-wide Council of Social Agencies. Not until 1937 was this achieved. Meanwhile, Roman Catholics and Jews further developed their welfare services. The *Star*'s Fresh Air and Santa Claus appeals continued. Social welfare remained a matter of charity, of privilege, hardly a basic right for all citizens.[9]

If a desire for social planning influenced action in education, health and, to a degree, welfare, in housing this was not the case, except momentarily. The pressure for subsidized housing was apparent between 1907 and 1914 and had resulted in Spruce Court and Riverdale Court. It was renewed toward the end of the war as veterans returned. The cost of living had risen, rents were very high, and real wages fell over much of the two decades to 1921, all of which meant that ordinary working people, and not simply the poor living in the city's slum areas, were feeling the pinch. A good deal of doubling up occurred; in March 1918 at least 8,000 houses were said to be overcrowded. Housing had "emerged as the most serious domestic problem" facing the provincial and federal governments. Between 1913 and 1918, 1,600 houses had been demolished at the behest of the Health Department. In May 1918 it was claimed that over 5,000 families required "sanitary dwellings," while shack towns continued to spring up on the periphery of the city. By 1921 the number of persons per dwelling may have still been nearly as high as in 1911.[10] (Table XIV)

In 1918 the provincial and federal governments undertook modest and temporary initiatives for subsidizing housing. The city responded by setting up the Toronto Housing Commission. Composed of five businessmen who saw their work as a "regrettable intrusion into the free market," it built only 236 houses. The planning profession was not amused: 50,000 houses might have been built by the commission "if narrow-minded business doctrinaires had not killed the movement." Toronto and Canada would continue to follow the American way of letting the market provide rather than emulating Western European council housing programs. But as the economy improved, if only slightly, the problem of slums slipped from view. It would be 1934 before the issue of public housing again became a central concern.[11]

Middle-class Torontonians may have been better housed by 1929 than a decade earlier, though census and assessment data are contradictory. If the situation had improved slightly generally, the availability of apartments toward the end of the decade made a contribution. In 1921 there were only 2,188 apartments, but by 1931 there were nearly ten times as many. The 1912 city bylaw preventing apartment construction was being circumvented by numerous exceptions, especially after 1924, despite a warning in *Saturday Night* that apartments would lead to a higher divorce rate. But even though rents fell, Toronto remained a high-rent city. The market had been building enough units, but they were not distributed evenly enough among income groups. Finance Commissioner Ross's claim of 70 per cent home ownership was an exaggeration: the census suggests that fewer than half the householders owned their dwellings in 1921 and in 1931.[12] (Tables XIII, XIV)

While the city was making some strides in improving social services, it did not ignore the social life of its citizens. The city significantly increased its support for leisure activities and to a much higher level than did poorer Montreal. New libraries were built, and books circulated at three times the 1918 rate. While in 1914 Mayor Horatio Hocken could boast of nine supervised playgrounds, by 1929 there were six times as many, as well as thirty-eight neighbourhood parks, plus more picnic areas and skating rinks. Despite the haggling over the financing of education, schools and their yards were increasingly turned over to the community for recreation and other uses.[13]

In 1922 Sunnyside Bathing Pavilion opened, spelling doom to the less accessible Hanlan's Point Amusement park on the islands, and also replacing Scarborough Beach Park at the far east end of Queen Street. Sunnyside was built on reclaimed muck from the Humber Bay, in accordance with the 1909 Guild of Civic Art's plan and the 1912 waterfront plan. (Lakeshore Boulevard—then one leg of the "Marginal Boulevard" proposed to encircle the city—was also built on reclaimed land.) With a rollercoaster and merry-go-round, games of skill, shooting galleries and boat rentals, Sunnyside attracted visitors and their money. The boardwalk drew the Easter Parade. The *Telegram* sponsored the Water Nymph Carnival "to encourage girls and young women in the art of swimming," obviously a daring move for Toronto. The Miss Toronto contest started in 1926, an event that reflected the times: the political gains by women were stymied and deflected in the 1920s.[14]

Nearby was the Canadian National Exhibition (CNE), "unquestionably the world's largest annual exposition." In increasing numbers over the decade, people thronged the midway and the exhibits that introduced them to more and more consumer gadgets. The Royal Winter Fair, in 1922 located in the new Coliseum, was praised as "the world's greatest indoor livestock and Agricultural Exhibition."[15]

All told, in 1930, the city spent $19 million on social and recreational needs—nearly double the 1920 level. While education accounted for more than half the gain, advances were still achieved in other fields.

In the 1920s the line between amateur and professional sports was not hard and fast, nor were athletes particularly specialized. "Big Train" Lionel Conacher, called in 1950 Canada's greatest male athlete of the half-century, graced the gridiron, rink and diamond. But the trend to professionalization and standardization was apparent. In 1927 Conn Smythe took over the St. Patrick's team of the National Hockey League and renamed it the Maple Leafs. He began to build the team and to plan Maple Leaf Gardens. By then, the voice of "Hockey Night in Canada," Foster Hewitt, was already being heard. Successful University of Toronto teams were remolded as the Varsity Grads which took the Allan Cup in 1927 and the 1928 Olympic Gold Medal.[16]

In rugby football, still a distinctively Canadian game, Varsity won the Grey Cup from the Argonauts in 1920. The next year, in the first east-west game, Conacher led the Argos to an easy win over Edmonton. With another of Toronto's famous athletes, Ted Reeve, Balmy Beach of the Ontario Rugby Football Union played in the Grey Cup finals several times, winning over Hamilton in 1927.[17]

Like most Canadians, Torontonians enjoyed their baseball. While sandlot hardball flourished, the Maple Leafs won International League pennants in 1918 and 1926. Playing in the stadium at the foot of Bathurst (which replaced the Hanlan's Point grounds), the 1926 Leafs went all the way to win the minor league laurels in the Little World Series. Well-known stars such as George "Moony" Gibson, one of Canada's greatest baseball players, stopped on their way up to or down from the majors. Other sport heroes of the 1920s earned their laurels in the Olympics, such as 1928 medal-winner Bobbie Rosenfeld, and George Young won his by swimming the Catalina Channel.[18]

Other groups catered to the recreation needs of young people. For the many attending Sunday school, there were house leagues. Scouting and the "Y's" expanded, providing summer camps for some of the less privileged, just as private camps catered to the elite. Cottages of Torontonians continued to spring up around the lakes of the Canadian Shield.

American influences insidiously worked their way into the entertainment of Torontonians, but also gave rise to creative rebuttals. Musicals and revues at the Royal Alexandra and movies, particularly the talkies which arrived in 1927, were considered immoral by many. Others worried about the commercialization of entertainment. But these reactions produced beneficial side-effects. Amateur theatre flourished as churches sponsored at least fifty groups. Hart House, donated by the Massey Foundation and completed in 1919, increased the influence of live little theatre, which previously had been largely restricted to the Arts and Letters Club. The Players Club, which included Raymond Massey, and other groups (all unpaid) performed British and promising Canadian plays. The Shakespeare Society of Toronto was begun in 1928, and The Chester Players, founded in

Toronto's network of neighbourhood parks grew in the 1910s and 1920s. Above, a musical parade at the Elizabeth Street playground in the Ward. At left, a balloon man at the gate to Riverdale Zoo.

Sunnyside, 1922. The crowds were enormous on the "poor man's Riviera". Special streetcars transported children free of charge.

The Canadian National Exhibition's Dufferin Gates. Since the 1870s, the late summer trade and agricultural fair was a highlight for Ontarians. By the 1920s "national progress" had overtaken the glory of the British Empire as a central image.

Lionel Conacher, Canada's athlete of the half-century, was a star in many sports. Here he is honoured by the Hillcrest baseball team in 1920.

Amateur athletes still dominated the scene. These speed skaters belonged to the Old Orchard Skating Club.

Old-style "rugby" football at Varsity Stadium in 1923. Helmets were leather — but the ball carrier has only a cap.

1918, evolved into the Dominion Drama League in 1930. The University Alumnae, Toronto Children's Players, and Yiddish theatre rounded out the limited number of amateur companies. However, Canadian playwrights did receive a boost, and with Shakespeare timelessly transcending the decline of the British Empire, theatre became more firmly entrenched in the cultural life of the city. Music too, mostly European and British and mostly consisting of concerts by large church and school groups and by the Mendelssohn Choir, took the edge off Toronto's dour side.

Popular culture got a significant boost when radio (CFCA) made its first appearance at the CNE in 1922 under Toronto *Star* auspices. The number of radios increased through the decade. Ted Rogers's batteryless radio helped launch CFRB.[19]

THE POLITICS OF EFFICIENCY AND RESTRAINT

After the flurry of debate in 1920, city-spending settled down for several years. Between 1923 and 1928 expenditures remained virtually constant and the mill rate hovered just above 30. As the panic of 1920 subsided, the finance commissioners' reports became quieter and, as we have seen, even glowing by 1927. But a new growth impulse among the city's politicians, which surfaced with the election of Sam McBride in 1928, called forth the rhetoric of 1920 from the new finance commissioner. All the gains of the decade were dismissed as "prodigal Capital Expenditures" leading to "burdens of debt and attendant oppressive taxation."[20]

However, certain achievements in efficiency could not be ignored: a substantially increased assessment; by 1924 a mill rate lower than the next three largest cities in the province; lower per capita debt payments and far better services than Montreal; nearly half of the city's 1929 expenditures invested in revenue-producing areas; $16 million of the previous decade's borrowings "extinguished" ahead of schedule; $72 million retired—"a unique record;" borrowings well below the limits imposed by the province; and, finally, freedom from bank borrowings because of sound debentures.[21]

Through the decade the expanding power of civic and appointed officials reflected the drive for more efficiency in civic administration. In 1922 the finance commissioner found the power wielded by some appointed officials particularly worrisome. The TTC, Toronto Hydro, Harbour and CNE commissioners handled more revenue than the city itself. According to the finance commissioner, "Bulk applications from these outside bodies, involving many millions, have been passed [by council] almost without question, although no capital expenditure proposed by a [city] committee was too small to receive the most careful scrutiny." Yet, two years later, the same finance commissioner claimed that, among North American cities, "Toronto was one of the first to appreciate the value of [the commission] system in promoting general administrative efficiency." In 1926 Horace Brittain of the Bureau of Municipal Research pushed the efficiency line further by arguing for even more streamlining of city departments. But the politicians, and perhaps officials concerned for their turfs, were opposed. Besides, few in the public sphere, and certainly not the provincial government, would have endorsed another American solution, autonomous "home rule" based on a civic charter.[22]

The power of the bureaucracy may have grown in the 1920s, but the city was still governed by politics, by a struggle between the finance commissioner and his empire-building colleagues and between politicians and the people. John Ross Robertson's assertion in 1901 that "municipal government is a question of business not politics" may have been an article of faith at City Hall in the 1920s but practice did not square with it. The heat generated at council meetings, in the press, by community groups, and the fact that elections were held yearly (often with referenda) show that bureaucrats were not totally in charge. Nor were politicians. Flamboyant Tommy Church may have titillated voters with his beguiling yet contradictory rhetoric and by winning the mayoralty an unprecedented seven times, but even he lost in a comeback attempt in 1924. In fact, two incumbent mayors lost during the 1920s: the able William Hiltz was defeated by penny-pinching Thomas Foster in 1925 and Foster in turn fell to Sam McBride in 1928.[23]

During this decade of searching for stability, women were not well represented in the political life of the city. In the wake of the successful suffragette movement, Constance Hamilton and Ethel Small briefly served on council after 1918, but few women ran after 1923. Apparently, the pursuit of efficiency excluded women anxious to spend on social services. At the same time, women had been prominent among school trustees. But after 1922 only one or two women, notably Ada Courtice, were able to win. Nonetheless, there was no total retreat to the nineteenth century; though they may have been quieter than in 1920, many women's groups persisted.[24]

Attendance at an official opening is de riguere *for the mayor. Tommy Church may have preached restraint in school building, but showpieces like the* CNE *Coliseum — the 1921 cornerstone ceremony is seen above — could be afforded. The other dominant local politician of the era, Sam McBride, presided over the more growth-minded late 1920s. At left he joins J.E. Atkinson of the* Star *in starting the presses in the paper's new skyscraper on King Street, 1929.*

Though heated and noisy among men, Toronto's politics then exhibited little of the boodling of pre-1900 Toronto, nor of the patronage often associated with the Tammany Hall ward-heeling style that led to drives for purification in the U.S. Some well-placed individuals, such as Robert Home Smith, a harbour commissioner and land developer, could use politics for their own ends. But an efficient civil service, comprised of well-organized civic employees (among the strongest supporters of the local Trades and Labour Council), reduced substantially the potential for patronage. Workers at city hall were paid relatively high salaries for the time, and the city not only increased their numbers but also raised their fringe benefits.[25]

The newspapers were fervent participants in city politics. Not only did the newspapers offer detailed reports on council and School Board meetings, but they also provided their readers with a good deal of evening entertainment as they attacked one another. The *Telegram* and the *Star* framed much of the debate of the 1920s, certainly outdoing their more respectable morning rivals, the *Globe* and the *Mail and Empire* (which absorbed the *World* in 1921, a paper supporting development at any cost). The *Telegram* was the most outspoken. It represented Church and Foster; restraint in taxation and spending; the Orange Order, at least in presenting its slates for City Council; the workingman, particularly in the British east end; the Conservative Party; protectionism; and public ownership of utilities. The *Telegram* viewed big business as an enemy; it could be racist, and certainly it was anti-red. The *Star* had labour beginnings and, under Joseph Atkinson, it generally supported the federal Liberals, notably W.L.M. King, and, locally, Sam McBride. It favoured economic growth; freedom of speech; social welfare to a degree; free trade; and, for a while, the provincial United Farmers party under Premier E.C. Drury. On the public ownership of utilities and, more generally, on the rights of property, the two papers could agree. But overall the *Telegram* won most of the electoral battles in the silver age of restraint from 1918 to 1929.[26]

This was the heyday of ratepayer associations, which brought Torontonians directly into the political arena. The first association had been formed at the turn of the century in Rosedale, and since then the ward and neighbourhood associations representing property owners had spread. The newspapers and city council committee reports were filled with the generally conservative and protective positions taken by these groups. For example, in 1925 when Trinity College was moved from Queen Street to Hoskin Avenue, the local association working with the churches prevented the building of a stadium on the old site. To signify its legitimacy, the Central Council of Ratepayers met at city hall, and its constituent groups were listed in the annual city handbook.[27]

The Board of Trade and the Toronto Trades and Labour Council also spoke out on many city issues. The former influenced more decisions directly, as its general manager sat on committees and commissions dealing with traffic, the harbour and the like. The latter made its mark in many municipal affairs, from advocating free milk for undernourished children to the building of a baseball stadium. The Labour Day parade continued as a respected event, even if the 1920s were not easy years for labour. The labourite former controller and future mayor Jimmie Simpson failed to win during the period, a sure sign of caution in the electorate.[28]

The Home and School Associations were another group that held some sway in city politics. Beginning also in Rosedale, by 1916 there were enough associations to form a Toronto-wide body, which by 1930 had managed to get a foothold in sixty-four schools. The associations did not hesitate to speak after the war, and they had taken a strong stand in favour of opening the schools for community use. But they became less explicitly political after 1922.[29]

The drive for efficiency and restraint within the city was confirmed by the lack of expansion without. Much of contemporary Toronto's suburban-city split in civic politics dates back to the city's failure to annex expanding residential areas. In 1911 only 33,454 people lived beyond the city's boundaries, in what is now Metropolitan Toronto, because annexations had largely kept up with growth. But by 1921 the number had risen to 89,550 and, by 1931, to 187,141. The city's share of the metropolitan population thus fell markedly. Even before the war, city officials had been warning the generally expansionist politicians about the drain on city resources. In 1912 the annexation of North Toronto and Moore Park would be the last major annexations until 1967. In the intervening years, only bits and pieces were added. Much of the opposition in the 1920s was based on the widespread belief that the great land speculators would benefit if annexation brought city services to such areas as the Humber Valley Estates of Robert Home Smith, the York Land Company's and Canadian Northern Railway's new town of Leaside, founded as a municipality in 1913. This left the newly urbanizing areas on their own. The city's continuing refusal—and, one should

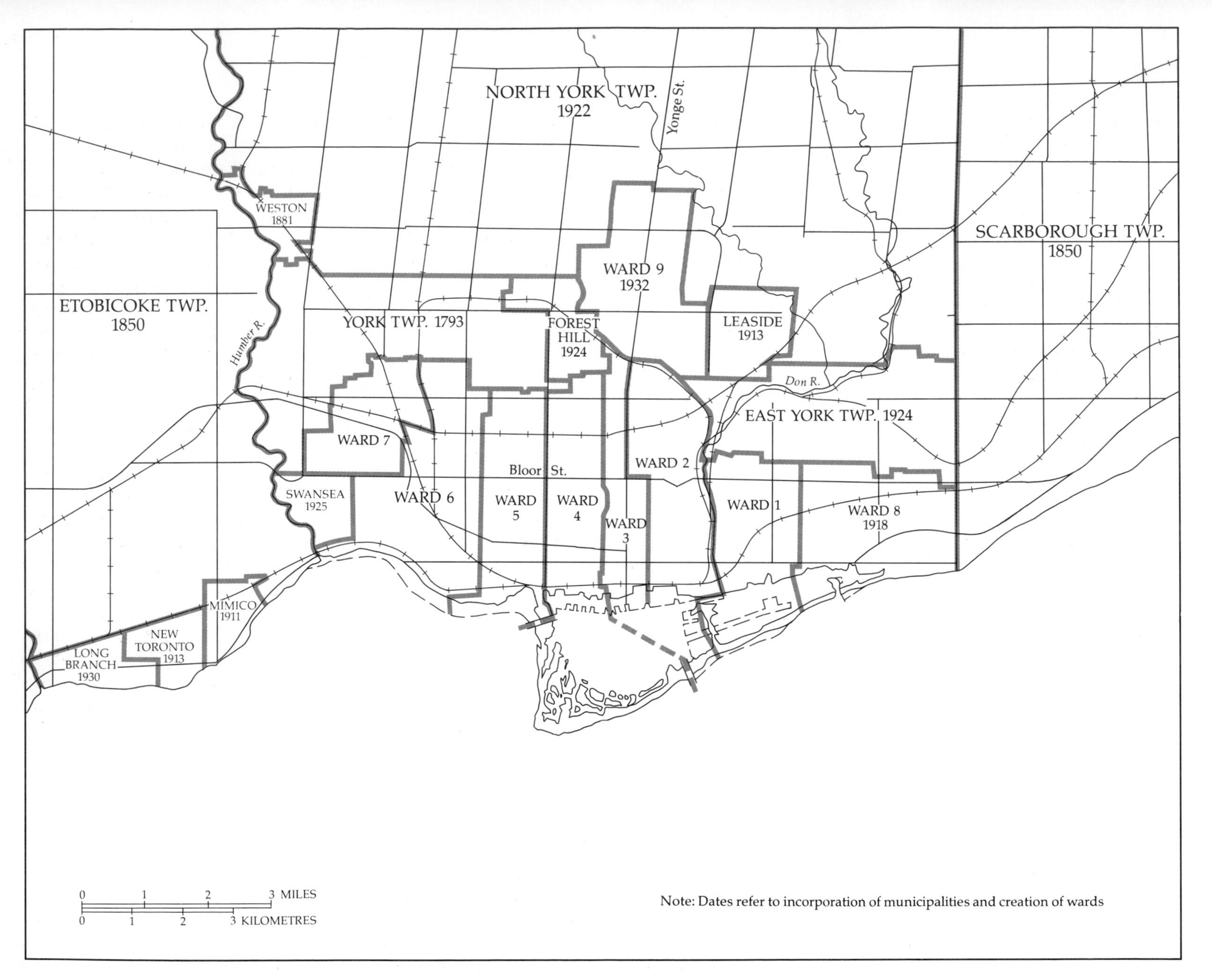

1 City Wards and the Balkanization of the Suburbs in the 1920s: In 1891 the City of Toronto was redivided into Wards 1 through 7. The north-south strip configuration favoured northern districts. Wards 8 and 9 were carved out of existing wards in the east and north ends in the years shown, completing a pattern that lasted until 1969. The city stopped annexing suburbs in 1912, leading to the fracturing of York Township evident here.

add, the unwillingness of the province to act—led to the breaking up of York Township (leaving it poor) and the creation of new municipalities.[30] (See Tables I, II and Map 1.)

The initiative came from the rural areas and from small villages along Yonge Street north of Hogg's Hollow. In 1922 farmers and their supporters, complaining of paying for urban services on the south side of the township adjacent to the city, successfully appealed to the province for separate status as North York. In the wake of this, another citizen movement tried to bring city status to York. Some within Spadina Heights, North Wychwood, Oakwood, Fairbanks and Mount Dennis argued vigorously for the creation of a city. But this movement was defeated overwhelmingly by York electors who feared that taxes would rise and provincial rural school subsidies would dry up.[31]

As a result, further splits ensued. In 1924 the Village of Forest Hill was created largely from affluent Spadina Heights. In the same year East York achieved separate township status. With Swansea's withdrawal in 1925, York Township appealed to the province to prevent more divisions, which would further cut the assessment base. The outcome resulted in the very modestly endowed York and East York townships, which included a good deal of working-class housing. In 1930 Long Branch was formed next to Mimico and New Toronto along the Etobicoke lakeshore.[32]

These places, together with other towns organized earlier within the urbanizing area, were pointing Toronto toward American-style balkanized metropolitan areas. The idea of a metropolitan county, floated within the Ferguson cabinet by George Henry, the East York member in 1924, fell on deaf ears. The same fate had met a similar proposal in 1913 by Morley Wickett, a reformer associated with the Bureau of Municipal Research. The consequences of inaction would be felt by the early 1930s, when most suburban places defaulted on their borrowings. But the 1920s were not a time for innovation.[33]

The politics of restraint and less obviously efficiency also reigned on the provincial scene. In 1919 a decaying Conservative government under William H. Hearst was replaced by E.C. Drury's reform-minded United Farmers of Ontario, who formed a coalition with eleven Labour members. Not to be swept up in reforming zeal, Toronto went only part way, electing five Liberals out of eight city members. Although the farmer-union government passed much advanced legislation, the coalition's internal contradiction between free-trade-minded farmers and protectionist workers could not stand up to a revived Conservative Party and the clear shift already apparent in Toronto, a shift toward restraint and efficiency in government, toward free enterprise in the resource industries, and away from prohibition. So in 1923 Drury went back to his farm and Howard Ferguson and the Tories assumed power, holding all Toronto and suburban seats. In the 1926 election they took all Toronto seats but one. While ending prohibition, Ferguson's government continued to be a regime which, on social matters and particularly on old age pensions, "was moved to open its heart... with a maximum amount of prudence and minimum generosity." It again recorded a resounding victory in the midst of the Great Crash of late October 1929 taking all fifteen city and three suburban seats. Ferguson was soon appointed High Commissioner in London by R.B. Bennett, leaving George Henry to face the Depression as premier.[34]

Tory domination was also apparent federally. In 1917 all nine city and county members sent to Ottawa were Conservatives. In 1921, 1925, 1926 and 1930, save for one county Liberal in 1921 and one from the city in 1930, all were Conservative. Tommy Church returned to the House of Commons in each election, except in 1930. As on the provincial scene, labour's attempts to organize parties, let alone do well at the polls, were hampered not only by the communist-versus-socialist debate, but also by the question of whether or not labour should be involved in electoral politics. On this question, practice tended to favour the stand of Sam Gompers of the American Federation of Labor, who advocated keeping labour out of politics, even though sentiment pulled toward the British way of direct party involvement.[35]

ECONOMIC LIFE: APPARENT STABILITY TO CRASH

Restraint in politics partly reflected the struggle in the immediate postwar years to get the economy moving again. In large part, judging from the rhetoric of the time, it was a struggle to thwart bolshevism, the great bugbear of the age. From 1922 to 1926 conditions looked better, though unemployment, which remained serious throughout the decade, rose again in 1925. By 1929 real wages had risen, but people toward the bottom of the income ladder had to be largely content with improved municipal services and none of the luxuries. From 1926 to 1929 optimism was more visible, but for some the explosion of speculation was worrisome. The Great Crash in the stock markets in October 1929, following three years of

FORTY PAGES

THE EVENING TELEGRAM

5 O'CLOCK EDITION

VOL. LIV. NO. 149 — TORONTO, TUESDAY, OCTOBER 29, 1929 — PRICE TWO CENTS

SELLING AVALANCHE TOPPLES MARKET PRICES

Slides, Bulletins and Broadcasts Will Keep Readers of Telegram Up to Date on Election Returns

The Evening Telegram's election service to-morrow evening will consist of stereopticon bulletin service and moving pictures, screened from the main office only, at Bay and Melinda streets, beginning at 7 o'clock. A program of popular selections will be given by the band of the 48th Highlanders.

At eight o'clock bulletins from Toronto and outside points will be broadcast by radio by CJBC (The Evening Telegram) using the transmitter of CKGW.

A Special Edition of The Telegram will be issued when the returns indicate definitely the results of the day's voting.

Get your election results from the "Tely."

Fight Gale to Rescue 55 From Sinking Lake Liner; Deaths Placed at 10 to 15

Captain's Body Found by Coastguards — Several Die Later of Exposure — Passenger Swept Overboard — Another Liner Makes Port After S.O.S Call

[illegible], Wis., Oct. 29.—With all but [illegible] persons of a crew of over 60 [illegible] the steamer Wisconsin sank off [illegible] early to-day in a storm that [illegible] damage all along Lake Michigan [illegible] the second time in a week [illegible] officers of the Wisconsin stuck [illegible] craft until it sank and were [illegible] from life rafts by rescue boats [illegible] of which rushed to the steamer [illegible] after the Kewaunee lifeguard had [illegible] off most of the crew. One man [illegible] reported to have fallen overboard [illegible] the rescue was in progress. Eight [illegible] to have lost their lives, but [illegible] death toll is placed at 10 to [illegible]

[illegible] of fifteen survivors were [illegible] later to-day by the fishing [illegible] and taken to Milwaukee [illegible] raised the rescued list to [illegible] Early check-ups along the [illegible]

CAPTAIN SANK WITH SHIP

The body of Captain Douglas Morrison was picked up by guardsmen [illegible]

REPORT THREE DIED

[illegible]

NOSE, THEN POCKET SUFFER INDIGNITY

Chicago, Oct. 29.—Walter Nolak, blacksmith, weighs 200 pounds and his wife, Eleanor, weighs less than 100. She appeared in court to-day to answer his charge of assault with intent to do bodily harm.

She put a bowl of cold water on the table, Nolak said. "I remarked it didn't look like soup to me. She dumped it on me. I dodged into the bathroom. She rained dishes at the door.

"When I thought she was out of ammunition I peeked out. She broke a plate on my nose."

Judge Herbert G. Immenhausen assessed a $100 fine.

Mrs. Nolak broke her silence. "My husband will pay it," she said. He did.

Curious Tale Nearly Snares Vote For Grit

Looks as If Speaker Had Confused Liquor Stores With Pawn Shops

Kemptville, Oct. 29.—(Special)—The ring of a true election campaign was sounded in Grenville County this evening when Rev. Thomas A. Bradley, prohibition candidate opposing Premier Ferguson, held a meeting in the town hall at Oxford Mills.

Mr. Bradley was supported by Rev. H. H. Beach and Rev. R. W. Armstrong. Rev. Armstrong, a firm prohibitionist, brought the meeting to a climax when he stated as a fact that bread and milk tickets were taken in exchange for beer and liquor at the Government liquor stores in Toronto, and that a vendor of one of these stores had stated that a man had offered to leave his false teeth in exchange for beer. At this juncture Gordon Sheppard, a native of this county, but now a resident of Toronto, and a keen supporter of the present administration, jumped to his feet and asked if that were an absolute fact, and if Mr. Armstrong were prepared to have it in the press over his own signature. Mr. Armstrong stated that he was still would immediately check its validity through the young man who had told him. Mr. Sheppard branded the assertion as wholly untrue, and stated that on his return to Toronto he would enquire of Sir Henry Drayton if this was the case, and if so, he would vote for prohibition.

Higher Wages For Carpenters

Builders' Exchange Reported to Have Made Offer to Union at Conference

The Telegram understands on the most reliable authority that a conference was held yesterday afternoon at the Builders' Exchange, Bay street, between the business agents of the Amalgamated Carpenters' Union of Canada, all Canadian, and the executive of all the sections of the exchange, when an offer was made of an increase in wages for 1930 and a further increase again in 1931.

The present wage scale of the carpenter [illegible] $1 an hour for a 44-hour week [illegible] contract expires December 31 [illegible] offer made to the [illegible] asking for an in-[illegible] hour some work [illegible]

Three Women Communists Sent to Farm

J. Corbin, Leader, 30 Days — D. Leibovich Fined $25; E. Chaihoff 10 [illegible] D. Bisgould 15 [illegible]

CHEERFULLY CONFIDENT, AWAITS THE VOTE

HON. G. HOWARD FERGUSON, Prime Minister of Ontario, is asking for popular support of the electorate at the polls to-morrow, says: "Our sole aim is to serve you faithfully and usefully in the future as in the past."

Election Machinery Ready To Handle Big Toronto Vote

Officials Prepar[illegible]-Party Forces Lay P[illegible] Out Most Voters—[illegible] a.m. [illegible]

CODY, FINLAYSON TO BE BROA[illegible]

Many Low Records for Year as Wall Street Trades Madly at Twenty Million Share Rate

New Lows on Toronto Market Include International Nickel, Brazilian Power, Massey-Harris, Walkers, Ford "A", Page Hersey—Wall Street Sales at Noon Total 8,000,000 Shares

By B. P. WEBBER, Financial Editor The Evening Telegram.

The stock Markets opened to-day with a crash that rocked the continent. Prices went crazy. Noranda sold at $10 a share at the opening in New York; Nickel was just above 26. Radio Corporation touched a low at 32. Chrysler at 31 and General Motors at 37. City Service was down to [illegible]. Blocks of shares were turned over ranging from 5,000 to 50,000 shares.

Sales on the New York Exchange crossed eight million shares around noon. This is at the rate of over twenty million shares a day, compared with just below thirteen millions during the previous record day last Thursday.

At one p.m. the New York ticker running an hour late showed prices at their low point for the day. Flashes from the market, however, stated that there were feeble signs that the selling was drying up.

George F. Baker, Jr., of the First National Bank, joined the conference at the Morgan offices in the early afternoon.

Officials of the New York Stock Exchange again delayed the delivery time of securities purchased and sold yesterday, from 2.15 to 2.30 p.m. to-day.

After the opening on the local market, in which scores of issues were far below their low points for the year, there was a decided upturn, but progress was very slow.

New York was in a turmoil with the ticker running an hour late. After the opening crash it was hard to determine the trend. Rallies would break out, followed by fresh selling. The market was demoralized and one financial man pointed out that only millions thrown into the market by cool-headed financial leaders would save the situation. It was apparent that these millions were waiting until the weak holders were cleaned out.

DRAWN, ANXIOUS FACES

Drawn and [illegible] faces jammed the gallery of the local Exchange and the watchers overf[illegible] also lined the doorway of the main floor. Every few minutes a [illegible] was called to the door to answer some client's question [illegible]

Many [illegible] evidence coming and going to local [illegible]

[illegible] very, but did not appear to [illegible]

WHEN MONEY IS REAL MONEY

Word came up from New York today that a man flashed a $5 bill while walking through Wall Street this morning, and was immediately offered a Rolls Royce and a palatial yacht for it.

Mayor Decides Police Building Chief's Affair

Choice of Site and Plans Not Matter For Board of Control, He Now States

Plans for the new police administration building are being held up by the Police Commission. This morning Mayor McBride unexpectedly took the view that the Police Commission and not the Board of Control and Council should decide where the police building is to be located. He said the Police Commission have not yet decided on the location.

Other members of the board were astonished at the Mayor's change of front to-day.

Two months ago the Mayor was very enthusiastic for [illegible] of the old Victoria School [illegible] on Victoria street as a site for [illegible] police headquarters.

[illegible]

The Telegram *of October 29, 1929 — "Black Tuesday" — broke the news that ushered in a decade of depression. Tory Premier Howard Ferguson "cheerfully" awaits the result of the election the following day — and his optimism was proven well-founded by voters.*

increasingly rampant speculation, marked the end of the superficially prosperous 1920s.[36]

The stock exchanges reflected — in an exaggerated fashion — life at the time. After a rise in 1919 from the doldrums of the Great War, the number of shares traded through the Toronto Stock Exchange and the Standard Stock and Mining Exchange fell off in 1920 and 1921, jumped suddenly in 1922, weakened slightly in 1924, and began a dramatic take-off in 1926: 132 million shares traded and a Standard value of $125 million. Following New York, up they went. In 1929, 318 million shares (19 million industrial) were traded and mining shares reached a bloated value of $710 million. When the Great Crash came, the collapse was apparent enough: in 1930 the value of mining stock shares fell to $140 million and the volume of industrial shares was cut in half.[37]

The serene picture of Toronto painted by Finance Commissioner George Ross had failed to include the storm clouds on the horizon. The city was bullish. Caution was thrown to the winds even by careful Torontonians as they got caught up in the speculative maelstrom. Just after the crash, the *Financial Post* complained of "markets ruthlessly manipulated by short selling." Even electorally, by voting for Sam McBride in 1928, Torontonians signalled to the world that they wanted growth. Certainly new skyscrapers dominating the downtown landscape reflected the impulse.[38]

The banking system, however, had become more stable during the 1920s, at least for those with safe money and a job. In November of 1929 Sir Joseph Flavelle, chairman of the board of the Canadian Bank of Commerce (by then Toronto's largest), could claim that "not a penny" had been lost in the crash because the bank had not invested in stocks. None of Toronto's brokers and investment dealers were forced to declare insolvency, and because banking was concentrated in the hands of a few, Canada was spared the American experience of small banks going under.

During the decade, bank mergers virtually completed the process of centralization that was quite apparent between 1900 and 1913. In 1923 *Saturday Night* was still asking whether small banks would survive: the answer was no. The Canadian Bank of Commerce's absorption of the Bank of Hamilton and the Standard (which in turn had taken over the Sterling) was the most significant development in Toronto banking. The Commerce increased its number of branches, especially in the west and Ontario, by a quarter (to about 800). With the disappearance in 1931 of the last tiny western bank into the fold of the Imperial, the financial empires of chartered banks had become totally concentrated in Toronto and Montreal. But the Commerce, the Nova Scotia (effectively a Toronto bank since 1900), the Imperial, the Toronto and the Dominion were in position to withstand the trials to come.[39]

Banking stability was also achieved through federal legislation that created the office of Inspector General of Banks. The legislation came in 1923 in the wake of the failure of the Home Bank. It had been started by a bishop in the mid-nineteenth century and many of the depositors at its eighty-two branches were working-class Roman Catholics. The failure resulted from shady dealings by the bank's officials, from bootlegging operations it financed into the dry U.S., and above all from the risky loans made to Henry Pellatt for speculating in real estate and other fields. Neither Casa Loma nor a knighthood saved Pellatt or the bank from bankruptcy. The Home Bank failure, which led to a temporary run by small depositors on the Dominion Bank, severely shook Canadian banking, and resistance to banking reform giving the federal government explicit power could hardly be maintained after that. The hand of government in the economy became conspicuously heavier: the system had to be controlled.[40]

The longstanding rivalry between Toronto and Montreal was heightened in the 1920s. Both cities were major manufacturing, wholesaling and retailing centres, but their most important role lay in organizing the financial life of the country. Although Montreal continued to house more headquarters of large corporations, the two cities remained fairly balanced through the decade. In 1920 the value of assets of Montreal's two giant "English" banks ran only slightly ahead of Toronto's big five; in 1930 the value of assets had increased relatively more. By then, altogether the seven banks held well over 90 per cent of all bank assets. Montreal's Sun Life also gained in assets significantly over Toronto's more cautious life insurance companies. But eight of thirteen of the leading insurance companies operated their head offices in Toronto. Activity at Toronto's stock exchanges was more brisk: in the late 1920s trading in industrial shares passed Montreal's. Toronto's brokers were busier partly because American investment increased, as Britain was supplanted as the chief source of foreign capital. In 1914 the American investment share was less than a quarter; by 1930 it had reached three-fifths of all foreign investment. Canadian banks invested successfully in the U.S. and staked Canadian corporate enterprises in other western countries. All told, Toronto and Montreal increased their financial hold over the rest of the country during the 1920s.[41] (Table XII)

By 1929 Toronto was surging ahead in the anglophone publishing business. Half of the business journals and a clear majority of monthlies came out of downtown Toronto, but the city's weeklies had fewer readers than Montreal's *Family Herald and Weekly Star* and had stiff competition in rural areas from London's *Farmers' Advocate*. Maclean's Publishing was the leader in the periodical field, but it was not as dominant as it would be later. Its flagship, *Maclean's*, competed with *Saturday Night*, the city's other national magazine. *Everywoman's World* gave way to the *Canadian Home Journal* and *Mayfair*, but they had to compete with the American *Ladies' Home Journal* in persuading women to buy more consumer goods. Nonetheless, many new periodicals appeared during the decade, testifying to greater middle-class affluence, reflected also in the opening of many new Eaton's and Simpsons stores across the country.[42]

Although growth in other economic activities was less vigorous than before the war, an increase was certainly noticeable. Tonnage through Toronto's harbour grew from about 250,000 tons in 1921 to 1.3 million in 1930. Electricity consumption outstripped population growth, and the rates were "among the lowest on the Continent." Tourist traffic increased. The Tourist and Convention Bureau, set up in 1926 to counteract the impression that Toronto was "possibly the poorest known big City" in North America, could report that in its first four years tourist spending had doubled. The city's charms and attractions were advertised at a kiosk in Niagara Falls, New York, and American motorists began discovering Toronto.[43]

Increased construction activity was reflected in the rising value of assessments. While the population of the city rose less than 25 per cent between 1918 and 1929, the value of assessments rose 60 per cent, from $606 million to $967 million. Assessments actually peaked in 1932 when the downtown buildings started before the 1929 crash were finally completed. Although in every year assessment expanded, as reflected also in building permits, construction was most rapid between 1920 and 1923 when subdivisions within the city's boundaries were filled in. The slowing of the pace thereafter, except just before the crash, signalled, however, a weakening economy. (Tables XII, XIV)

Although the rising assessment helped to hold the mill rate down and ensured more tax money for the city coffers, some concern was expressed over the type of construction. In his 1921 report the finance commissioner warned that the "industrial progress of the City is being retarded by a high tax rate" and, more ominously, that too much construction was occurring in "non-productive" sectors, such as offices, and not enough in manufacturing. Firms were either moving to or establishing themselves in suburban towns and villages such as Weston, New Toronto and Leaside (areas that Toronto was reluctant to annex).

Despite the finance commissioner's worries, the manufacturing sector apparently remained structurally stable. In 1922 the value of products made in the city reached $371 million, then pushed to a peak of $593 million in 1929. This expansion substantially exceeded the relatively high overall growth in Canadian industry: from 1923 to 1929 Canadian manufacturing output rose by 37 per cent, considerably surpassing both the U.S. and Britain. This exceptional record was partly the result of more American branch plants moving into the country, and many into the Toronto area.[44] (Table XI)

Although the city's labour force expanded fairly constantly in each sector, manufacturing's share fell slightly over the decade, though most of the loss occurred between the crash and the census. In 1931 manufacturing continued to employ nearly 30 per cent of the work force. The retailing and wholesaling trades remained the second largest group, with the wholesaling proportion falling as big department stores increased their share of retail sales without the services of wholesalers. A substantial increase occurred in the mixed census category of "community and business industries," from over 10 to over 16 per cent, indicating an increase in the number of professional and business support firms and of clerical workers. The financial, insurance and real estate fields expanded sharply, reflecting a shift in the city's economy. Public employment grew modestly to 1929.[45]

The number of women in the labour force increased slightly over the decade. In 1931 about a quarter of all women — most of them single — held jobs. However, the definite shift in women's employment from manufacturing to services continued, though less strongly than between 1911 and 1921 (excluding the war years). In 1921, 30 per cent of women workers were found in factories, close to half of them in textile and clothing sweatshops; ten years later, the proportion had fallen to less than a quarter. By 1931 nearly half the clerical workers were female; more women had become typists,

GOWNS ALL SPARKLE AND GLITTER

Are Easily Made With These Beaded Tunics

A SILKEN SLIP—that's all you need to evolve a gorgeous gown out of these indescribably beautiful tunics! They are exceedingly fashionable, with the present vogue for beading, and the essence of grace, scintillating with the lights from a thousand sequins, glowing with the color of a thousand beads—

You must see them for yourself among the trimmings on the Third Floor, where many other styles are gathered, beside the five shown here.

Clever beading gives a side draped effect to this tan tunic, patterned in light and dark gold, and cascading at the side in tiers of net. Price, $50.00.

Like the mist above Niagara, this simple straight tunic, beaded in white, and shimmering with opal lights, from the sequins spattered over it. Price, $19.50.

One of the loveliest for older women—a solid ground of black sequins, vividly splashed with round, richly shaded roses. Price, $75.00.

Perfectly simple, yet gorgeous, in stripes of glinting blue sequins and a quaint pattern of dull rose beads on black. Price, $29.00.

Dainty—exquisite—quite beyond description, this dull blue tunic, where slender petalled blossoms sprawl over a delicate floral pattern ground. Price, $40.00.

1919 marked Eaton's Golden Jubilee, celebrated above by Lady Eaton (at centre) and company staff. The vast Eaton empire, like Simpsons, retailed goods in its department stores and through mail-order advertising vehicles like the Eaton News Weekly *(left). Much of the clothing the company sold was manufactured in its factory lofts.*

Toronto's industry maintained its strength in the postwar years. Ship launchings became more rare, however, and expectations of heavy industry for the waterfront faded.

Industry's resilience owed much to the continuing influx of American branch plants, like that of Colgate-Palmolive Canada. The workforce here, as in many clothing factories, is largely female; but many women were finding service jobs.

retail clerks, telephone operators and teachers, though fewer held jobs in 1931 than in 1929. If women were now an "acceptable part of the paid work force," gains in status were not great. The image of women in major magazines was contradictory: should they stay at home or should they work?[46] (Table X)

The higher levels of inflation toward the end of the war and up to 1920 resulted in agitation for higher wages. From 1921 to 1929, a period of low inflation, the payroll in manufacturing rose from $84 to $134 million, matching the increase in value of products. Average annual earnings rose modestly from $1,261 to $1,306. However, wage gains relative to the value of the products slumped late in the decade, suggesting that workers retained a smaller share of the growth than their employers, increasingly more interested in gains through mergers than improved machines to raise productivity per worker. Cost of living and wage indices suggest more improvement over the decade for workers outside manufacturing, though women's wages did not improve.[47]

Employment insecurity persisted. Unions' efforts to counter the malaise were ineffectual as their membership fell during the decade. Indifference was so great in Ottawa that in 1928 the director of the Employment Service of Canada could not "hazard a guess" on the levels of unemployment over the past five years.[48]

The vulnerability of workers and the paternalism of industrialists during the uncertain 1920s were illustrated by the operation of the Industrial Council at Massey-Harris. With assets of $53 million in 1931, this multinational firm ranked thirty-first among all Canadian-owned companies and first in metal fabricating, and was recognized as one of the world's leading farm-implement manufacturers. Working conditions in the company's plants and its treatment of employees were among the best in the country, largely because of improvements toward the end of the war.[49]

In the spring of 1919, during the most turbulent time of industrial unrest in Canada, some workers at the Massey-Harris King Street plant went out on strike. The company then invited the workers to join management in forming an industrial council. After starting auspiciously with frank discussions on working conditions, by 1921 the council's weakness was becoming apparent. Because of the recession that year implement sales flagged and wages were cut without consultation with the workers on the council. From then on it became clear that the whole exercise was largely one in public relations. Although modest gains were registered in safety and in some other plant amenities, even vacations for a favoured few with seniority, management clearly reserved the right to control wages and terms of employment. Only in 1943, when industrial unions were recognized, did collective bargaining begin. In 1924 a protracted walk-out by typographers striking for a forty-four hour week also failed. Paternalism still remained the style of operation.[50]

A SLOWLY CHANGING CITYSCAPE

In 1929, 340,000 plants, 115,525 bulbs, 934 shrubs and evergreens, and 5,345 trees were set out in the parks and along the streets of Toronto. Clearly the city was affluent and it was indeed, as Commissioner Ross had boasted, "in splendid condition." Besides its beauty and cleanliness—a quality Charles Dickens had noted back in 1842 (he missed the March mud!)—the city's transportation system was working very well by North American standards. During the decade, the downtown was partly rebuilt and was moving upward. The waterfront passed through yet another extensive landfill and, except for a few slums, residential areas with their brick, semi-detached houses and tree-lined streets exuded stability. Development filled virtually all the prewar subdivisions within the city and spilled beyond the well-preserved boundaries. Strips of new shops appeared along new streetcar and bus routes: on the Danforth after the Prince Edward Viaduct over the Don was built in 1918, on Bayview and Eglinton West. Luxury shops opened up on Bloor west of Yonge. On the city's fringes, market gardening declined as vegetables and fruit began pouring in from the Holland Marsh and Niagara. But city hall found in this postwar growth certain features that were worrisome, such as the speculation that continued at the city's boundaries, automobile traffic, and indiscriminate intrusions of factories and warehouses into residential areas.[51] (Map 2)

The lines of the Toronto Transportation Commission (TTC) tied the city, if not the northern suburbs, together. On September 18, 1921, the TTC officially took over the creaking Toronto Railway Company (TRC) from the Mackenzie-Mann utility empire. Torontonians had spoken out in favour of the municipalization of their transportation system as far back as 1891, but City Council had ignored their views and opted instead for a thirty-year franchise agreement with Mackenzie-Mann. In the last decade of the TRC's monopoly franchise, there were signs of deteriorating service.

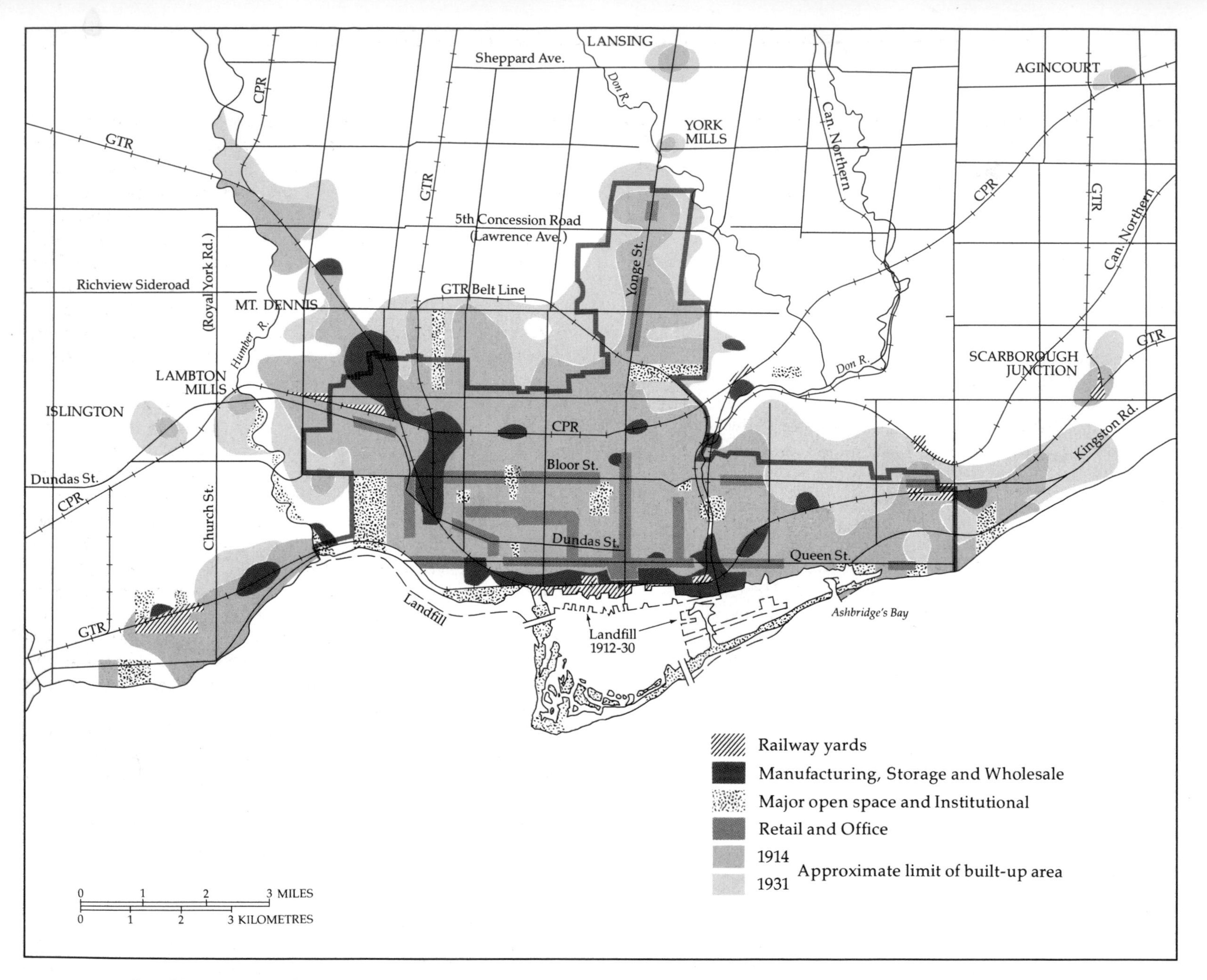

2 Land Use 1914 and Built-up Area, 1914 and 1931: In 1914 there was still some unoccupied space within the city's 30 square miles. By 1931 growth was only occurring beyond its boundaries. Among the major changes underway were landfilling in the harbour; further industrialization along rail lines; an increase of open space (such as at the Western beaches); and the development of commercial "streetcar strips."

Streetcars were crowded and busy. But the city's long-suffering strap-holders were told by TRC General Manager R.J. Fleming that they would simply have to "take the next car." Obviously the TRC had decided that there would be no improvements in the final years of its agreement with the city. The company even ignored an order from the Ontario Railway and Municipal Board to add cars to the system, electing to pay fines instead.[52]

In 1915 Tommy Church, a rather reluctant supporter of increasing funding for education and social services, dramatized the need for municipalization. At midnight on June 25 Mayor Church and a band of workers marched to the CPR crossing at Yonge Street and began tearing up a stretch of tracks on the Metropolitan branch of the Toronto and York radial line up Gallows Hill to Woodlawn Avenue at the 1891 city boundary—a line whose franchise, held by Mackenzie-Mann, had at that moment expired. The time had come to reassure restless residents in the north end, already tempted to secede, that they were part of the city and deserved cheaper and better transportation services. But they had to walk up and down the hill for a few years yet. In Toronto's New Year's Day elections between 1918 and 1921, voters overwhelmingly approved the takeover not only of the transit system but also of the hydro-electric company, also held by Mackenzie-Mann. Municipalization, through which, according to the *Star*, "service and dividends" were "synonymous" as "the people themselves are the shareholders," was the answer for transportation and electric power, if not for gas and telephone.[53]

In the U.S. and in Canada, municipalization was a holding action for streetcars as buses and automobiles increasingly took over the streets of the 1920s. But in Toronto it was confirmed that rails were here to stay. The TTC spent over $50 million, most of it by 1923 and with heavy backing from city hall—to the tune of $44 million. In the 1920s the city's high debt was largely the result of its commitment to the TTC and to Toronto Hydro. But the TTC single-zone fare in the city of seven cents or four for twenty-five cents eventually paid off the debt by the mid-1940s, even though the system was saddled in that short term with debts on failing radial lines beyond the built-up area, taken over in a "clean-up" arrangement with Mackenzie and Mann. Also, in a brilliant if controversial move, the TTC bought out five private intercity bus lines and amalgamated them into Gray Coach. The bus line proved to be profitable and the TTC gradually shed the interurban rail lines.[54]

By 1923 the TTC was running over 230 miles of track, by 1930, 254 miles. It had rebuilt most of the old TRC lines and interurbans in the city's built-up area, taken over the 1911 civic lines and added 43 miles. Ridership had increased to 200 million passengers by 1929 and, in terms of rides per capita, the TTC had surpassed all other systems on the continent, with the exception of New York's, Chicago's and San Francisco's. It had purchased 575 new steel Peter Witt cars and gradually scrapped over 400 draughty and ill-lit TRC cars. In 1930, 987 cars were in use. Unlike many U.S. systems, it added only a few bus and trolley bus lines. In 1929, along with over twenty other street railways, the TTC committed Toronto to the development of a streamlined car.[55]

But while the TTC integrated, rebuilt and expanded within city boundaries, like the TRC, it was reluctant to extend lines beyond them. Cars were operated on the old radials to the north, north-west and on the lakeshore, but there was little expansion. Three streetcar lines were added in York Township and a bus line in Forest Hill. With only the Leaside bus, which ran over the new Confederation bridge built over the Don Valley in 1927, East Yorkers had to rely on either a private bus firm or their legs to get to the Danforth. Those living outside the city had to pay a double fare because of a zone system that would persist to the 1970s. As a further blow, these lines were contracted and the municipalities through which they ran were responsible for any debts. The TTC thus followed the city in excluding suburbanites from full and equal participation in Toronto's life.[56]

In 1921 the growth-oriented *Star* argued that the TRC had "retarded the natural growth of Toronto and repressed the city as within iron bonds," despite the fact that public transportation "ought to be our most useful instrument in shaping the city's growth and development ...." By the end of the decade, the same accusation could have been levelled against the TTC as subdivisions languished far beyond city boundaries. Although York and East York were deprived of good service, the medium-density housing that resulted undoubtedly contributed to the financial success of the systems. By North American standards Toronto may have remained relatively dense; according to one calculation, it was exceeded only by New York and Jersey City.[57]

While Torontonians were already entrenched in the transit habit by the 1920s, the TTC had to increasingly share the city's streets and its commuters with the automobile. In 1916 there were

In the 1910s riders on the Danforth civic line had to get off at Broadview and pay a second fare to ride the overcrowded Toronto Railway Company (TRC) cars downtown. Poor service and TRC intransigence persuaded ratepayers to vote for a public system.

There are more free than paying passengers on this Toronto Suburban Railway car on Davenport just west of Bathurst, seen in 1923. This privately-owned line, which ran to west-end suburbs, was later taken over by the TTC.

Old lines were renovated and new ones added in the wake of the TTC's takeover of the TRC in 1921. This is the labrynthine junction of Queen, King, Roncesvalles and Lakeshore in 1923.

Commuting downtown by streetcar induced outlying streetcar shopping strips between 1880 and 1930. This scene at Bloor and Dundas West is from 1927.

10,000 cars in the city, in 1928 over 80,000, surpassing the ratio to population in big cities in the eastern U.S. and in generally poorer Canadian cities.

The number of vehicles entering and leaving downtown each day had tripled since 1915. Trucks were replacing horses (which meant fewer flies and fewer sparrows); in 1928 there were over 13,000 commercial vehicles compared to about 1,000 in 1916.[58]

City officials listened to calls for action and to proposed solutions, such as the *Star Weekly's* idea of limited access "speed highways" built over railway lines. In 1926 the Joint Traffic Committee (later the Traffic Advisory Board) was set up. Some street widenings were completed, as were the connecting links for Dundas Street to the east, underpasses beneath railways, bridges to Leaside and over the Moore Park Ravine, high level bridges over the Don and Humber, and new arteries on the waterfront to the west and east, allowing easier access to downtown. Traffic signals were installed, but aside from restricting parking, little was done downtown where streetcars competed with cars and trucks on narrow streets.[59]

Despite arguments that new office buildings would add to congestion and "menace the proper functioning of the whole civic transportation system," new skyscrapers were built and more were planned. Seven went up between 1922 and 1927 and, in 1928 alone, seven more were added. To the delight of some city officials, four buildings—Canada Permanent, Northern Ontario, Atlas, and Sterling Tower—tripled the assessment of their lots. The twenty-three storey *Star* building on King opened early in 1929, and though another tower was planned it was never built. The tallest building in the British Empire, the thirty-four storey Bank of Commerce, opened the same year under Sir John Aird's presidency. The massive Royal York Hotel and Canada Life Insurance building were already under construction. Along Bloor Street East in "midtown," insurance blocks appeared, while the Park Plaza and the Medical Arts building were under construction to the west. The provincial government contributed the Ontario Hydro building on University and the Whitney Block east of Queen's Park. Expansion upward, though modest at first, was soon running neck-and-neck with the mania for speculative stock gains.[60]

All this construction and the 1928 election of growth-minded Sam McBride to the mayor's chair seemed to signal a new era for Toronto's downtown. The idea of planning had been largely dormant in Toronto since 1913, but early in 1928 City Council appointed the Advisory Commission—Toronto's first since the province had approved planning boards in 1917 and 1918. The commission was composed largely of businessmen who shared Mayor McBride's dreams of growth, and was aided by city officials. While members deliberated in 1928, the *Telegram* and the politicians it supported darkly but inaccurately predicted that certain interests, including the *Star* (a McBride supporter) and the *Mail and Empire*, would gain if the rumoured "crooked lane" were run southeast from Queen and University, then south between the new *Star* building and the one planned by the *Mail and Empire*.[61]

In March 1929 the commission presented its downtown plan and it was nothing less than grand, naming major improvements after Great War battles in which Torontonians had fought. University Avenue was to run southward at a slight angle and around Vimy Circle, like Piccadilly. Cambrai Avenue was to run north from Front to a plaza bounded by City Hall, Osgoode Hall and the Registry Office. The scheme would rid the city of a lot of tatty buildings, including those in The Ward. New diagonals as in Detroit and street widenings would improve traffic flow into the downtown.[62] (See p. 47.)

It was expected that the plan would be fulfilled in fifteen years for a cost of $19 million. The city would retire the debt at the same time the plan was completed by following the European practice of expropriating the property for these streets and selling it at a profit. Debate raged over the issue of expropriation: who would benefit? Not surprisingly, the *Telegram* and *Globe* opposed the plan, the *Star* and *Mail and Empire* supported it. Bert Wemp, city editor of the *Telegram*, challenged both Mayor McBride and the plan. All the planning effort came to naught. In the wake of the Great Crash, on January 1, 1930, the voters narrowly came out against the plan (29,680 to 27,277) and turned out McBride. Patriotic invocation of Great War battles did not persuade quite enough voters to support this plan, by far the most extravagant in a Toronto rarely moved by civic grandeur. Only the extension of University Avenue was built.[63]

As in the nineteenth century and up to 1912, the waterfront remained a fertile ground for political action. The Board of Toronto Harbour Commissioners' 1912 plan set the framework for development to 1930, and included proposals to make Toronto an important port, to attract industry to the waterfront, and to

The finishing touches are put on one of the enduring skyscrapers of the late 1920s, the Canada Life Building at University and Queen. From this vantage point, the rise of commuting by car is obvious from the parking lots straddling York Street. Land speculators who anticipated further skyscrapers created the lots, which would largely remain just that for many years.

Originally "Macaulaytown" in St. John's Ward, the slum in the shadow of City Hall came to be known as "The Ward." It was an ongoing embarrassment to Torontonians, despite a scorching indictment of public neglect issued by the Bureau of Municipal Research in 1918. In the 1920s Chinatown would take over part of the area.

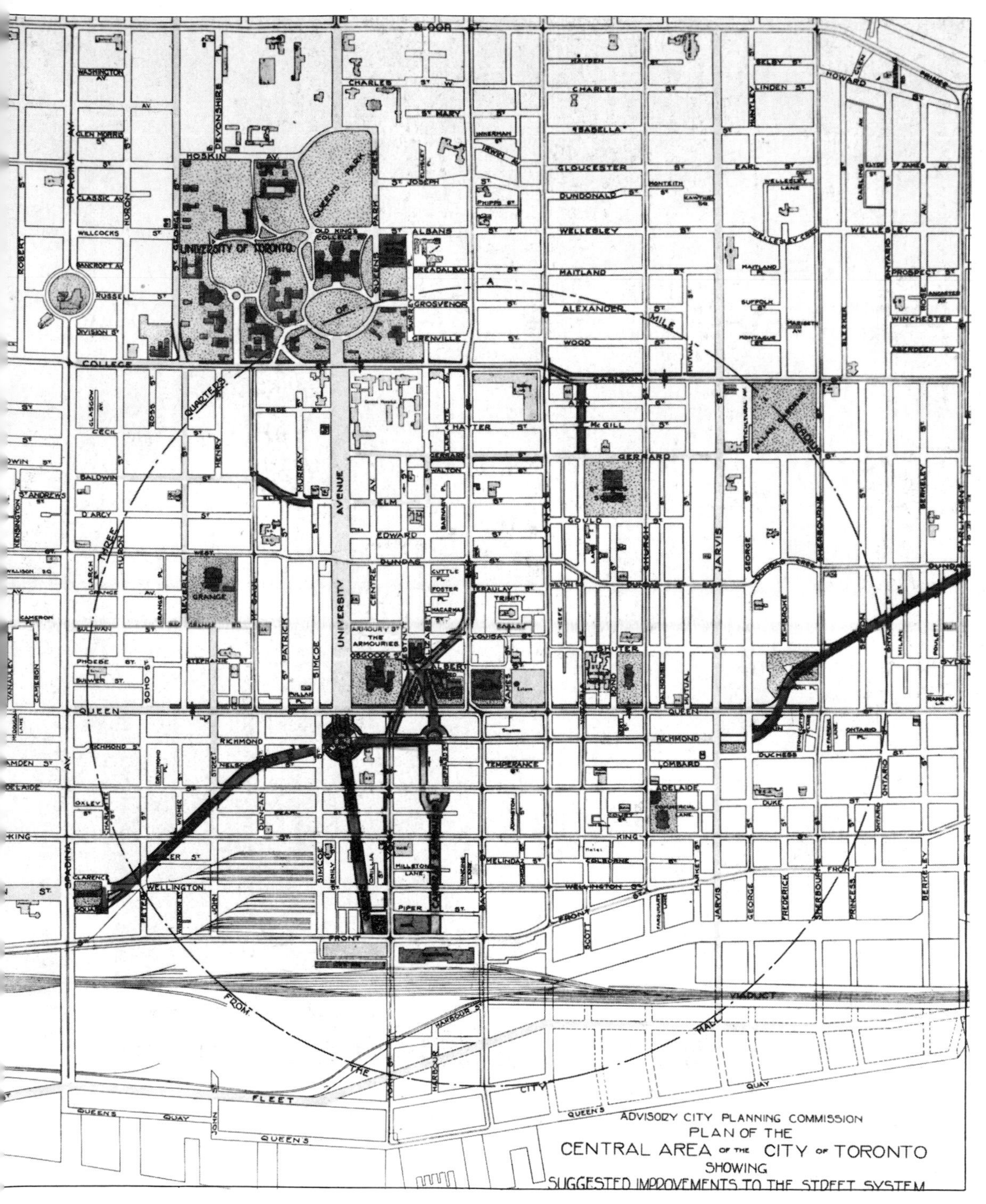

The speculative late 1920s led to visions of grandeur. The city's 1929 plan directed automobile traffic along grand avenues blazed mostly through low-income areas like The Ward. (These "motor boulevards," all named after battles of the Great War, are shown in dark shading.) But in the depressed early 1930s only some jog eliminations and the extension of University Avenue south of Queen were carried out. Even then, Vimy Circle, shown above, was not included in the extension.

From 1913 to 1930, Toronto's waterfront was reshaped. New industries, shipping berths and railway tracks gradually appeared on landfill in Ashbridge's Bay and the central waterfront. While the Great Hall of the new Union Station (foreground) was finished by 1919, the viaduct bringing in tracks (beginning in background) was only begun in 1924 and not finished until 1931. Visible to the left are the old tracks along the Esplanade and the old Great Western terminal at Yonge, by this time in use as a wholesale fruit market. The monumental federal Customs Building of classical design would replace the parking lots between Yonge and Bay in the early 1930s.

In its early years, Union Station saw one historic Toronto hotel fall and another rise across Front Street. The Queen's Hotel, a Toronto institution since 1856, was replaced in 1929 by the Royal York, the largest hotel in the British Empire. Most of the buildings in the foreground were built from the ground up after the 1904 fire.

promote leisure activity, all within eight years. It was 1930, rather than 1920, before the landfill for industry, port facilities and railways was completed. Yonge Street to the Don was the last section filled by the two dredges — named *Cyclone* and *Tornado* — which became familiar to everyone. Parkland and Lakeshore Boulevard, from the Western Gap over to the Humber, and Cherry Beach were completed. By 1930, 1,448 acres had been reclaimed, but leasing continued at a slow pace, so much so that the commissioners sold land to bolster revenue. The 1912 plan, conceived at the peak of the prewar boom, had depicted rows of factories adjacent to the shipping berths of a reshaped Ashbridge's Bay. But most of them never materialized. Oil storage tanks had appeared and coalyards were expanded, however. Grain elevators, the Terminal Building, and the Harbour Commission Building became prominent landmarks on the newly expanded central waterfront.[64]

Together with the war and the slower economy, two confrontations held back waterfront and downtown development. The first and most prolonged was over the viaduct planned to raise the railway tracks and allow easier access to the waterfront. Begun in 1913 after years of debate, the final piece, the York Street underpass, was not opened until 1931. Even though the great hall of the new Union Station had been completed in 1919, the railways refused to co-operate on the viaduct until 1924. And, although officially opened with great fanfare by the Prince of Wales in August of 1927, the station was not fully operational until 1931. The second confrontation was over whether electrical radial entrances should be permitted on the waterfront leading to a terminal near the new Union Station. In 1916 Toronto voters had agreed to Adam Beck's grand vision of a vast interurban network throughout southern Ontario, but by 1920 the tide was turning toward the car. The rural-dominated legislature saw the Model T, not the radial, in the farmer's future. But City Council persisted, and the issue came to a final vote in 1923. Warnings from the *Telegram* — that workingmen would be deprived of country cottages and sick children would be denied the healing powers of country air — fell on deaf ears. The "waterfront grab," as opponents dubbed it, was defeated handily. Gray Coach buses, not toonerville trolleys, were to carry central Ontario's travellers to and from Toronto.[65]

TORONTO'S SETTLED POPULATION

Finance Commissioner George Ross's "settled" and "contented" population grew from 489,681 in 1918 to 606,370 in 1929. While the growth rate was considerably lower than it was during the years before 1914, virtually all the areas annexed by 1912 were full by the end of the 1920s. Beyond the city's boundaries, the number of suburbanites more than doubled, contributing to an increase in the metropolitan area's share of Ontario's population. The slowed rate of immigration contributed to a decrease in the proportion of young children, though schools remained crowded. (Tables I-V)

The ethnic composition of the city remained overwhelmingly British. In 1931, 81 per cent of Torontonians claimed British origins, which led local historian Jesse Middleton to assert that "no other city of comparable size... is as homogeneous...." The number identifying themselves as English grew slightly, while fewer reported Irish roots. Of the native-born Canadians almost all were from Ontario. The non-British "element" (a term used at the time) grew modestly, by less than 5 per cent over the decade, to about 19 per cent. Jews remained the largest ethnic group, increasing slightly to just over 7 per cent; Italians were the only other group to reach 2 per cent. Of the foreign-born (as distinct from the ethnic category), only those from Poland jumped markedly, to over 3 per cent. Particularly after the United States virtually closed its borders in the early 1920s, some immigrants arrived from other parts of eastern Europe, such as the Ukraine and Hungary.[66] (Tables VI-VII)

The city's religious affiliations perpetuated its British tradition, while also reflecting North American denominational pluralism. Although in 1925 the Methodists, more than half of the Presbyterians and a small number of Congregationalists joined to form United Church congregations, in 1931 the city's Anglicans still outnumbered them three to two. Roman Catholics registered a modest increase. (Table IX)

Between 1916 and 1918 in the *Star Weekly* reporter W.A. Craick described sixty-four public elementary schools and their residential districts (about four-fifths in the city). From his articles emerges a picture of the city's class and ethnic composition. In class terms, Craick considered some local populations as "floating", others as "solid" working-class; "solid" middle, and well-to-do. His chief ethnic distinctions were British and Hebrew, but Craick makes clear where mixing and expansion were taking place.[67]

The lower-income districts with floating or transient populations were largely adjacent to the central business district and toward the east in Cabbagetown, to the northeast, and in Yorkville. Shack towns outside the city boundaries continued to spring up, as portrayed by Lawren Harris in his painting "Outskirts of Toronto." But the neighbourhood most in the eye of Toronto, and especially its social reformers, was The Ward. Located west of Yonge and above Queen and focussed on Hester How School, named after a concerned reformer, by 1918 The Ward was the poorest Jewish area, where rag-picking was the chief male occupation and garment-making in sweatshops, such as Eaton's, the main source of income for females. Perpetuating prewar reform concerns, the Bureau of Municipal Research published a strong indictment of conditions in 1918 with graphic evidence of low incomes, wretched housing, inadequate diets and disease in an area being held by speculators awaiting further institutional and business expansion. The "social gospel" waned, however, and by 1922 conditions had not improved much. By 1930 fewer people were living there, even though Chinatown was appearing west of City Hall.[68]

Other downtown neighbourhoods were also under pressure from the advancing factories and office buildings. Victoria Street, York Street, Duke Street and George Street schools disappeared in 1930 and were combined into the new Duke of York School. Chicago sociologists of the day would have recognized the invasion-succession pressures induced by the expansion of the downtown and resulting in rundown zones of transition. The sociologists would also have seen the transient floating population who lived in boarding houses in areas like Wellesley at Bay as evidence of *anomie*, of an atomized urban population. If these sociologists tended to see the processes as "natural" to cities, clearly the tenacious reformers of the time did not. Yet, despite improvements in the 1920s, not until the 1940s did Toronto seriously confront the problems of poverty.[69]

Regent Park in Cabbagetown contained a poor British and native labouring population, which was "constantly shifting." Around Sackville School was located "one of the dingiest districts" where smoke poured over the mixed English, Scottish, Irish and Jewish population; and, although not noted by Craick, here sojourning Macedonians were crowded into rooming houses, though fewer than before 1912 because they were moving elsewhere or returning home. Despite the poverty of these areas, Cabbagetown managed to produce notable Torontonians in this era, such as Mayor Horatio Hocken and labour leader Jimmie Simpson.[70]

West of downtown were modest neighbourhoods where transiency was less apparent. By 1912 the Jewish Kensington Market had developed. Many Jews were working in the factory-loft district that had crystallized around Spadina and King by 1921. The Jewish ghetto embraced a large area, with Spadina Avenue as the axis. Although not all Jews were segregated, most of the expansion of this community was to the west and north. At College and Grace, Little Italy was well established.[71]

The largest number of school areas described by Craick were working-class, some "solid" if they were British. Many of these were east of the Don; some were rather poor, such as around Morse and Queen Alexandra schools. More affluent were the neighbourhoods surrounding such schools as Duke of Connaught (though recently an "object of charity"), Norway, and Earl Grey, where growth had "mushroomed." To the west were the Junction and Parkdale area schools, where residents worked in the CPR railyards or the factories. A small Jewish enclave had appeared in the Junction area. Closer in were Manning (now Charles G. Fraser) and Grace, then beginning to take in Jews and Italians. The children of Givins School near Massey-Harris were already on their way to fifty years of athletic superiority.

Moving up the ladder to "solid" middle-class areas, Craick noted that the school children in the Brock Avenue and Clinton area in the west came from the homes of artisans and some business and professional employees. The Dufferin-Bloor area, High Park and parts of Parkdale were also middle-class areas. The Eglinton community was considered "fairly well to do," with most families owning their own homes. The Beaches was another middle-class neighbourhood.

Only a few upper-class districts came under Craick's scrutiny, though some were cheek-by-jowl with less affluent areas and some were mixed. Rosedale was the neighbourhood of the wealthy who sent many of their children to private schools, such as Upper Canada, Bishop Strachan and Havergal. As the rich moved north to the "hill district," Huron Street School in the Annex was "now more for the masses." Nonetheless, many Annegonians in the 1920s still

There were many faces to Toronto. Above left, Rosedale children in 1920; above, youngsters downtown pick among cinders discarded by the gas company in 1923. Downtown was an ethnic mosaic, symbolized in the photo at left, where York Street School pupils from fourteen different nationalities were posed beneath the Union Jack. York Street was closed in the 1930s, one of three inner-city schools that disappeared as the expanding central business district invaded neighbourhoods.

bought subscriptions to the *Blue Book* to advertise their names. In the west end near High Park was an "excellent class of population." Finally, an apparent anomaly in the downtown was the McCaul Street area with a "bon-ton" Jewish school, just west of The Ward, though many Jewish children also attended religious or ethnic schools. Segregation by class within the Jewish community had already occurred. Upper-income districts not noted by Craick were well underway, such as Lawrence Park and Kingsway Park just over the Humber in Etobicoke. Wealth from northern Ontario mines created some areas: "It is a well-authenticated legend that Cobalt built up the St. Clair Avenue district, Noranda and Hollinger built Moore Park, and nickel, Forest Hill." Restrictive covenants maintaining high quality housing and, beginning in 1921, residence-only bylaws protected the class, if not totally the ethnic, homogeneity of these neighbourhoods.[72]

What emerges from these snapshots by Craick are several conclusions. First, many of the city's residential districts as they are known today were apparent during the First World War; if the ethnic character of some areas has changed, the relative income levels have persisted in many cases. Second, despite many areas being described as "solid," considerable mixing was obvious. Fixed enclaves of affluent and working-class existed side-by-side, as in the new Wychwood district and adjacent to Pellatt's white elephant, Casa Loma. Third, the invasion-succession pressures, while apparent near to the downtown and toward the west during the prewar period of rapid growth, seemed to lose steam because of slower growth in the 1920s and 1930s and also because of the strong political action of residents' groups, home and school associations, and the work of City Council.

In the 1920s, throughout the western world, antagonism toward Bolsheviks and discrimination against foreigners were rampant. In this very British city the same impulses surfaced, and were so intertwined that it is not clear which was the cardinal sin. During the war Germans carried the burden of the stranger, so much so that between the 1911 and the 1921 censuses half of them stopped declaring their ethnic origin. A few Greeks had suffered during a riot in 1917. Some Finns and Ukrainians felt the stings of discrimination, and the Chinese marked July 1, 1923, as "Humiliation Day" when the Chinese Immigration Act excluded any more Chinese from entering the country, guaranteeing that men in Canada would forever be separated from their families.[73]

Yet it was the Jews who bore the greatest burden. The small number of Jews who saw socialism as an answer to economic problems were tagged Bolsheviks or Reds. The large numbers involved in the needle-trade unions, most of whom spoke only Yiddish, contributed to the view that most Jews were card-carrying Communists. Discrimination against them was blatant. In 1920, for example, the city's legislative committee debated whether or not to prohibit non-English—meaning Yiddish—advertising signs. And according to Alderman John Cowan, "If foreigners who came here to make a living could not conform to English ways and customs they could return to their native countries." This kind of comment was mild compared to *Saturday Night*'s continued attacks in the early 1920s: Canada had become the "dumping ground for the 'scum of Europe'." Referring to Jews the magazine exclaimed, "Imagine a gang with names like that running a white man's country!" *Saturday Night* also worried about the Bolsheviks in labour; beginning in 1923 under a new editor, it identified a new enemy, the Ku Klux Klan. The chickens were coming home to roost.[74]

In late 1928 and 1929 the issue of free speech severely divided Toronto. Chief Constable Denis C. Draper, with the support of the Police Commission, prohibited Communist public meetings in foreign languages. Street-corner meetings were banned, and in August 1929 Communist meetings held at Queen's Park ended in arrests. While the *Telegram*, the *Globe* and the *Mail and Empire* applauded these efforts to prevent Queen's Park from becoming a replica of Hyde Park, other journalists, like Joseph Atkinson and Salem Bland, writing in the *Star*, were among those who fought against this kind of repression; the *Star* was dubbed "the Big Brother of the Little Reds" by the *Telegram*. The *New Outlook* of the United Church also shared misgivings. Although the Toronto Trades and Labour Council had been locked in a bitter battle with the Communists, it too opposed these strong-arm tactics. *Saturday Night* now worried about the dismissal of human rights. After a Hart House debate on the motion that "Toronto is deserving of her reputaton for intolerance," students voted overwhelmingly for the yea side and against Mayor McBride, who tried to argue otherwise. The free-speech crisis would deepen into Canadian-style McCarthyism in the early 1930s. That Torontonians resisted Bolshevism is understandable enough. That they were so willing to abrogate the right of free speech and to link foreigners and Communists is less so. But, as Michiel Horn argues, "Kicking the Reds was, it seems, for some

The largest "ethnic" group in still very British Toronto was the Jews, who even before 1914 had been leaving behind the storefronts of The Ward for Kensington Market, Spadina Avenue and other districts to the west.

Italians were the second-largest group of non-Anglos. Family picnics on the Humber were a favourite past-time in the 1920s.

Gypsies, if few in number, were highly visible. This family's campsite is also by the Humber.

people a thinly-disguised way of kicking aliens in general and Jews in particular."[75]

The fear of strangers was obviously upsetting, particularly as the economy signalled distress in the speculative fever of the late 1920s. The great prewar influx of non-Anglo-Saxons, while nowhere on the scale of immigration into New York, must have been unsettling to a city so devoted to things British. In the 1920s it may well have been a sense of a slipping empire that gnawed at Torontonians. The decline was partially offset by rising signs of a Canadian identity. The Orange Order began its long slide into obscurity, though the *Telegram's* Orange slates still dominated. Nathan Phillips, who would become Toronto's first Jewish mayor, knew in his first run for alderman in 1924 that he would have to join the Conservative Party to win. Returned Canadian soldiers and English immigrants in the 1920s were appalled enough by the slaughter in France to show less willingness to wave the Union Jack as fervently as before. The invasion of American investment and culture added another dimension to the identity problem. The theatre began to show inklings of a Canadian presence; the formation of the United Church and the Group of Seven would as well, though with some uncertainty.[76]

As the cultural centre of anglophone Canada, Toronto was appropriately the locale of the first assembly of the United Church in 1925. The coming together of Methodists, Congregationalists and many Presbyterians was of major importance to Toronto and Canada where religious views were strongly held. The quest for union had taken decades. Union created considerable bitterness within families and among friends. Disputes over property were particularly charged. Knox College remained with the Presbyterians, though it obviously became a much less significant institution than Victoria College within the University of Toronto. What was especially important in the formation of the United Church was the establishment of a nearly national church. If the continuing Presbyterians drew on their Scottish tradition to sustain their identity, those who joined the United Church now could claim that Canada was not just an English colony. For the Methodists the union offered a leg up over Anglicanism, that bastion of empire. The Ryerson Press was a major force in Canadian publishing.[77]

In the 1920s religious and moral issues often divided Torontonians. Though the "social gospel" of prewar days had slipped, it was sustained through the decade by the founding of the university's Student Christian Movement and by the appearance of the *Canadian*

The inaugural service of the United Church of Canada was held 10 June 1925 at the Mutual Street Arena. Front and centre seats were reserved for officials — the sprinkling of women's hats farther back shows where seating for others begins. The union of Methodists, Presbyterians and Congregationalists was a singular event in the Protestant world.

Forum. Both appeared in 1920 and would focus the left intellectuals for several decades. On the right were men like T.T. Shields of Jarvis Street Baptist Church (the wealthiest in Ontario) who thundered the invectives of American fundamentalism against his modernist liberal colleagues (many could be found at McMaster University, located until 1928 on Bloor Street). Even the Anglicans experienced schismatic impulses as evangelicals and Anglo-Catholics railed against one another. When arguments failed, the evangelicals resorted to stealing the high-church vestments from St. Thomas's and trampling them in the mud.[78]

The Group of Seven, which was based in Toronto, pointed indirectly to the new nationalism. Lawren Harris painted working-class homes in Toronto and Halifax. But even in these paintings, people were largely absent or just as diminutive as they were in vast numbers of portraits of the northern Ontario landscape. Though the Group's artists may have complained of "urban materialism" and the horrors of war as did Fred Varley, their pictures of the north largely failed to capture the human and environmental exploitation caused by mining and lumbering ventures which were financed by Toronto's bankers. To Barker Fairley, "the characteristic work of the Group is as empty of humanity as an extinct volcano." Nonetheless, in the midst of a not very creative decade, these painters developed a distinctive Canadian (or at least Ontarian) style that eased the transfer of emotional attachment from the British Empire to Canada.[79]

But Toronto was hardly any more cosmopolitan in a cultural than in an ethnic sense. To Ernest Hemingway, the young *Star Weekly* reporter in the early 1920s, Toronto's population was all too settled. In 1923 he complained in letters to friends: "Christ, I hate to leave Paris for Toronto the City of Churches" where "85% of the inmates attend a protestant church on Sunday. Official figures." Not only that, he had to buy a box of chocolate peppermints for a friend in hospital from a bootlegger because the drugstores "cannot sell candy on Sunday." Quiet, Orange, British Toronto could not nourish a Hemingway, nor an Emma Goldman who, a few years later, was told by a Toronto librarian: "No, we do not censor books, we simply do not get them."[80]

Toronto's continuing dourness, its xenophobia, the inability of women to establish themselves firmly in politics or in economic life, the controversies within the labour movement, unemployment, the exclusion of the growing suburbs, caution turning to speculation, the decline of the reform impulse with its ideological base in the "social gospel" were all part of Toronto life in the 1920s. But they cannot detract from the high sense of civic responsibility and a strong concern for the fabric of the city. Toronto had developed certan mechanisms to deal with the running of the city, such as commissions, a strong civil service, ratepayers' groups, newspapers that paid close attention to city affairs, though not always rationally. Less was left to chance in sorting out the city's landscape than in American cities; the municipalization and orderly development of the street railways in the 1920s were a sure sign of order. But in the 1930s Torontonians would be forced by conditions to debate new ways, ways that would bloom in the 1940s.

The skyline of 1931 would change little until 1960. From the right, the highest buildings are: the Royal York, the Star, *the Bank of Commerce (standing tallest), the pre-1914 Royal Bank building at King and Yonge, the recently finished Sterling Towers and, across Richmond Street, the uncompleted Victory Building, which remained empty until 1938, thanks to the Depression. At thirty-four stories, the Commerce building was the tallest in the Empire — but only a third of the height of the Empire State Building, constructed at the same time. The photograph on page 46 was also taken from this vantage point.*

Chapter Two

The Dirty Thirties

> We have a great and beautiful city... blessed by honest and efficient government... but I fear... [it] has acquired the inevitable "slum districts."... Would it not be a splendid thing to commemorate this, our hundredth civic year, by the creation of a large and noble plan conceived in a spirit of fellowship? A plan that would mould this city more nearly to our heart's desire, a plan that would recognize the inalienable right of every man and woman and child to a decent and dignified and healthful environment.

To the assembled dignitaries at the centennial luncheon in 1934, Lieutenant-Governor Herbert Bruce's sudden reference to "slum districts" must have come as a shock. These elite Torontonians, though not lulled by wine, had already been soothed by the bland praise of high officials such as R.B. Bennett and Mackenzie King. They then heard Bruce call for "planned decentralization" of "outmoded" industry and new suburbs so that workers' "children would learn by experience... that there are really and truly other and lovelier flowers than those on the lithographed calendar that hangs on the cracked, crumbling and soiled wall of a murky room into which the sun's rays have never penetrated." Not for a decade and a half had such a clarion call been heard from an establishment figure. Many of those assembled in the ballroom would not have agreed that all Torontonians possessed the "inalienable right" to an environment of decency, dignity and health. Slums had existed for decades and the Depression exacerbated conditions.[1]

The celebration of Toronto's birthday symbolized, nevertheless, a turning point in the bleak thirties. The worst was passing, even though economic recovery would be slow and another sharp setback would strike in 1938. Many would remain on relief. Bruce's remarks and those of others did move city officials and citizens to search more seriously, if haltingly, for solutions to economic, social and planning problems.

THE UNSUSTAINING ECONOMY

The Depression hit Toronto hard. According to the 1931 census, 17 per cent of Torontonians were unemployed; by January 1933, 30 per cent were jobless. In early 1935, a quarter of the population of Toronto and suburbs was on relief. Most suburbs suffered more than the city; in East York 45 per cent of the population was on the dole and working residents paid much of the cost. The social results were disquieting, to say the least. While describing the human tragedies, novelist Hugh Garner also observed that "there is love in Cabbagetown:"

> Behind the front windows... lies drama, pathetic or shocking. There are innumerable quarrels and bickerings, drunken fights, sordid tragedies. There are the quarrels of worn-out parents with the idle and blasé sons and daughters, who, unable to find work, must need lie about the house all day sunk in cynical boredom.... There are tragic arguments over the birth of illegitimate children to the unmarried daughters of the household.... If young girls and boys spend their evening hours making love, who can blame them, and what else is there to do?

Remembering those days of her childhood, Bernice Hunter recalls the ferocity of the squabbles between her parents after her father failed to find work, of his shame in not providing for his family, and of his resentment toward those handing out Christmas charity. Only the single drifters had it worse. As in seventeenth-century English parishes, they were forced out of even the worst sort of shelter, such as the abandoned brick kilns in the Don Flats; they were insulted for not getting work; their relief funds and few hostels were threatened. They were isolated—unable even to share the collective anguish of Cabbagetown families. But while scapegoating them as "slackers," the finance commissioner could argue that the city's finances were beyond its control. Despite the inability of the economy to sustain working people, many others did well, and Toronto increased its economic strength in relation to Montreal.[2]

Several sectors of the economy were hit harder than others; those sectors with wage earners bore the brunt of the Depression. Construction almost stopped. The number and value of building permits fell to the lowest level in the century, and the best the industry could manage was a recovery that matched only half of the weakest year of the 1920s. In the city the number of houses in 1939 barely exceeded the 1929 level. In only one year did the number built reach 300. As in the late 1920s, the late 1930s saw the revival of apartment construction, so that by 1940 there were 60 per cent more units than at the beginning of the decade. The semi-detached city was resembling Montreal more and more as 28 per cent of all units were apartments. After 1931 commercial and industrial construction virtually ceased. Office vacancy rates remained high.[3] (Tables XIII, XIV)

Manufacturing was cut back, hitting a low point in 1933 and 1934; even by 1939 activity had not quite regained the peak levels of 1929. The value of products fell by half to 1933, then slowly recovered, only to slow down again in 1938. Many more firms appeared so that their average size fell dramatically between 1929 and 1933, and would not rise significantly until the war. The drive toward mergers and larger firms had been reversed, if only temporarily. The Toronto Industrial Commission claimed that it encouraged the setting-up of new factories. Yet by 1938, though 500 acres had been leased or sold on Harbour Commission lands created after 1912, nearly twice as many sites were still available.[4] (Tables X, XI)

For workers in manufacturing, conditions deteriorated. They might have been worse if manufacturers had reduced the number of employees as sharply as the values of their products fell. In 1933 three-quarters of the workers employed in 1929 were still on the job and, in 1939, about as many as in 1929. But, partly as a result of underemployment, in 1933 wages dropped to 60 per cent of 1929 levels—though rents remained at nearly three-quarters. Salaried teachers whose incomes were cut fared better than wage workers—and anyone with a job certainly survived more easily than the unemployed.[5] (Tables X, XI)

In the sweatshops like Eaton's, which had earlier been a model for the industry, piece-work wages were cut drastically, and the women were forced to work faster, with their pace being timed by stop watches. They could expect to be fired if they did not reach the production level of the minimum weekly wage of $12.50 established in the 1920s. As one testified before the Royal Commission on Price Spreads in 1935, "You were driven so fast that it just became impossible to make $12.50, and you were a nervous wreck.... It almost drove me insane." Of course, if a woman "were starving, she could have reported to the welfare office at Eaton's.... It had a generous welfare office." Turn-of-the-century conditions again prevailed, particularly in the low-wage sectors.[6]

These conditions were scant comfort to the unemployed. Although the city and Toronto's business community responded to the unemployment problem at the onset of the Depression, as the crisis deepened innovative (but unsuccessful) notions gave way to the dole. If economic planning solutions, proposed by the democratic left through the CCF's Regina Manifesto and the League for Social Reconstruction, failed to take hold, at least headway was made when some of the burden of welfare was shifted from local government to higher levels. Although relief recipients still bore the greater burden, the Elizabethan Poor Law model of purely local responsibility was beginning to crack.[7]

In January 1930 the city set up a Civic Unemployment Relief Committee to survey the possibilities of relief jobs. The Board of Trade and other groups organized through a Joint Committee on Unemployment asked employers to avoid layoffs if they could. The city also established a Civic Employment Office and a Central Bureau for Unemployment Relief. Early in 1932 the new Public Welfare Department pulled together these activities, and non-profit charities struggled to contribute.[8]

Following federal government proposals, public works were pursued initially by the city and the adjacent municipalities. In 1930 the city spent three times as much on outdoor work as on the dole. Mimico sold debentures to put men to work on sewers and watermains; Etobicoke laid watermains; New Toronto gave the men sledgehammers to break up rocks for road metal—a time-honoured path to bread and virtue for the male poor. The two upper-level governments together contributed half the cost. But it was soon argued that using unskilled labour instead of machines was inefficient and more costly and, as the crisis deepened, public

Lieutenant-Governor Herbert Bruce and Mrs. Bruce leaving Chorley Park, his official residence. Far from merely being a ceremonial figurehead, Bruce called for action to rid the city of slums in 1934.

works could hardly handle the growing ranks of unemployed. Another problem made this kind of solution increasingly unfeasible: except for Forest Hill and Swansea, other adjacent municipalities headed into bankruptcy. Even Toronto, with its rich commercial and industrial tax base, saw its assessment fall, its line of credit recede, and its first deficits since 1914.[9]

In 1933 Harry Cassidy, in his *Unemployment and Relief in Ontario, 1929-1932*, could still argue for relief "providing it is applied in the right way." Cassidy was striving for providing a shred of dignity through hard work on useful civic projects and on farms, at least for single men. But after that, imaginative solutions largely vanished as married men went on the dole in droves.[10]

So people lived on the lowest possible guaranteed income, chiefly vouchers for low-nutrition food and inadequate clothing, and they suffered the indignity of means tests. Since the Dominion government provided only a third of direct relief funds, the provinces were reluctant, even unable, to give more than another third. For the other third, the municipalities had to either use current funds or borrow, which was beyond the ability of many places. In better-off Toronto, the cost reached $6.7 million; the city's share was borrowed on 5-year instalment debentures at 4.5 per cent. The peak of almost $10 million was reached in 1935 when 23 per cent of the population was on relief. (The city's proportion amounted to about half of its total budget for 1900.) With about 8 per cent of Canada's population, Toronto paid out 19 per cent of the national relief bill—a sure sign of its great affluence, if less clearly of its generosity. In 1936 East York residents contributed one week's pay a year to relief costs; Torontonians, only one day's.[11]

After 1935 the annual amounts decreased slowly. But by 1939 a total of $61.3 million had been spent on direct relief in Toronto and, for the city's part, $14.9 million had been borrowed. Although in the latter years of the decade better economic conditions generated higher taxes and allowed the city to pay more from current revenues, the taxpayers had to pay off the debt. By 1939 relief costs were taking nearly eleven cents of every city tax dollar spent. Funds for other services dwindled. Public works and the police, rather than education and health, took the greatest cuts. The city administration had weathered the storm; the mill rate rose only to a peak of 36, and by 1945 all of the debts of the 1930s had been paid off.[12]

The federal government's parsimony was a block; neither R.B. Bennett nor Mackenzie King would act with Roosevelt's vigour, despite appeals from the provinces and hard-pressed cities and towns. A 1933 proposal to impose a special tax on incomes higher than $10,000 was resisted by the Board of Trade and by the *Financial Post* in the fashion of supply-side Reaganomics: Have faith in the rich to invest and buy, they will lead us out of the Depression. But the burden remained overwhelmingly on regressive property taxes. How many low-income people lost their homes and how many renters were evicted during the decade is not clear, but the refusal of affluent businessmen to pay higher taxes undoubtedly placed a greater burden on them.[13]

Non-governmental agencies were unable to ameliorate, let alone resolve, human service needs. In the fall of 1933 the agencies operating with funds from the Federation for Community Services submitted budgets of $1.7 million, of which nearly half was expected through the federation. The financial campaign brought in only $406,000, down from the previous year. Although the city contributed directly to some agencies and miscellaneous sources covered half of the shortfall, the federation faced a deficit of nearly one-quarter of what was required. The painful process of cuts meant no repairs to buildings, no new equipment and reduced salaries. Even worse, staffs were pared: the Visiting Housekeepers' staff was reduced from 32 to 27; the Children's Aid Society's share was lowered; and Victorian Order Nurses took a month's holiday without pay.[14]

During 1933 the Public Welfare Department began to take over family casework from the Neighbourhood Workers' Association, and the association became responsible for meeting the special needs of the unemployable rather than spending its "whole time in administering unemployment relief alone." The administration of welfare was finally being shifted, but agency staffs were now working, it was said, with "*sweat-shop methods*." In a belated response to a 1925 suggestion, in 1938 the Welfare Council was created. Composed of seventy-two organizations, it took on a mandate to co-ordinate conflicting and overlapping voluntary efforts and to engage in research, such as family budgeting. To maintain a modicum of well-being for the dispossessed, centralization of non-profit and public sectors became necessary.[15]

The unions responded to the Depression first by taking its lumps but eventually with increasing aggressiveness. The construction workers never regained their militancy of the late 1920s when they were needed to build the office towers downtown. Overall union

A march of the unemployed arrives at Queen's Park, 1935. Like many newspaper photos of the period, this picture was boldly retouched.

Two men were needed for cleaning chores at the Canada Steamships Lines docks one day in the spring of 1932, and this crowd of unemployed applied. One of the lucky applicants climbs aboard a freighter to start work.

membership fell. But in 1934 the organizing of workers in the needle trades marked a change. Strikes in Toronto reached a maximum in 1934 and 1936, compared to a peak in Canada as a whole in 1937. The East York Workers' Association, employed by the township, struck when relief benefits were cut. But most strikes in Toronto occurred in manufacturing plants, and also increasingly in trades and services. Newspaper reporters organized.[16]

The most significant development was the arrival of the Congress of Industrial Organizations (CIO) in Oshawa in 1937. By then, thanks to the Wagner Act of 1935 which was part of the U.S.'s New Deal and allowed workers to organize closed shops and to engage in collective bargaining, the United Auto Workers of the CIO had forced General Motors in the U.S. to recognize it as the bargaining agent. Bitterly opposed by Premier Mitchell Hepburn, the CIO successfully organized the auto workers at General Motors in Oshawa. After the depression of 1938 weakened efforts, the CIO and its industrial model for organizing—in contrast to the craft-based American Federation of Labor (AFL)—appeared in Toronto at the end of the decade at Canada Packers (through the Packinghouse Workers' Organizing Committee) and in the electrical manufacturing field. The Toronto and District Trades and Labour Council welcomed the CIO and the necessity of union solidarity. The AFL, through the national Trades and Labour Congress, however, eventually put irresistible pressure on the Trades and Labour Council to expel CIO locals. As a result, for sixteen years a separate Toronto Labour Council represented industrial unions, all because Canadian unions were dependent on American organizing strength and strike funds. Even so, unions were on the verge of making their voices heard, both politically and on the shop floor, as never before.[17]

While construction and manufacturing languished, Toronto's economy was faring well on other fronts. The employed middle class enjoyed greater prosperity as prices fell and remained low. Electricity consumption expanded considerably faster than the population, especially in the residential sector, indicating more affluence. The opening of the new Welland Canal in 1931 doubled the tonnage into the harbour within two years; much of this was coal from Pennsylvania. The number of conventions continually increased and estimated tourist spending picked up markedly after 1933, though in 1940 the mayor was worrying about the "adverse propaganda . . . about Toronto still very prevalent in the United States."[18]

As saving rather than investing in industry became the norm, the strength and stability of Toronto's financial fields were apparent and some gains over Montreal were registered. In 1939 the *Financial Post* asserted that Toronto had "passed Montreal as a centre of finance, commerce and industry." While this was more justified than the *Globe*'s similar pronouncement in 1906, several more decades were to pass before Toronto could claim outright pre-eminence. As private financial power became centralized in Toronto, government agencies, especially the Bank of Canada, doubled their share of the Gross National Product.[19]

In 1934 Toronto's stock exchanges combined, partly as the result of failures of brokerage firms in the mining sector. The tight auditing control by the Ontario Securities Board helped to prevent bankruptcies in the Toronto board so that the markets encountered "little disruption." Northern Ontario gold, sought for its supposed security, contributed to the recovery on Bay Street. But the assertion by one mining magnate that mines were "the Hinges of Prosperity" was more than optimistic as manufacturing investment lagged. Nonetheless, largely because of liquor and beer production, Toronto's stock markets moved ahead of Montreal's. As for banking, although the ratio of assets between Montreal's two large banks and Toronto's five held up, increasingly more cheques were cleared through Toronto. Also, despite shaky investments in common stocks, Sun Life maintained its lead over the several large Toronto companies. The middle class was saving even if at low interest rates: in 1934 the assets of the chartered banks and life insurance companies peaked as a ratio to the Gross National Product. In short, the financial sector suffered little in comparison to wage workers. But it would not lead the way to recovery, nor would direct American investment which slowed down a great deal during the decade.[20] (Table XII)

The Toronto media strengthened their metropolitan power over English-speaking Canada. Although many periodicals went under in the early 1930s, an equal number appeared later. In 1939 six of the nine top anglophone general magazines, with *Maclean's* leading, were published in Toronto. The *Star Weekly* surpassed *The Family Herald and Weekly Star* of Montreal with a circulation of 325,000. The *Northern Miner* and *Financial Post* easily led the financial papers, and trade journals were overwhelmingly Toronto's. The creation of the Canadian Broadcasting Corporation put Toronto's CBL at the forefront of radio productions including the famous Happy Gang and Andrew Allan's plays.[21]

SLUM DISTRICTS AND DAMPENED SOCIAL LIFE

Lieutenant-Governor Bruce's comments brought the housing of the poor and even the not-so-poor to the surface. Soon after his speech and at his behest, the Board of Control approved an enquiry into slum conditions and asked for recommendations. In the fall the Bruce Report was issued, largely the work of Harry Cassidy and Eric Arthur, two indefatigable workers for improving Toronto's society and environment. As expected, it laid out in verbal and numerical terms the wretched quality of housing for "at least 2,000 families." A survey of more than 3,600 dwelling units in the central area showed that three-quarters fell below minimum standards, two-thirds needed repairs, and outside toilets were still too frequently found. The problems had worsened, despite marginal gains in the 1920s following the Bureau of Municipal Research's 1918 report on The Ward, the demolition of low-quality housing by encroaching industry, and orders by the Board of Health. In response to conditions, one person was moved to write:

Here the Crowded Hovels Squat

Rattling sash and broken pane,
Rotten sill and creaking floor,
Sodden roof and stinking drain,
Mildewed wall and sagging door—
Here where little children sleep
Rats abound and vermin creep.

This went on for three more verses. Unable to pay the rent and pursued by the bailiff, the poor often moved. Hugh Garner could describe Cabbagetown houses as "supposedly easy to heat. That is why the landlords refrain from the expense of providing a furnace for them. Most of the heat is derived from large coal ranges.... Most houses have no bathtubs.... Until poverty is ended there will always be a Cabbagetown. It might move up to Rosedale."[22]

In a real sense Cabbagetown was moving up to South Rosedale, to the Annex and out to South Parkdale, as it had earlier moved up Jarvis and Sherbourne streets. It was moving wherever substantial houses could no longer be maintained without servants or afforded as single-family dwellings. Despite bylaws prohibiting multiple occupancy, non-occupying owners had to leave them empty, break them up into flats, rent them as group homes, to fraternities and non-profit organizations, or fill them with roomers or boarders. Not a few resident owners were forced to double up.[23]

By 1931 the correspondence of the Annex Ratepayers' Association (ARA) was filled with graphic tales of illegal occupancy. The ARA, trying to protect S.H. Janes's late nineteenth-century homogeneous neighbourhood of the East Annex for the now dwindling rich, fought vigorously but unsuccessfully to stop the conversions. Combing the newspapers for advertisements, complaining to the city about window signs for room and board and, in one case, even hiring a Pinkerton detective to watch a shady house on Bedford Road, the ARA demanded that the reluctant city take these offenders to court and pass tighter bylaws. But by the fall of 1932 the cause had been lost. President George Gooderham, a well-known businessman, reflected that "in these very strenuous times I would not want to prevent people who really require it, from getting assistance in the way of boarding a few people, but I would like to be sure that permission is only granted...during these hard times...." With that the ARA began to fade away, afterward protesting only in a desultory fashion.[24]

Lady Eaton had moved in 1931 from the mansion at Lowther and Spadina to Forest Hill, making it clear the process noted by Craick in 1918 was moving a step further. Attempts at city-wide organization failed as the Central Council of Ratepayers petered out. With the return of prosperity in the 1940s, most of the substantial and elegant houses on St. George and adjacent streets did not return to the commercial elite.[25]

Housing was a problem not only for the poor. Families doubled up and young people stayed home. Despite the construction of more apartments, no clear reduction in the number of people per occupied unit occurred over the decade; in 1941 the official average still hovered around 4.5, although the actual number was probably higher. Vacancies remained high until 1937, especially in apartments, though they decreased after a peak of nearly 16 per cent in 1933. Many households could not sustain rents even though the index dropped from 100 in 1926 to 74 in 1933. Houses owned by

Despite continued calls to eliminate slums, they persisted. During the Depression, housing for the poor deteriorated even more.

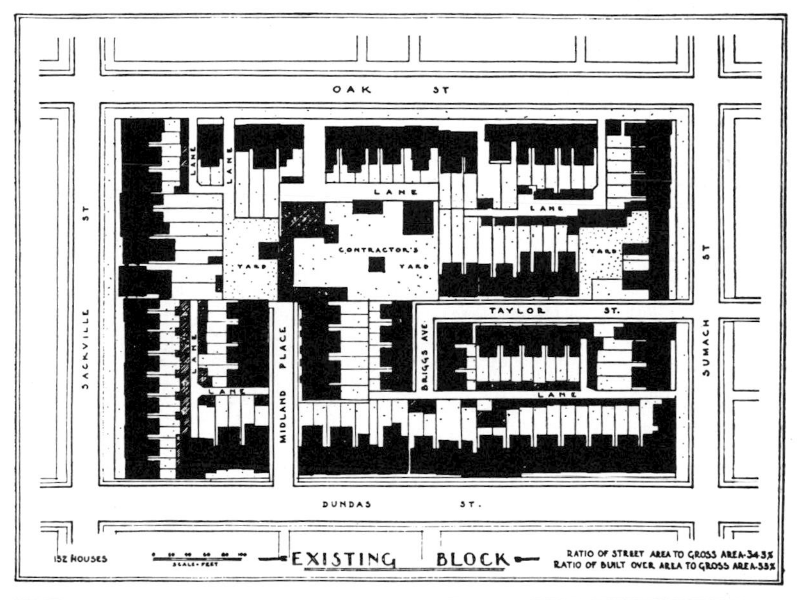

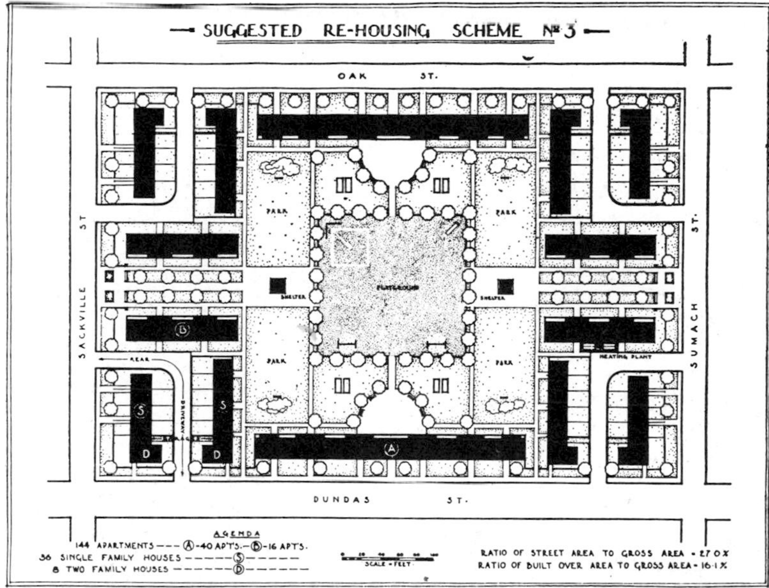

The Bruce Report of 1934 suggested three "garden city" models for part of Cabbagetown. The housing density of the existing block (top) would have been halved in scheme 3 (bottom). The proposals failed, though from 1936 to 1939 the city did help to finance renovations. Not until the early 1950s would families move into Regent Park, a redevelopment of the same area.

occupiers fell from 60 to nearly 50 per cent, and the number of households renting rose from 50 to 60 per cent between 1931 and 1941, a level reached once again in the 1970s.[26] (Tables XIII, XIV)

A variety of solutions to the housing problems of low-income families appeared from 1934 onward: the demolition and rebuilding of slums through public housing, improved borrowing standards for the construction of new middle- and modest-income houses, and renovation. The motivation of all legislation and action was to reduce unemployment rather more than to fulfil Bruce's "inalienable right." Much fruitless debate revolved around whether low-income housing should be provided by units constructed at low cost or by subsidizing rents. In the late 1930s renovation proved to be the only comfortable path, though both easier mortgages and the agitation for public housing were harbingers of the future.[27]

To alleviate slum-housing conditions and to create employment, the Bruce Report recommended to the Board of Control the replacement of unfit slums with low-cost houses and apartments, the establishment of a city planning commission to guide land-use change, and legislative and financial support from the federal and provincial governments. Gone was Bruce's earlier plea to move industry and working peole to the suburbs; instead, urban renewal was proposed to keep people close to their work. Three graphic designs using the garden suburb model of Radburn, New Jersey, were drawn up for the Oak, Sackville, Dundas and Sumach block in Cabbagetown. (See at left.) Other groups had already proposed similar schemes.[28]

The early responses to the Bruce Report were guarded. Getting rid of slums and slum landlords was a fine idea but, in his response to Bruce at the centennial luncheon, Mayor William Stewart had indicated resistance to tampering with private property rights, as had A.E. LePage. As Garner asserted, without a guarantee of new housing, Cabbagetowners themselves were apprehensive. The Central Council of Ratepayers' Associations opposed the idea on the grounds of tight money and class distinctions: "The situation will not be improved by spending twelve million the taxpayers cannot afford, for the plan would mean segregation of the poor in one district which is even worse than the old feudal system." Tracy leMay, planning commissioner since 1930, attacked the report for stressing density, since the average in the city was already less than one person per room. He scoffed at its preoccupation with health. Dilapidated housing was scattered; it was nothing like the situation in some British cities where council housing was replacing obsolete back-to-back houses and where action had been taken to "stave off a revolution." To Controller William Wadsworth, leMay expressed what was undoubtedly a widespread view:

> Improper living conditions in Toronto are very largely caused by the tenants rather than the houses, and it is a question to what extent the habits of people can be changed by improving their houses, and it is certain that if they are rehoused it can only be done on the basis of a substantial subsidy.

The poor had only themselves to blame.[29]

Not surprisingly, subsidies for renewal were not forthcoming from higher levels of government. In 1935 the Bennett regime passed a lukewarm Dominion Housing Act — one element in Canada's belated New Deal — more to put construction workers back to work building middle-class housing than to provide directly for the poor. The poor and unemployed received no real benefits under this scheme, nor did they under the National Housing Act of 1938. The middle class and the affluent were the main beneficiaries of these modest acts.[30]

But because housing reformers persisted, in February 1936 the city passed what was to be its major response to poor housing (which was not quite the same as responding to housing the poor). The city's Standard of Housing bylaw, a pioneering one in Canada, helped to provoke the Federal Home Improvement Loans Guarantee Act of 1936. By June 1939, of the 9,038 houses inspected, over a half were repaired at a cost of just under $1 million. Although demolitions exceeded new construction under this 1936 federal act, by October 1940, 16,400 loans totalling $5.6 million had contributed to improvement of housing stock. With less than a tenth of Canada's population, Toronto had garnered at least a fifth of the money. To Toronto's commissioner of finance these renovations had "undoubtedly obviated, to a considerable extent, the necessity of a low-cost housing programme, which would have involved an expenditure of millions of dollars in the erection of buildings." Reformers, however, pressed for more action. But in January 1938 the electors overwhelmingly rejected their scheme for slum clearance and low-income housing, which would have cost the city $2 million.[31]

Between 1934 and 1939 housing for the poor had generated a great deal of debate and a modest degree of action. To conservatives, renovation was seen as the chief answer and, up to a point, it worked. Provision for cheap low-rent housing was less successful. To reformers, the renovation solution was still inadequate: housing was not tied to planning nor was it seen as a social right, at least when it came to action, and the remedies seemed directed more toward alleviating unemployment than to encouraging low-rent housing. In June 1939 E.J. Urwick, honorary chairman of the Ontario Housing and Planning Association, ruefully commented to leMay that Canada was the only western country not organized to build low-rent housing, largely because the three levels of government had failed to co-ordinate their efforts.[32]

Grinding poverty reduced the ability of many Torontonians to take any pleasure in the city's social life; even the Santa Claus parade embarrassed parents who could not afford to buy toys. Better-off Torontonians, however, continued to enjoy what the city had to offer. Attendance at the Ex fell slowly and recovered. The churches flourished, if with less money for the clergy. Trump Davidson and Bert Niosi played at the dance halls. The *Cayuga*, *Northumberland* and *Dalhousie City* still ran excursions across the lake. The rich hunted foxes and frequented their clubs.[33]

Professional sports continued to engage the city. In November 1931 Maple Leaf Gardens opened after only five months of construction. Perhaps inspired by the move from the Mutual Street Arena, that season the Maple Leafs won their first of eleven Stanley Cups. But the bloom faded: the team reached the finals every year in the 1930s, except 1934 and 1937, without winning the cup again. Those were the years of Red Horner, King Clancy, Hap Day, the kid line of Joe Primeau, Charlie Conacher and Busher Jackson, Ace Bailey, Syl Apps, Gordie Drillon, Sweeney Schriner and Turk Broda. Boys traded corn syrup labels for hockey cards of their heroes. Football came more to resemble the American game with forward passes and downfield blocking. The west was more competitive, but Balmy Beach won the Grey Cup in 1930, as did the Argos under Lew Hayman in 1933, 1937 and 1938. The baseball Leafs did not do well in the 1930s; but fans of the game saw some of the greats coming and going, such as the Twinkletoes Selkirk and Phil Marchildon.[34]

Group of Seven member Arthur Lismer gained an international reputation for his children's art classes. This is a Saturday morning class outside the Toronto (later Ontario) Art Gallery in the Grange.

A slightly less refined recreation — free seats to CNE motorcycle races, 1938. The bandshell was the only addition to the grounds that the Ex could afford in the 1930s.

SLOWED POPULATION GROWTH AND THE DECLINE OF DISCRIMINATION

Demographic changes reflected a depressed decade. The number of marriages fell (by 40 per cent), as did the birth rate. Few immigrants arrived, so the number of foreign-born dropped over the decade from 38 to 31 per cent. Toronto lost some of its more ambitious young people to places like New York and Detroit, as Canada experienced more emigration than immigration for the first time since the 1890s. The conspicuous drifters were mostly from Ontario; the 1941 census showed only a very modest number of people born on the prairies or elsewhere. As the population aged and the number of children declined relatively, public school enrollments slowly declined after 1933. However, the number of high school students continued to rise to 1939 (the year of the highest ratio to population), as young people flocked into technical and commercial programs hoping to improve their job prospects. Population growth was therefore slower: the built-up city grew by only 6 per cent from 1931 to 1941 and the suburbs, by 30 per cent, ranging from 16 per cent in the older townships of York and East York, to a doubling in Forest Hill, and to more than 500 per cent in small but dynamic Leaside. The affluent could afford to buy new houses there and in central Etobicoke.[35] (Tables I-VII)

For North Americans, the birth in May 1934 of the Dionne quintuplets was a diversion from the trials of the Depression. With its typical razzle-dazzle aggressiveness, the *Toronto Star* (along with the American press) fostered and exploited the public's curiosity by sending hordes of reporters into a poor francophone community near North Bay. Eventually the quints were separated from their parents and siblings so that tourists from Toronto and elsewhere could gawk at them. They were also separated and, in fact, made wards of the province to keep them healthy. Dr. Alan Brown of the Hospital for Sick Children and Dr. William Blatz of the city's Institute of Child Study took over a large share of the quints' upbringing. Dr. Brown had earned a solid reputation in the reduction of infant mortality in Toronto and in the promotion of better infant diets, which included the nutritious biscuit and Pablum developed by researchers at Sick Children's Hospital. While Dr. Brown oversaw the quints' diet, Dr. Blatz worked on designing a proper environment and a disciplined routine, which was carefully followed by the quints' nurses and teachers. However, the prescriptions of Toronto's doctors did not prepare the quints particularly well for adulthood. As one of them commented later, "There was so much more money than love in our existence." Interestingly, they sought anonymity in Montreal rather than in Blatz and Brown's Toronto.[36]

At a time when it appeared to be an economic necessity to limit the size of one's family, a bizarre stork contest was underway. In 1926 Charles Vance Millar had left well over a million dollars for a mother who in ten years had given birth to the most children. One woman was denied the prize in 1936 because only five of her ten children could be verified as having been sired by her husband. Toronto the Good had to be sure, so four other women split the prize. Thomas Foster, a mayor in the 1920s, also set up a series of stork derbies which continued to 1964.[37]

In times of trouble, scapegoats as well as diversions are sought. A few months before the quints were born, Bunty Hillier was murdered in east Toronto. Two young boys, aged four and seven, accused one another of the crime and, as everyone seemed to believe he was to blame, the older one was sent to the Ontario Hospital in Orillia. In 1935 Red Ryan, a notorious gunman and bank robber, had been welcomed back to Toronto from his eleven-year stint in Kingston Penitentiary. But the welcome did not last long and the city turned against him, as described in Morley Callaghan's novel *More Joy in Heaven*. A few months later he was shot to death while involved in a robbery. Every era has its strange affairs, but the 1930s seemed to have had more than its share.[38]

Antagonism toward Jews intensified and reached a crescendo in 1933. But as the Nazi spectre rose, attitudes softened. Early in 1933 an insurance company cancelled many policies held by Jews but was forced by the legislature to reinstate them. Jews were denied apartment leases and entry into resorts, hotels and dance halls. Signs such as "No Jews, Niggers or Dogs" were posted intermittently for several years at Balmy and Kew beaches and triggered a number of incidents between young Jews and members of the Swastika Club. In August 1933 at Christie Pits, the swastika was again displayed and a six-hour battle ensured between the "Pit Gang" and young Jews. Although the *Telegram* blamed the Jews, the *Star*'s support of civil rights, a better-organized Jewish community behind the League for the Defense of Jewish Rights, and general disgust at the antics of local Nazis reduced but did not altogether dispose of the problem. The identification of Jews with Communists continued, though only a tiny minority were members. Jews actively promoted

The newsroom at the Globe and Mail *in 1938, soon after George McCullagh combined the* Globe *and the* Mail and Empire.

The Globe *was outshone by the* Star*'s aggressive style, which involved dispatching reporters like young Gordon Sinclair (left) on daring assignments around the world. But as fellow reporter Art Wells (above, in fedora) discovered, the realities of early spring could slow local news.*

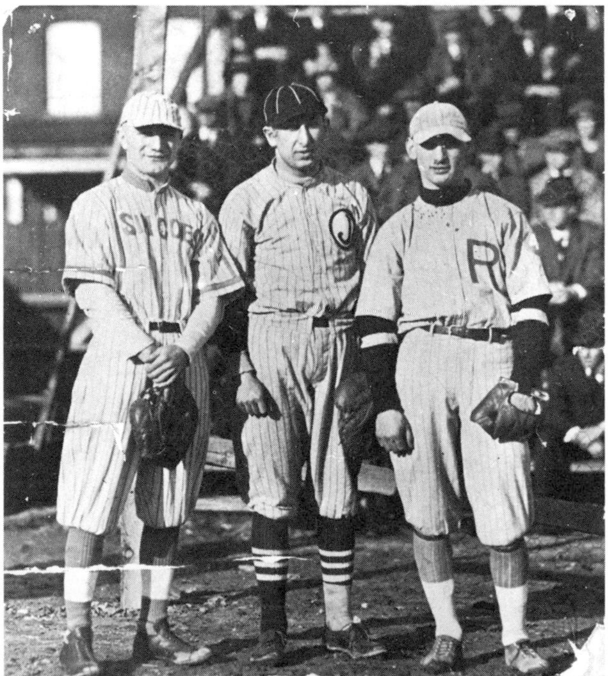

While the 1920s and early 1930s were characterized by anti-semitism, Jewish cultural life was vibrant and diverse. Above is the Peretz Shiel Orchestra in 1936; at left, members of three Jewish senior baseball teams — probably at an all-star game.

unionization, particularly in the needle trades, and were no doubt inspired by protest productions of the Yiddish theatre at Spadina and Dundas and the Workers' Experimental Theatre. Without new immigrants, other ethnic groups saw their institutional fabric losing strength.[39]

UNCONFIDENT POLITICS

The promotion of annexations or metropolitan area organization did not bear fruit, nor did the issues disappear. Interest in annexation was expressed in York and East York, as the problems of the poor suburbs became magnified. They were broke. York's taxes for schools were higher than Forest Hill's, but its schools were far less well equipped and staffed. York residents paid more for water than Torontonians did though it was all from the same source, that is, Toronto's system. As early as 1930 York suffered tax arrears of almost one-third. In 1931 the Township of York electors voted eight to one in favour of annexation to the city, a result largely ignored by the press.[40]

In March 1931 city department heads reported their views on annexation. For the first time since the end of the major annexations in 1912, officials were divided, with several in favour of further exploration of the issue, largely because of the strong desire for annexation in York and East York. However, by the fall they had retreated. The works commissioner successfully warned the others and council that annexations of these weaker townships would be "altruistic" with no financial benefits to the city. As the situation worsened, the reorganized Ontario Municipal Board put York and several other suburbs under boards of supervisors from 1933 until 1941. But the city remained adamant: in 1939 again the city (and the *Star*) opposed the annexation of "the semi-circle of bankrupt municipalities on its borders."[41]

York County and the province nibbled at the metropolitan problem throughout the decade, however. In 1932 the county established the Metropolitan Area Committee; it heard Mimico Council, for example, plead for a metropolitan county which, in fact, the county supported. As a result the Ontario government, then led by G.S. Henry who had proposed a similar idea in 1924, set up a special committee and then a commission on the Government of the Metropolitan Area of Toronto. In 1935 A.F.W. Plumptre recommended to the new Liberal minister of municipal affairs that the province should enforce annexations and promote comprehensive planning. The report was never even printed. Without enthusiasm from a premier who was antagonistic to Toronto and its problems, another attempt from within the ranks of Ontario Liberals floundered just as the war began. As in housing, reformers and dispossessed municipalities recognized the need, but few others did.[42]

Municipal electoral politics reflected this period of austerity in public spending. However, after 1934 a shift in public opinion was apparent. In the city, as Bert Wemp ended his 1930 stint, McBride's attempted comeback was narrowly thwarted by William Stewart who was, perhaps appropriately for the times, an undertaker. He would preside ineffectively over the decline of Toronto's economy for the next four years with virtually the same Board of Control. Among these was labourite and future member of the CCF Jimmie Simpson, who had been off council since 1914. In 1935, despite Liberal and Conservative opposition, Simpson won the mayoralty, and labour finally had one of its own in the top position. His defence of more hostels for single men against Hepburn who accused him of "doing everything in his power to assist men who refuse to work" probably contributed to his loss in 1936, though the *Star* withdrew its endorsement after accusing him of devoting too much time to labour issues and too little to civic affairs. Two years later, Simpson was dead. McBride did come back but died in office soon after, and was replaced by another but less vigorous friend of labour, William Robbins. In 1938 he was defeated by Ralph Day, also an undertaker, who held the seat for three years.[43]

The deaths of McBride and Simpson marked the end of an era in Toronto's electoral politics. Both had been active since the first decade of the century and had fought many battles, often on the same side on the issue of growth if not on welfare and civil rights. And both were usually out of favour with the Tory electorate and the *Telegram* whose slates won more often than not. Tories continued to dominate council numerically, though the flamboyant newspaper rhetoric became somewhat more muted. (In 1939 at least twenty-four local weekly newspapers operated in various districts of Toronto and suburbs, several of which were new in the late 1930s, signalling new local political energy.)[44]

New faces and new stances appeared on the council. After several years on the School Board, Adelaide Plumptre successfully ran for alderman in Ward 2. She was the first woman on council since 1923 and the only one until after 1945. Like Constance Hamilton in the

The Telegram*'s view of Jimmie Simpson and the CCF, 1935: "Jimmie had a little ram/The CCF you know/And everywhere that Jimmie went/The ram was sure to go." The* Tely*'s support of the working man did not extend to trade unions, any party of labour, or politicians like Simpson. Electorally unsuccessful but still influential in the first two decades of the century, Simpson finally became mayor in 1935.*

early 1920s, and with the support of the Association of Women Electors formed in 1937, she brought a reforming enthusiasm, particularly on housing questions. Apart from Simpson and Arthur Williams, elected as reeve for a year in East York, the CCF party failed miserably. Its time had not yet come. But two Communists from the west side managed to get elected in the late 1930s: Joseph Salsberg for one year and Stewart Smith for three. Tim Buck collected many votes in controller races. Although forced to retreat in the 1940 elections because of the Ribbentrop-Molotov deal over Poland, the Communist presence pointed to increased public concern, if hardly polarization, on social and economic questions.[45]

The election of Communists to City Council signalled something more: a relaxation of political censorship. Until 1934 Communists had been unable even to hold public meetings. In fact, using Section 98 of the Criminal Code, in 1931 the federal government jailed Tim Buck and seven others on a charge of sedition. Others were deported. The oppression initiated in 1928 by Chief Constable Draper and the Police Commission extended to those considered fellow-travellers. In January 1931 a newly formed pacifist group, the Fellowship of Reconciliation, attempted to rent a hall only to find the police again warning the hall owners, this time about "thinly veiled Communists." But against this blatant McCarthyism, sixty-eight faculty members of the University of Toronto signed a protest because the police were attacking colleagues. The *Globe*, originally the bastion of liberalism, hastened to push the university administration to reprimand the faculty. But the university administration resisted. By 1934 advocates of free speech successfully managed the release of Buck and the others, who later appeared at a tumultuous rally of 17,000 in Maple Leaf Gardens. Along with Herbert Bruce's speech on housing, this event indicated significant change. Even if for a while single men seemed to replace Jews and Communists as scapegoats, a shift in the awareness of Torontonians occurred. In 1934, as the economy finally improved slightly, higher levels of government were now blamed for the woes of the time.[46]

Both provincial and federal elections signified dissatisfaction with Conservative regimes. Provincially, in 1934 hapless George Henry gave way to the popular but inconsistent Hepburn who, as it turned out, showed only modest interest in social or economic legislation. But Hepburn's Liberals broke the Tory stronghold in Toronto, winning six of thirteen city seats in 1934 and seven in 1937. The recently formed CCF failed to win a Toronto seat in either election.

Federally, the Liberals were not very successful in Toronto. Although in 1935 Mackenzie King returned with two-thirds of Ontario's seats, only two in the city (Spadina and Trinity) and only York North and York West in the suburbs were won. In 1940, while picking up Eglinton, the Liberals lost York West. In Trinity former provincial Attorney General and Minister of Labour Arthur Roebuck, having broken with Hepburn over the Oshawa labour dispute, went over to the premier's fellow Liberal but arch-enemy Mackenzie King. If Torontonians had shown their displeasure with the provincial Tories, they were not convinced that Mackenzie King would help matters very much. By 1939 they were discovering that Hepburn was hardly the solution. Few took seriously the proposal in the late 1930s for a union government put forward by George McCullagh (who pulled together the *Globe* and the *Mail and Empire* in 1936).[47]

Eaton's College Street store, as proposed in 1929. The first uptown move of a department store was largely unsuccessful. The late 1920s enthusiasm embodied in this plan was only partially fulfilled.

A STATIC LANDSCAPE BUT AN URGE TO PLAN

The physical fabric of Toronto changed less in the 1930s than in any other decade of the twentieth century. The Royal York Hotel, Eaton's College Street, Maple Leaf Gardens and the Customs Building on Front Street were all finished by 1932. The Bank of Nova Scotia postponed construction of a tower. Following the failure of the 1929 redevelopment scheme, these projects marked the end of downtown development for many years. Initially planning attention was fixed on improving traffic flow into the centre, with musings over expressways along with arterial improvements. To show that Toronto was serious about planning, City Surveyor Tracy leMay was the first person elevated to the position of commissioner of planning. If the Bruce Report failed in its housing redevelopment proposals, it did rekindle enthusiasm for the planning of land use. The hodge-podge of zoning bylaws was recognized as a problem by city officials and so the preparation of a comprehensive zoning system was undertaken in 1937.

Early in 1930, in response to a general desire for a city master plan and in line with Mayor Wemp's position, the Advisory City Planning Committee (composed of department heads) brought in a "comprehensive" plan for Toronto. Unlike the grandiose 1929 downtown plan, this one combined the "greatest utility with the maximum of safety and economy." Without even a touch of elegance, the plan pulled together many of the ideas on street improvements that had been bandied about for some time. References to aspects of land use were scant. Proposed were street widenings and extensions and the separation of streetcars from automobiles, mostly outside the downtown area. A central notion was the connecting of disjointed east-west streets parallel to the main arteries to expedite the flow of automobile traffic unhindered by streetcars. Since car traffic from the north was becoming increasingly heavy, several extensions were proposed. Because it was a flexible scheme and could be dealt with on a piecemeal basis, council unanimously supported the plan, a plan designed for a city of a million and a half and one expected to catch up to Los Angeles in the number of automobiles.[48]

Only easy and inexpensive jog connections, such as Dupont and Harbord, and the extension of Church to connect with a widened Davenport through a poorer part of Yorkville were completed in the 1930s. The proposed Jarvis Street extension to Mt. Pleasant was opposed by the affluent residents of Rosedale. Their Don Valley Association, which promoted an alternative roadway in the valley, tied the project up for years. Then, in 1940, despite the support of all three newspapers, electors rejected both the Jarvis extension and a Nordheimer Ravine streetcar route. The north-south flow remained a problem. The inability to act on the traffic issue indicated the shift of the city's expenditures into direct relief measures, a failure to use the unemployed in road building, and a slower than anticipated use of cars for commuting.[49]

The public transportation system was also set back by the Depression—many of those with jobs had to revert to shank's pony. The number of passengers fell from more than 200 million in 1929 to a low in 1933; from then to 1939 the level hardly exceeded 150 million. The TTC added to the unemployment rolls by reducing the number of its employees by a quarter throughout the latter half of the decade, in part by shifting to one-person operated vehicles. However, in 1934 an American efficiency expert found the TTC in healthy shape:

> There is no comparable system where the entire personnel appears to be working so harmoniously to the one end of furnishing the best possible transportation service in the most economical manner... none with records and data so complete... none in better physical condition... none with lower fares; under comparable conditions... none with higher average speeds or with better frequency of service... none with a better safety record.[50] (Table XV)

The TTC reduced its debt over the decade, partly because of Gray Coach revenues. In the fall of 1938 it enlivened the streets with the first modern Presidents' Conference Cars, after observing their successful introduction on the streets of some large American cities. It also added more buses. Of greater future significance was the proposal for a north-south subway, lying fallow since 1915, and the suggestion of another to the northwest. In 1937 planning experts Norman Wilson and Arthur Bunnell detailed the route north to Heath Street, which would take the streetcar tracks off Yonge Street and Avenue Road between Bloor and St. Clair. During a period when officials enjoyed a good deal of legitimacy and longevity in their positions, they could introduce or reintroduce notions and proposals hoping that the right time had finally arrived.[51]

In 1937 two airports were added to Toronto's landscape. In the 1920s seaplanes had begun to land in the bay, and the question of whether an island or an inland airport should be run commercially was debated. In 1937 the city and the federal government decided to build both airports, but only Malton became a commercial facility for Trans-Canada Airlines because of the frequency of fog on the waterfront and the presence of skyscrapers downtown. The city put up half of the $1.9 million, one of the few major capital works expenditures of the decade. Three side-effects flowed from these decisions: without a large airport on the island, neither a bridge nor a tunnel (both debated on and off over the years, and the latter even started in 1935) was needed; cottages were removed from the Hanlan's Point airport site to Sunfish (later Algonquin) Island—the first disruption of the island community; and the aircraft industry began to develop at Malton as two firms moved in.[52]

Although actual public investment was minimal over the decade, Toronto maintained its physical fabric. But with a sense that it could be better, citizen and professional interest in planning was resurrected from a "stand-still" in the early 1930s following the Bruce Report recommendation that a planning commission be set up. For some, planning had to include housing and social development. In his 1935 report on Metropolitan Toronto, Plumptre criticized both the 1929 and 1930 proposals as plans for motorists, "not a city plan." He promoted the idea of a long-term advisory citizens' planning

Despite the restful appearance of the junction of the Bloor Street car and the Jane Street bus in 1937, the 1930s were a time when problems of transit, roads and traffic got worse rather than better.

While the public transit system suffered setbacks, north-south traffic congestion worsened: Avenue Road looking south from St. Clair, also in 1937. Despite the economic slump, those who had steady jobs bought cars.

commission composed of professionals with an independent planning staff to deal with all land uses, including slums. The formation of the Ontario Housing and Planning Association in 1937 signalled continued concern about the issues.[53]

City officials resisted the call for a planning commission just as they resisted calls for a housing authority and for public housing. They eventually admitted, however, the need for a comprehensive zoning bylaw. In response to the Bruce Report, leMay had pointed out that Toronto had generated a whole series of plans and, by implication, that his department had matters well under control, which to him largely meant improving traffic flows. While noting the "wave of zoning" still passing through the U.S., he argued that Toronto was different because its bylaws did, in fact, protect 70 per cent of residential areas "against intrusion of industry." The industrial "absorption of obsolete housing" areas located in the other 30 per cent might help the city.[54]

In 1936 City Council asked leMay and the property commissioner to consolidate and revise the zoning bylaws. Finally leMay was forced to admit that the bylaws had "largely failed to restrict," at least in poorer areas. In 1939 after the draft zoning scheme was presented, the Board of Control ordered the formation of the Independent Committee of Zoning to review the provisions and conduct hearings, though, in the Toronto tradition of making haste slowly, it was not appointed until February of 1940. Composed of two architects, two engineers and a real estate agent, the panel did not hold hearings until 1941, and then the system was not put finally in place until 1952. The late 1930s thus saw greater interest in controlling the use of land. But, as leMay noted in 1937, reformers could not decide whether a housing commission "would be divorced from that on zoning and planning, whether these two should act in common, or whether one commission would be sufficient," reflecting the continuing disjointedness of approaches. Given the slow pace of change and the failure of reformers to gain significant ground electorally, he was not about to resolve these conundrums.[55]

TORONTO THE LESS GOOD

In early July 1936, during the worst heat wave ever (40.6C/105.1F), thirty men were arrested at Sunnyside for indecent exposure because their bathing suits failed to cover their chests. Toronto the Good still looked after appearances. As local historian Jesse Middleton claimed in his *Toronto's 100 Years*, the city had few "determined *poseurs*" among its artists "to afflict the police by doing paper chases at three in the morning," and no "criminal quarter filled with Apaches . . . preying upon decent society." The *Globe and Mail* pointed out that without Bohemians, the Gerrard Village around Mary John's tearoom was about as radical a place as could be found. To writers, Toronto was still not a warm place. The world was changing just the same: the bathers were not convicted. Men's topless suits had come to stay, and so had women's pants just because Marlene Dietrich wore them.[56]

In 1939, when Torontonians celebrated the royal visit, they were poised not just for another, if more justifiable, sacrifice of their sons. In the wake of the Great Depression, enough of them were also ready to consider new politics and dramatic changes in the ways the city was run.

During the 1920s, despite brash rhetoric and unbridled speculation, Toronto—along with the whole of the western world—was on the downside of a long cycle of growth. But unlike many other North American cities, Toronto emerged from the immediate postwar years in relatively good shape. And, through the decade, it managed to enhance its status as a financial, industrial and cultural centre, to extend its public services and to make modest improvements in the quality of life of its citizens.

On V-E day, Torontonians took to the streets to celebrate the defeat of the Nazis. But the outpouring was far more subdued than in places like Halifax, where rioting broke out.

Chapter Three

Planning for Growth, 1940–1953

"The eyes of the whole city are upon this district! [Oriole Park] has awakened a city-wide demand for expert, over-all city planning . . . . WE WANT PLANNING FOR THE PEOPLE—NOT JUST THE T.T.C."[1]

In April 1947 the Oriole Park Neighbourhood Association (OPNA) organized a mass rally to protest TTC plans to construct subway yards on the Belt Line lands south of Chaplin Crescent just west of Yonge Street. OPNA argued that the proposed yards violated the city's Master Plan, as well as the zoning bylaw protecting stable residential neighbourhoods, and threatened to eliminate a playground in a city with "already grossly inadequate park area." One member went so far as to equate the TTC with a secretive New York Tammany Club, "pampered and overfed too long at the expense of other city departments." The rally—"the most dramatic community effort in recent years"—drew 500 people and widespread support from North Toronto Community Council, aldermen, ratepayer groups, newspapers and planning reformers. In typical Toronto fashion, the debate dragged on until September 1948 when, after the mayor interceded, the TTC agreed to a north-south realignment of what became the Davisville Yard. OPNA was satisfied, calling this simple solution "a great improvement."[2]

The OPNA fight was very much like previous struggles by ratepayer groups. Yet there were important differences. Not only did this affluent neighbourhood retain planning experts of its own, but it also appealed to a city-wide concern for planning. Planning, it appeared, had become entrenched in the public mind and citizen action was in the air.

The 1940s were years of debate and of political turmoil, of sorting out to what degree goverments should directly intercede in the affairs of society. It was an era of rising expectations that repudiated the conditions of the 1930s. During the period, the CCF was a major catalyst and a vehicle for change with its call for economic, social and land-use planning. When the CCF narrowly missed winning political power in the province and lost ground federally, it failed to convince others of the need for serious postwar economic planning. Following a vigorous British lead, CCF members, some businessmen and experts did succeed, however, in bringing a measure of social and, more clearly, land-use planning, which was implemented haltingly by the Liberals federally and the Conservatives provincially. In the end, what stuck the most was land-use planning (that is, the public hedging in of property rights to increase efficiency and reduce waste). For Toronto, the culmination of the 1940s was the formation of Metro with an appointed chairman holding great power. But if local neighbourhood democracy was maintained, and even revived, the CCF hope for social democracy floundered. Too many Torontonians wanted domestic and neighbourhood stability, not limitations on free enterprise. Nevertheless, Toronto was more open in 1953 than it had been in 1940.[3]

A TIME OF POLITICAL TURMOIL

Striving for stability and organizing for growth resulted in a roller-coaster of electoral politics. On the provincial scene, the 1943 election threw Toronto into turmoil. George Drew's Tories ended up forming a minority government with only a four-seat advantage over the CCF, which won all four Yorks—a sign of acute suburban dissatisfaction—and took four of thirteen seats in the city. The Communist Labour Progressives won two; the Liberals, now discredited by Hepburn's erratic, anti-labour stance, were shut out in the Toronto area. The party was also excluded in the 1945 election, but so was the CCF, which lost most of its seats in the province for a number of reasons. The turnout for the Tories was much larger than it had been in 1943 and, even though the Toronto Labour

Council which represented industrial unions supported the CCF, many trade unionists did not, nor did the Toronto Trades and Labour Council which represented more traditional craft unions. As well, Communists were out in force running in CCF-held ridings, even combining with Conservatives and Liberals in a few ridings in the province. Just before the election, CCF leader E.B. Jolliffe accused the Tories of gestapo-like spying on his party, ironically resulting in more Tory support. Finally, the Tories had brought in some reform legislation for labour and land-use planning, which had been built on the CCF platform. In the election of 1948 the CCF recovered somewhat, winning twenty-one seats in the province, eight in the city and three of the four Yorks — a resurgence that was partly the result of high prices, high rents and housing shortages (which helped spark the drive to Metro's creation). Deep resentment over Colonel Drew's permitting of cocktail lounges in 1946 contributed to his loss in High Park to Bill Temple, a prominent dry. In York East Agnes McPhail, one of the few women politicians of the time, was returned to the legislature. The Tory majority in 1948 was followed by another in 1951 when astute, small-town lawyer Leslie Frost virtually swept the province. Prosperity and order had returned. In the Toronto area only the very capable Communist Joe Salsberg survived the onslaught.[4]

The results of the federal elections obscured the volatility of public opinion. After Joe Noseworthy's win in the 1942 York South by-election, the CCF kept rising in the federal opinion polls; a year later it actually led the Liberals in Canada. However, promising a "New Social Order," Mackenzie King's Liberals pulled off a win in June 1945. In Toronto, rather than moving either to the CCF or the Liberals, thirteen of fifteen Toronto area seats went Tory. Only servicemen overseas, undoubtedly affected by the British move to Labour, voted CCF. In 1949 the Liberals broke through to win seven of eleven seats in the city, their largest proportion since 1918. The electors not only rejected George Drew again (this time as leader of the federal Tories), but his loss was a signal that, federally, Toronto no longer belonged to the Progressive Conservative Party.[5]

The city's annual elections also reflected the shifting electoral sentiment of the era. The 1941 and 1942 elections were relatively quiet; Fred Conboy was re-elected mayor by acclamation in 1942. Two groups ran partial slates: the CCF and the Association for a Better City (ABC). For its effort, the CCF lost its only alderman, William Dennison, and the ABC elected only Controller Lewis Duncan, already established as a vigorous reformer. The *Globe and Mail* and particularly the *Telegram*, an undying devotee of localism and Toryism (if now less so of Orangeism), did not take kindly to this "organized opposition." Undeterred, the CCF and the ABC ran partial slates again in 1943 focussing on problems of housing, day care for children of mothers working in war industry and the shortage of electricity. However, without a challenge to Mayor Conboy, the voter turnout was low. The CCF elected three aldermen, the ABC, only Duncan, and Communist Joseph Salsberg returned.[6]

The 1944 election was the most dramatic. The ABC did not run, but Duncan unsuccessfully challenged Conboy. The CCF ran a full aldermanic slate, but all twenty-three candidates were defeated. How persuasive the no-holds-barred advertisements of M.A. Sanderson, head of a pest control company, were is not clear, but they were graphic: "THIS IS THE SLATE TO RUB OUT NEW YEAR'S DAY!" CCF candidates were called Communists but, ironically, Communists (officially, Labour Progressives) Norman Freed and Charles Sims won aldermanic seats.[7]

In 1945, when the CCF did not stand as an organized body, Tory dominance was restored. The vote was lower, despite a mayoralty contest in which Controller Robert Saunders successfully challenged incumbent Conboy. According to the *Star* and the *Globe and Mail*, Saunders was the most able politician of the day — the right Tory at the right time in the right place. Like the metro chairman of the 1950s, Fred Gardiner, he could get things done: positive votes on the subway, incipient expressways, Regent Park and the civic square all happened during his four years at the helm. It was a time to vote for projects and for action, and Saunders's reward from the Tories was top job at Ontario Hydro and his name on a dam in the St. Lawrence Seaway. In the 1945 and 1946 elections, the Communists backed several candidates and one, Stewart Smith, successfully returned to a controller's seat, only to lose in the rising anti-red tide in 1947.

Hiram McCallum, another Tory who replaced Saunders, won easily in 1949 and 1950. In 1950 the turnout was heavy when the issue of Sunday sports was on the ballot. Controller Leslie Saunders, one of the last conspicuous Orange enthusiasts, helped to rally the anti-forces, but unsuccessfully as it turned out. Election day was shifted to early December, and the turnout in December 1950 too

As before, political battles were often fought on the editorial pages of the daily papers. To McCullagh's Globe and Mail, *the CCF represented oppressive centralization rather than the greater democracy it promised. This cartoon, captioned "The Mask is Off!", is from November 1943. The* Star *was more sympathetic but stuck with the Liberals at election time.*

On January 1, 1950, voters went along with Allan Lamport's advocacy that commercialized sports should be allowed on Sunday, despite a vigorous "anti" campaign by church leaders and others. The Star's *editorial and cartoon of December 29, 1949 warned innocent and puzzled voters against opening the door.*

was heavy: those who had been opposed to Sunday sports came out to defeat Allan Lamport who had spearheaded the pro-forces. Nonetheless, Toronto the Good was modernizing itself.[8]

In December 1951 Tory control was weakened slightly when Lamport defeated McCallum and Nathan Phillips who split the Tory vote. Lamport was clearly a leader for wide-open growth. He repeated his win in the next two elections though, according to the *Globe and Mail*, he lacked the "dignity" of Nathan Phillips. While the last Communist faded away, labour did elect a few of its own, notably Ford Brand as controller.[9]

The topsy-turvy electoral politics of the era reflected fear of a return to the Depression and the search for mechanisms to ensure growth and stability. Transferring taxation and control of money away from the municipalities and toward the provincial and the federal governments was a major issue. In contrast to the post-First World War experience, it was not quite as easy to end the centralized war economy of the early 1940s nor for the provinces to hand back social and welfare costs to the municipalities. The ratchet of history, it seemed, had locked the scale of living and actions at a point "higher" than before, even if at a point "lower" than the CCF advocated. Given a history in which the collective day-to-day experience of Torontonians and others had been sustained chiefly through the municipality and its taxes, the shifting of power was unsettling. To transform the provincial government into something more than a super-county council, even with its constitutional authority over municipalities, was a daring step the majority would entrust only to the Tories. To give the federal government powers akin to a centralized British government under the Labour Party was taking the matter too far. To the majority, the CCF meant state control, not democracy, and the end of freedom. Just the same, the process of centralization would continue.

Ironically, there was less centralization in Canada than in the U.S., where continued war production, inner-city redevelopment and the interstate highway system were financed by the federal government, despite free-enterprise rhetoric. Torontonians did not talk of freedom so glibly. They had become accustomed to commissions, boards and authorities, and local democracy remained sufficiently intact to persuade people that they had more control over their collective environments. At the same time, growth had to be sustained: the small affairs of city, town and township government were transformed into vast businesses. With appointed Fred Gardiner in the driver's seat of Metro, John Ross Robertson's 1901 assertion that "municipal government is a question of business and not politics" had finally come true.[10]

ECONOMIC RECOVERY: WARTIME PLANNING AND POSTWAR KEYNESIANISM

The CCF's call for centralized economic planning was answered during the Second World War, as regional interests were submerged under C.D. Howe's federal Department of Munitions and Supply. Canada became the fourth most important Allied supplier of materiel. By 1944 the federal government had built ninety-eight new war production plants while subsidizing additions to private plants. The slackness of production in the 1930s was replaced by full use of capacity and full employment.[11]

Most industrial production went on in central Canada, with Toronto as a major centre. By 1943 eighty-seven large plants and many smaller ones were mobilized for war work in the Metro area. National Steel Car at Malton, taken over by the government as a crown company in 1942 and reorganized as Victory Aircraft, was a key producer of Lancasters for the Commonwealth air forces. Leaside's Research Enterprises, an experimental crown company, manufactured optical equipment and radar. Massey-Harris made wings and spars for Avro Anson planes and anti-aircraft shells; produced tanks for the American army in Racine, Wisconsin; and manufactured self-propelled combines in Toronto for the "Massey-Harris Harvest Brigades," which were familiar sights in small towns from Texas to North Dakota. Sales of $21 million in 1939 rose to $75 million in 1946, and employment from 5,141 to 11,321. While Massey succeeded in this major foray into the American economy and Research Enterprises was inventive, the war led to even greater dependence on American technology.[12]

In countless other ways, Toronto contributed to the war effort. If fewer died than in the Great War, many Torontonians served overseas. Widely heralded was Toronto's contribution to Commonwealth air-training schemes, particularly in Little Norway at the Island Airport where Norwegians were prepared for RAF service. Women of the Red Cross knit stockings and sweaters and other items for Canadian servicemen and British citizens. As elsewhere, Torontonians lived with rationing and gasoline shortages. Nevertheless, even in the darkest days of 1940, 1941 and early 1942 there seemed little doubt that the war would soon be over: rising expectations were being expressed in politics and planning.[13]

Planning for postwar reconstruction began in 1943, though the federal government was slow in taking the lead. W.A. Mackintosh's White Paper on Employment and Income was presented as the basis for growth although, as it turned out, his hope for "full employment" was watered down to "a high and stable level of employment." The Industrial Development Bank was set up to help private industry; Central Mortgage and Housing Corporation was established to spur housing starts; and extensive public works were planned. But at the behest of Minister of Reconstruction C.D. Howe, many crown corporations were sold: Research Enterprises was purchased by Corning Glass in the U.S. at a fire-sale price and Victory Aircraft was bought by A.V. Roe of Britain. In Ontario Drew's Twenty-Two Point Program, a "counter-answer to socialism" and containing many CCF ideas, provided a partial basis for provincial reconstruction plans.[14]

The Toronto Reconstruction Council was established in 1943 on the recommendation of Controller Lewis Duncan. A major concern was the shifting of employment to the peacetime economy: industry surveys indicated that 330,000 to 350,000 more jobs might be expected. Because commercial enterprises showed increasingly less interest, by 1945 direct economic planning petered out (as it did in Ottawa). The proposition that "private enterprise" would "provide full employment" overrode the view of leaving "this problem in the . . . hands of the State." Few, if any, recognized at the time that the American "state" would increasingly lay its hands on the economy through "military Keynesianism."[15]

After shortages were alleviated, the Canadian postwar economy boomed, particularly after 1949, with several years of help from Korean War demands. Unemployment had fallen to 4 per cent by 1941; it increased after the war, but dropped again to an historic "peacetime" low of 1.3 per cent in 1951. Manufacturing wages, which increased greatly during the war, continued to rise. The labour force in the city expanded from 285,778 in 1941 to 338,576 in 1951, and even more noticeably in the suburbs from 94,253 to 188,252, especially between 1948 and 1951. Since 1921 women had been increasing their share of the city's work force; even if the proportion fell after the war from a high of more 40 per cent, in 1951 it still remained high, at 33 per cent.[16] (Table X)

Manufacturing was considered to be the sector that would lead the way to recovery. The number of manufacturing firms in the city did increase from 2,762 in 1939 to 3,622 in 1946, which caused some planners to worry, as they had in the 1920s, that too much was concentrated in the centre. By 1951 manufacturers of iron and steel products, electrical goods, clothing, food and beverages, and printing and publishing firms were the city's major employers, and workers' wages had increased substantially. While the number directly engaged in manufacturing was the same in 1951 as it had been in 1941, the number of white-collar employees rose by 12 per cent. Although the proportion of women directly involved in production increased, a great number of those who had worked on production lines during the war were absorbed into the new or expanding offices of processing companies. The Toronto Reconstruction Council's concern for the need to plan postwar manufacturing jobs and production of public works had been allayed by the availability of capital for expansion.[17] (Tables X, XI)

Despite planning fears, most of postwar expansion in manufacturing occurred in the suburban municipalities, which undoubtedly helped convince reformers and politicians of the need for a metropolitan form of government to provide services that would sustain growth. In 1946 more than 90 per cent of all manufacturing firms in York County were located in Toronto, by 1954 that figure had fallen to 77 per cent. Joining the large, sprawling suburban factories were many relatively small branch plants — said to already number 400 in 1948 — which established themselves on agricultural land on Toronto's fringe, the favoured Canadian location in American corporate eyes. Even if some larger firms migrated from the core and the city's manufacturing sector began its decline to the present, the pre-1900 centralization of Ontario's industry in the Toronto region was renewed.[18]

In 1948 it was claimed that Toronto had "undoubtedly taken from Montreal the title of Canada's most important money market." However, not until 1950 did the stock exchange recover its 1936 levels in values and shares sold. From then on the trend was upward until the depression in 1957. Although the number of cheques cashed in Montreal closed the gap somewhat, Toronto held its strong lead in insurance and gained on Montreal in head offices, an indication of its financial strength. Ottawa's involvement in the economy during the war and its postwar Keynesian policies, as well as Canada's dependence on American investment, would eventually alter these relationships. But Toronto's image as a money-making

The fortieth Lancaster bomber completed at Victory Aircraft in Malton supports sixty-five women workers on its wings. Crown corporations such as Victory were sold to the private sector after the war, as the wartime belief in the efficiency of public production faded.

The drive to victory was aided by Massey-Harris and its workers. Tanks were made in Wisconsin; the Toronto works made wings for Mosquito bombers assembled by de Havilland. Massey-Harris combines, which formed "The Harvest Brigade" of the American wheat belt, also contributed to the company's postwar success. This ad reflects widespread confidence in the war effort.

Workers in all plants further contributed to the war by devoting a share of rising wages to Victory Loan Bonds. In this promotional photograph the pitch is made at the entry door of a Mosquito at de Havilland. These two women had between them seven brothers in the service.

Secretarial jobs continued to expand in the 1940s. Although many young women had been trained in the public high school system since 1915, private schools like this one — the Katherine Gibbs — were needed to keep up with demand for typing and shorthand skills.

The transformation of postwar suburbia owed much to industrialization. IBM was one of the first large companies to spread out its one floor at Don Mills in the early 1950s. Parking lots for commuting workers had become as important as railway sidings.

machine was already well established by 1947, the year Lister Sinclair's CBC radio skit, "We All Hate Toronto," had Torontonians going off to work chanting:

> Sing a song of moola
> Pocket full of scratch
> Piling up mazuma
> Watching nest eggs hatch!

Certainly some Torontonians revealed an understanding of the postwar world. In 1951 Marshall McLuhan interpreted the rise of the consumer society in his *Mechanical Bride*. Soon after John Seeley and his colleagues told Americans in *Crestwood Heights* how postwar affluence wended its way through suburban families in not altogether typical Forest Hill.[19] (Table XII)

Higher wages gained by unions during the war and after were reflected in the rising wages paid to salespeople, and in a virtually proportionate increase of receipts to retailers. In the city, although the number of retail outlets began to fall in the 1940s, sales and other receipts rose from about $400 million in 1941 to $1 billion in 1951 despite only a slight rise in population. Even more dramatic was the increase in suburban sales.[20]

Another indication of prosperity was a postwar increase in the number of conventions, conferences and tourists. By 1949 it was claimed that as a convention centre Toronto trailed behind only New York and Chicago on the continent. Since facilities had "reached the saturation point," the Civic Advisory Council (CAC) was asked to develop a proposal for an auditorium and convention hall. In 1950 the CAC recommended a 12,000 seat auditorium and 80,000 square feet of exhibition space. As well, more hotels were needed. The O'Keefe Centre and other facilities relieved some of the pressure a few years later, but the number of conventions continued to grow. In its inimitable fashion, Toronto would have to wait another thirty years or so for its convention centre.[21]

The clear measure of increased prosperity was electricity consumption, which doubled in the city between 1940 and 1954. During the war the strongest demands came from the commercial sector, yet the longer-term increase was greater in residential use and commercial lighting. The black-outs of 1948 only pointed to increasing demand for "living better electrically." Consumerism had hit Toronto harder than ever before.[22]

While Toronto's manufacturing, financial and tourist industries boomed, the housing construction industry lagged until 1950. During the war people could tolerate doubling up and so could municipalities. The Wartime Prices and Trade Board countermanded zoning bylaws, thus encouraging conversions. But fifteen years of little action on the housing shortage problem and the postwar "baby boom" produced increasing pressure, which was expressed electorally in 1948 when the CCF gained a majority of seats in the Toronto area. The number of persons per unit had increased since 1939; vacancies were virtually non-existent by the late 1940s; and the Central Tenants Association complained that the city had substantially raised rents on emergency housing. Toronto was the most critical area in the country: it still had 30,000 doubled-up families. People lived in crowded tarpaper huts, reminiscent of pre-First World War shack towns.[23]

In 1946 Humphrey Carver and Robert Adamson reported the results of their CMHC-financed survey in *How Much Housing Does Greater Toronto Need?* and *Who Can Pay for Housing?* Besides arguing for subsidized housing, they calculated that metropolitan Toronto would need 50,000 units by 1956. The goal of 5,000 per year was not reached in 1947, nor in 1948, and builders fell further behind in 1949. By May 1949 only 17,643 units had been built, a gain of only 9 per cent which compared unfavourably with 14 per cent in Montreal and 22 per cent in Vancouver. The shortage of materials after the war was considered a major factor in slowing production and, of course, prices were up. The high cost of serviced land was another serious restraint, as it had been in the 1920s and earlier. A CMHC spokesman at a 1948 conference also pointed to the lack of cooperation among governments, noting that the city had actually offered to pay half the cost of serviced land in the suburbs for rental housing, only to be ignored by the other municipalities.[24]

In *Houses for Canadians*, written with Toronto in mind, Humphrey Carver observed that the small speculative builder puts up only a few houses at a time, and that "fundamental changes . . . can only be brought about through the entry of large-scale producers into the housing industry, and they can only enter upon such a business if they could anticipate a continuing market which would justify the necessary capitalization . . . ." Similarly, through large-scale organization, labour costs could be reduced and more "imaginative planning" of whole communities pursued.[25]

After 1948 the situation improved substantially: 4,143 completions in 1948 were raised to more than 13,000 in 1951 before being

Even in the postwar boom, some veterans could not make ends meet: a veteran's family is evicted in 1951. This street in North York is typical of the federally-funded housing put up in the the less accessible areas of the suburbs during the war and postwar years.

Like the family above, most households had an electric washing machine and other such appliances by the early 1950s. Ontario Hydro encouraged consumers to "live better electrically," even though demand exceeded supply in the late 1940s, leading to promotions like this.

dampened somewhat by Korean War materiel needs. CMHC financing was finally taking hold. Home ownership jumped to an historic high of 82 per cent in the metropolitan area (62 per cent in the city), reflecting affluence and productive capabilities. Political agitation therefore receded as shown by the 1951 election results. Like other aspects of the economy, housing production had entered the halcyon days of the 1950s.[26]

The 1940s were a momentous decade for trade unions in Canada. Memberships doubled, a delayed effect of the U.S. Wagner Act of 1935 which guaranteed union recognition, the closed shop, and the rights to collective bargaining and to strike action. But it was only through strikes in 1943 and again after the war that Canadian workers gained recognition. The handwriting was on the wall in 1943 when the fading Ontario Liberals, desperately seeking labour votes, passed Canada's first legislation on compulsory collective bargaining. In 1944 the federal government finally granted sweeping rights temporarily as a trade-off for wage controls. After the postwar strikes, most of the rights were entrenched federally and provincially. Wages, fringe benefits and shorter hours came to be the focus of strikes. This turbulent period did result in an uneasy but relatively stable era in the 1950s. As government, management and labour settled into the Keynesian era, labour continued to agitate for improved public social benefits for everyone.[27]

Toronto experienced none of the landmark strikes of the era. In 1947 the country-wide strike of packinghouse employees involved Toronto workers at Swifts and Canada Packers. In 1950 the traditionally conservative "non-operating" railway workers in Toronto and elsewhere went out. The transit workers struck for three weeks early in 1952 for higher wages and fringe benefits. Although the TTC resisted on the grounds that fares would rise, an arbitrator's compromise ended the strike. The three-year campaign to organize 15,000 Eaton's employees was energetic, "the closest thing to a crusade in the English-speaking union movement." But it failed because of wage increases, a pension plan granted by Eaton's, and rapid staff turnover. Unlike industrial workers, most service employees would have to wait. With prosperity in the 1950s, the unionizing impulse weakened.[28]

In the volatile 1940s, the two local labour councils managed to co-operate on a few issues, though the craft unions (AFL) largely stayed out of electoral politics while the industrial (CIO) unions supported the CCF. As elsewhere, they had to deal with the contending forces on the left, the Communists and the CCF, which were both trying to strengthen links with the unions. By the early 1950s, as the Communists largely disappeared, a softening of attitudes between the craft and industrial councils was apparent, though unity would not come until 1956.[29]

POPULATION GROWTH: THE GATES BEGIN TO OPEN

Toronto's shaking up in the 1940s owed something to population shifts as well as to immigration from overseas. With the city already filled, the suburbs added nearly 200,000 between 1940 and 1953. Although by 1951 other industrial cities in southern Ontario were taking a larger share of the final push toward the urbanization of the province, the metro area was still increasing its share of the total population. Some of the growth come from other parts of Canada. Many came to work in war production, so by 1951 the proportion of those born elsewhere in Canada, particularly in the Maritimes, had risen. (Tables I, VI)

Undoubtedly, the most significant sign of change in Toronto's culture was the arrival of immigrants from overseas. They came haltingly in the late 1940s, but the flood was well underway in the early 1950s. In the postwar era immigrants, like everyone else, sought urban jobs: the rural solution had had its day. Ottawa policy-makers decided that Canada's economy needed people and Toronto was the chief beneficiary.

In 1945 and 1946 there was still little indication that Canadians wanted new people, especially Japanese, Germans and Jews. The British war brides were obviously acceptable but, fearing another depression, nearly half of Canadians did not want even British immigrants. In 1946 and 1947 the labour shortage became pronounced; so, as in other countries, the King government issued several orders-in-council to allow "displaced persons" to immigrate. But, as always, caution in selection would prevail: British, American and French immigrants first, then European relatives of Canadian residents (though not German citizens until 1950) and, last, Orientals. A "fundamental alteration in the character of the population" had to be avoided. This 1947 position essentially remained in place until 1962.[30]

External pressure from the United Nations and its International Refugee Organization (IRO), as well as the labour shortage, eventu-

Labour union membership shot up thanks to sweeping changes in labour law. Labour Day parades were more enthusiatic, the floats more expressive, as in this effort by the UAW local from Massey-Harris in 1953.

Infighting still continued. The United Electrical Workers, here at their 1948 annual meeting, kept strong ties to the Communist Party while most other unions moved to support the CCF. But many in the rank and file were hesitant to support labour-based parties once the Depression was licked.

ally led to Canada's acceptance of Poles, Ukrainians, Jews, Yugoslavs, Estonians, Latvians, Lithuanians, Hungarians, Czechoslovaks and Rumanians. Of those who began arriving in 1947, many at first turned to farming and lumbering, but some came to urban jobs as domestic and textile workers. Parallel to the IRO program was the *Volksdeutsch* program for ethnic Germans, who began arriving in 1948. Not until 1950 were many of the "forgotten elite" of intellectuals allowed in. By 1953 more than 165,000 "displaced persons" had arrived in Canada.[31]

How many of them came to Toronto is unclear. Some came under programs for domestics, garment workers, furriers and as close relatives. In October 1949 more than 4,000 were enrolled in 130 special classes for immigrants. The 1951 census recorded substantial increases of those born in Russia, Poland and other eastern European countries while, by ethnicity, Ukrainians, Poles and Germans were substantially higher than in 1941. After 1950, German and Italian citizens were admitted, and the latter began their great influx. The Roman Catholic population showed a substantial gain in the city, up by 5 per cent from 1941 to nearly 20 per cent. Lutherans doubled their proportion.[32] (Tables VII, VIII, IX)

The city's population also grew simply because Torontonians begat more Torontonians. By 1947 the birth rate had peaked and would remain high for a decade. The effect on the public school system was not immediate: not until 1951 did elementary school enrollments reach the low point from their prewar high in 1933. Enrollments in elementary separate schools, however, grew after 1947 partly in response to the new immigration. Both systems were on the verge of phenomenal growth. (Tables IV, V)

Even if Canada would not explicitly eliminate racial distinctions for immigrants until 1962 and did not open its door to "displaced persons" as widely as other countries did, clear advances were achieved in civil rights. The various factions in Toronto's Chinese community united to lead the way to the partial repeal of the harsh 1923 Chinese immigration act. With the help of the churches, the press, the labour councils and the CCF, the act was softened in 1947 to permit Chinese citizens to bring over immediate family members, thus wiping out the 1923 "Day of Humiliation." The effort in Toronto was "uniquely a joint White-Chinese enterprise." A similar effort by the Toronto Joint Committee to Combat Racial Intolerance and the Jewish Labour Committee of Canada, which began in 1947, resulted in the Ontario Fair Employment Practices Act and, in 1954, the Fair Accommodations Act. Though racism would not disappear, these were at least steps toward a more open multicultural Toronto.[33]

The arrival of "displaced persons" challenged Toronto's social service network. Those coming through the garment workers program were well integrated through the efforts of Jewish organizations. The Catholic Women's League and ethnic organizations helped Roman Catholics; the YWCA and the Interchurch Committee helped Protestants. Those who came under the Domestic Service Programme were the least satisfied because they had no protection against capricious employers. Since most were single women, they were isolated from their ethnic peers, at least until they were able to move on after fulfilling their contract. The University and St. Christopher Settlement Houses in west central Toronto renewed their work among minority groups. This area, losing Jews northward to Bathurst and Eglinton, was becoming the major immigration area for a generation.[34] (Map 8, p. 176)

SOCIAL PLANNING AND NEW PLEASURES

Social planning moved ahead, but its pace was agonizingly slow. Although in the early years of the war social spending fell as employment rose, by 1943 the issues of postwar social welfare spending and which level of government would pay were clearly on the agenda. Municipal governments hoped to move the costs of welfare, social security and, to a degree, social services—particularly education—to higher levels of government. Public attitudes toward collective responsibility for the first time seriously shifted toward the need for positive government action to promote consumption and to foster a higher degree of equality. The individual and the family were finally recognized as social and not simply private entities. The state representing society as a whole would provide minimum support. If in housing the principle was hard to establish, at least some positive moves occurred.

In 1940 the federal government enacted unemployment insurance for 75 per cent of the Canadian population. In response to the rising popularity of the CCF and to the Marsh Report of 1943 (based on the widely publicized Beveridge Report in Britain), which advocated a comprehensive and universal social security system, family allowances were instituted in 1946. This was Canada's first universal welfare scheme and was mainly responsible for raising federal

After a final postwar bout of reluctance, Canada allowed immigrants from continental Europe. For "displaced persons" from central and eastern European countries, the point of arrival was Union Station. Where Western homesteads had been the final destination of many turn-of-the-century immigrants, by 1948 most new Canadians — like this Dutch family — were settling in Toronto and other cities.

per capita expenditures on social welfare from $19 in 1943 to $50 in 1947. Some improvement in unemployment insurance, some "meagre" initiatives in the health field in 1948, the Old Age Pension Act of 1951 and the Blind Persons Act showed that *ad hoc* responses to pressures had shoved aside the notion of comprehensiveness in social security. The next major federal advances would not occur until the late 1950s.[35]

Higher-level inaction left the municipalities still paying for a large share of family social services from property taxes. Indeed, in 1950, despite the city's "very enviable financial position," the finance commissioner could argue that the city was bearing a "disproportionate share" of the costs of education, relief, hospitals and care of dependent children. Despite the marked drop in the city's expenditure on education, owing to a major rise in provincial grants in 1945, by 1950 costs had crept back up. Even more obvious was the rise in the cost of social services. The proportions drifted upward despite some conditional grants from the province for Children's Aid and Homes for the Aged from 1949 to 1953. Further, the spectre of the 1930s haunted the scene. After 1951 relief payments rose with unemployment and for unemployables: by 1953 the city's share of $1.2 million of the $2.2 million spent showed that the system had not really changed since 1932. Of course, greater wealth and lower unemployment allowed the city to handle the burden out of the current account. But it is little wonder that the commissioner complained; in the near future Toronto would see only gradual and certainly incomplete relief from these costs.[36]

Voluntary social welfare agencies were caught up in the enthusiasm for reform between 1942 and 1946. The Welfare Council's budget jumped from $8,600 in 1941 to $62,000 in 1947. The vastly expanded staff contributed vigorously in pushing for the goal of social security. A reorganized fund-raising body, the United Welfare Chest, began in 1944 to raise more money for the Welfare Council and for a wider range of agencies. Catholic and Jewish agencies co-operated with the city-wide body. The 1946 annual report of the Welfare Council described the vast increase of work in referral services, child and family welfare, day nurseries, health, old age care, recreation and research. By 1948 activity had levelled off and the impulse of collective action had waned. Nevertheless, the Welfare Council had more firmly embraced the Marsh Report's position of social welfare as a right rather than as a matter of relief.[37]

The Regent Park North public housing project was Toronto's most visible expression of the revival of social welfare planning. However, the enormous organizational energy poured into the planning of this project and of other central redevelopment areas indicates how difficult it was to establish the principle of social housing. Agitation for low-rent housing had intensified between the late 1930s and 1947, when ratepayers voted for Regent Park. The 1942 Lewis Duncan committee report on housing had estimated that 1,500 units were needed for the war effort, 1,000 to raise vacancy rates, 1,000 "to remove a menace to health," and 3,000 "to remove a menace to family and social life," that is, overcrowding. Duncan minced no words on the failure of private enterprise to supply adequate housing. But the reactions of the mayor and Board of Trade were not positive, even though the federal government was financing some wartime housing.[38]

So armed with the 1943 city plan and the federal Curtis Report on housing, the reformers started to press harder in 1944. The Toronto Housing Association (later, the Citizens' Housing and Planning Association) proposed direct involvement of government in redevelopment; the federal government's counterproposal was limited dividend construction through Housing Enterprises backed by largely reluctant insurance companies. But reformers persisted; that fall they convinced the Board of Control and many citizens. The *Star* and *Globe and Mail* were on-side, though the *Telegram* was not. In December 1945, with Mayor Saunders clearly in charge, City Council approved unanimously the "Regent Park Rental Housing Project." After another year of debate, including numerous, largely unsuccessful forays to Ottawa, the city went ahead on its own.[39]

In 1947 the city created the Toronto Housing Authority. Following the commission tradition in keeping with a more democratic era, the housing authority was composed of a wider variety of people than earlier bodies had been, though no citizen from the area was appointed, nor would tenants be appointed later. This was still largely social housing as a privilege.

The design was an austere garden-suburbs superblock model based on American precedents. Most of the 854 units were to be in apartment structures with a few row houses. As for money, the

At Gerrard and University, soon to be the site of the Sick Children's Hospital, wartime workers had to live in these tiny "mobile homes." In the right background are the elegant Alexandra Palace Apartments, which gave way to Mount Sinai Hospital.

A barometer of the economic climate through the decades, the Scott Mission as it appeared in the early 1950s. It was later rebuilt.

authority eventually had to raise the number of units to 1,056 to meet building costs, and City Council had to go back to barely supportive ratepayers for more funding in 1952 (one of the last times a referendum on money questions was put to voters). In the meantime, the authority persuaded the reluctant federal government to put up nearly $1.4 million and the province $1.3 million. The total cost was finally about $16 million. The first families moved in in March 1949. Since the construction was phased so as not to displace anyone, the last tenants occupied their units early in 1957. Even then, 5,000 families were on the waiting list. Regent Park had not solved the housing problem, but it obviously pointed to the need for more. By then the federal government had become willing to finance more projects. Although the reform sentiment in the city had already weakened, largely because the private sector with CMHC help was producing suburban houses at a prodigious rate, more inner-city projects were to come.[40]

Between 1946 and 1949 the Toronto Reconstruction Council and its successor, the Civic Advisory Countil (CAC), devoted a good deal of energy to the development of community councils. Rising juvenile delinquency and gang organizations (like the Beanery Boys); the awareness of declining and vulnerable neighbourhoods; increased action by residents' groups; social surveys; and the advocacy of census tracts, all prompted the CAC to hire an energetic community organizer to report to a committee chaired by George Hees. Despite an enthusiastic delving into various neighbourhoods, attempts to organize councils where there were not organizations already failed to produce very much. In fact, north Toronto was better organized on the council model than west Toronto was where considerable survey work was conducted.[41]

At the CAC's Working and Living Conference in 1949, organizer Hugo Wolter summed up his frustrations: Toronto was still very British and not very open to foreign immigrants, especially "displaced persons" who were then arriving in substantial numbers; religious "conflicts" were marked; young people, especially ex-servicemen, were rebelling against "traditional policies." In fact, Torontonians were experiencing a

> deep inner conflict. Everything seems to weigh so heavily on the people resulting in a characteristic dourness. Indecision is evident and leadership seems to be lacking. In the face of Toronto's alleged "goodness" why this apparent insecurity?

The poor of Cabbagetown took on the guise of a tycoon in this ad placed by the Property Owners Association of Toronto to protest the expansion of public housing in Regent Park. The ad went on to give the association's side of the debate, ending with an unsuccessful appeal to vote "no" in the December 1952 plebiscite on adding more public money to the project.

Toronto hopes it is doing the right thing but seldom gets beyond a promise to itself.

Because the "geographic unity of neighbourhoods no longer exists" and there was an absence of "long range planning," so much was being wasted. Community councils bringing together all interest groups in particular districts would, Wolter silll thought, be a "constructive means." After comment by other delegates, the matter was left there.[42]

Nonetheless, Toronto took two major steps away from Toronto the Good: cocktail lounges in 1947 and Sunday commercial sports in 1950. Liquor by the glass returned to Toronto and a few other cities. In 1927 the Liquor Control Board of Ontario had been set up to sell packaged liquors, as much to ensure a lucrative source of revenue for the province as to control drinking. Seven years later hotels began to sell beer and wine in dingy beverage rooms. After the experience of the war, people who had served overseas, among others, were in no mood to keep to old ways. So in 1946 wetness advanced. Despite dry resistance as before and a last ditch opposition move to require local option votes, Drew's provincial government approved cocktail lounges. As of April 1, 1947, 123 applications from Toronto had been received by the province; 41 had been granted. But rigid inspection rules slowed down preparations. On that day the frustration level was high: only one place, the Barclay Hotel, was actually ready at noon, although the Silver Rail and others soon followed. Only West Toronto retained the local option, a right dating back to annexation in 1909, and indeed has remained dry. Elsewhere the lounges had come to stay, and the province would reap great profits as a result.[43]

In January 1950, a bare majority of Torontonians voted for Sunday sports. This vote, and a positive one in Windsor, resulted in provincial legislation allowing municipalities to hold referenda for Sunday afternoon amateur and commercial sports. (In the 1960s, theatre performances, horse racing and evening activities were finally permitted.) The 1950 vote had been preceded by a debate that was as long and rancorous as that over Sunday streetcars in the 1890s. Opposition had been strong enough in 1941, for example, to persuade the government to drop a Sunday Ski Train bill. Moves in 1947 and 1948 to put Sunday sports on the ballot were turned down handily by City Council following pressure from the churches and the Lord's Day Alliance. But the fight heated up in January 1949 when Allan Lamport proposed "Sensible Sunday." Long a leading proponent of open Sundays, this often flamboyant controller sensed that the time had come. Despite fierce lobbying, City Council approved the vote, but only after deleting other types of entertainment from the motion. Expecting a close vote, both sides fought fiercely. The Toronto Citizens' Committee set up a $25,000 fund to get out the No vote. Cardinal McGuigan supported the No side. One clergyman invoked God to send his Son to Toronto. Another feared that the "liquor interests" would next ask for Sunday opening of bars, thus "debauching the youth of the Dominion." All was for naught: residents of the city's west, east and north extremities (then, Wards 7, 8, 9) voted against, others came out in record numbers to vote for the Yes side. Later, a United Church minister warned the province that the pro-vote came from Wards 4 and 5 "where there are many Communists and foreign-born people," even worse, from the "gangster-plagued slums." The province obviously did not agree. Lamport had reached his greatest moment, but his malapropisms would continue to enliven council meetings for two more decades. "If someone stabs me in the back, I want to be there," he once told council.[44]

Toronto's professional sports teams also reached their greatest heights. The Argos won the Grey Cup five times between 1945 and 1952. Under coach Teddy Morris, Joe Krol and Royal Copeland led the team to three consecutive championships over Winnipeg. Frank Clair coached two more winners in the finals, all played before capacity crowds at Varsity Stadium. One winning team Toronto could not quite claim as its own was the RCAF Hurricanes in 1942, composed of players stationed in Toronto. In 1940 Balmy Beach won the cup for the last time; after the war the semi-pro Ontario Rugby Football Union was gradually squeezed out of the football picture by the pros.[45]

Canada's anglophone ears were glued to the radio on Saturday night listening for Foster Hewitt's exclamation: "He shoots, he scores." It was more often for the Leafs than for their opponents, as the team won the Stanley Cup six times between 1942 and 1951. The first and last were probably the most exciting: in 1942 Toronto overcame a three-game deficit to defeat Detroit. In 1951 Bill Barilko beat the Canadiens in seventh-game overtime. The farm system developed by Conn Smythe and judicious trades produced outstanding stars such as Ted Kennedy, Wally Stanowski, Babe Pratt and dipsy-doodling Max Bentley.[46]

Baseball was revived. After record lows in the early 1940s, crowds reached record highs in 1949 and in 1952. Only part of the success could be attributed to the team—only in 1943 did the baseball Leafs manage a first. The rise in enthusiasm reflected the rising ebullience of the postwar era. So strong was the pull that entrepreneur Jack Kent Cooke bought the team in 1951 and turned the stadium at the foot of Bathurst into the greatest show in town with fireworks, giveaways and stunts. Returns at the turnstiles finally began to pay off with a string of winning teams in 1954. Ralph Kiner, Toronto's Goody Rosen and Ingersoll's Oscar Judd were among those stars who donned Leaf baseball uniforms.[47]

During the war, Sunnyside—the "poor man's riviera"—was a popular playground of Torontonians. The Easter parade on the boardwalk continued, though uniforms were more prevalent than new coats and hats. After the war, cars clogged Lakeshore Boulevard on special days. At the Seabreeze, people continued to dance. Les Brown, Harry James and Toronto's Trump Davidson played at the nearby Palace Pier, which was originally planned as a pier of the likes of those in Atlantic City and Brighton. The Community Sing Song sponsored by People's Credit Jewellers attracted many on Sunday evenings. However, by the late 1940s Sunnyside's future looked grim. In 1949 what became the Gardiner Expressway was proposed and threatened to cut through the amusement park. In 1950 the TTC ended the fine, longstanding custom of free streetcar rides for children. Over the next half decade, Sunnyside declined further as other amusements became more attractive. When demolished in 1955, its merry-go-round was shipped to Disneyland. Somehow by renaming it King Arthur's Carousel, it acquired a special aura for postwar North Americans.[48]

The theatre went through only a modest revival after the war. By 1953 the University Alumnae, Hart House, Toronto Children's Players and the fading Canadian Drama League had been joined by Dora Mavor Moore's New Play Society (famed for *Spring Thaw*), the Earle Grey Players and the Jupiter and Crest theatres. The effect of the 1951 Massey Commission on the Arts in Canada was not immediate, though the opening of the Stratford Shakespearean Festival in 1953 indicated a remarkable achievement for prosaic Ontario. All the while, the *Star*'s Nathan Cohen chastised local professional efforts for their derivative mediocrity. In the face of

Bill Barilko scored one of the Maple Leafs' most famous goals, beating the Canadiens in overtime in the seventh game of the 1951 Stanley Cup.

Servicemen and their partners could dance cheek-to-cheek at Sunnyside in 1942 — but the notice at the ticket booth says there was to be "no jitterbugging or fancy dancing allowed."

In 1949 Toronto's worst human disaster occurred when the cruise ship Noronic *went up in flames, taking 118 lives.*

more exciting, realistic and funny American and British movies and, after 1950, television, serious interest in live theatre was yet to come.[49]

PLANNING THE URBAN ENVIRONMENT

The CCF's call for economic planning may have been reduced to a degree of Keynesian pump-priming and its social security proposals only modestly fulfilled, but Torontonians embraced, almost as a panacea, the party's concern for a well planned urban environment. In the heady years from 1940 to 1953, Toronto revealed an instinct for order that was as strong as its demand for growth. A zoning system, comprehensive plans and the formation of a metropolitan government would guarantee greater environmental stability as well as a more balanced allocation of public services.

The war effort did not deter interest in stability and growth. In the bleak fall of 1941, the city's Independent Committee on Zoning (ICZ) took its proposals for a comprehensive zoning system to the public. Under a plethora of bylaws and amendments, 39 per cent of the city was already covered by residential restrictions, but nearly 33 per cent was still available for commercial and industrial activities. The committee suggested the stabilization of land use to stop "industrial infiltration" so as to "make this City of Toronto the best place on the North American continent and perhaps the best place in the world to live in." Within each category of use were to be graded zones of use and density: four residential and three commercial.[50]

At the public meetings the problem of fitting neighbourhoods into these categories created a good deal of heat, particularly where South Rosedale and other high-status areas were involved. The ICZ recognized the reality of rooming houses and institutions in areas with large houses that were no longer attractive to affluent families and suggested easing restrictions.[51]

A larger question was the connection of zoning to planning. According to one member of the ICZ, J.S. Galbraith, "Zoning is a department of planning. Planning has to do with all land including streets and all the services they carry .... A city plan, a comprehensive plan, must therefore precede a zoning by-law ...." Without a plan, decentralizaton would be accelerated: people would move to the suburbs "because taxes are too high." "A city plan can become a tax control plan," resulting in efficient and prudent use of public funds. To zone without a plan would be "not only useless but dangerous." Planning Commissioner leMay agreed; City Council had embarked on the exercise not only "to consolidate and codify existing bylaws" but also "to produce a firm basis for further town planning efforts ...."[52]

With the support of the Board of Trade, Bureau of Municipal Research, Trades and Labour Council and Ontario Association of Architects, in 1942 Galbraith and others persuaded a still somewhat reluctant City Council to set up the City Planning Board of Toronto to consider housing, transportation, business areas, public services, annexation and other matters. After hearing from experts and commissioners, the new board proceeded with a plan, which was made public in December 1943.[53]

And a sweeping plan it was. More comprehensive than earlier American city plans, it was a proposal for thirty years of development. (See opposite.) The most important feature of the plan was the system of "superhighways." Toronto would thus follow New York's 1929 and Los Angeles's 1939 expressway plans. A close look at the freeway plan reveals both what was accepted and what rejected. Connecting with the already constructed Queen Elizabeth Way were expressways on the waterfront (A) and through midtown, a depressed route just north of Bloor and down Rosedale Valley (E). The route of the Brown's Line-401 bypass, now 427 (D), was already being planned by the province. The Barrie highway and its extension would cut a swath across York's working-class areas and down the Garrison Creek bed, also through Toronto's neighbourhoods, to the waterfront (B). This would appear in later plans as the 400 extension and the Christie-Grace Expressway. Superhighway C, the predecessor of the Don Valley Parkway, would cut north along Coxwell, then along Don Mills Road. New arterials would be the long-discussed Don Roadway-Beltline route westward along Eglinton; Eglinton east from Leaside; Spadina through a tunnel at Casa Loma; an improved Kingston Road; the Jarvis extension (again); and a Mimico Creek route to the airport.

Several principles were invoked in this scheme: the expectation of increased urban and interurban auto traffic; the use of obviously cheap ravines; and the removal of through traffic from neighbourhood streets. (The destructive midtown superhighway, later moved north as the crosstown to Dupont and then to the CPR line in later plans, would become the route of the Bloor-Danforth subway.) Another assumption was that certain neighbourhoods were ex-

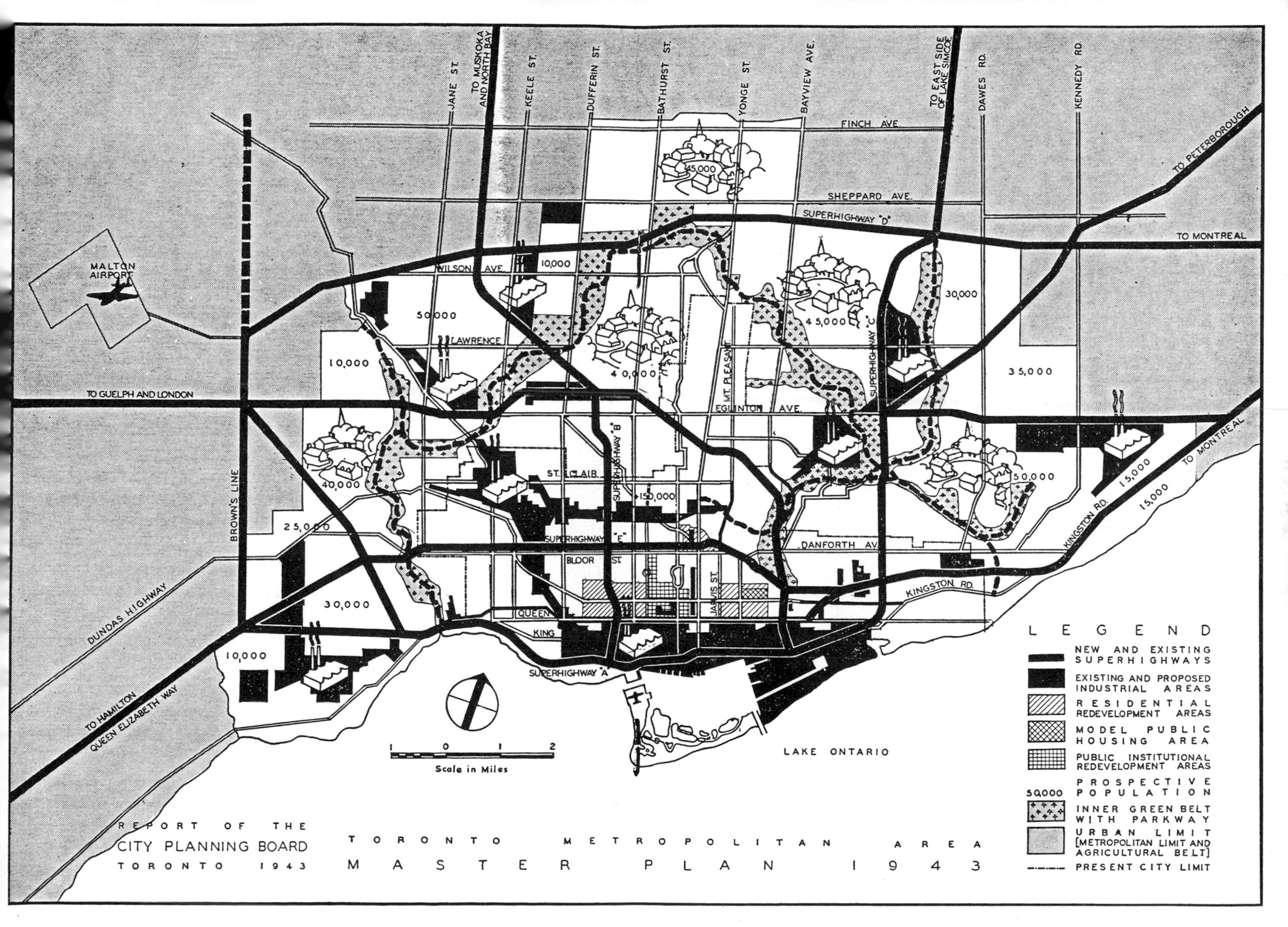

The city planning board scheme of 1943 was arguably the most important plan for Toronto in this century. Prominent features include expressways on the American model, a "Green Belt," surburban communities with industrial districts, and a central redevelopment area.

pendable: existing housing was not to stand in the way. A final principle was modal separation: the Planning Board endorsed the TTC's 1942 decision to proceed with the Yonge subway and the removal of streetcars from Yonge, Sherbourne and Avenue Road. A Queen Street subway line was supported. Following earlier plans, some ravines were also deemed useful for an inner greenbelt with parkways (for Sunday drives, it seems). Although the parkways and the northwestern section of the greenbelt were never completed, this innovative scheme did raise public awareness about the potential for ravine recreation and conservation.

The central area was singled out for special attention. From the Don to Ossington south of Carlton-College and Yorkville, residential districts were marked as "redevelopment areas," with Regent Park in Cabbagetown clearly marked as a "model public housing area." Lands straddling University Avenue and to the west of the University of Toronto were defined for "public institutional redevelopment areas." A civic square (once again), a new city hall and an auditorium were proposed.

Although the board accepted the continuation of existing industrial areas, and designated most of the area south of Queen between Dufferin and Coxwell and along railways for such uses, it argued for decentralization because the city had enough industry for tax revenue and employment. Any more would strain mass transportation facilities. Hence, the board advocated that the metropolitan area be zoned for neighbourhoods with "each providing all the essentials for satisfactory living, employment and recreation." Thus, on the map were shown new suburban districts with specified populations and, in most cases, industrial zones. This almost "new town" notion would be especially challenging for future planners, developers and politicians.

Overall, the plan foresaw suburban expansion based on a 1974 population of between 1,250,000 and 1,500,000, and therefore proposed a planned area of 100 square miles, nearly half as much again as the existing built-up area. The members wanted to control and restrict "straggling" fringe development, which had plagued Toronto since about 1850, because the 1912-1918 subdivision control law was not working well enough. The Planning Board foresaw the future urbanized area in a rough semi-circle along eighteen miles of waterfront between Etobicoke Creek and Markham Side Road and extending nine miles north on Yonge. While taking in Weston on the northwest, the board clearly wanted to shift greater growth toward the northeast, countering the historically stronger trend to the west and northwest. An almost symmetrical Toronto was envisaged, though very much still focussed on the central area.

The board underestimated population growth by nearly a million: in 1974, 2.1 million lived in Metro. The extent of spatial expansion was underguessed even more: in 1974 the built-up area was closer to 200 square miles. The board could not foresee the increased impact of the car, of cheap gasoline and of the giant development corporations.

The plan played down municipal boundaries; to make the plan work required a "partnership" among municipalities. Without question, the Planning Board's scheme was an argument for the creation of Metro (though not yet clearly recognized as such). The board members also expressed a desire to balance growth, order and populism: "It is . . . a people's plan aimed at meeting the crisis created by the necessity of building a modern city on the framework of the old pre-machine age town." With planning recognized as "the most valuable tool in civic development," the plan was widely circulated for comment.[54]

Another sign of quickened interest in planning was the wide mandate granted to the Toronto Reconstruction Council (TRC) by the city in 1943. Although the TRC's main problem was postwar employment, it also had under its purview social welfare, provision of social security and the powers of government—a breathtaking range of issues for a municipality. Since public works were regarded as a regulatory mechanism to maintain full employment, the TRC gave early support to the 1943 Master Plan. After the war, the TRC was transformed into the Civic Advisory Council, which focussed on housing and especially on the metropolitan structure, and not directly on economic structure.[55]

The Planning Board continued forging ahead. Its most significant work in 1944 was "The Neighbourhood Plan of Toronto," which defined seventy-eight city neighbourhoods in terms of socio-economic homogeneity, similarity of housing stock and physical barriers (Map 3). The neighbourhoods were also categorized. The "sound" districts (16 per cent) had modern housing, low land coverage, low population density, no through traffic, and local ratepayer associations. Most of them were in north Toronto. "Vulnerable" (32 per cent) and "declining" (50 per cent) neighbourhoods were closer to the centre and, of course, older and more densely settled. "Blighted" neighbourhoods—or "zones of transition"—and "slums"

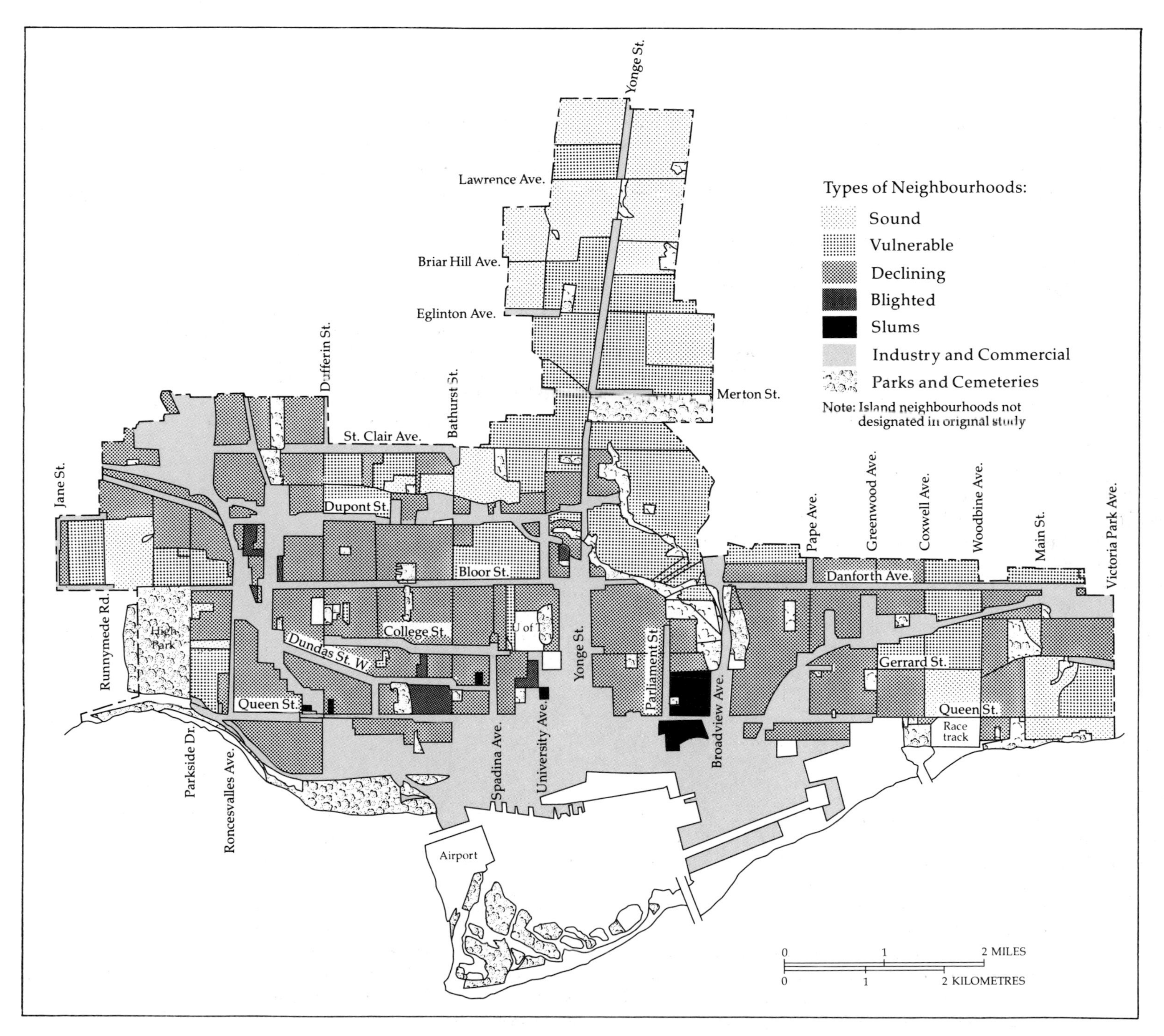

3 City Planning Board's Neighbourhood Classifications, 1944: The first attempt to sort out districts by housing quality was largely based on the age of homes. "Blighted" and "slum" areas caused concern, as did the wide extent of declining and vulnerable housing. But after 1965 many of the "old" areas would become attractive.

(2 per cent) required zoning control and redevelopment.[56]

This model of 1944 signalled that the board was interested not only in regional planning but also in districts within the city, whether deemed good or bad. Indeed, these seventy-eight neighbourhoods provided the template for planning districts in the 1950s and for tracts for the 1951 and subsequent censuses. Academic and lay reformers pushed for the latter as a source of data for research and hence for social planning. Thus the plan was an extremely significant document.[57]

No one was more resolute about preserving those neighbourhoods than the people who lived in them. In 1946 "The First Tidy Block" association was formed. By 1948 the Annex Ratepayers' Association, among others, was revived. And Oriole Park residents were hard at work fighting the TTC to preserve their neighbourhoods and to create playgrounds. In 1950 leMay complained to an American audience that "citizen participation... is certainly not spontaneous. A mere handful of people who make a hobby of civics can always be relied upon to take an active interest...." But that handful of hobbyists had been making some difference, tenaciously hanging on to their neighbourhoods.[58]

Not until 1944 did the provincial government step gingerly into land-use planning. The Conservatives set up the Department of Planning and Development and passed legislation to co-ordinate planning among government departments. Although the slow process temporarily halted initiatives in Toronto, including the zoning system, the Planning Act was finally passed in 1946. The Tories invested strong powers in the minister and the Ontario Municipal Board, particularly over subdivisions, and allowed private enterprise plenty of room. The act allowed the minister to set up planning boards across municipal boundaries (a step in the direction of Metro), and permitted municipalities to set up local planning boards to develop official plans. Although "designed to secure the health, safety, convenience and welfare of the inhabitants," local planning was to focus primarily on public works, only indirectly controlling development. Unlike British acts since 1919, explicit references to public housing were excluded.[59]

There were further limitations. Little concrete guidance on planning was provided by the act. It did not embrace zoning, which remained under the municipal act. Though planning boards were not supposed to deal with zoning, they had to in order to conform with plans declared official. Unlike commissions such as the TTC, planning boards were not granted any financial powers. Although independent of councils which supposedly kept politics out of planning, boards had to rely on councils for the money to hire staff. Another delicate balance among electoral politics, expertise and direct elite citizen input was struck.

Under the Planning Act, the city reconstituted its planning board, and the official plan that emerged was less than visionary. Since the 1943 plan had been "in no sense adopted as a pattern for the future growth of the city," it was more comfortable to be practical once again, this time with price tags. Passed by City Council in 1949, the new plan was a very practical series of thirteen maps and a long list of public works priorities, totalling $145 million. Despite complaints regarding municipal support of welfare and social services, the finance commissioner boasted that the city could handle the new thirty-year program because of its "sound debt position." A major reason for the rosy picture was the massive reassessment of the city in 1948 that raised the value from $985 million in that year to $1,356 million the next, the highest level since 1932. As a result, politicians were happy too because the mill rate fell (temporarily) almost to 30, which had been Tommy Church's sacred level in 1920.[60]

The Toronto and Suburban Planning Board which covered up to Steeles Avenue and its successor which took in York County provided a major impetus toward the creation of Metro and hence a Metro Planning Board. By 1948 the Toronto and York Board had developed a draft official plan which included major arterials, greenbelt development and industrial land use. It was also required by the province to "comment" on all subdivision plans in York County. Major studies were completed on transportation, on water and sewage disposal and on York County land use. Local plans were supposed to fit within the large regional plan. Also in 1948 Humphrey Carver, in *Houses for Canadians*, provided the basis for neighbourhood planning in the suburbs. As a major spokesman for the revived and dynamic planning movement, Carver subscribed to the British concept of new towns and proposed new communities of 50,000 people grouped in several neighbourhoods. Each neighbourhood would need one public school and five would be combined for one high school. He went on to discuss a heirarchy of playgrounds and parks following current theory, and the compact but auto-

"Beautify Toronto" campaigns of the late 1940s and 1950s featured outbursts of collective enthusiam like this instant paint job on a poor pensioner's cottage.

Lawrence Plaza is opened in 1953 at Bathurst and Lawrence. This was one of the first shopping centres in Toronto designed for access by the family car; it would be dwarfed by later centres such as nearby Yorkdale.

oriented shopping centre of forty stores, which was clearly a departure from Toronto's streetcar strips.[61]

Frederick Gardiner was a key actor in the regional planning initiatives and the creation of Metro. Gardiner had been an isolationist, serving as reeve of Forest Hill. But in 1942 two significant events persuaded Gardiner to become a centralist. The first was the CCF victory in York South (embracing Forest Hill), which pushed him to lead the Tories in a more progressive direction on social and labour rights; and the second, his experience as chairman of a committee investigating an inept and ancient Toronto and York Roads Commission. "Unsettled" by the lack of planning and confusion in regional services generally, Gardiner recognized the need for co-operation among governments and gradually the need for overall planning and development. In 1946 the provincial cabinet appointed him to the Toronto and Suburban Planning Board, and in 1947 he was responsible for creating the new Toronto and York Planning Board.

By this time Gardiner was very expansion-minded and, like the 1943 Toronto Board, he saw municipal boundaries as a hindrance. He proposed large projects—the greenbelt, a unified system of arterial roads—and the need for a single public transportation network over the region. But if the city was willing to pay its share for the greenbelt start-up costs, the county was not. Convinced of the need for expressways and arterials, he pushed hard but, because of suburban resistance, without success. "We hadn't gotten a bulldozer or a steamshovel into the ground," he complained.

In late 1949 and with Gardiner now chairman, the board released its first report on planning programs. Most important was the report's insistence that amalgamation of the city with the suburbs was essential in order for Toronto to move ahead. The former reeve of the American-style suburban community, Forest Hill, had thus finally reached a diametrically opposed position: "Amalgamation is as inevitable as the law of gravity." Planning frustrations provided a major impetus for the creation of Metro.[62]

THE FORMATION OF METRO

Gardiner and the Toronto and Suburban Planning Board were not alone in pushing for a metropolitan government. In the early 1940s some of the poorer municipalities had fought amalgamation, soon afterward city officials and the Bureau of Municipal Research argued for it. By 1948 the city's newspapers were advocating amalgamation and blasting away at intransigent suburban politicians. The Toronto Reconstruction Council had broadened its scope to include metro area issues and had passed this mandate onto its successor, the Civic Advisory Council (CAC). In 1948 Albert Rose and others undertook a comprehensive study of metropolitan problems and in their first report, published in 1949, the CAC made it clear that some kind of union was necessary.[63]

In marshalling its argument for a union of the city and suburbs, the CAC noted "the economic interdependence" of the area, the inequities in costs, the patchwork of numerous agreements between the city and suburban municipalities, and the difficulty of implementing the Toronto and York Planning Board's plan in a "divided" metropolitan area. Financing and administrative structuring were the keys. The city spent only a third of the civic tax dollar on education; North York, a half. Scarborough and North York still ran local rural school sections, though others had finally erected overall school boards, and the province had brought together the Separate School Board in 1941. The results were "widely divergent standards of education" and extremely unequal teacher salaries.[64]

The litany of inadequacies continued. With "rapidly changing standards" in public health and welfare, the suburbs were ill-served. Despite legislation in 1937 and 1943 (which Hepburn could rightly claim among his modest achievements), only four had set up boards of health. More hospitals were needed. In the suburbs, welfare was poorly handled, if handled at all, which meant that people in need "gravitated" toward the city. Public recreation and libraries were poorly developed. Fire departments co-operated but lacked water and equipment, and some still relied on volunteers. The prolonged summer drought of 1949, creating a water shortage in North York, showed that action was needed. Arterial roads did not connect, creating "chaotic conditions." As the 1949 Gore and Storrie Report had noted, the inadequate sewerage system put "serious limitations on the development of new residential areas." Perhaps most scathing was the criticism of the police: eleven separate forces by then had radio-equipped cars, but all operated on different frequencies, a veritable "Babel."[65]

At bottom, the problem was tax structures. Revenue raised per capita ranged from $29 in relatively poor East York to $51 in the city to $64 in Forest Hill. Mill rates varied greatly, from 30.5 in the city to 98.4 in Etobicoke. Clearly, Toronto's rich taxation power must be

Population, and services, were still relatively sparse in the suburbs. When Elizabeth II was crowned in 1953, North York celebrated at its community hall in Willowdale, above. (The North York City Centre could hardly have been foreseen!) Advocates of a metropolitan structure pointed to inadequate social services, like the travelling dental clinic seen at left.

tapped. And something had to be done to serve and house the growing population, which by then had reached one million.[66]

The CAC report of 1949 explored seven alternatives for governing the metro area. Aware of the need to balance efficiency through unification with local autonomy and democratic participation, the committee seriously considered a variety of federated schemes. Defining the key problem as "demarcation of function," members debated the question in forty meetings over another year and a half. In its final report of 1951, because of divided opinion, two alternative systems were drawn up: one more clearly unitary with most of the power residing with the overall "county;" the other more federal with divided but balanced powers for the two levels. How these powers could be divided was considered in detail.[67]

Before the appearance of the CAC's final report, the politicians had taken action. Early in 1950 Mimico applied to the Ontario Municipal Board for a regional board covering major services, and Toronto City Council overwhelmingly voted to apply for amalgamation. Gardiner's appearance before the council was persuasive. As chairman of the Toronto and York Planning Board, he argued that the only thing standing in the way of a quarter century of development was the present fragmentation of government, "a barrier that must be broken." About the same time Premier Leslie Frost met the heads of the thirteen municipalities. But Mimico and Toronto were aligned against the other eleven.

As a consequence, the debate was shifted to the Ontario Municipal Board (OMB) where Lorne Cumming, board chairman and a key actor in Windsor's amalgamation, considered the Mimico and Toronto applications. For a year the OMB heard over three million words of testimony. All the facts in the CAC report and more were laid out: growth was dramatic, housing was scarce and services unequal. Cumming had to reconcile these problems, and he took his time.

In his 1953 report Cumming chose a federated system — a metropolitan council. This body would deal with certain key functions, leaving the residue to existing municipalities. With Gardiner he stressed efficiency and with the suburban politicians, accessibility and representation. The CAC's preoccupation with equal quality of service was a lesser concern. Development was the overriding issue. Despite opposition, mostly from the city and the three newspapers, Premier Frost quickly guided the Municipality of Metropolitan Toronto Act through the legislature. On April 15, 1953, Metro was created and assumed full powers in 1954.[68]

The act defined representation and functions. Metro Council was to be composed of local politicians: twelve for the city (the mayor, two controllers and the nine senior aldermen) and an equal number from the suburbs (the mayors and reeves) to balance interests, even though the suburbs had only reached 42 per cent of Metro's population. The chairman, however, was to be appointed rather than elected. The first one was appointed by the province, so anxious was it to ensure efficiency and development. The chairman's role was not defined: this was done by Fred Gardiner, its first and most aggressive chairman, who took on the role of public developer and urban manager. The act provided for a Metro School Board, again with equal representation, but with a chairman chosen from among the trustees appointed by local boards. This would guarantee a degree of equality in education.

In keeping with the devotion to development, hard services were stressed. Metro was to be in charge of pumping stations, treatment plants, trunk mains and reservoirs. The longstanding problems of expressways and roads would be Metro's responsibility. As advocated by Norman Wilson in a 1948 report, the Toronto Transportation Commission became the Toronto Transit Commission; it covered the whole area and reported to Metro Council. The Metropolitan Planning Board was created, embracing an area of 720 square miles and 26 municipalities. Metro Council was given the same powers as all other municipalities in housing and development. On the social side, Metro could establish parks; it was empowered to maintain a courthouse and jail, and was given limited health and welfare functions.

Crucial were the financial powers of Metro. It was to assess property and do it uniformly. Although the local municipalities were to collect taxes, the needs of Metro were to be levied against them. Debenture financing for Metro itself and for all the localities, including the school boards, was placed in Metro's hands. These powers pointed to a vast change from the old, weak county system.

Area municipalities retailed water and collected sewage. Garbage collection, fire and police remained with them as did public health, unemployment relief and welfare. Local planning boards were required and their plans, as before, were supposed to conform with the region's. Local school boards were responsible for education programs and had the right to raise extra taxes beyond those allocated by the Metro Board.

Even though the legislation attempted to define separate powers carefully, overlaps led to conflicts between Metro and the municipalities. Metro's creation did not by any means wipe out city-suburban differences. Even so, Metro was the key structural change for ordered growth, for planning and housing. Without question, the creation of Metro was North America's most notable municipal experiment of the postwar period. American experts would look northward for a change. The drive for order and, only modestly, for equality had resulted in an odd local government, odd by the nineteenth-century standard of local autonomous democracy. Metro was to be as much a provincial commission as a municipal government.[69]

MANUFACTURING A NEW LANDSCAPE

On April 30, 1953, Tracy leMay, who was approaching the end of his long and distinguished service to the city and soon afterward was chief planner for Metro, took the new Metro politicians and planning board members on a "tour of inspection." In all, he showed them nearly a hundred projects and problems in Metro. Some of these problems were old, largely insoluble ones but others were on the way to solution. In the west end, the waterfront (Gardiner) expressway was being planned and the new Parkdale pumping station was under construction. In Etobicoke the Humber Valley Golf Course was recommended as a site for low-rent housing. Finally, after twenty years of discussion, the new wholesale produce market at the Humber was finally becoming a reality. One of the early suburban large-scale apartment developments was underway: Parklawn with 2,100 units on 81 acres. Unfortunately, too little housing had been built adjacent to the A.V. Roe plant in Malton, thus generating far too many commuters. To the east, leMay praised the nearly completed bypass (401) and the Barrie (400) highway. New industrial areas were planned for the Crang Estate and for Rexdale. However, Wilson Avenue was fast becoming a "commercial ribbon development seriously detracting from its value as a through highway." Obviously, the automobile was creating problems as well as blessings.[70]

Traffic flows in and out of the central city still presented challenges, particularly toward the north. Even though leMay had been an author of the 1930 road plan, some of its proposals were still hanging fire. He still clung to the southeast extension of the Barrie highway via the Don Valley Roadway to downtown. A more recent solution was getting nowhere: the Spadina Road Extension, "delayed because of failure to secure support from all the municipalities through which it passes"—meaning York and North York townships. To the northeast, helping the Don Mills development then underway, was the proposed extension of Eglinton eastward. Golden Mile on Eglinton east of Victoria Park was already a reality, and the Don Valley Parkway a serious proposal. The downtown was largely ignored. At that time little redevelopment was happening: only the Bank of Nova Scotia and the Bank of Montreal had built significant structures in the financial district since the war, and these had been planned in the late 1920s.

LeMay's stress was thus on the growing suburbs. Not since 1912 had activity on the fringe been so tumultuous. This would continue during the next period, though gradually more attention would be focussed on the centre. The planning act and Metro under a czar (as the *Globe and Mail* had advocated) represented forward steps in controlling the pace and spacing of growth. The hodge-podge of disconnected subdivisions and the frequent lag of years, even decades, between servicing and building—a problem leMay and others had struggled with for years—would be largely overcome. Despite this, because density would be lower than in the older city, the cost of transit would rise and the car would be more dominant, even though the opening of the Yonge subway in 1954 would help sustain the public system. In the words of leMay's successor, Murray Jones, the new suburbs were expected to be "more and more distinct" from the city as they became "almost purely middle or upper class." If this turned out to be an inaccurate prediction, in the rest of the 1950s and early 1960s it seemed that many ordinary people rode a wave of affluence to the expanding edges of the city. As the condition of most people improved, poor immigrants were already piling into the older city.[71]

Workers doff their hardhats after a goldplated bolt completes the superstructure of the fifty-six-storey Toronto-Dominion tower in 1966. Beams frame the recently completed City Hall and Court House.

Chapter Four

Toronto's Mosaic, 1954–1966

"Where is the Old Torontonian today? . . . I understand that one or two are being mounted and stuffed for posterity at the Royal Ontario Museum." By 1961 strangers were the new Torontonians who had changed the city into a "turbulent" cosmopolitan place. Those old Torontonians in the "comfortable pews" were, to a Pierre Berton impressed by the transformation, "out of step with the times."[1]

The flood of immigrants certainly challenged the old ways of what had been the Belfast of North America: the sun had set on the British Empire and Orange antagonism to Roman Catholics was disappearing. Toronto the Good was fading, and new symbols of a more liberalized Toronto were appearing. The tremendous growth of public spending on roads, sewers, schools and their social support; of manufacturing through American branch plants; of the mile upon mile of new suburbs, all pointed to an era of affluence in which, according to Metro's planning commissioner, "man 'never had it so good'."[2]

But the golden era of consumer goods actually lasted only until 1957: homeownership began to slip, multiple high-rise apartments became more obvious, relatively fewer cars were bought. As if on signal, the birth rate levelled off in 1957 and then fell. By 1960 the political era under Metro Chairman Frederick Gardiner and Premier Leslie Frost had begun to appear less benign.

Pierre Berton should not have discounted the old guard. Even while some economic power was drifting more into government hands, the corporate leaders, largely of British ancestry, strengthened the corporations as Toronto gained on Montreal. Indeed, the old elite might have switched the Queen's Plate from old to New Woodbine in 1959, but it would carefully ensure that royal visitors knew who counted.[3]

IMMIGRATION, THE BABY BOOM AND IDENTITY CRISIS

It was clear to everyone by the early 1950s that Toronto was and would continue to be one of the fastest growing cities in the western world. About 2.7 million immigrants arrived in Canada between 1945 and the mid-1960s and at least a quarter came to Toronto. Contributing even more was a natural increase that continued to be higher than before the war. While the population increased by 23 per cent in Metropolitan Toronto in the ten years before 1951, it doubled over the next decade, nearly equalling pre-First World War days. By 1961 Metro had reached a population of more than 1.6 million; by 1966 it was up another 16 per cent. The municipalities adjacent to Metro expanded from 48,000 in 1941 to 291,000 in 1966, raising once again the question of how the Toronto area should be organized. The city itself, however, grew very little and its share of Metro's population fell from 59 to 37 per cent. But North York, Etobicoke and Scarborough pushed Metro's share of Ontario's population to 27 per cent in 1966 from 24 per cent in 1951, no mean feat in a rapidly growing province.[4] (Tables I, IV, VIII)

The foreign-born population rose in the city from 31 per cent in 1951 to 42 per cent in 1961, and in Metro up to 35 per cent. Though many returned home or moved on to the U.S., the net increases remained impressive. The trend continued in the 1960s though the gains were less dramatic. As for ethnic origins, the imprint of eastern and southern Europeans was clear by 1961. The total number of those identifying themselves with the British Isles fell markedly in Metro from 73 per cent in 1951 to 59 per cent in 1961, despite many British arrivals. Jews apparently declined even more. Italians quadrupled their numbers to 78,000, which was nearly 12 per cent of the city's population in 1961. Another 57,000 were already settled beyond the city's boundaries. Poles and Ukrainians and many "displaced persons," who had doubled their prewar numbers by 1951, were overtaken by an increase of Germans and French-speaking Canadians by 1961. As a result, Toronto was well on its way to becoming the home of the largest concentration of "ethnic" people in the country. Among large groups, only Vancouver's Chinese and Scandinavians and Winnipeg's Ukrainians were more numerous than those in Toronto.[5] (Tables VII, VIII)

By 1961 the Hungarian community in Toronto had become the largest in the country, primarily because of the arrival of refugees of the Hungarian Revolution in 1956. The number rose to 11,000 in 1961, as compared to only 3,000 in 1951. In contrast to the immediate postwar reluctance to accept refugees, the federal government quickly responded to pressure: Canada and Toronto were obviously more open than earlier, largely because economic conditions had improved. About a quarter of the refugees coming to Canada settled in Toronto, where organizations cushioned the adjustment. The infusion helped in the development of new cultural organizations and a revived Hungarian press. One internationally distributed Hungarian newspaper, *Magyar Élet* (*Hungarian Life*), actually moved from Buenos Aires to Toronto. The Soviet invasion of Hungary also had a more directly political effect on the city: the Communist Party in Toronto, already badly eroded by the Cold War, was weakened even further.[6]

Perhaps most striking, though hidden in this "foreign-born" data, was the dramatic increase in the "other" category, from 7 to 12 per cent, testifying to Toronto's sudden cosmopolitanism. Through the 1960s the mix became even richer. In 1962 the federal immigration policy was altered largely to eliminate ethnic distinctions and to favour those with skills needed for Canada's increasingly sophisticated economy. In fact, immigrants designated as farmers and labourers were already declining as more with manufacturing, clerical and even managerial and professional skills arrived. If, as a Social Planning Council conference was told, "immigration stimulates employment" and expands the economy, Sputnik and the recession of 1957 forced a reconsideration of who should come. These newcomers would also balance "so many of our bright and promising young people" who were going off to the U.S. To fine-tune the policy, a systematic point evaluation was worked out by the mid-1960s. The emphasis on skills still discriminated against those from poorer countries. All the same, the number of ethnic groups subsequently increased: Portuguese immigrants and the more visible minorities, such as West Indians, South Asians and Chinese, would push Toronto closer to defining itself as the most multicultural city in the world.[7]

Restrictions could not, of course, hinder the movement of Canada's poor seeking economic opportunity. Maritimers showed up in substantial numbers. As the film "Goin' Down the Road" portrayed, the trip meant first trying out Toronto, then taking off to the golden west. (Tables VII, VIII)

These great changes were reflected in the religious mosaic of Toronto: in the city, the proportion of Roman Catholics rose from one-seventh in 1941 to one-fifth in 1951 to more than a third in 1961 and, in the suburbs, to more than a quarter. The other major denominations fell proportionately. From 1941 onward the number of Anglicans and Presbyterians slipped relatively; the United Church made the greatest gains among Protestants in Metro by appealing to more of the new suburbanites. By the 1950s, as it became more tolerant in a decade of higher religious interest, the United Church came to be recognized as the anglophone national church. But by 1958 protestant zeal was waning and by 1965 even the United Church was losing more adherents than it gained. By 1971 only one in six in Metro considered himself a United Church member. Roman Catholics, on the other hand, reached the level of one in three.[8] (Table IX)

The ethnic map of Toronto changed dramatically in the west-central immigrant area, west Toronto, and from there a wide swath to the north roughly between Spadina and Keele where the proportion of people of British ancestry declined greatly (See Maps 8, 9, 10, pp. 176-77.) But almost everywhere, except in affluent North Toronto and adjacent tracts in North York and Leaside, the proportion of British fell below 80 per cent. (In 1951 about two-thirds of Metro's area had been still above this level.) Despite the residential concentration of some ethnic groups, immigrants were settling nearly everywhere in Metro.[9]

Filling the expanding suburban swath to the north and north-west were the two largest groups, Jews and Italians. By 1951 Jews had been moving north in city wards 4 and 5 and up to Eglinton, with the affluent occupying Forest Hill west of Spadina. Especially after 1956, expansion was rapid to the Bathurst-Lawrence area. This movement north and the decline in west-central Toronto led to an increasing degree of Jewish segregation. Even though they were rapidly losing Yiddish and were acculturated to the norms of the middle class, conservative and even some non-religious Jews depended on institutions, networks and residential clustering for cultural survival. Expansion to the north continued and, not surprisingly, Jews became prominent in North York politics as their involvement in the City of Toronto weakened.[10]

By 1961 Italians had replaced Jews as the largest non-British group. They too were strongly segregated residentially with considerable "institutional completeness"—churches, clubs, shops, professionals, social welfare agencies, newspapers, youth groups and separate schools. Largely because of Italian immigration, the Separate School Board increased its enrollment by 113 per cent between 1954 and 1962 and the number of schools from 49 to 85. One-sixth of Italian males were employed in the construction industries either as contractors or working for contractors in very risky conditions. By 1951 the new "Little Italy" on St. Clair around Dufferin had emerged, partly drawn from the original and long-established concentration at College and Grace. But by 1961 Italians were already settling in the Dufferin corridor to the north. Of the 135,000 Italians in Metro, two-fifths already lived in York and North York. Second and third generations showed less propensity to congregate.[11]

Other moderately large groups showed a strong tendency to cluster. By 1961 Ukrainians were moving westward from the Bathurst-College area toward High Park; the Poles were also moving westward from essentially the same area, and would congregate in Parkdale. The Chinese were moving west from old Chinatown on Dundas Street in the city's core, partly because many were displaced by the new civic square.[12]

The other two largest non-British groups, the Germans and French-speaking Canadians, were not nearly as segregated. Despite a rapid increase in their numbers and strong institutions, Germans spread out. Presumably because they were lower-income Quebecois and Acadians, French-speaking Canadians showed some clustering in the Cabbagetown area but were hardly concentrated. Toronto's francophones, it appears, expected to be bilingual.[13]

The sheer size of the non-Protestant and non-British immigrant population altered Toronto in a way that no one could have foreseen in 1945. Many Torontonians were dumbfounded by the phenomenon of immigration and what it signified. Reflecting old Toronto, Berton expressed amazement over a visit to Little Italy where "nobody rushes."

> And this is odd for these people are surely the hardest pressed in all Toronto. They tumble from the immigrant ships with a single suitcase, often in debt for their fare. Yet in five or six years they own their own house and car. They do this by sacrificing their leisure, their privacy and their comfort—everything indeed but their dignity. They crowd into ancient houses, so heavily mortgaged that for almost anybody else the investment would be insane. They accept, without whimper, the crushing discounts and exorbitant interest rates that are the shame of the city. They work long hours and their children work long hours and they rent out spare rooms and paint their houses and fix the stairs and scrub the interiors and pay off every cent often at thirty per cent interest. And they still make time to saunter in the spring sunlight.[14]

Since 1957 the Metro Social Planning Council (SPC), which had been born out of a reorganized Welfare Council and supported by the United Community fund, had been concerned about settling the great flood of immigrants. In May 1959 the SPC's newly founded Immigration Section drew together many community leaders and immigrant representatives "to explore the area of attitude and adjustment and to try to discover some of the real needs of immigrants beyond the basic physical needs of housing, employment and other immediate matters." An eastern European immigrant who had lived in Toronto for ten years told the council that "too much stress" had been laid on the "material welfare of immigrants;" a "glass curtain" prevented the "harmonious integration" of immigrant families. Even a spokesman for the British immigrant suggested that Torontonians were "difficult to get to know." Another commentator agreed that there was "insufficient effort to welcome and understand immigrants at the neighbourhood and community level." The search for "real needs" was a difficult one. The "glass curtain," a phrase widely used in the press and in government over the next few years, was not easy to pull aside or shatter.[15]

Discussions of the SPC over the next few years raised more tangible and immediate issues. In 1960 it was argued, unsuccessfully, that the Housing Registry at Union Station, which had officially received the Hungarian refugees and given them "the first taste of life in our community," should have been continued. In the first ten months of 1959, 2,200 unsponsored immigrants without relatives had been helped to find their "bearings" by this federal program. Advocacy of similar travellers' aid at the airport would come soon after, as more arrived by air. Night and day English classes had been offered for many years and increasingly by the school boards, west-central settlement houses and churches, but the problem of wives learning English remained a problem. Ensuring that immigrants were aware of all available community services needed attention. Material conditions in housing and at work were serious, especially for low-income Italians and others. "Substandard accommodation" found in "sardine-tin flats in remodelled houses" was serious in the reception areas of west-central Toronto. Worse, "the sweatshop, the kickback and the job agency racket are still with us." And the high unemployment of 1958 and 1959, conspicuously among Italian construction workers, had strained low-income budgets. Finally, the danger of deportation remained a threat, if only seriously for a few.[16]

Lying behind these concerns over the condition of "New Canadians" was also the large question of the Canadian identity. The cultural needs of older Canadians, it seems, were as "real," if less visible. Old, British Toronto the Good was changing dramatically and traditional attitudes were being challenged. The election in 1954 of Nathan Phillips, an offspring of the earlier Jewish migration, symbolized another step in that direction.

Phillips had failed in two previous bids at the mayoralty and in 1954 he had to depend on a very close three-way split to beat two Protestants. One was Leslie Saunders, who was temporarily mayor in 1954 after Allan Lamport moved to the TTC. Saunders represented the last hurrah of Orangeism. Indeed, in July 1954 Saunders not only marched as usual in the annual parade but issued a statement that the Battle of the Boyne had been more than a religious event—it resulted in "civil and religious liberty for all." When the votes were counted, Saunders had not fared particularly well in North Toronto where Toryism had lost whatever Orangeism it had once had, but he had done well in east Toronto, the final stronghold of Britishness and the Orange Order, and in the High Park area because of his opposition to booze and Sunday sports. Phillips's pluralities were in central and west-central Toronto, where he overwhelmed the Communist standard-bearer, Alexander McLeod. The three major candidates did reasonably well everywhere, however, indicating that political regionalism was no longer as homogeneous. Equally significant was the *Telegram*'s endorsement of Phillips. Gone were the days of the Orange slate![17]

Phillips remained mayor until Controller Donald Sommerville defeated him in December 1962. What kept Phillips in office was continuous campaigning as "mayor of all the people," a sure sign of cosmopolitan consciousness. Duncan Macpherson's cartoons in the *Star* captured Phillips's intent: with fork and knife in hand, the mayor set forth to conquer by attending, it seems, every luncheon and dinner of every conceivable community group in the city.

A liberal and cosmopolitan Toronto can be detected in the fiction of the time—though in 1960 Dennis Braithwaite still asserted that the "face of the city leaves uncertainty," and Al Purdy still followed the time-worn theme of Toronto's coldness in his "Towns." Novels pointed to change. In *In Praise of Older Women* Stephen Vizinczey depicted a quite dramatic shift in the late 1950s. When he arrived in 1957, people were still agog with television, basement recreation rooms, backyard barbecues and new cars. But by 1960 they "had got used to their standard of living and suddenly became interested in life:" boutiques, art galleries, book shops and outdoor cafés had sprung up. Soon after, the village on Gerrard was being superseded by Yorkville. It was as if Torontonians were finally realizing that they had been "hiding new energy and growth under the ivy of tradition," to quote Jeann Beattie. Breaking from her high-status, North Toronto, Anglican upbringing, a young woman in still another novel registered at University College rather than at Trinity and decided she "liked living below the Hill" in an Annex rooming house. Phyllis Young's protagonist asserted: "Toronto—and you could sense this everywhere but the Hill—was becoming increasingly restive under the yoke of traditions that it had outgrown." Life in the inner city was beginning to appeal to more than a handful of stalwarts in the Annex; North Toronto and the new suburbs had begun to lose their hold. Indicative of a change of attitude was the rapid turnover of editors of *Maclean's* in the early 1960s, as if no one person could capture the shifting ground of attitudes. Toronto's mediation of Canadian impulses had to be sorted out.[18]

But the "glass curtain" would not fall away easily—Berton's amazement at life in Little Italy reflects this—and the "core" elite of North Toronto would not relinquish its control over social welfare,

The 1950s brought the greatest number of European immigrants to Toronto. The single largest group were the Italians, for whom arrival at Union Station often meant reunification of a family.

While the station was the traditional point of arrival for new Torontonians, it was increasingly replaced by the Malton airport after 1960, the year these Italians landed.

much of "high" culture and the economy. Indeed, despite the depression of the late 1950s, growth was renewed and Toronto was jubilant. Quite uncharacteristically from an historical viewpoint, in 1960 the city's finance commissioner could argue that "the 'growth money' of a municipality—the means for providing and extending those services and facilities required by the residents and taxpayers—comes, in the main, from the sale of debentures." The keeper of the purse was now an enthusiastic Keynesian. Whereas suburbanization was an engine of growth from 1949 to 1957, in the 1960s the central city became more and more the focus. In its 1963 report called *Boom Town Metro*, the *Toronto Star* unabashedly praised growth.

> Entering the bigtime with a bang, Metro Toronto boasts: It's growing faster than New York, is richer than Montreal, is the brightest, boldest, lustiest city in Canada... and, 10 years after its formation, is just beginning to come alive.

Toronto was not quite there, but it was close.[19]

STRENGTHENING METROPOLITAN STATUS AND THE BOOM ECONOMY

In 1961 Allan C. Burton, chairman of the city's Redevelopment Advisory Council, claimed that Toronto was the financial centre of Canada and was "the reason why Metro grows." Certainly by 1965 Toronto's share of financial activities had grown enormously and at a faster pace than Montreal's. Bank clearances in Toronto ran further ahead. The assets of Toronto chartered banks caught up with Montreal's as the Bank of Nova Scotia and the Toronto-Dominion (merged in 1954) gained. The Bank of Commerce (having joined the Imperial Bank in 1960) maintained its level and replaced the Bank of Montreal in second place. While the growing trust companies were shared nearly equally, Toronto's life insurance companies continued to improve their position. As Sun Life, Montreal's and Canada's largest, lost ground, Toronto's eight largest (by assets) pulled up to about 40 per cent of Canada's total. Toronto passed Montreal in the number of head offices of large corporations.[20] (Table XII)

More striking than changes in these operations, which were conspicuous to ordinary Torontonians, was the increasing power of other financial intermediaries in Toronto, which set it off against Montreal and other cities. The assets of finance companies, investment funds and the like grew far more rapidly than those of insurance companies and chartered banks. By the early 1960s their assets were more than four times greater in Toronto. Toronto investment dealers, such as Wood, Gundy & Co. and A.E. Ames and Company, captured more of the expanding specialized underwriting activities. After 1955 mergers among investment dealers increased. The relative importance of the stock exchange changed dramatically: Toronto's pulled away ahead of Montreal's though much of Montreal's decline was replaced by Vancouver's. The ratio of the labour force in finance was also substantially higher in Toronto.[21]

Far outweighing Vancouver's modest gain were two other developing trends. Increasingly, Canadian issues were listed in New York and Canadians became more interested in U.S. stocks, and the Toronto Stock Exchange lost ground as a result. In sharper contrast to the past, municipalities and provinces began borrowing more in New York. In 1961 in front of a Detroit audience, Frederick Gardiner praised the "facilities of the money markets of the United States." It is easy to see why: Toronto possessed a high rating with Moody's Investment Services on Wall Street. Ottawa and Queen's Park also expanded their role as financial intermediaries. By 1966 the federal and provincial governments had increased their share of assets held by intermediaries to 30 per cent, after a postwar decline. Thus, while considerable concentration occurred in Toronto at the expense of Montreal, Bay Street had to share the stage. After 1965 the trends would be even sharper.[22]

Toronto's already formidable presence in the anglophone media was strengthened considerably in this period and far outstripped the expanding institutions of higher education and weakening churches as "main loci of power within the ideological system." In the newspaper field, the huge amount of capital investment needed pulled more and more small city newspapers into chain ownership. Southam, originally based in Hamilton, and Thomson chains, with head offices in Toronto, bought up more newspapers across Canada. Falling circulation of dailies in the face of television, and an attempt to steal a march on the *Star* and *Globe and Mail*, led the *Telegram* into an ill-fated Sunday paper in 1957, yet all three

Though more Canadians read Time, Maclean's *was preeminent among Canadian magazines, and was the flagship of the growing Maclean Hunter group of publications. The ability of cover artists like Peter Whalley (left) and Rex Woods (right) to capture the mood of the times probably contributed to success. Toronto writers dominated the pages inside.*

remained powerful. *Star Weekly* circulation reached 900,000 in 1959. The ethnic press came to be more concentrated in Toronto, overshadowing Winnipeg's prewar prominence.[23]

Toronto strengthened its hold on other areas of publishing in anglophone Canada and even invaded francophone homes. Its roughly thirty-five periodical and book publishers in 1959 far exceeded the number in other cities, and Toronto contributed half of Canadian periodicals (even though a few were officially published in Montreal to allow liquor advertising). In the 1950s Maclean-Hunter increased its share of revenues from advertising in Canadian magazines from 56 to 78 per cent, and in the early 1960s established French-language versions of *Maclean's* and *Chatelaine*. In the trade and professional journal field, Maclean-Hunter and Southam increasingly dominated English-speaking Canada and the former began some new journals for francophones. But, while only five of Canada's consumer magazines could claim a circulation of more than 20,000, at least fifty under American auspices captured as much, while taking 40 per cent of all magazine advertising revenues. The Royal Commission on Publications in 1961, under Grattan O'Leary, could head off neither the concentration of Canada's print media in Toronto's corporate hands nor the continued influx of American ideas.[24]

Television emerged very quickly as the great soporific of the age. By 1960 three in four Canadian households owned sets. The first American television programs arrived via Buffalo in 1948 and would continue to attract Toronto viewers. The Massey Commission of 1951 was successful in persuading Canadian politicians that the CBC should move into televison. The first two stations opened in Montreal and Toronto. Yet in 1954, when the Buffalo newspapers praised Canadian productions as "unusual, interesting and highly entertaining," two-thirds of Torontonians watched U.S. channels. A forest of antennae had grown almost overnight on Toronto's roofscape.

The continued success of commercial radio stations, such as CFRB and CKEY, and the federal Conservative intent to reduce the CBC's status led to private television. In 1960 the largest number of applicants for new stations came from Toronto; it was "Canada's richest market, was the largest commercial and advertising centre, and a centre for publishing and English-language performing talent." Emerging out of the competiton among corporate giants was CFTO. The station was controlled by a group headed by John Bassett (owner of the *Telegram* since 1952) and soon became the flagship station of the new CTV network. Despite claims of Tory favouritism toward Bassett and a shaky start, by 1965 CTV, which relied heavily on imported American programs, was challenging the CBC for a large share of the viewing audience. Thus, through television, Toronto strengthened its control of the anglophone media.[25]

Concentration of ownership and power became more evident in the manufacturing and resource fields. Canada's pre-eminent holding company was the Toronto-based Argus Corporation. In 1950 it controlled ten dominant Canadian corporations. Through mergers this number was reduced to larger units by 1960: Massey-Ferguson, Domtar, Canadian Breweries, Dominion Stores, St. Lawrence Corporation, and B.C. Forest Products. Only 10 to 20 per cent of the voting stock ensured that Argus could appoint enough directors to control their boards and executive committees. Sometimes vicious proxy battles were fought to gain control, but there was little doubt that men like E.P. Taylor, W.E. Phillips, J.A. McDougald and W.M. McCutcheon held the purse strings of a large part of Canada's economy through interlocking directorships. In 1961 Argus not only extended itself into media but also acquired shares in several large mining companies. Only Montreal's Power Corporation could vie for industrial and mining control among strictly Canadian corporations. Of course, neither could contend with American economic power in sectors such as automobiles or burgeoning Canadian oil. Canadian subsidiaries were firmly under U.S. corporate control. Unlike many American corporations, however, Canadian companies rarely bothered to promote an image of people's capitalism to persuade the public of widespread common stock ownership.[26]

Despite the setback during the recession of the late 1950s, manufacturing expanded greatly. Although the city's share continued to fall after 1951, by 1961 Metro's nearly 5,000 establishments employed 224,000 workers. In the early 1960s employment in the whole metropolitan area increased by a quarter, though by 1965 Metro itself had virtually peaked. Massey-Ferguson continued to be a major force with 4,500 Toronto workers on its payroll, and Canada Packers was a "mighty power" with 3,500 employees. Oil refineries became conspicuous near Port Credit and Oakville. The region comprising the counties of York, Ontario, Peel and much of Halton increased its part of Ontario's manufacturing employment from 39 per cent in 1946-50 to 46 per cent in 1961-65. Most of the

E.P. Taylor established himself as one of the world's major industrialists and financiers, first through Canadian Breweries and then Argus Corporation. Taylor turned to horses for a past-time. The star of his stable was Northern Dancer, winner of the Kentucky Derby in 1964.

remainder of southern Ontario actually lost manufacturing establishments.[27] (Table XI)

The great influx of branch plants made its mark during the heyday of direct investment in Canada. While in the rest of southern Ontario generally the percentage of foreign-owned plants established between 1954 and 1967 was 31, in the Toronto region it was 48. More than half of the new foreign plants started in Ontario came to the area. Large operations, such as Ford in Oakville and American Motors in Brampton, were only among the most conspicuous. Many were little more than warehouses. American companies obviously preferred the Toronto area because of its large market and its airport. One study concluded that those American companies more distant from Ontario's border were most likely to set up subsidiaries in the Toronto area than those in Detroit and Buffalo. More than two-thirds of companies in the New York City region, the largest contributor, sought sites in and around Toronto. The Toronto region was preferred to Montreal: according to one U.S. branch plant manager from New Jersey, "We chose Toronto because the living conditions, the labour market and the growth rate were better.... Toronto had an edge."[28]

Despite the tremendous growth, not everything hummed on the manufacturing front. The British-owned A.V. Roe in Malton built the all-Canadian supersonic fighter plane, the AVRO Arrow, using Canadian Orenda engines, and after a lot of hullabaloo it turned out to be a failure. Although by 1957 federal Liberals had virtually decided to abandon the project, it was left to Diefenbaker's ill-fated government to act decisively in 1959. As a result, 14,000 of Toronto's manufacturing workforce had to seek new jobs. If Toronto's de Havilland and Montreal's Canadair would maintain a Canadian presence in the aircraft industry—eventually as crown corporations—the Malton plant ended up in the hands of Douglas Aircraft. After the glory of the Arrow, the plant more prosaically produced wings for the world's commercial fleets.[29]

The Arrow issue was only a dramatic example of the inability of Canadian industry to take the initiative and of its dependence on American capital. Canadian entrepreneurs were less inclined to take risks. The Arrow showed how difficult it was for the federal government to enter the frontline of risk-taking in league with foreign profit-making corporations subsidized by their own governments. A "formidable technical team" developing the Arrow could not obscure "a depressing record of profligacy and budget overruns." Perhaps it was not surprising then that a few Torontonians, such as Walter Gordon and Mel Watkins, were in the forefront of questioning foreign influence in Canada's economy, challenging the "branch-plant society." If some Torontonians worried, and Torontonians Gordon and Mitchell Sharp, as federal finance ministers, sought to guide Canada's economy through federal budgets that never seemed to satisfy anyone, American influence continued unabated, even if direct investment fell.[30]

Boomtown Toronto was fed by the world economy and in turn created its own economic growth through construction. Under Gardiner, Metro delivered the major infrastructure of roads, water and sewer lines, while local services were built into the price of buildings, replacing the archaic local improvement taxes. In the 1950s small developers and builders still dominated. But as advocated by Humphrey Carver in 1948, large companies slowly emerged to organize the legion of builders and workers. E.P. Taylor of Argus Corporation developed Don Mills. Principal Investments Limited emerged as a major builder of shopping centres. In the 1950s companies now familiar to Torontonians were formed: A.E. Diamond's Cadillac in 1953 and Greenwin, Belmont, and Meridian in 1961—all formed, it seems, by Harbord Collegiate graduates. Montreal's Cemp Investment Limited, Sam Bronfman's family trust fund, in 1959 became involved with Cadillac. Some large foreign concerns, such as British-controlled Trizec, showed strong interest. Economies of scale began to take hold. Major developers also found ways to write off or defer taxes with the approval of agreeable governments.[31]

These corporations were able to assemble large amounts of capital, hence large amounts of land, at lower rates than small builders. The development industry was the "joint creation" of government and Canada's financial intermediaries. Even after chartered banks entered the mortgage field, CMHC remained involved in more than a third of new-house financing, and guaranteed loans for developers. British and American financial institutions lent money to developers for big projects, providing, according to one estimate, more than a third in the 1960s. The speculative urge before 1957 and again after 1962 undoubtedly drove up the price of land and therefore the price of the final product: housing, schools, offices and shopping centres. This process maintained traditionally high housing costs in Toronto compared to other cities; by the late 1960s housing in Toronto was more expensive than anywhere else on the continent.[32]

The builders and developers, however, delivered an enormous number of dwelling units: between 1954 and 1966, almost 240,000 in Metro. Even in the slacker years between 1959 and 1961 the level did not fall back to the 1953 figure.[33]

As striking as overall production was the shift from single-detached units (and a modest number of semi-detached) to apartment types. Construction of single-detached units peaked in 1955 in the booming suburbs. In 1958 rental apartment units exceeded single-family houses. The innovations of prestressed concrete and of bonusing—that is, of granting developers higher densities if more open space is provided—resulted in apartment structures reaching twenty and even thirty storeys, compared to mostly six or eight in the 1950s. Nowhere else in the Western world would high-rises be so conspicious. In the suburbs the production of single types paralleled multiple units between 1962 and 1966. But, in spite of federal government policy favouring home ownership at least until 1964, the golden age of endless new, American-style tracts was indeed shortlived, extending only from 1949 to 1957—about the time the birth rate began to fall and the first major postwar recession struck. Recovery of overall production in 1961 could not hide the changing realities, nor could the very small number of public units. Although the number of persons per dwelling unit fell in the 1950s and 1960s, crisis conditions for low-income households never did disappear.[34] (Table IV)

The relative peace between management and labour established by the 1950s continued generally until the recession of 1957. In 1956 the CNE grounds were the venue of the inaugural national meeting of the new Canadian Labour Congress, which united the Trades and Labour Congress and the Canadian Congress of Labour. A similar trend toward co-operaton between the AFL and CIO in the U.S. had helped the process along, but just as important were events in localities such as Toronto.

One sign of a softening of tensions in the city was the increased co-operative participation of both labour councils on issues such as housing, community services and public ownership of gas and telephone. Mutual support in strikes and for municipal candidates became more frequent. So Toronto was well prepared for unity. Most leaders and many of the rank and file in Toronto's new Labour

The Avro Arrow's first public appearance, at Malton in 1957. The innovative fighter seemed to herald a new presence for a middle power. Its subsequent scuttling by Prime Minister Diefenbaker was a symbolic turn toward even greater dependence on U.S. technology and military power.

Italians built postwar Toronto. The work was often risky, insecure and poorly paid, leading to a unionizing drive. In 1961 Bruno Zanini, through the "Brandon Hall" organizing group, almost achieved the goal before the group fell apart. At left Zanini is cheered by strikers.

Council and a hundred of its affiliates supported the move when the New Democratic Party emerged in 1961, but many unionists were not convinced. The British solution to electoral support had not quite been reached: American individualism outweighed solidarity.[35]

As for industrial unrest, the CPR railway walkout in 1957 and the teamsters' strike in 1959 stirred up Torontonians. Beginning in 1957 the construction industry went through considerable turmoil as workers in the residential sector struck. The slowdown of 1958 put many workers into even a worse plight. Cut-throat competition among mainly Italian contractors led them to accept bids that were too low and then to exploit the workers, mostly Italian immigrants in a variety of skilled and unskilled trades. Italians died tunnelling sewers. Frank Drea's revelations in the *Telegram* of their atrocious working conditions unsettled complacent Torontonians.[36]

Largely unprotected, these workers were subject to "kickbacks" and short payment. The pay for a couple of hours was assessed "for the Queen," they were told. Against what seemed insurmountable odds, the Brandon Hall Union Group organized many workers into a number of unions, which led to more strikes and violence in 1960 and 1961. Despite a one-man royal commission appointed by the province to investigate the residential building industry, the 1961 victory of Brandon Hall was shortlived. From 1962 onward the solidarity of these residential construction unions eroded, and by 1965 apartment builders were able to cut wages as they had in 1957. The people who built Toronto brick by brick and concrete pillar received no thanks for their efforts.[37]

Although strikes were rare in most manufacturing sectors, in 1964 the International Typographical Union struck. New technologies in printing lay behind the upheaval. But Toronto printers might have accepted modernized equipment and come to terms had not the American headquarters made Toronto a test case for Luddite resistance. The three major dailies were well prepared with other personnel trained to work the machines. Other unions at the newspapers and elsewhere offered little support. Even when the union offered a conciliatory package in 1966 the papers would not resume negotiations. The failing strike dragged on until 1971. Similarly, half of the low-paid employees of the Royal York Hotel lost their jobs after a year-long strike, begun in May 1961. Increased militancy could not bring the gains achieved by industrial workers in the 1940s. Part of the reason was that unemployment, which had increased during the recession, did not recede to the level of the halcyon late 1940s when it seemed everyone had a job.[38]

The experience of the typographers indicated changes in employment patterns. Substantial shifts in the labour force occurred. Despite a golden age of manufacturing, employment in that sector began to fall proportionately later in the period, as in the city after 1951. More people pushed paper, fewer produced goods. The largest gains were made in finance and business services and in social services and education, much in direct government employment. The creation of Metro and the expansion of federal and provincial initiatives became particularly noticeable after 1957. The formation in 1963 of the Canadian Union of Public Employees, bringing together a variety of old and new groups, signalled the increased importance of public and semi-public workers.[39] (Table X)

THE SOCIAL SERVICE STATE IN AN AFFLUENT SOCIETY

As Canada's economy, particularly its financial sector, showed signs of being more and more concentrated in Toronto, its elite increasingly dominated the national scene. Although elites persisted in all sectors of society, all were subservient to a small core which held the reins of capital. A major study of Toronto's elite structure in the mid-1960s concluded that the leading financial institutions were under "tight control." Indeed, "the stock exchange and the banks have something of the character of a private club. They operate, within their top ranks, more by trust than by contract."[40]

Toronto may have developed into Canada's clearest melting pot, yet non-Anglo-Saxons were acculturated but not assimilated. Even if in a growing economy some of them could rise into functional economic elites or succeed politically, the "core" elite remained the preserve of a small group composed of Tory, Anglo-Saxon men. In Britain a more secure elite allowed Jews onto boards of top-drawer schools and colleges. Not so here: influential Jews had to be content with backroom power-broking or take a lead in dirtier fields such as the development industry. Italian aspirants had to be content with lower and riskier parts of the construction business. Much of the *ressentiment*, a mixture of hostility and attraction, of ethnic leaders and followers was siphoned off into votes for the federal Liberals. Rarely did anyone of low or foreign birth make it to the central core of financial power. Upper Canada, Ridley and Trinity College remained the chief avenues to high status.

Not only did members of this economic core elite increasingly dominate Canada's economy, but they were also prominent in the social service field, at a time when Keynesian notions had pushed such concerns closer to the centre stage of public action. How seriously the elite considered social programs on the local scene was indicated when Wallace McCutcheon, managing director of Argus Corporation, took the mantle of president of the Social Planning Council. Similarly, Edgar Burton, president of Simpsons, was a key figure in establishing the United Way in 1956, a partially successful attempt to render the voluntary social service sector more efficient and effective. If financial goals were not always reached, far more money was raised than earlier. It was another step on the way to centralization and corporatization of society generally and the building of a social security safety net. At the same time the professionalization of various social work fields was largely completed and programs rationalized. In 1962 the casework of the forty-five-year-old Neighbourhood Workers' Association was taken over by the Family Service Association of Metropolitan Toronto.[41]

The concerns of the Social Planning Council remained largely focussed on the poor, including the provision of public housing—still a controversial matter. Despite the massive construction of new housing, early in 1966 a housing policy committee reported that Toronto was facing its worst crisis since the immediate post-war period. As many as 20 per cent of all families were "unable, with their own resources, to provide decent, safe and sanitary housing." Making matters worse, redevelopment for apartments and offices had removed a large amount of the old housing stock.[42]

It was obvious something had to be done: the slums described by the Bureau of Municipal Research in 1918 and Herbert Bruce in 1934 were still there. A sensational series of articles in the *Telegram* in October 1955 highlighted the "notorious slum empire," replete with prostitutes, "vice syndicates," shadowy companies and even a "mystery woman of Panama," in the skid-row Jarvis-Sherbourne-Parliament area. In 1956 Toronto's Planning Board's report, *Urban Renewal*, raised the 1944 estimate of blighted and slum housing from 2 to 8 per cent. In 1961 the Lower Ward, west of University and south of Queen, was described as "a hidden 'no man's land'" sheltering "a beaten down group of mostly Anglo-Canadians."[43]

This was not for want of concern among reformers and certain city officials. In 1955 Albert Rose reported to the Community Planning Association that the "impasse" of several years over developing Regent Park South had been "broken" when the Federal-Provincial Partnership finally acted. But that this would "pave the way" to ridding Toronto of the "broad band of blight" was optimistic. Regent Park South with 732 units was completed in 1960. Moss Park's 900 units were provided in three high-rise slabs, the closest Toronto would come to American-style, inner-city public redevelopment. More appealing architecturally, and mostly low-rise, Alexandra Park was underway by 1965 and Don Mount was in preparation. Some limited dividend housing, with federal financial aid for developers to keep rents down, had been constructed. Although 2,200 public units had been built for the elderly by 1965, even Metro admitted that, though the stock of low-rent public housing for families had increased seven-fold since 1953, the 3,900 units were "far from adequate." The promise of Regent Park North had only marginally been fulfilled. The waiting lists were still growing.[44]

Superblock slum clearance was also being questioned. As early as 1959 a shift to smaller scale improvement was already apparent in the City Planning Board's *The Changing City*. In 1966 a Metro planning study reported that the nearly 10,000 structures in poor condition were not concentrated, even if many families were still doubling up. While Toronto was quite well off compared to American cities, the Metro report advocated phased and limited "spot" clearance and renewal; a new approach—at least in the public sphere—had begun.[45]

In the suburbs a modest number of public housing units were built on vacant land at the insistence of the province and Chairman Gardiner. Although resisted by neighbours, 1,108 units were completed in Lawrence Heights, and the Metro Housing Company developed other projects for senior citizens, mostly on land assembled in the early 1950s by the Federal-Provincial Partnership. But, even if the new suburbs were targeted for most public housing, the goals were not fulfilled and hardly solved the crisis for low-income people. The projects too created as much a psychological wall as the "glass curtain" separating new immigrants from old Torontonians.[46]

The shortfalls and jurisdictional problems did induce the province to create the Ontario Housing Corporation (OHC) in 1964. By 1967, 11,000 public units had been built and another 6,000 were under construction. The suburbs finally were taking more than half of the new units. For a decade OHC was the main force in building and

Redevelopment of slum areas was still on the agenda after the completion of Regent Park South in 1960. But politicians such as Jean Newman (above right) worried about the high cost of land held by speculators — in 1960, said to be $500,000 an acre. Little wonder that by then only 7,500 people had been rehoused.

managing the public housing sector, but primarily in the suburbs. In the city, private developers were the major actors. Even though few families were now without television or indoor plumbing, housing for the poor remained a problem.[47]

If poverty remained a problem the rise of tenancy signalled a decline of status for many more people, at least if they believed that home ownership was the norm of social well-being. From an historic high of 82 per cent in 1951, suburban home ownership receded to 67 per cent in 1961. Although this level hardly shattered the image of the suburban dream, the trend would continue downward to 50 per cent before levelling off in the 1970s. In the city the proportion fell from a high of 62 per cent in 1951 to 56 per cent in 1961 to 42 per cent in 1971, when it began to stabilize. The contrast with Montreal was perpetuated as its rise and fall of home ownership (at a much lower level) paralleled Toronto's. (Table XIV)

By 1966 half the dwelling units in the city were tenant-occupied. Realizing that tenancy was again becoming a way of life for many, Alderman William Dennison, with the firm backing of the Association of Women Electors, persuaded City Council in 1957 to expand the municipal franchise to include all tenants. Another indication of tenants' rights was the recognition that neighbourhoods were inhabited by people and not just by property owners. In the Annex in the mid-1950s, two spontaneous neighbourhood improvement associations merged with the ratepayer association after agreeing that tenants should be allowed membership, albeit in a special category until 1969. Times were changing. In contrast to previous days, the rights of people seemed to be gaining on property rights.[48]

The setting up of the Ontario Housing Corporation was only one example of accelerated government action as the welfare state expanded not only for the poor but for everyone. The federal government still approached social security issues in a halting and *ad hoc* way. In 1952 old age security was expanded as was unemployment insurance. In a further move toward universality, in 1957 hospital insurance was introduced on a cost-shared basis with the provinces. Besides contributing to public housing, for a while the federal government helped to finance the building of schools, especially high schools and universities. In 1966 through the Canada Pension Plan it began providing modest support for retired workers. (Hardly foreseen at the time was its subsequent importance in financing the country.) Finally, following the Saskatchewan experience, a universal medical care program was set up in 1966, though not until 1968 did all provinces agree to participate.[49]

The take-off to the "service state" in Ontario occurred between 1957 and 1962. The province increased its spending from $420 million to $1,791 million between 1953 and 1966, which was much faster than municipalities other than Metro increased theirs. As a percentage of personal income of Ontarians, net provincial expenditures nearly doubled. Education replaced highways in taking the largest part. The call of the city's finance commissioner in the late 1940s for relief from education, health and welfare costs had, in fact, been fulfilled to a degree, though in 1965 low-income families were still receiving welfare from the city and Metro's role was expanding. Social questions heavily influenced the restructuring of Metro in 1966. Unemployment was creeping up. Canada's expenditures in 1966 on public social security (as a percentage of the Gross National Product) was still modest by western European standards, but it was about 2 per cent above the U.S.[50]

Schools and schooling came to dominate the social scene after 1960, as vocational concerns came to the fore and spending increased enormously. Justice Hope's report on education in 1950 was a virtual retreat to the 1920s, and Frost's minister of education until 1960, W.J. Dunlop, sounded as though he were the Howard Ferguson of the era: the goal of education was to train "loyal, intelligent, right-thinking, religious, and freedom-loving citizens." In a decade of complacency, when high school youth dutifully attended formal dances and university students joined fraternities, building new schools or expanding old ones seemed to be all that was necessary to maintain pedagogic health. In the late 1960s the normal schools and the College of Education (at Bloor and Spadina) pumped out hordes of new teachers.[51]

Under new education ministers, John Robarts and then William Davis, Ontario jumped on the vocational bandwagon which started in 1960 when the federal government passed the Technical and Vocational Training Act "to foster national development." More high schools were built and secondary streams restructured to give as much encouragement to students in technology and trades and in business and commerce as to the university-bound in arts and science. The vocational emphasis led to even more young people remaining in high schools: public enrollment in Metro tripled over the period, while Metro's population rose by about 50 per cent. But that was not enough to solve the vocational issue and to develop "human capital," a code phrase for the time. In 1966 post-secondary

The Baby Boom strained school facilities. Even though trustees seemed to attend opening ceremonies for new and rebuilt schools weekly, portables were brought in.

Physical education was considered important for high school students, as at this open house at Edith L. Groves Vocational School (later Heydon Park Secondary).

Colleges of Applied Arts and Technology were established in the Toronto area—Centennial, George Brown, Humber, Seneca and Sheridan—and Ryerson Polytechnic was strengthened. Technology was riding high: Marshall McLuhan speculated in *Understanding Media* for the U.S. Office of Education on how to live in the brave new world.[52] (Table V)

The vocational emphasis, since it smacked of earlier progressive concepts for the whole child, was not greeted with unanimity in Toronto. University academics, elementary and secondary teachers came together through an unprecedented Joint Committee of the Toronto Board of Education and the University of Toronto to sharpen the goals of education. In their report in 1962, *Design for Learning*, they criticized some prevailing methods but promoted a still largely elitist view of education. Condemned were rote learning and province-wide standarized examinations; in these respects they were in the vanguard of liberalizing an educational system that W.J. Dunlop had called "the best in the world." From junior kindergarten to university, the aim of education was the training of the intellect, not the whole person, through structured disciplines. That science was separated from technology and English was emphasized meant that functional concerns were played down. Even though critical thinking was to be encouraged it was not clear why. Elementary texts in social studies portraying "rosy-cosy" suburban life were considered damaging because they failed to describe inner-city life. This was not surprising: the committee members were from Toronto and thus in tune with local issues. American norms of life could be rejected. But what wider moral or social purposes were intended is not clear. The introduction by Northrop Frye, Toronto's renowned literary critic, suggested that the primary concern was educating the mind as an end in itself and with the university as the pinnacle. A "very small number" of university students were "enough to keep our society's head above water."[53]

The committee seems hardly to have been prepared for the sudden influx of students. Indeed, Frye cautioned: "One hardly dares speculate about what might happen if the numbers were suddenly to increase." But the masses did descend on the University of Toronto, forcing it to reconsider its curriculum. Even it was becoming more of a vocational institute. Expansion planning had already begun in 1957 and physical extension was considerable in the early 1960s.[54]

York University would also draw a mass of new students. Breaking away from traditional curricula, York was founded in 1959 to stress innovative interdisciplinary programs. In 1961 its Glendon College was operating. In line with provincial imperatives to expand higher education, the Keele Street campus was opened in 1965. Although corporate executives dominated the boards of new and old universities, on the assumption that they could raise money from their peers, the public purse provided the bulk of funds. As students began to arrive in droves—in part because fees were held down, which suggested an edging toward universality—Ontario's version of California-style multiversities were, it seemed, in safe corporate hands. But the universities could hardly remain quiet enclaves for Frye's scholars: they were designed in large measure for learning corporate ways. So long as corporate executives favoured the training of engineers, lawyers, and geologists, as well as general and malleable arts and science students, the government would respond. In the mid-1960s the Ontario Institute for Studies in Education showed how seriously the Tories and their brethren took the educational research industry. When the impulse weakened around 1970, a staggering investment could not be dismantled easily.[55]

While Toronto's corporate donors were reluctant to risk their money supporting higher education, with a flourish Ed Mirvish supported the start of Trent University in Peterborough. Honest Ed also refurbished the Royal Alexandra and started the Poor Alex to promote off-Broadway shows. The former was so successful that E.P. Taylor's O'Keefe Centre, opened in 1960 and already heavily subsidized, was forced into Metro's hands. Mirvish had simply outhustled the O'Keefe management in booking Broadway shows. Even though the theatres in the Central Library and the Colonnade and the Theatre-in-the-Dell joined the Poor Alex, the take-off of alternative theatre was yet to come.[56]

As for sports, the Argos floundered after 1952 but so did the hockey Leafs, until Punch Imlach came along to rebuild teams that won the championships of 1962, 1963, 1964 and 1967. A curious team, the Leafs were serious contenders only in playoffs. The only close competitor historically to the Montreal Canadiens in playoff competition, Toronto lagged far behind in regular season play. Johnny Bower, Carl Brewer, Tim Horton, Red Kelly, Dave Keon and Frank Mahovolich were the greats of these years, though Toronto never mustered a scoring leader and, indeed, had not since Gordie Drillon in 1938.[57]

To Americans, Toronto's — indeed Canada's — most famous citizen was Marshall McLuhan. From The Mechanical Bride *to* War and Peace in the Global Village, *the University of Toronto seer dazzled readers with his interpretations of the world of mass communication.*

Despite Jack Kent Cooke's addition of fireworks and other entertainment touches, fewer and fewer attended Maple Leaf games in the stadium at the foot of Bathurst. The majors on television dampened interest. But in 1977 Toronto finally achieved big-league status with the Blue Jays.

Marilyn Bell became the nation's top sports hero — and a symbol of Toronto's self-esteem — after she swam Lake Ontario and then the English Channel. With fellow swimmer Cliff Lumsden, she received the first of the city's Awards of Merit.

This era saw the last hurrah of the baseball Leafs, who folded in 1967. Ironically, though Jack Kent Cooke built contending teams from 1954 onward, attendance started to fall—presumably because of the attraction of major league television sports. In 1954, 1956, 1957 and 1960, the Leafs won the pennant and came second five more times between 1954 and 1966—a splendid record achieved with many future major league stars. Even four league playoff champions, four finalists and one Junior World Series finalist in 1960 could not stem the decline. Although amateur baseball waned, interest was kept alive through the Intercounty Leafs and a few other local leagues. By contrast, minor hockey came to be more strongly organized; suburban parents followed the American preoccupation with their children's success. Sunday sports and community centres eroded the church leagues and Sunday schools at the same time.[58]

Toronto doted on individual sports heroes and cultural celebrities. In 1954 Canada's "sweetheart," Marilyn Bell, swam forty-two miles across Lake Ontario with the support of the *Star*. The *Telegram* financed her crawls across the English Channel and the Strait of Juan de Fuca, as well as Cliff Lumsden's long-distance swims. Bill Carruthers, Abby Hoffman and Bruce Kidd competed with some success in the Commonwealth Games and Olympics. Singer Lois Marshall and pianist Glenn Gould impressed the music world. And Harold Town was one of many rising painters who ventured into the abstract. By the mid-1960s the Beatles were better known to far more, as the baby boom generation became a mass of teenagers. The youth culture would soon flower. For most, the affluent society was realized.[59]

THE SUBURBAN BOOM AND INNER-CITY REDEVELOPMENT

Suburbs were hardly a new phenomenon. What was new about postwar growth was its scale in terms of population and, even more so, in the consumption of space for housing and schools, shopping centres and industrial estates. What was often referred to as "sprawl" was, of course, largely the direct instrumental result of the automobile. Metro's planning commissioner from 1955 to 1962, Murray Jones, pointed to the dramatic shift to commuting. In this era of the car, symbolized by tail-fin flashiness (at least in the 1950s), arterials blossomed with car dealerships. Although the increase in the number of cars in Metro slowed down after 1960s, public transit travel fell, even after the opening of the subway in 1954. In the 1950s Torontonians came closer than ever to accepting the American style of suburban growth. This too was the heyday of the suburban ideal of family-centred living for raising baby boom children. In 1953 half of Metro's 240 square miles were occupied by urban uses; by 1965 three-quarters: two more Torontos area-wise to house one more Toronto population-wise suggests the magnitude of development, especially when compared with the city's 35 square miles which took decades to build. Just the same, when Jones asserted that the city was becoming "more and more distinct" from the suburbs, some differences were already becoming blurred.[60] (Map 4)

Don Mills, the Golden Mile, Yorkdale, indeed the Golden Horseshoe wrapped around the western end of Lake Ontario, all conjured up images of the heroic era of mass suburbanization. Don Mills was a major pacesetter. By 1952 E.P. Taylor had assembled 31 parcels of land totalling 2,063 acres. On the question of suburban design, a Canadian compromise—between an American plan for a dormitory town and the European solution of a self-contained town replete with industry and all services—was worked out. Though the vast majority of workers would have to commute, as in the U.S., a more balanced assessment base was achieved. In 1952 the Don Mills Development Corporation began to build; by 1962, 3,630 houses, 3,683 low-rise apartment units for a population of over 25,000, offices and 2.5 million square feet of floor space for 63 industrial firms had been constructed.[61]

Following in many respects the ideas of Humphrey Carver, the planners introduced many innovations to Toronto. Four neighbourhoods focussed on elementary schools surrounding a regional shopping centre, an apartment cluster and a high school were laid out. Architect-designed, ranch-style housing was the norm. Even colour control was introduced. A hierarchy of streets was created. Bounded by arterials, the neighbourhood and its children were protected from through traffic. Inside the neighbourhood, the local curvilinear streets and cul-de-sacs fed into collectors to reach the arterials. A ring road ran around the thirty-six acre shopping centre. Three hundred acres of land was set aside for two industrial zones on the northern and southern edges. Lots of green space was provided, largely in ravines.

The success of corporate development in Don Mills set a pattern

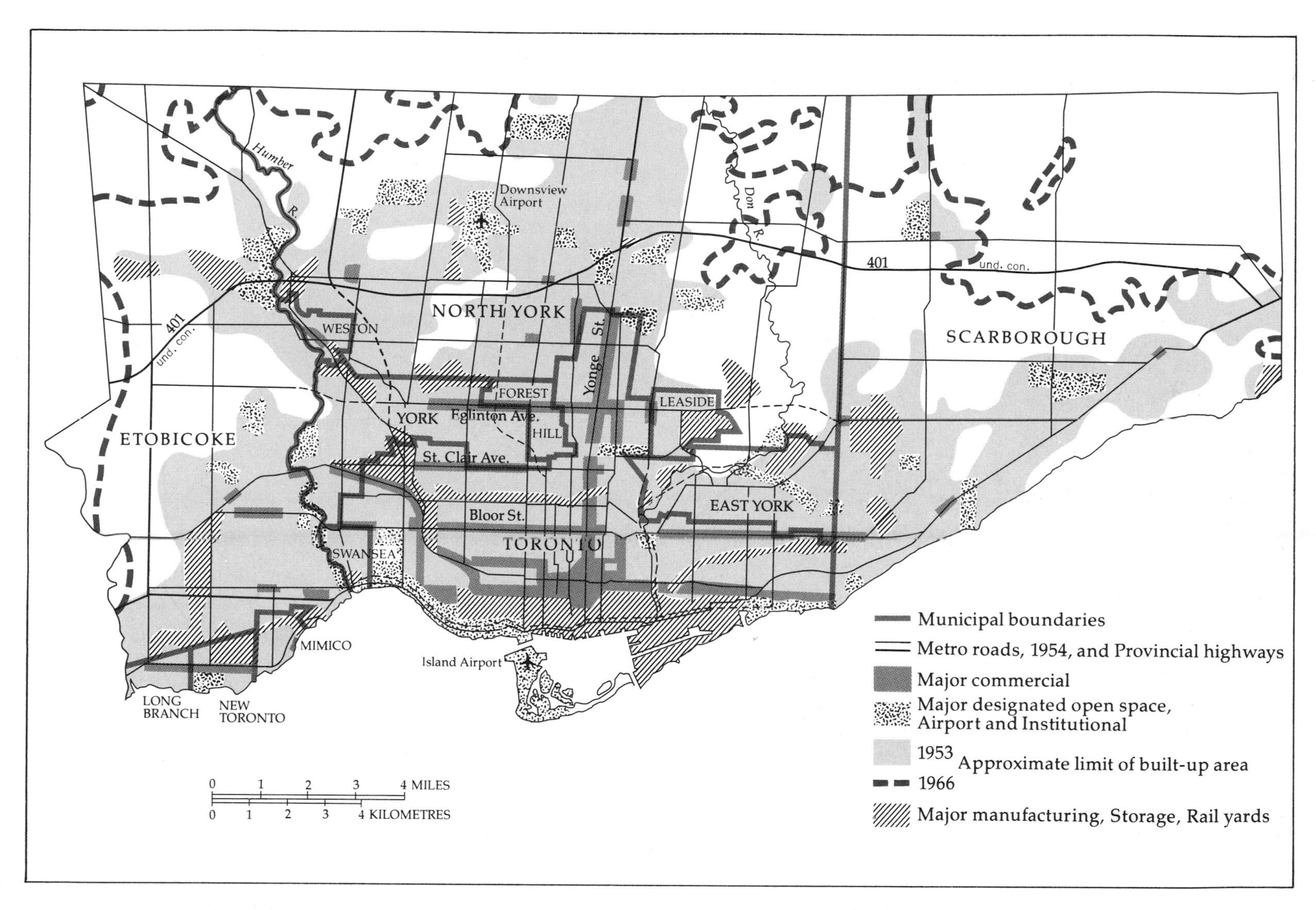

4 Metro Toronto in 1953, and Built-Up Area, 1966: With 13 constituent municipalities at the time of its creation in 1953, Metro Toronto was eight times the size of Toronto proper. Since Metro "assumed" the roads shown here in 1954, it has taken on additional ones and handed others back to the municipalities. Outlying shopping centres and industrial sites are only beginning to appear here; great expansion of the built-up area in outer townships occurred between 1953 and 1966.

for future, large land assemblies. More articulated than Los Angeles-style sprawl or early postwar Toronto suburbs, it also went beyond Home Smith's large Humber Valley Surveys of the 1920s by providing for a wider range of housing and industrial and commercial uses. Don Mills's achievement persuaded Taylor to begin assembling 6,000 acres in 1955 for what eventually became Erin Mills and for others such as Bramalea. Corporate planning of Toronto's suburbs was arriving in a big way. But many suburbanites and exurbanites moved into modest subdivisions built by small operators. Many pre-existing places like Agincourt and Weston were engulfed.[62]

In the early 1960s the corporate developers altered their planning to include high-rise apartments and to provide for more modest-income earners and smaller families. Illustrating this shift was Flemingdon Park just south of Don Mills, where maisonettes, terrace and "garden" apartments were built. But the great majority of units were put in high-rise blocks: people had to live vertically if profits were to be made. Flemingdon was planned to be totally rental units — pointing to another trend, one that went against the aspirations of most Torontonians. Flemingdon and other high-priced rental housing belied Jones's assertion of suburban distinctiveness.[63]

Education was a major concern of suburban living. In 1956 in the three outer suburban townships of Etobicoke, North York and Scarborough, there were 108 public elementary schools; in 1966, 238. Even more dramatic was the increase in the number of high schools: from 8 to 49. Suburban enrollments shot up — a tripling in elementary schools and nearly an eight-fold increase in high schools. The separate system expanded markedly in response to the suburbanization of Roman Catholic immigrants, and many new Jewish schools appeared in the Bathurst corridor. The spiritual life of the suburbanites was also a concern: for a while the United Church built churches at the rate of five a year.[64]

Shopping centres were conspicuous, new features of the suburban landscape. Between 1953 and 1966 the number rose from 5 to 227, to provide a third of all retail floor space in Metro. In the three outer suburbs, not surprisingly, floor space in centres expanded enormously, from 414,000 to 9,136,000 square feet. So important were shopping centres that by 1965 developers and planners had worked out a three-level hierarchy of centres: local, intermediate and regional, after a great deal of *ad hoc* planning.[65]

Yorkdale was the glorious culmination and model for the few subsequent large centres. In 1955 the T. Eaton Company bought the largest part of the seventy-eight acres that eventually comprised the site. In a departure from the Don Mills model, Eaton's asked Simpsons to share the centre — on the downtown principle that two department stores together would bring more trade to both and to small stores. For the first time too the mall would be enclosed. The plan was made public in 1958 and immediately received enthusiastic support from North York Township, which rezoned the site, and from ratepayer groups, which called the project "a wonderful thing for North York's assessment." A subsidiary of the large Trizec Corporation developed the site.[66]

The site was splendid: adjacent to the 401 and the projected Spadina Expressway. Two expressways, like two department stores, were better than one. Spadina was moved up on the agenda of public works: in 1961 Metro Council finally approved nearly $74 million for its construction. Yorkdale opened in 1964. The largest regional shopping centre in Canada, it provided for a breathtaking 6,500 parking spaces and its 1.1 million net square feet housed more than 100 stores. To an "unrepentant Downtown Snob" like writer Harry Bruce, however, Yorkdale's scale was bewildering.[67]

In this golden age of manufacturing, the suburbanization of industry created a new industrial landscape, as more capital-intensive and space-consuming industries moved to the periphery. The pattern set in 1953 by Maclean-Hunter at 401 and Yonge and IBM at Eglinton and Don Mills would be followed enthusiastically. In 1959 Metro planners noted that space-per-worker, the use of horizontal conveyors demanding one-storey buildings, truck-loading facilities and parking space and a desire for green space had increased greatly and was expected to "continue to grow" to 1980.[68]

These assumptions led planners to project what turned out to be an excessive amount of land for industry in the Metro planning region. Optimism rose to greater heights as the levels were increased in the 1966 plan. If the 1959 estimate of increased manufacturing employment (50 per cent) over twenty years was close to being realized, the estimate of needed land was very high. The politicians and planners did not realize that the limits on the postwar style of production and space consumption had nearly been reached.[69]

The postwar population surge, though less strong relatively than the boom early in the century, gobbled up far more agricultural land. Large developers put up instant houses on large lots, creating new communities somewhat in the style of garden surburbs advocated by reformers in the late nineteenth century. Don Mills, the first "new town," included a shopping centre and walk-up apartments.

Within the region the three outer suburbs of Metro — North York, Etobicoke and Scarborough — absorbed most of the new manufacturing, largely in industrial parks. In 1964 Metro accounted for more than three-quarters of employment within the arc enclosed by Oshawa, Newmarket and Oakville, though the fringe was gaining more. Together with commercial retail and office additions, manufacturing helped to strengthen the assessment base for these suburbs, from a quarter to nearly a half of Metro's total, with North York achieving the largest share.[70] (Tables XI, XIII)

The appropriation of ravines for public parks and flood control was a major innovation in the suburbs and beyond. By 1966 Metro Parks controlled nearly 5,500 acres of parkland, of which two-thirds lay in the three outer suburbs. Local municipalities held nearly as many. Formed in 1957, the Metropolitan and Region Conservation Authority was responsible for 950 square miles in twenty-three municipalities, extending from Ajax to Long Branch and north to the Oak Ridges glacial moraine and the headwaters of the Humber in Mono Township. By 1965 it had developed eleven sites for outdoor recreation and Black Creek Pioneer Village, which drew more than a million visitors annually. The authority took over flood plains in the Humber and Don valleys and leased them to Metro Parks, finally realizing the hopes of earlier plans.[71]

The authority's chief job was flood control. Although some action had been taken since the mid-1940s, the horrendous flood in October 1954, when Hurricane Hazel dumped on the area, showed how poorly prepared the region was for such an onslaught. In all, eighty-one people died, most of them residents of an ill-advised subdivision just south of Weston on the west bank of the Humber. Property damage was extreme in both city and country. Spurred on by this disaster, the authority moved ahead on flood and erosion control, especially on the Humber, the Don and Highland Creek. Plans were drawn up for thirteen dams and limitation placed on construction in flood plains.[72]

The residential, educational, industrial and recreational expansion of Toronto depended on vigorous programs for water, sewerage and roads. Conspicuous in the glossy brochures published almost annually by Metropolitan Toronto were water supply and sewage disposal, which ranked high on Metro's agenda. It was in this area that Fred Gardiner would make his greatest contribution. By 1964 Metro had spent $72 million in distributing and storing water and on water treatment, all through sales to local municipalities which retailed to consumers. Metro, together with the conservation authority, had cleaned up the streams. By 1964 Metro had also invested $85 million in new and expanded sewage treatment plants and trunk sewers. Even though construction of the Humber Sewage Disposal Plant was temporarily resisted by area residents, by 1965 the water and sewerage systems were almost totally directed from and to Lake Ontario.[73]

Roads, as always, were intensely political. Since everyone was an expert on transportation matters, controversy was frequently generated. Up to 1965, however, the debate was muted compared with the controversy that would rage over Spadina, largely because Metro's road program was favourably received. In 1953 Metro took over arterial roads, thus in one stroke solving the jurisdictional problem that had pushed Gardiner and others into Metro. In suburban areas Metro widened and resurfaced roads, and built grade-separation bridges, underpasses and expressways. The Belt Line-Moore Ravine parkway was dropped and the Bayview Extension constructed instead. The Don Valley Parkway was gradually built. In 1955 the Queensway and the Lakeshore Expressway (named after Gardiner in 1957) were begun, the latter generating considerable debate over its route around the CNE and Fort York. Eglinton, as the main arterial crosstown route which would improve access to Don Mills and other large developments, was extended. The arterials were linked to the 401 and 27 bypasses and the 400 to Barrie.[74]

In 1959 Metro planners unveiled the draft official plan of the metropolitan area, in which the expressways were more systematically arranged and the "inner box" of the 1943 plan was resurrected but redesigned somewhat (Map 5, p. 140). This is largely the plan Toronto lives with still, but it was refined further in Metro's 1964 transportation plans. To aid the movement of cars, which doubled in Metro between 1953 and 1964 (compared to a population increase of 50 per cent), a computerized traffic signal system was initiated in 1960 and completed in 1966. Uniform traffic bylaws were instituted in 1958, as were crosswalks for pedestrians.[75]

The TTC took over the four private bus companies operating beyond the city boundaries and added new lines for the suburbs. Despite the connection of surface suburban lines with the increasingly successful Yonge subway, ridership fell overall from a peak in 1954 (when the subway opened) until 1964. Fare increases needed

Eighty-one lives were lost in 1954 when Hurricane Hazel turned the flood plains of the Humber into a disaster area. Above, homes on Fairglen Road in Weston jammed together by floodwaters; at left, a cave-in on Royal York Road.

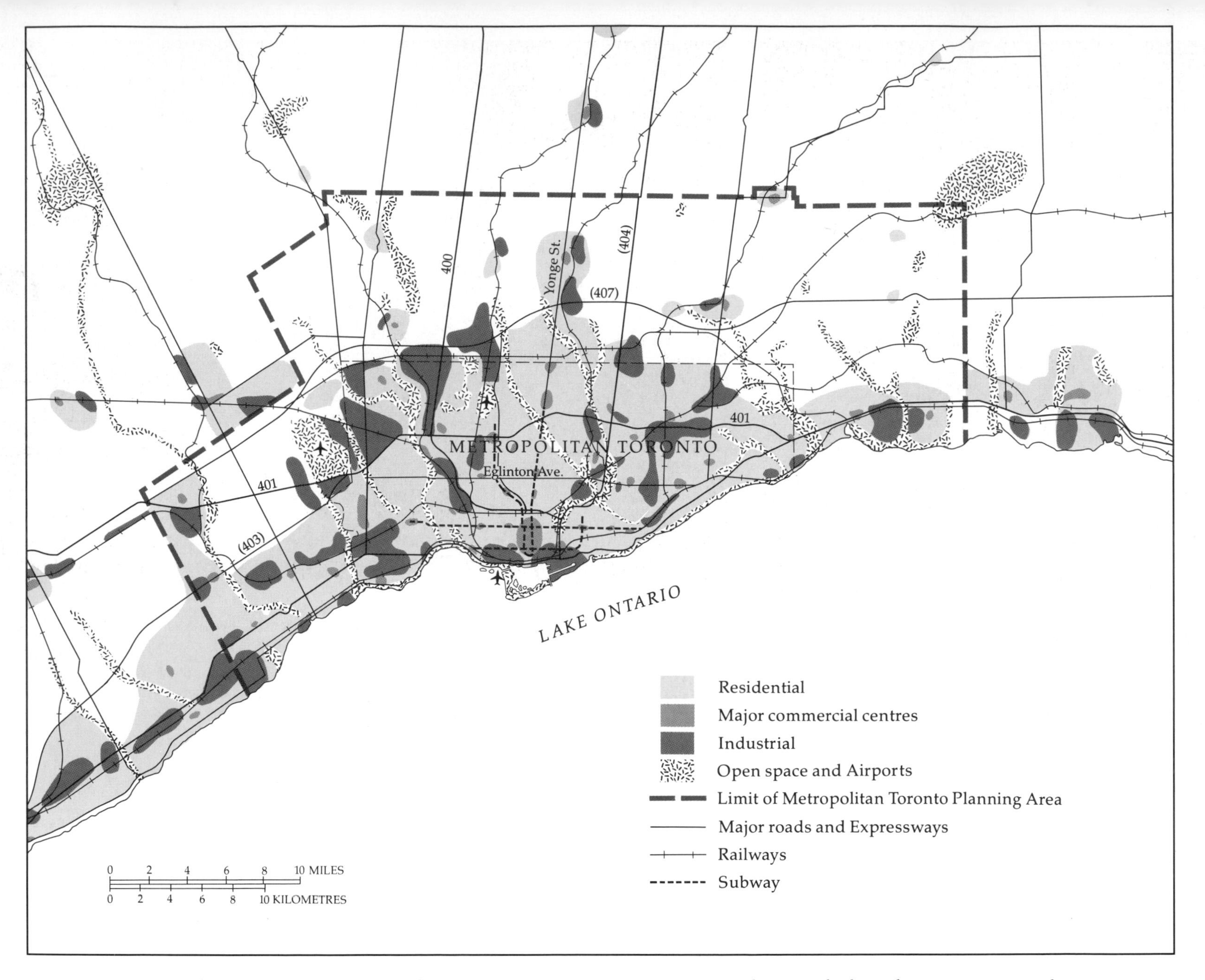

5 Proposed Metropolitan Toronto Plan, 1959: From 1953 to 1970, Metro planners dealt with a 720-square mile area, three times that of Metro. This scheme overoptimistically allotted too much land to industry. Subsequent planning made only modest changes, altering expressway and transit routes somewhat (note the Queen Street subway), and in the mid-1970s finally supporting outlying office concentrations in the town centres of North York and Scarborough.

Major construction of one type or another dominated the landscape. Provincial expressways built in the 1950s were redone in the 1960s, as at the junction of Highways 400 and 401, left. Construction of Yorkdale Shopping Centre, the largest of its kind, started in 1962 (above). For Eaton's and the developers, the Spadina Expressway was part of their plan — and thus of public plans too.

to pay off the debt on the subway undoubtedly contributed to the decline, as did the zone system forcing suburbanites to pay more. The decline and the vicious circle of infrequent service in the thinly settled suburbs, which resulted in more debt, were not lost on Gardiner. Despite his enthusiasm for the Spadina Expressway, in 1956 he argued that "a succession of new expressways is not the answer to efficient movement of traffic. Each successive one is filled the day it is opened .... Additional rapid transit is the only answer." In 1961 he audaciously repeated this to a Detroit audience.[76] (Table XV)

To promote transit, money was needed. Since TTC loans could no longer be supported from the fare box, Gardiner appealed to the federal and provincial governments for capital funds. Although in 1955 the province granted a one-year subsidy to stave off a fare increase temporarily, not until 1961 did it agree with Gardiner. A low-interest loan of $60 million was provided for the more expensive University line, opened in 1963. In 1964 the province picked up one-third of construction costs for the Bloor-Danforth line, opened in 1966 and extended in 1967, as Metro assumed the TTC's other debt charges. The costs of low-density suburban development and better roads had become obvious: suburban bus lines did not pay. By 1966 ridership was again rising. By then, downtown parking charges and the already large number of low- and modest-income suburbanites dependent on the TTC increased ridership. It was the continued insistence, especially of city politicians, for public transit that prevented Toronto from going the way of Detroit and Los Angeles. Seventy per cent of commuting workers came downtown by subway or streetcar; only New York City was relatively more dependent on transit. As in social services, the province was now a major financier of the urban scene.[77]

The Yonge subway induced new apartment and office construction around the "regional" centres at Eglinton, St. Clair and Bloor and Yonge. The last area to feel the full effects of the redevelopment impulse was the downtown. Even as late as 1965 the skyline was hardly distinguishable from the skyline of the early 1930s: from the bay, the Bank of Commerce and the Royal York still dominated the scene. But enormous change was underway, starting with the new city hall opened in 1965. Even while Toronto's share of assessment fell, its proportion of the value of Metro's building permits actually rose from a quarter to a third, reflecting massive redevelopment and a shift toward greater office employment. (Table XIII)

The 1966 Metro Urban Renewal Study noted that private enterprise had shown little interest in redeveloping the swath of poorer housing in the east-west axis because "properties are very costly and difficult to assemble, and because they do not contain attractive locations for the current apartment market." Instead, private redevelopment had pursued higher-income small families and individuals, primarily in a north-south corridor straddling Yonge Street over to Bathurst Street. (Map 11, p. 177) In April 1965 nearly three-quarters of 46,000 apartment units were concentrated in 9 major clusters in this sector. (Map 7, p. 167) Only modest groupings were found elsewhere in the city, except a very large one of 6,000 units in South Parkdale. In these areas, large lots could easily be pulled together for high density. The higher-income north-south band coincided with the Yonge subway, and 60 per cent of the units in major concentrations in the city were close to it. It had obviously been built to relieve longstanding commuting problems from the north to downtown, despite the fact that the east-west routes, such as Bloor-Danforth and Queen, were nearly as heavily used. High-rise apartments encouraged more riders and attracted more of the young affluent, many of whom undoubtedly expected to marry and raise families in single-family houses.[78]

The 1956 city study, *Urban Renewal*, an interim plan for the city, had clearly advocated higher densities around Eglinton and Yonge, in the Annex, and south of Bloor Street and east of Yonge over to what became St. James Town, where some structures such as City Park Apartments had already been built. (See at right.) In that same year the Parliament Syndicate submitted its proposal for a predecessor of St. James Town. Even if access made it attractive to developers, small lots would, the group suggested, require the help of the city in expropriating land, but in turn the city and Metro would realize higher assessments. That proposal did not pass, but in the early 1960s another did. Only in that quadrant south of Bloor and east of Yonge would the developers show interest in redeveloping low-income areas with small lots. The area could be transformed to fit into the northern higher-income corridor. The east-west subway later produced some clusters, most conspicuously at Broadview-Danforth and High Park.[79]

By 1966 apartment units constituted 46 per cent of all dwellings

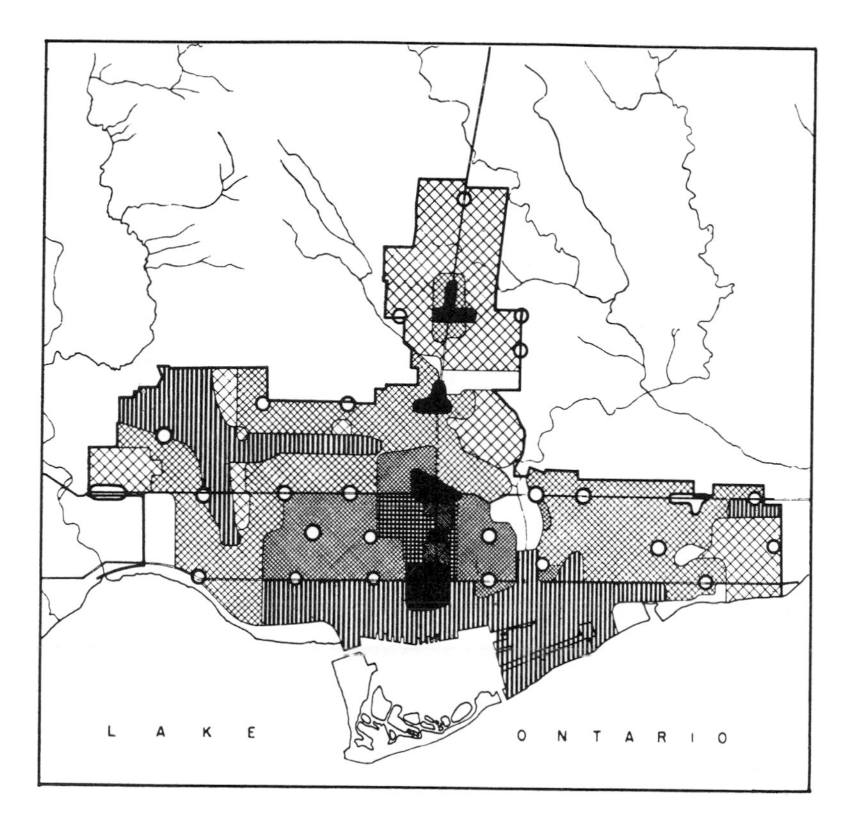

Toronto's future land use, as envisioned in the 1956 interim plan of the Urban Renewal Study. Cross-hatching shows increasing residential densities; a grid, institutional areas; white, "major open spaces"; vertical lines, industry; and black, major commercial centres. The plan stressed renewal, including the commercial centres up Yonge, and the elimination of housing south of Queen, where industry was expected to thrive.

in the city, up from 30 per cent in 1951. The high number of demolitions of older buildings and of building permits for high-rise redevelopment in the mid 1960s triggered opposition. Central neighbourhoods, which were attracting new residents, formed a large part of the resistance. In contrast to many American inner cities, a major strength of much of inner Toronto was the availability of mortgage money, including vendor "take-back" mortgages. Although to a lesser extent than in the U.S., institutional mortgage lenders and the federal government largely supported new housing in the suburbs. In the city confidence in buyers, in older housing, and thus in neighbourhoods was expressed by sellers. Another sign of this came in the late 1950s when planners and residents began drawing up neighbourhood plans; significantly, the first plans were for vulnerable parts of the northern corrridor. It could be argued persuasively that "it's smart to live in the Annex," partly because of the heterogeneity of life styles and ethnicity. However, the peak of citizen action was still to come.[80]

Commercial office construction was the second major redevelopment activity and much was closely correlated to apartment construction and to subway access. By 1962 the Bloor, St. Clair and Eglinton regional office and shopping nodes on Yonge were conspicuous, as was considerable new building by insurance companies on Bloor East and by the province east of Queen's Park. In Metro as a whole, net office floor space between 1953 and 1965 increased from about 8 to 21 million square feet, most of it in the Yonge corridor up to Eglinton. Outside this sector, only Don Mills and adjacent districts along the Don Valley Parkway contained significant concentrations.[81]

After a relative lull in the construction of offices between 1960 and 1963, the downtown landscape was in the process of being dramatically transformed. Although it had added the most commercial floor space of any district in the 1950s, much more was expected, and concern was expressed over how this would happen. The selection of Finnish architect Viljo Revell's spectacular plan for a new city hall and square in 1958 was a clear indication that affluent Toronto wanted to express its rising power, cosmopolitanism and civic pride. The design, selected by an international panel from more than 500 entries, was recognized as a dramatic departure from Toronto the Good and from its stodgy, smoke-blackened, downtown skyscrapers. The twin towers, curving around the clamshell council chamber and set in the large plaza, symbolized a host of

Downtown around 1960, as the great building boom is just beginning. The Gardiner Expressway has not yet arrived. The only striking additions to the financial district since the early 1930s are the Bank of Montreal and the larger Bank of Nova Scotia, facing each other across Bay on the north side of King, just right of centre. The Royal York has gained an addition, obvious by its unblackened state, and the Lord Simcoe is conspicuous just to the left.

contradictory ideas: development upward but surrounded by open space; politicians in the centre of a towering bureaucracy. The square represented something new for Toronto, an open place for celebrations, demonstrations and recreation, a return to a market square or *agora* as the focus of public activity. Despite a leaking roof, City Hall inspired a sense of cosmopolitanism, ebullience and even grandeur, sentiments rarely experienced in Toronto.[82]

Sparked by the 1959 decision to proceed on the new City Hall, Mayor Phillips, the council, Chief Planner Matthew Lawson and downtown businessmen decided that Toronto needed more of this kind of redevelopment. Believing that "private enterprise is more efficient than government" or, more precisely, that "private enterprise can be depended upon for redevelopment if there is encouragement on the municipal level," a Redevelopment Advisory Council (RAC) was set up, with Allan G. Burton of Simpsons as chairman and composed only of businessmen. In 1961 Burton claimed to the Downtown Businessmen's Association that Toronto's problem was one not of growth but of planning growth "so it doesn't strangle us." Already the RAC and the planners were projecting a near doubling of office space downtown, from 14 to 24 million square feet, a 50 per cent increase in employment (despite recent declines), and a modest increase in traffic to the area.[83]

The new City Hall was thus a fillip for rising expectations of more building and of more sophisticated design. In 1962 and 1963 two studies on central Toronto appeared, both concentrating on the downtown core. The first was put together by five architects, the second by the Planning Board. Like the RAC, they both projected growth, particularly in finance (banking, trust, investment dealers) and associated business services (mining, accounting, corporate law). More pointedly than the RAC, the plans emphasized grand, even futuristic, design in the Corbusier mold with buildings on stilts on spacious lots, as had been achieved in Montreal's Place Ville Marie. One major proposal suggested grade separation of traffic: pedestrian malls (which did happen) and cars and public vehicles travelling underground (which did not happen).[84]

In 1963 development began in earnest. Simpsons decided on a tower. The Toronto-Dominion Bank started the T-D Centre project of three towers on plenty of open space. The tallest tower would reach halfway up the Empire State Building, perhaps signifying that Toronto was halfway to the top. Thus started the race in the financial district to see which bank could build the tallest tower. Offices, hospital additions and the shortlived and misnamed Lord Simcoe Hotel were built on University. The Royal York regained its status as the largest hotel in the Commonwealth with an eastern addition. Reflecting Toronto's culture was the construction of the O'Keefe Centre for the Performing Arts with 3,200 seats and the planning of the centennial projects, the St. Lawrence Centre and a renovated St. Lawrence Hall. But lost in the process, and to the chagrin of many, was the old, classical Toronto-Dominion office at King and Bay, another sign of things to come. Only concerted campaigns would save other splendid old structures, such as the old City Hall.

On the waterfront, the area east of Yonge Street was transformed in anticipation of world traffic through the St. Lawrence Seaway. The Harbour Commission opened the Queen Elizabeth Docks between Jarvis and Parliament and subsequently a container facility. The Redpath Sugar refinery received ships directly from the West Indies. By 1966, of the 5.7 million tons of cargo passing through the port, a quarter was foreign cargo, and a third of the ships came from overseas. Despite slower growth than anticipated, bullishness had led to plans for an outer harbour enclosed by a spit created by landfill from the massive redevelopment of the city. Island houses were disappearing as the parkland expanded. Of equal significance were plans for the central waterfront, west of Yonge. By 1965 Harbour Square had been planned. Offices and apartments would appear on a waterfront that, since 1850, had been the preserve of manufacturing, railways and ships. A 1962 architects' plan for the central area foresaw the potential for recreation. Though the railways were in the process of moving their yards to Maple and Agincourt and the city's manufacturing base was declining, by 1966 the waterfront—and indeed all of Toronto—was distinctly changing its face.[85]

THE POLITICS OF GROWTH

The Gardiner years (1953 to 1961) were not very controversial: Toronto succeeded in doing better than other North American cities in fostering and distributing growth. The task of providing a public built-environment of new roads, sewers, watermains and schools was tackled with gusto and general agreement. Gardiner has been likened to Robert Moses, New York's famous twentieth-century public developer. They both acted as tough entrepreneurs

Several proposals were made for an Eaton's Centre in the mid-1960s. They saw not only the elimination of the Eaton factory lofts but also the old City Hall — except the tower. This model shows one of the redevelopment schemes seen from a point just northwest of new City Hall. Citizens rallied to save the grand old building and a new scheme emerged — one that neither destroyed the old city hall nor dwarfed the new one.

pushing ahead to get things done: in private, they could boast to one another of five-year plans while the western world denounced Reds and Soviets. They both predicted the growing corporatization of the public sector. But the salient difference was that, as the "Maharajah of Metrostan," Gardiner acted straightforwardly and publicly while Moses operated in an almost clandestine manner. Unlike Moses, who contributed to the "fall" of New York, supermayor Gardiner built with order and stability in mind, even while claiming to give free enterprise the initiative. If local nineteenth-century democracy was overriden for the broader public good, the people were generally in agreement. Not until Gardiner left office were the limits of his vision recognized: perhaps he left on the cue that social services and protection of the urban environment, not the full head of development steam, were gradually becoming the order of the day.[86]

While Gardiner dominated the Metro scene in a very functional fashion, Mayor Nathan Phillips acted more as symbolic head of a rising cosmopolitan and ethnically diverse city. Perhaps too many banquets and—despite his advocacy of the new City Hall—too little drive for downtown redevelopment led to his defeat by Donald Sommerville in 1962. As the heroic era of suburban development wound down, city voters backed politicians who more clearly favoured private redevelopment. In 1962 Walter Manthorpe was appointed development commissioner to promote and implement construction. However, the style of growth in the next era — under mayors Sommerville, Givens and Dennison — would be challenged.[87]

In 1962 Metro Council elected William Allen, a Toronto controller, as chairman. Continued city-suburban differences meant that Allen just barely beat North York Reeve Norman Goodhead. Allen was a city manager who avoided controversy in his seven years as chairman. He accepted provincial initiatives on the much needed restructuring of Metro. Despite some changes since 1954, notably the consolidation of police forces in 1957, a study had revealed a good deal of complexity and overlap in the operation of departments of Metro and the municipalities. Inadequacies in the welfare system had reappeared and the city was supporting the greatest number of the poor, even though some of the costs for social and family welfare had been transferred to Metro in 1954. The city's share for welfare rose sharply from 1957 to 1963 during two sharp recessions. Thus, in 1963 a one-person royal commission was appointed by the province to consider Metro's structure. After hearings arousing little public interest, H. Carl Goldenberg reported in mid-1965.[88]

The province acted on Goldenberg's recommendations in 1966. Although his proposals were watered down, Metro was restructured from thirteen municipalities into one city and five boroughs (Map 6, p. 154). The result was a thirty-three member council, with twenty members from the growing suburbs. A balance was struck by giving the city greater weight on a stronger executive centred around the chairman. Major steps included putting welfare and the growing problem of waste disposal in Metro's hands. The Metro Library Board was set up to co-ordinate and supplement local systems. Metro School Board was strengthened by acquiring the right to review and co-ordinate all local budgets. Metro Council's take-over of local school debts smoothed out the confusing bookkeeping. Finally, on Goldenberg's recommendation, the province took over more of the courts. Despite rhetoric to the contrary, local autonomy was cut back. Metro chairmen still had a great deal of power, even if not exercised as vigorously by Allen as by Gardiner. Symbolically, the expressway named for Gardiner extended a lot farther than the one eventually named for Allen. But both reached dead ends.[89]

Growth meant public spending in unforeseen quantities: between 1954 and 1966 the gross current expenditures of Metro, local municipalities and schools increased almost 300 per cent. Outstanding net debt for capital expenditures went up even more. In 1965 capital expenditures were $182 million, well above the $100 million barrier that had, as recently as 1963, been considered the sacred limit.[90] (Table XV)

As expenditures rose so did taxes and government grants. Property and business taxes still provided more than 70 per cent of revenues; the difference was largely made up by provincial grants, such as capital grants for hospitals and roads in the 1950s and then increasingly for schools. By channelling federal support for welfare, by moving from unconditional to conditional grants to Metro, and by entering into subway building in 1963, the province signalled a widening but unavoidable provincial interest in Metro. Premier Robarts moved much more vigorously than Frost had. By 1966 the province was recognizing its budget as a social support and as a device to control the economy (in contrast to the 1950s when it had been primarily devoted to building roads) and to promote develop-

Fred Gardiner was the dominant political figure of the period, using Metro's clout to get the steam shovels into the ground. At left, he relaxes at the Glen Haffy Conservation Area, one of several run by the Metropolitan Toronto and Region Conservation Authority. Above, the Star's *Duncan MacPherson captures a Toronto-Metro dispute over sharing the new City Hall.*

Nathan Phillips, the first non-Anglo-Saxon Protestant to reach the city's top office, was "mayor of all people" from 1954 to 1962. The mayor's chair is vacant at Phillips's last Board of Control meeting, following his defeat at the hands of Donald Summerville.

ment by private companies. The rhetoric of free enterprise would continue. So would development. The growing role of government was partly the result of increased restiveness among citizens. The 1964 NDP by-election win in Riverdale indicated that a renewed left would push the Tories toward even more equality and a wider range of services. Electoral democracy was being renewed after more than a decade of provincial rule by management.[91]

Dramatic changes had happened since 1953. Despite the pains of readjustment, the multitude of immigrants were absorbed—far more easily than were those who came before 1914. Toronto's citizens survived the identity crisis brought on by these strangers. They looked forward confidently to achieving world-city status for Toronto. The affluent were jetting around the world in DC-8s. At the same time, as a fragment in McLuhan's "global village," Torontonians expected more of their local environment. New ways of dealing with the public environment would appear soon after 1966.[92]

Yet old ways hung on. Public outrage stopped CBC's "This Hour has Seven Days" in its tracks for its critical commentary. Growth in a business-like fashion far outweighed any urge to extravagance. In the wake of Expo, extolled by Berton and nearly everyone, Gardiner told Percy Saltzman that he would "never" have agreed to a world's fair in Toronto. It

> would have cost us millions of dollars that are a damn sight better invested in sewers and water pipes and roads which are a permanent value instead of one year's bust. Then you won't wake up next morning with a hell of a headache and find that you haven't got the money to pay for the drunk you were on last night.

Toronto may have been parsimonious about financing the spectacular but, apparently unlike Montreal, it had little to prove. Besides, Toronto was growing more rapidly. The unstoppable monied elite was involved in a corporate merger splurge in the U.S. in the mid- and late 1960s, investing rather less in Canada than good Tory nationalists should have been. The old core elite still prevailed even while economic decisions were gradually drifting more and more into unsure government hands.[93]

The skyline of 1983, looking northeast. Enormous change is evident since the early 1960s (page 144). In the immediate foreground the Harbourfront project is still being transformed. In early 1985 the railway lands just west of the CN tower were chosen as the site of the city's domed stadium.

Chapter Five

Multicultural and Financial Metropolis, 1966–1984

On the evening of June 3, 1971, joy was unbounded—or as far as could be in Toronto—as hundreds of central-city residents who had spent hours cooking up strategies and organizing rallies to stop the Spadina Expressway converged on the Yonge Street mall to celebrate Premier Davis's decision. "If we are building a transportation system to serve the automobile, the Spadina Expressway would be a good place to start. But if we are building a transportation system to serve people, the Spadina Expressway is a good place to stop." Suburban politicians were stunned; they could only sputter that the decision was "a disaster."[1]

The great expressway fight was a milestone in the fervent and powerful reform impulse of the time. The mid-1960s to mid-1970s witnessed a massive outpouring of citizen participation against the Viet Nam war, urban renewal and pollution, as "small is beautiful" became the credo for many, and more saw the virtues of old houses. Redirecting power in land-use planning, social services, schools and universities was exhaustively pursued. Reform was a drive to restructure the way people were governed—from the neighbourhood level up to the federal level. The reform movement did transform some ways of running the public world—most clearly in Toronto if less so in the suburbs. For its part, the province became more active in proposing the Toronto-centred region and completed the "service state."

But reform had limits. After 1975 Ottawa and Queen's Park imposed restraint. Regional planning was largely forgotten. Early 1970s predictions of vast population growth in Metro and the region fell by the wayside in the face of census results. Metro's suburbs, not the inner city, now presented the severe social problems. By 1980 weaknesses in the unplanned economy had become visible, especially in manufacturing. Unemployment came to be a more central concern. Yet, as the economy faltered, Toronto ever more markedly took over much of Montreal's economic power. At the same time it had to share its financial power increasingly with New York and governments that became more direct actors in the economy.

CITIZEN PARTICIPATION, REFORM AND THE RUNNING OF THE REGION

By 1966 citizen action entered a new and more intense phase with the Trefann Court fight against an urban renewal scheme. This reform impulse eventually extended to restructuring the city's ward system, opposition to expressways, to private apartment redevelopment, to University of Toronto expansion, to downtown office reconstruction and to the city plan (declared official in 1969) that allowed the zoning of chunks of low-rise residential areas for high-density development. There was as well a democratizing of ratepayer associations, social agencies and educational institutions. Pierre Trudeau's call for citizen participation in public affairs during an appearance in Nathan Phillips Square in June 1968 further pumped up enthusiasm.

Local folklore has fixed on John Sewell as the central figure in the Trefann Court fight (and in others, such as South St. James Town). While Sewell was a dominant figure after 1966, the reform upsurge was underway when he joined local residents in Trefann and other organizers to fight the renewal scheme which had almost universal support from politicians. Concern was also focussed on Don Mount where the city was expropriating property for another renewal scheme. There, with widespread support, the few holdouts, such as Dorothy Graham, argued successfully for compensation on the value of a "home for a home." The expropriation act of 1963 was finally changed in 1968, after five years of allowing the city to bulldoze poor owners — far too cheaply — out of Alexandra Park and Don Mount. Buying out absentee speculators holding land in Cabbagetown slums had been one thing; turfing out low-income owners was another. Community organizing extended into adjacent areas of South Riverdale and elsewhere. With the help of organizers, low-income neighbourhoods became particularly energetic in fighting city hall, as did the middle-class residents of the Sussex area (west of Spadina) when they discovered what the city planned for their neighbourhood. Another sign of quickening change was the election of many more New Democrats in 1967, including the hell-raising Morton Shulman.[2]

Aiding the cause of reform was the Ontario Municipal Board's order in 1969 to redraw the city's ward boundaries. City Council had supported a strip system for dividing wards; citizen groups had argued for a block system. Since 1948 City Council had considered redrawing boundaries, but in 1969 most members held firm to the status quo of long strips. But citizens argued successfully at the OMB. Board Chairman J.A. Kennedy concluded that the block ward system would ensure that "the various conflicting problems for the different areas [would be] debated around the council table rather than . . . within the conscience, so to speak, of each individual alderman.[3] (Map 6, p. 154)

The restructuring led to representation from more homogeneous areas. It helped also to encourage party politics in the debate "around the council table," for the first time since the early 1940s. Liberals, New Democrats and a loose coalition group, CIVAC (Civic Action), tested the voters but with only very modest success: most politicians were elected still on their personal work in filling "pot holes." Even so, between 1969 and 1972 a few reformers of several stripes — left Liberals, downtown New Democrats, Red Tories and others of varying mixtures of radical, conservative and populist notions — very effectively exposed the shenanigans of developers and the politicians who supported them. The growing network of activists was informed and galvanized into action by *City Hall*, a periodical written by four reform aldermen, and the *Toronto Citizen*, a fortnightly midtown newspaper, and by several books. On this wave of reform, new resident associations were formed (with some ratepayer associations recognizing tenants as full members), and the Confederation of Resident and Ratepayer Associations (CORRA) became the central body, though a Metro-wide group failed to take hold.[4]

In December 1972 a heavy turnout of voters brought the reformers to power in Toronto, or so it seemed. Under the banner of "preservation of neighbourhoods," David Crombie easily won the mayor's chair. Because of the pro- and anti-development split on council, he held the balance of power. The most energetic and skillful mayor since Robert Saunders in the 1940s, Crombie pursued a moderate reform line. Some changes came quickly. Neighbourhood planning was played up as the planning staff was doubled. After a lapse of several years, the city revived its direct involvement in constructing housing. On the agenda was "social" housing, the mixing of people of different incomes, a sharp contrast to ghettoizing the poor in "public" projects. Since area municipalities continued to regulate development, controlling and diversifying central-area construction was also a focus between 1974 and 1976.[5]

Ironically, the reformers' victory led to a weakening of the reform impulse. After being consulted by all sorts of groups throughout the province in the wake of the successful 1972 election, CORRA gradually became a rump group. For many, control of development was in the safe hands of council, so action was no longer needed. After 1972 at least some developers were more inclined to consult planners and residents' groups. Undoubtedly, most residents believed the central city's environment was better managed than before 1972. But some reformers sought further improvements.[6]

So in 1978 John Sewell shed his leather jacket in favour of a three-piece suit to run successfully for mayor. To many of the conservative-minded, Sewell overstepped on civil rights questions, which resulted in his losing to Arthur Eggleton in 1980. As a moderate, Eggleton could hardly retreat to quite the same pro-development stance he had taken before 1972, at least regarding high-rise intrusions in neighbourhoods. Energy, civil rights, job creation and social questions came to share with development the agenda of a still very busy council. Much of the reform action in Toronto and North York came through the work of the NDP, which gradually renewed its effort to elect members to all municipal councils and school boards in Metro.

Collective democracy continues to be served by a wide range of community groups that cut across party lines. Although citizen involvement has been less intense than during the reform outburst between 1965 and 1973, special interest groups have persisted, criticizing the increasing disarray in the environment, defending

The transformation of Moss Park from rundown working-class homes (left) to apartment buildings that stood out in stark contrast from the surrounding landscape (below left) was the only totally high-rise renewal project in the city. Subsequent efforts like Don Mount returned to a more human scale. But protests, like the one at bottom right, arose over the entire approach to renewal.

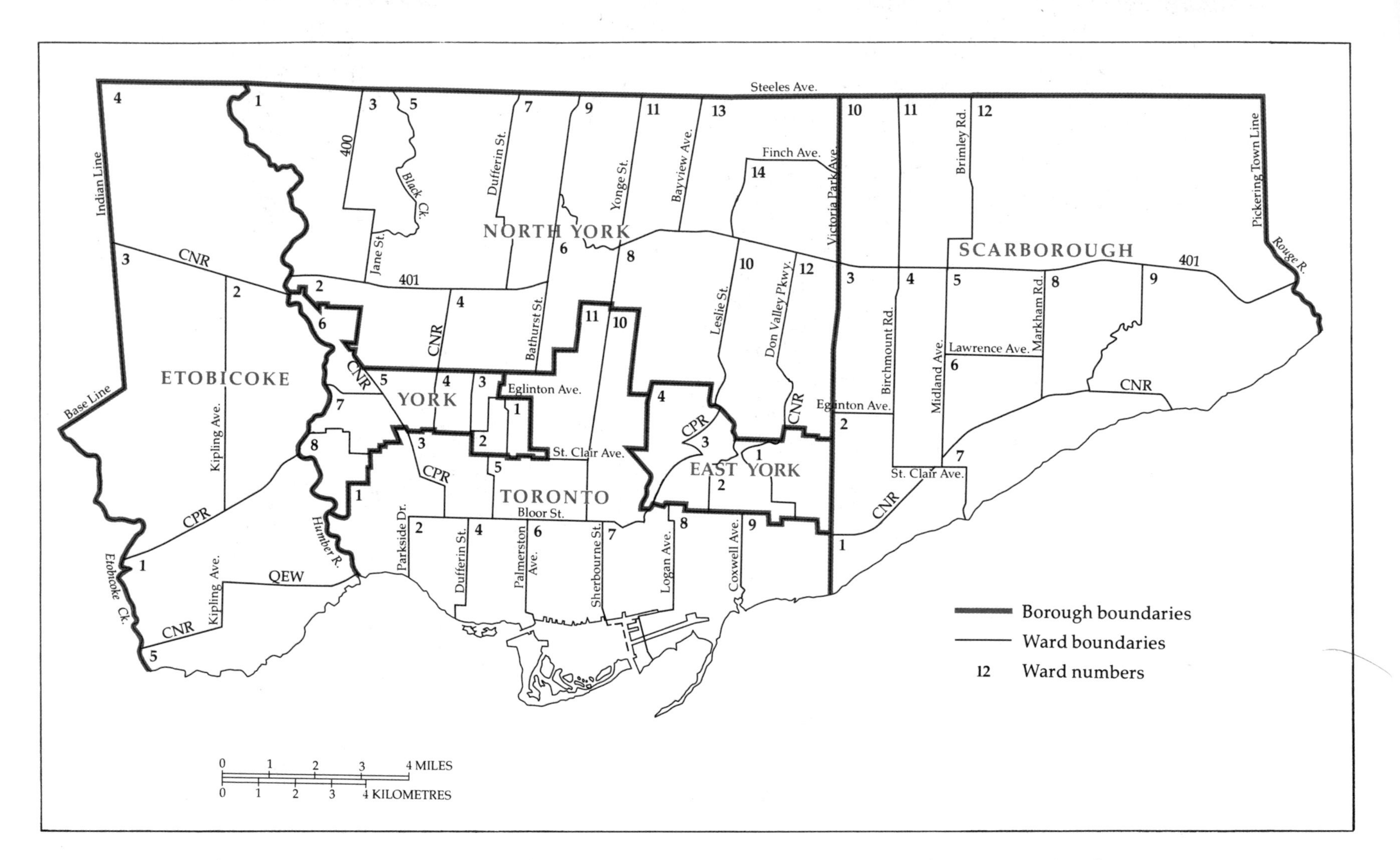

6 Metropolitan Toronto and Municipal Wards, 1975: In 1967 Metro's thirteen municipalities were reduced to six boroughs (since cities, except East York) and the city of Toronto. The population base per ward and number of representatives varied by municipality. In Toronto, ward boundaries were redrawn from strip to block format in 1969, on the orders of the Ontario Municipal Board (compare to page 34). The northeastern corner of Metro was the only largely unoccupied area, as the size of the Scarborough's Ward 12 suggests.

The 1969 election saw a small but vocal reform contingent elected to city hall. John Sewell criticized development schemes such as the Eaton Centre (above; with Sewell are fellow reform aldermen Karl Jaffary and William Kilbourn). The reform breakthough came in 1972 when a fourth member of the group, David Crombie, was elected mayor. But in practice Crombie proved conciliatory in negotiating with developers.

Contentious for a decade and a half, the Spadina Expressway met its fiercest opposition from 1969 to 1971. The "Stop Spadina" coalition achieved apparent success in 1971 when the new premier, Bill Davis, opted for people, not cars. In fact the logic of Spadina had been undercut as early as 1962 by the implicit but little-heralded deletion of the Crosstown Expressway from plans.

the rights of women, the handicapped and tenants, organizing food and housing co-operatives, dealing directly with the problems of education.

Like Toronto's City Council and School Board, the Social Planning Council was transformed by the reform movement. Between 1968 and 1971 business involvement weakened, and it expanded its interest in community action and, more recently, in the problems of unemployment. The running of the University of Toronto, which had been long in the hands of cautious corporate businessmen, was at least modified by the addition of a new governing council, a change in 1968 that was partly the result of faculty and student action. The businessmen's hold on social services and education, if not entirely pried loose, has certainly been relaxed.[7]

Even though Metro lost the Spadina debate, it operated relatively efficiently under its chairmen—William Allen (1962-1969), Albert Campbell (1969-1973) and Paul Godfrey (1973-1984)—though the province increasingly fired the crucial shots. Despite the continued suburban-city split, during Metro's second era after 1967, a greater measure of equality among local municipalities was achieved. The reduction of thirteen municipalities to six, and a larger number of factories and offices in the suburbs, brought greater equalization in assessment, though York and East York remained weaker. Many social services centralized in Metro improved service throughout the region, but some areas in the postwar suburbs still lack Toronto's level of community services. The reform of the Metro School Board in 1967 led to greater equality of spending on education. But in practice, while suburban trustees on Metro pushed to reduce spending, Toronto's trustees, whether right or left, argued for more spending to improve programs. Metro itself eliminated unequal fare zones on the TTC in 1973, though by 1976 the province paid 30 per cent of its operating costs.[8]

Metro's workings continued to be remote from the people, nevertheless. In 1977 former Premier John Robarts, in another royal commission review of Metro, suggested a much larger council with councillors elected exclusively to Metro, a chairman selected by council from among these, and the enlargement of the two smallest boroughs, York and East York, to increase their taxing capabilities (to the chagrin of North York's mayor). Nothing happened. With (at least in 1968) the 101 commissions, boards and local councils within Metro's boundaries, Metro's structure remained a system that "breaks all the rules of democratic process" with the public "being deprived of a genuine local government." If Robarts's suggestions were followed, party politics would probably become more vigorous, possibly to the greater benefit of the community. Amalgamation, long advocated by Toronto and the newspapers, might also make sense. But the province did not act because the current structure has suited it better.[9]

In contrast to the Gardiner years, the province assumed control over Metro's finances, at least until the mid-1970s. In 1978 Ontario's municipalities supplied only 55 per cent of their needs. The province provided most of the rest, largely through conditional transfer payments. Even while municipal expenditures rose rapidly, the burden of property taxes on urban dwellers fell. But, as a result, governments, "to a considerable extent, are really acting as agents, spending provincial funds on provincially designated activities."[10]

As a city with a more affluent population and an office assessment that steadily pulled ahead of other municipalities, Metro needed less provincial support. By 1974 provincial support amounted to nearly 30 per cent of the Metro system's revenue—education and public transit included—up by a third from 1967. Provincial money went increasingly more toward operating costs and less toward capital projects. Health, education, social services and housing, in that order, were subsidized the most. Since 1978 the trend has reversed, so that more of the onus has fallen on local taxes.[11] (Table XVI)

The province's further intrusion into Metro's affairs was signalled by a limitation of its area. By 1966 Toronto's suburbs were spilling over Metro's limits and its commuter impact was felt even beyond its 720 square-mile planning area. In a series of steps the province expanded its role in the region. Between 1962 and 1968 the province's Metropolitan and Region Transportation Study, covering 3,200 square miles, analyzed wider regional problems. In 1966 it started to consider "Design for Development: Toronto-Centred Region," and in 1970, with a grand flourish, Premier Robarts unveiled a proposal covering 8,600 square miles that would "shape our future and that of our children and their children" (Map 7, p. 167). In the same year Metro's planning area was cut back to Metro limits and the creation of regional governments was just around the corner: York Region to the north in 1971 and Peel to the west and Durham to the east in 1974. Despite howls of protest from Metro politicians and ex-chairman Gardiner, the province asserted its control over the expanding Toronto region. After 1975, as population growth slowed down, the imperative to follow "Design for Development" trickled away.[12]

The identification of Premier Davis as "Mayor Bill" did contain some truth. The Spadina Expressway decision was only his most conspicuous act. Planning, the islands controversy, big cultural and recreational projects, even street widenings, more than ever became provincial matters. "He who pays the piper calls the tune" was the principle in force.

With massive growth of the civil service, the province became Metro's biggest employer. It would be a mistake, however, to see Metro and its municipalities simply as wards of the province. Toronto's governments and volunteer groups were innovative, advocating projects and legislation ranging from a domed stadium to a better deal for the elderly poor to improved school programs. "Mayor Bill" dispensed a lot, but he had to listen a lot as well to serious initiatives coming out of Hogtown.[13]

Many of Toronto's issues were strongly reflected in provincial politics. Increasing politicization in the early 1960s saw the weakening of Tory hegemony, but the electoral battles intensified as New Democrats articulated many social complaints. After substantial gains in Metro in 1967, they suffered a setback in 1971 largely because of the popularity of Davis's Spadina decision. In 1975, however, the party's support of rent control helped win almost half of Metro's seats, a victory that was repeated in 1977 and that left only one Liberal representing Metro—well established city reformer Margaret Campbell. In 1981 apartment dwellers apparently trusted "Mayor Bill" to keep rent control: they did not bother to vote and so the NDP fell to nine seats in Metro, as the Tories gained. Beyond Metro's fringe, the Tories took all seats, reflecting the area's largely affluent character. Provincial Liberals seriously declined in Metro over the period and the NDP was established as the alternative to the Tories. The persistence of Liberals, mostly in southwestern Ontario, maintained a three-way split so that the Conservatives remained in power.[14]

The federal electoral scene in Toronto from 1949 to 1984 was dominated by Liberals, except during the Diefenbaker sweep. By the mid-1960s the Tories had lost their hold on east Toronto to the NDP. From seventeen of twenty seats in Metro in 1968, the Liberals fell to ten in 1972 as the NDP, attacking "corporate welfare bums," gained and the Tories won seats for the first time in ten years—an astonishing fact considering Toronto of old when the Tories took all. In 1974 the pendulum swung back to Trudeau's revived Liberals, who took four-fifths of Toronto's seats. In 1979 the swing was toward the Tories, then back to the Liberals in 1980, and then to the Tories in 1984. In response to reform pressures in Toronto and elsewhere, for a brief while after 1972 the federal government sought a stronger role in cities through the Ministry of State for Urban Affairs. Central (more recently, Canada) Mortgage and Housing Corporation continued as a political football, its level of funding dependent on shifting moods to the right or left, moods not clearly connected to electoral results nor to needs. Nonetheless, its role in housing Torontonians expanded, at least until 1984. Beyond that, the increased involvement in the economy through taxation and crown corporations affected Toronto's performance.

In the politics of this period, two apparently contradictory trends stand out: a rising involvement of the higher levels of government, especially the province, in the affairs of Torontonians; and rising citizen participation as a counterweight to provincial and corporate power. The reformers achieved some modest elements of democratization, slightly stronger land-use planning controls, and thus stability at vulnerable neighbourhood margins. The changes were less marked than those initiated in the 1940s, but enough was accomplished for Toronto to earn the reputation of a "city that works." Although the reform impulse weakened in the mid-1970s, the network of citizen activists could rise again, if Controller Esther Shiner and other North York advocates and Metro Roads Commissioner Sam Cass have a chance of pushing Spadina southward and the Scarborough Expressway eastward. In the meantime, the mini-expressway—the Leslie Street extension—has appeared as a demigod in the pantheon of car worshippers.

THE DRAMATIC CITYSCAPE AND THE LIMITS OF REFORM

Since 1966, a spectacular new skyline, a waterfront transformed for recreation and housing, widespread renovation of old buildings, the appearance of new apartment and office clusters in the suburbs and of "new towns" beyond Metro's boundaries, according to the city's boosters, have lifted Toronto into the league of *weltstadts*—world-class cities.

"Mayor Bill" was a powerful presence in Metro politics, symbolized by ceremonies like the opening of Ontario Place in 1971.

The other dominant provincial politician of the reform era was the eloquent Stephen Lewis, who led the NDP to within a few seats of power in 1975. Provincial Liberals virtually disappeared from the Toronto scene.

There was an unprecedented sprouting of new downtown office towers between the early 1960s when the new City Hall was built and 1974 when the city attempted to control growth. Following the Toronto-Dominion's first of three black towers came the silvery Commerce Court, then the seventy-two storey First Canadian Place of the Bank of Montreal (and later another tower), and finally the golden Royal Bank Plaza, located on what had been wholesalers' territory for more than a century. Moving from Montreal to Toronto, Canada's largest insurance company, Sun Life, built two office towers which added a million square feet to downtown office development and contributed to a shift of development to the west, as did the construction of Roy Thomson Hall, the new CN hotel and the convention centre (finally completed in 1984 after years of discussion). Although these structures provided space for a wide range of ancillary business services, other less conspicuous buildings were added for growing needs. Other insurance firms expanded along University and along Bloor East. The province, before its spending retrenchment in 1975, had built up the area east of Queen's Park and constructed the striking Ontario Hydro building at University and College. The Eaton Centre, a super shopping arcade, brought the Yorkdale model downtown with Eaton's and Simpsons anchoring the ends. On the central waterfront, a new hotel and apartment tower and Harbourfront, a new recreation area, replaced derelict docks, and the new *Toronto Star* building created a totally new appearance. The 1912 plan promoting manufacturing is nothing but a memory, as is the 1959 assertion that Toronto would become a "major" world port. The most overwhelming structure built was the CN Tower to transmit electronic impulses and to persuade Torontonians in its shadow that they stood at the top.

By 1982 the central corridor north to Eglinton contained more than 50 million square feet of office space, up from about 20 million in 1962 — an increase planners in 1959 hardly predicted. The financial district contained nearly half of this. Especially after 1975, as the suburbs experienced more office development, Toronto's share of office space fell. Indicating shifting employment patterns, the office corridor expanded while manufacturing, warehousing and other districts declined in the inner city. But employment over the period did not grow as rapidly as floor space: Toronto's affluent head offices supplied more working space to employees. From another perspective, redevelopment for offices helped to stabilize Toronto's share of Metro's tax base at around 40 per cent after dropping rapidly between 1955 and 1965.[15]

Downtown, midtown and suburban office development was not shaped without political struggles. Although citizen groups were more concerned about residential high-rise intrusions, by 1970 the Metro Centre project had become a focus of controversy. Proposed by the real estate arms of the railways, it would have resulted in several office towers on the site of Union Station, a new transportation terminal, and housing on the now partly disused rail lands to the west. The vast majority of council members were enthusiastic and, as they did for so many developers between 1965 and 1972, made concessions in their head-over-heels pursuit of more and more. The Ontario Municipal Board, however, forced the council and the developer to accept the planning staff prescriptions for open space. Equally important was the stiff resistance by citizens to tearing down Union Station, a landmark of half a century. The railways backed off the project, though the CN Tower and convention centre were subsequently built.[16]

Eaton Centre was another focus of fierce debate particularly because several architects' proposals for the centre called for the demolition of the elegant 1899 City Hall. Again the heritage impulse galvanized action as a few stalwarts of preservation fought tooth and nail, successfully, as it turned out: Eaton Centre was redesigned. Another problem was access to Yonge Street, but a cold winter's day made the indoor mall more appealing. The "strip" north of Dundas Street remained for young people.[17]

By 1972 it was apparent to a majority of voters that downtown development was getting out of hand and threatening neighbourhoods. Politicians were ready to give away, it seemed, every old building. So the reform council slapped on a forty-five-foot holding bylaw, which the Urban Development Institute did not like. While it remained controversial and earned lawyers tidy sums in litigation, it did allow the city breathing space to proceed with the Central Area Plan. Completed in 1976, it moderated some of the outlandish pro-development features of the 1969 official plan for Toronto in the quest for stability. For the central area, following the reform agenda, planners argued for the retention of low-rise neighbourhoods, more core housing (to offset the after-hour bleakness of office districts), more parks and recreation, some building design guidelines, avoidance of transit and auto congestion and, not least, a decentralization of office development. The council's objective was

The great growth impulse initiated by suburban development after the war shifted to the downtown after 1960. Although the Bank of Toronto's classical 1912 head office was levelled to make way for the T-D Centre, the Bank of Commerce retained its tower of 1929 when it built Commerce Court.

The climax of downtown development was the erection of the CN Tower, the only clear effect of CN-CP's Metro Centre plan for the railway lands in the early 1970s. The scheme would have seen Union Station replaced by office towers and a new transportation centre.

to hold central area office development in 1981 to about 62 million square feet and to 75 million in 1991. Through *Metroplan*, Metro planners also took up the call for decentralizaton into outlying centres.[18]

Whether through the design of planners or of developers, a lot of deconcentration occurred: in 1981 the level reached downtown was nearly 10 per cent less than expected. At the current rate of activity, the 1976 prediction is not likely to be achieved. A.E. LePage projected that the 6 million square feet of new office space available in the central area in 1983 would contribute further to a rising vacancy rate. In fact, it concluded that "there may not be a single building completed in the Financial Core of Toronto in 1985!" The boomtown rhetoric still heard even in the crisis year of 1982, as Calgary and Edmonton were slumping, became muted by the summer of 1983. Expectations for "a giant downtown 'wonderland'" for the railway lands, however, still danced in the heads of politicians and developers. As a retiring gesture, Premier Davis unveiled plans for a domed stadium of debatable merit and likely excessive cost.[19]

The reformers' opposition to public redevelopment was transformed into a new style. Trefann Court was not totally razed but, after years of wrangling, only a few of the original protesters ended up in new houses. However, superblock public redevelopment in older residential areas ceased. In 1973 the city embarked on a housing program redeveloping derelict railway and industrial sites. On the old Esplanade, the St. Lawrence project of 3,500 units was constructed, only this time on the principles of architectural diversity, including people of differing incomes and a variety of tenures. Among other projects, several small-scale infill schemes were artfully constructed, thanks to residents and architects like Jack Diamond and Barton Myers. But the waiting lists grew longer.[20]

Massive private redevelopment for high-rise apartments generated even more opposition than public projects. Before 1965 there were no apartments over twenty storeys. Within Metro in 1965 there were 8; by 1973, 142. The city's 1969 plan promoted development by designating the land west of Jarvis to Yonge and between Bloor and Queen for high-rise. Much of the area west of Yonge to Spadina was reserved for what promised to be an ever-expanding university and for high-rise. And around subway stations the high-density blobs on the map spread outward. Sussex residents may have fought successfully between 1966 and 1969 to delete the designation over their area, but most other areas could not. William

The city's largest cluster of high-rise apartments, St. James Town, was a proud achievement for developers and their political allies but a source of alienation for reformers.

After 1973 a new style of public housing appeared. The St. Lawrence neighbourhood, straddling former rail lands on the Esplanade, mixed housing styles, types of tenure and incomes, as the city of Toronto once again became a public developer. In the early 1980s federal restraint policies slowed down social housing programs.

Dennison, the protector of the Sherbourne-Wellesley-Parliament-Bloor area in the mid-1950s (and ridiculed by the developers), became one of the most eager for private redevelopment. Most of City Council was hooked by the maxim that bigness equalled progress and the increased assessment it was thought to bring. A study of York Borough was to undercut this notion.[21]

St. James Town was only the most impressive array of clusters of high-rise apartments sprouting up everywhere. In tune with the Urban Development Institute's goal of providing a "total environment," the developers, Belmont and Meridian, decided to construct "a city within a city." The 15 buildings (including some already built) in the cluster provided nearly 6,000 units. The density of floor space to land area was very high. The YMCA was brought in to plan and run recreational facilities. Open space which counted for bonusing was not open to the public.[22]

By the time the reform battle had heated up in 1970, St. James Town was completed as were some other clusters. But Meridian was moving on West and South St. James Town, and several others—such as Lionstar, Quebec-Gothic and Windlass—raised the reform ire. In 1973 some of these were modified with lower structures. In the central area plan of 1976 and subsequent neighbourhood plans, some of the territory allocated in 1969 was deleted or reduced. Since then a substantial number of high-rise residential buildings were built in the central core, but most of them were luxury condominiums.[23]

The reaction to high-rise development arose because many people objected to this style of family living and especially because they wanted to keep Toronto low-rise at medium densities. Preservation of neighbourhoods meant also the preservation of older houses. The modest number of professionals who stayed in or moved into the Annex and some other districts before 1965 became a flood, especially after 1972. "Whitepainting" became widespread. Working-class houses were improved, and many were "gentrified," that is, gutted and redone by owners and increasingly by speculative contractors. To the planners in 1944, the older the housing the worse it was: this formula was turned upside down. Undoubtedly, this change clearly distinguished Toronto from most large American cities where gentrification and urban homesteading of abandoned housing was less noticeable. Private "vendor take-back" mortgages were common in immigrant areas and probably helped this process along. One of the results was a more affluent inner city with fewer people taking more space. Consequently, after peaking in the early 1970s, the population of Toronto and York and then East York fell markedly.[24]

The Toronto islands community stood out in the process of stabilizing neighbourhoods. The program of removing all housing (most of it originally built as summer cottages) to make way for Metro parkland began in 1956 and was resisted well before the reform impulse took a firm hold. When most leases for the remaining houses on Ward's and Algonquin islands expired in 1968, the people did not move. After more than another decade of wrangling, the province interceded in favour of the city and the islanders to the dismay of Metro politicians (though a final resolution of tenure issues has not been reached). However, conditions had certainly changed from the 1960s: the islands had become relatively less important for recreation than anticipated. They were no longer so clearly a cheap leisure spot for immigrants. Also, a strong reform notion of mixed land uses was clearly expressed on the islands: far more people by then agreed that the park was considered safer, and even more pleasurable, with people living there. In Toronto's inimitable fashion, ferries continued their runs and decades-old dreams of bridges and tunnels faded.[25]

Suburbanization continued on the fringe. But within Metro every five-year census after 1956 showed a slowing down of population growth. As in the inner city, however, development was aided by the relatively large number of new, if smaller, households that could afford more space. By 1971 North York and Etobicoke had virtually stabilized. In Metro only Scarborough, slower off the mark, continued to expand. Losses elsewhere brought Metro's population growth to a halt. In the boomtown 1960s, the cautious estimates of 1959 had given way to optimistic projections. Even as late as 1978, Metro politicians and planners were shocked when they finally realized what was happening.[26] (Tables I, II)

As manufacturing growth slowed, the most significant developments within Metro occurred in office parks and in nodal town centres. Office space in the metropolitan area outside the central corridor (up to Eglinton) increased from 12 per cent in 1967 to 36 per cent in 1982. Following the city's and Metro's decentralizaton policy of 1976, the Don Valley office corridor grew significantly, as did the North York Civic Centre, the Scarborough Town Centre and, more modestly, the Etobicoke Civic Centre. As for housing, by the early 1970s the rate of production had slowed. The Malvern

Since 1956, when Metro began to tear down houses and cottages, the Islands community has been a source of controversy. Advocates of pure parkland met increasing resistance from residents and their mainland supporters, as in this rally in 1980. The debate has been so divisive — like that over the Spadina Expressway — that Queen's Park has had to step in.

project in northeastern Scarborough on publicly assembled land provided a large number of moderately priced houses. Public housing for families was constructed by the Ontario Housing Corporation at a rapid pace between 1965 and 1975. And Metro built for senior citizens.[27]

Outside Metro's boundaries growth was substantial. Between 1965 and 1975 the province showed a strong interest in planning the fringe zone and the Toronto-centred Region through its "Design for Development" (Map 7). As announced in 1970, "Design" proposed three zones in an arc drawn ninety miles from downtown Toronto: Zone One, the "lakeshore urbanized area," which could expect 5.7 million people by the year 2,000 living in "identifiable" communities to the east and west of Toronto; Zone Two, the "commutershed," in which development would be severely limited to the Yonge Street axis to preserve good agricultural land; Zone Three included "growth poles" for industry at Midland, Barrie, Port Hope, Cobourg and other places.[28]

Spatial expansion was not uniform on all flanks of Metro. As earlier and always, the western sector was more attractive than the eastern, except in Markham. Gobbling up good farmland, Mississauga and Brampton in Peel Region were the fastest growing. By the mid-1960s, the large developers had hatched new towns, all to the west and all very large: Bramalea, Meadowvale, Erin Mills and Mississauga Town Centre. They were designed to house a considerably denser population in town houses and terraced apartments than Don Mills and other subdivisions of the 1950s. Square One in Mississauga not only surpassed Yorkdale's shopping space, it also became an office centre and the site of the City Hall. The corporate city had arrived![29]

There were several attempts to pull development to the east. The most striking proposal put forward by the province was a cluster of new towns such as Seaton in North Pickering. After debate over a number of sites, in 1972 the federal government announced plans for Toronto's second international airport just to the north of these new towns. Although vigorously opposed by a well organized opposition group, "People or Planes," both governments bought up thousands of acres for their respective projects. But as growth slowed, both sets of plans faded away, leaving bitterness among the expropriated and the agricultural land rented out to agribusiness. "Design for Development" was hardly more successful than Toronto's 1943 plan to create a symmetrical city. So the mayors of places adjacent to Metro continue to vie with one another for development with nineteenth-century boosterism and what regional planning remains is *ad hoc*, although still very much in the hands of the province.[30]

As for expressways, Davis's pronouncement against Spadina did make some sense from a traffic flow perspective. Without the 400 extension down Christie-Grace (through working-class, ethnic neighbourhoods) and, most importantly, with the already deleted crosstown link to the Don Valley Parkway, there could be no inner box or ring, no system. So the logic of the "balanced" transportation plan had been undercut. Wherever Spadina was stopped, it would dump cars into existing streets. Better to stop it at Lawrence—or at least Eglinton—than farther down. In the wake of the 1971 decision yet another transportation study rejected the Scarborough Expressway—to the delight of opposition groups solidly organized from Riverdale to Scarborough. The 400 extension, called Black Creek Drive, was extended to Eglinton. None of the proposed expressways was actually dead, and the roads lobby continued to mutter. Elsewhere, provincial expressways—a redone 401, 403 to Hamilton, 404, 407 northern bypass (pending), 409 to the airport and 427, all on the 1943 city plan or on provincial drawing boards soon after the war—were constructed when needed with little opposition. Car registration continued to rise, rush-hour congestion worsened at points, commuting from the Toronto region to jobs in Metro's outer suburbs and beyond rose, but the need for inner-city expressways was not established.[31]

Although Metro planners in the mid 1960s advocated a "balanced" transportation system, public transit would have come out much worse had expressways not been stopped. The TTC marched on as before, winning North American safety awards. In 1980 ridership rose in ratio to population for the first time since the 1950s. And in late 1981 Toronto passed larger Chicago in absolute numbers. In contrast to virtually all American cities, Toronto kept the streetcar, though the number fell. The TTC carried about half as many riders as New York's system, and Montreal's only half as many as Toronto's, and it compared favourably with some, but not all, systems in European cities. Permanent provincial subsidies for operating costs (though relatively lower than those awarded to other Ontario cities) helped. Since the 1966 opening of the Bloor-Danforth subway, the TTC twice added more track to both ends and built the Spadina line, which turned out to be less successful than

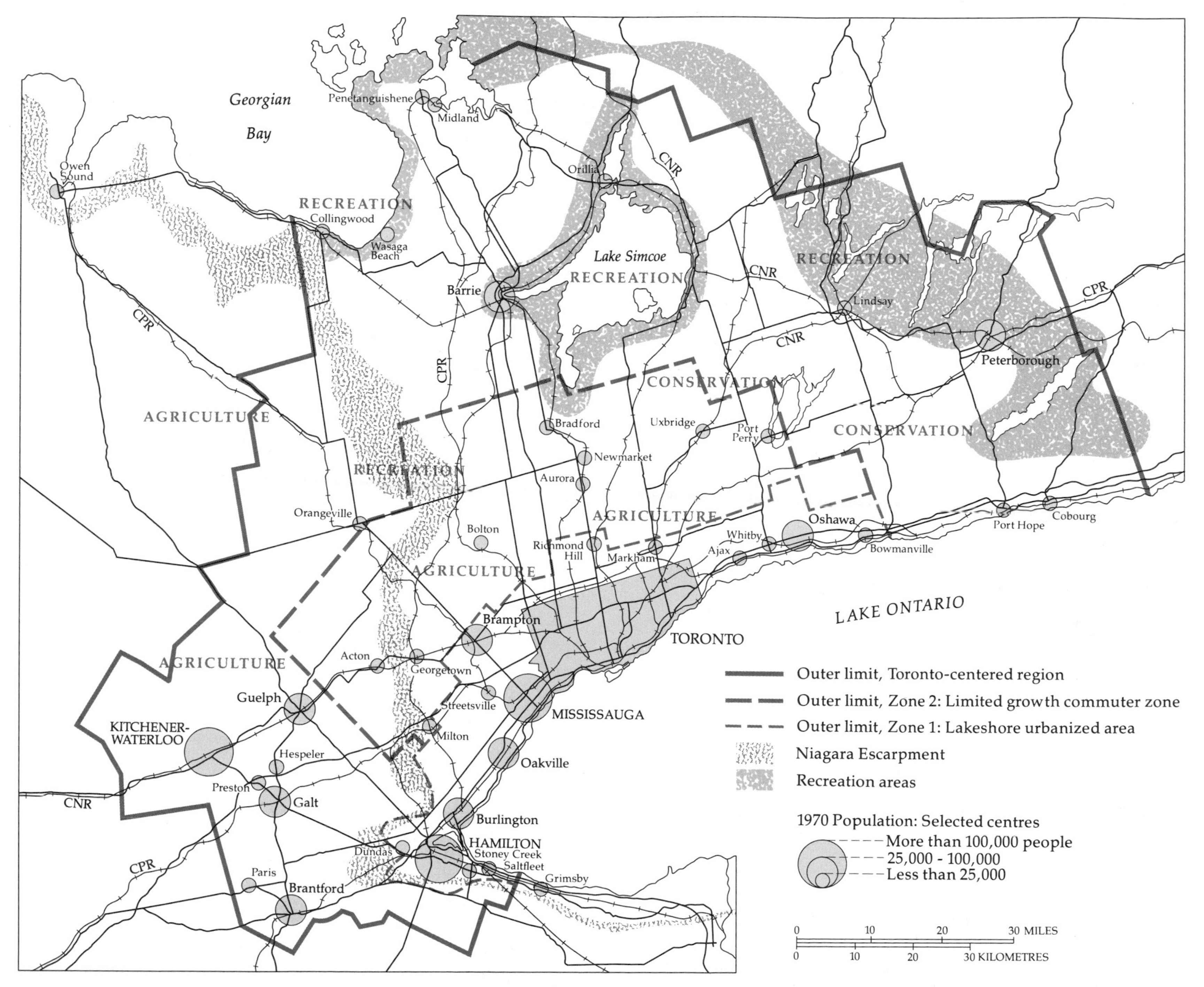

7 Toronto-centered Region Plan, 1970: The province's "Design for Development" was provoked by the expansion of Toronto's metropolitan area beyond Metro boundaries. This venture in large-scale planning was shelved in 1975, but some elements have been followed. Regional governments were set up in the early 1970s.

the others. With spiralling construction costs, "intermediate" lines were proposed. The Scarborough Town Centre line from the east end of the Bloor-Danforth subway will open in 1985; the location of a proposed east-west northern line continues to be debated. The province's entry into the transit vehicle-making business has been a factor in pressing Metro and the TTC to build a waterfront line and even another subway from the east into downtown. Beyond Metro's boundaries, municipal systems staked by the province connect to the subways. Heavily subsidized GO trains and buses, begun in 1967 and operated by the Toronto Area Operating Authority, passively encouraged living at a distance, big-city style.[32] (Table XV)

Energy conservation was a major factor in redirecting the 1950s pro-car attitude and even in encouraging commuting by bicycle. Although a total energy balance for the city and region was not worked out, among large North American cities, Toronto possessed a better record on waste than most, largely because of public transit. Unlike Los Angeles residents, Torontonians could at least choose whether or not to own a car. As elsewhere, hydro consumption per capita slowed down, and Toronto moved on several specific conservation projects, such as burning garbage to heat large buildings and introducing energy-saving features to the building regulations. Municipalities moved modestly on the recycling of newspapers, cans and bottles. They provided allotment gardens, though not nearly to the extent that European cities did.[33]

Yet the waste remained enormous. The energy companies, including an overly optimistic Ontario Hydro, encouraged more and more consumption — the cult of "moreness," to cite McLuhan. The Beare Road disposal site just east of Metro Zoo became a mountain. Chemical disposal problems in Stouffville and the Junction area affected health. The infamous Mississauga evacuation in 1981, after a rail accident threatened to let loose a cloud of chlorine, revealed the vulnerability of the population along rail lines. Residents of McClure Crescent in Scarborough realized the dangers of low-level radioactivity dumped on the site before their houses were built. Heavy metals sitting on the bottom of Toronto Harbour led to debates about whether dredging was safe or not. Even Lake Ontario, the great cleanser, was invaded by deadly dioxin from dumps in Niagara Falls, New York. Toronto's cottagers worried about acid rain on northern lakes. In the summer of 1983 Toronto beaches were polluted by faulty sewage disposal, a situation everyone thought had been settled in the 1950s by Gardiner's giant construction company — Metro.

DIVERSIONS AND BREAD

Visible on the cityscape are Toronto's elegant playgrounds for the affluent. Ontario Place, Harbourfront, the Ontario Science Centre, the Metropolitan Zoo, the planetarium, additions to the Royal Ontario Museum, an expanded Art Gallery of Ontario, Canada's Wonderland, a renovated Exhibition Stadium for baseball and Roy Thomson Hall show that Toronto has been getting more than the lion's share of Ontario's spectacles. Again the province was the prime mover, promoting and financing schemes to show that Toronto was a world-class city. Its role as an aesthetic and amusement entrepreneur was triggered by Montreal's Expo 67 and was in full flight just as it began to reduce the level of spending on education in 1970. By 1975 this thrust had largely run its course. Retrenchment in social services set in too. By then, some areas in the postwar suburbs were matching inner-city poverty pockets. Despite cutbacks, public agencies became more and more the financiers of housing as the crisis reappeared in 1980. By the summer of 1983 even emergency food supplies for the poor ran out: the lack of bread, in the most literal sense, loomed again. All the gains in human services seemed threatened.

Ontario Place opened in time for the 1971 election. As Ontario's "show case," it was also intended to be Ontario's response to Expo, to brighten up the CNE grounds, and to enliven the waterfront. A tour of the four exhibit pods was to provide an experience of the "Ontario personality." More successful, however, were Cinesphere, the Forum with its top-flight artists and the children's playground. Though it was not debated in the legislature, the entire project was wholly provincial; neither Metro nor the city was seriously involved in the planning. But, unlike Montreal's two spectacles — Expo and the Olympics — Ontario Place did not burden either the city or the province with awkward debts. The smaller scale of Ontario Place again proved Fred Gardiner's point that caution in spending is better — though he would have used the money on roads instead. The return to free enterprise brought yet another megaentertainment project in the late 1970s, Canada's Wonderland, an American corporate enterprise of the Disneyland genre.[34]

Rising incomes for everyone (up to 1975), fuller provincial coffers and the example of Expo in Montreal persuaded provincial politicians to provide diversions for the masses. Ontario Place was the most conspicuous. Across Lakeshore Boulevard, beer came to the ballpark in 1982, to Metro Chairman Paul Godfrey's pleasure.

Not to be outdone by the province, in 1972 the federal government handed over the waterfront lands between York and Bathurst streets to a crown corporation. Not nearly as spectacular as Ontario Place, Harbourfront has developed incrementally, with considerable public input. Besides recreation, housing is being gradually added, though the weakening of government support has limited the level of lower-income housing. Elsewhere along the lakeshore, more and more boats set out from more sailing clubs, and the Conservation Authority has added its tinier versions of landfill parks to the east and west. The gradually extended spit has become the home of Ring-billed Gulls (more than Toronto really needs), terns and Black-crowned Night Herons, as boaters and naturalists have continued debating its future uses.[35]

Several of the large projects were educational as well as recreational. The Ontario Science Centre—designed by Raymond Moriyama, one of Toronto's many creative architects—delighted hordes of tourists and busloads of school children. The Metro Zoo opened in 1974 and became known one of the world's best in preserving some threatened species. The genteel, expanded Royal Ontario Museum attracted many to see its totem poles and dinosaurs. And, as elsewhere in central Toronto's rich environment, the Portuguese peanut vendors outside suffered heat and cold to make ends meet.[36]

On the sports front, Exhibition Stadium took on a new aura. In 1977 the Blue Jays and baseball became the major attraction. The Argonauts, after three decades of floundering, finally recovered respectability in 1983. Professional soccer was only moderately successful in attracting fans. Meanwhile, neither Harold Ballard nor his players seemed interested in winning the Stanley Cup, which they last brought home in 1967. As for amateur sports, Varsity football hardly attracted anyone nor did other university team sports, though lots of players have been involved. For team sports, the University of Toronto budgeted only 5 per cent of the amount spent by the University of Maryland. More money, it seems, has been devoted more sensibly, if inadequately, to the fabric of the city and social programs rather than to sports.[37]

With the Art Gallery of Ontario (AGO) and the Ontario College of Art located in the heart of the city and the famous McMichael Collection of the Group of Seven located nearby at Kleinburg, Toronto was clearly the art centre of the province, if not the country. Additions to the AGO in the late 1970s allowed it to show more of its collection and more Henry Moore's sculptures, but the expansion also convinced the board of directors that the gallery should go mega too. The Van Gogh and King Tut shows were feathers in the board's cap, but the cost proved to be too high and retrenchment set in. As signs of Toronto's cosmopolitanism and economic success, the number of art galleries and art dealers increased enormously, especially between 1966 and the mid-1970s. Not all art was locked up in galleries: subway stations on the Spadina line and at Queen and Yonge stations began exhibiting exceptional art work to cheer up harried commuters.[38]

The performing arts expanded as never before until hard times hit the most financially vulnerable theatres. In 1965 there were only four small theatres; by 1976, twenty-two. The "surprising shortage" of small theatre space was solved by converting old warehouses. Government subsidies helped promote innovative theatre, as did the increasing affluent professional population in the central city where most of the action took place. The new theatres revealed a rising concern for Canadian plays at a time when Canadian nationalism was showing up in the writing of the burgeoning corps of such Toronto authors as Margaret Atwood. The great burst of theatrical creativity put Toronto among the top cities in the world, even if on a shoestring.[39]

In a seemingly more fun-loving Toronto, the tempo of music production picked up. The Mariposa Festival and Caribana on the islands brought popular folk music to the city. Rock concerts attracted hugh audiences to Maple Leaf Gardens and Exhibition Stadium. For the higher brows, the Toronto Symphony and the Mendelssohn Choir finally moved from Massey Hall to the new Roy Thomson Hall. Ontario or Toronto Hall might have been a more appropriate name since the taxpayers shouldered the biggest share of its construction costs. They now face appeals for a new opera house and ballet theatre.

The massive outpouring of public and private funds for entertainment showed that Toronto could be among the best. Old mores and institutions were shed, but not quite all. In 1984 the Royal Winter Fair was well into its second half-century and in 1978 the Canadian National Exhibition passed its century mark. While hands were wrung over the old-fashioned and shabby character of the place, the Ex lumbered on as the final summer escape for ordinary people. And if Sunday mornings were less sacred, Sunday store openings were still resisted by many. Nostalgia became an industry.

The ability not only to accept a diversity of cultures, but even to celebrate it, at least nominally, is a sign of how much Toronto has changed since it was "the Belfast of North America." With annual events like Caribana, a festival of Caribbean culture, Toronto celebrates its multiculturalism.

While Toronto scaled down its budget for its 1984 sesquicentennial, the province peddled once again the notion that Ontario has been the place to stand since 1784 when the first Loyalists arrived. While the diversions kept coming, lots of people still sat on their front porches (or, more often, on their balconies) on hot summer evenings, some because they could not afford much of what made Toronto an exciting and entertaining city to live in.

Poverty persisted for many Torontonians. Conditions worsened after 1975 as the province cut back support for the proportion of the population living below the Social Planning Council's, even Statistics Canada's, poverty line. It was not that the problem of poverty was ignored: in the late 1960s, federal government commissions on poverty and housing responded to yet another dimension of the reform wave. Alternative reports were more critical and the "Just Society" organized the poor.[40]

In 1962 Metro Planner Murray Jones expected a sharp contrast between the affluent new suburbs and a poor inner city. By the mid-1970s this was clearly not the case: the inner city was an appealing place to live for higher-paid professionals. In 1979 the Social Planning Council's *Metro's Suburbs in Transition* showed that the new majority in the three postwar suburbs was composed of poor recent immigrants, single mothers with young children, young people facing increasing unemployment, and elderly residents without term deposits to generate incomes. These people did not have the support of an institutional network which had developed over the years in the city. The image of the traditional family with two small children had to give way. Although a few suburban politicians were fully aware of these conditions, the planning council's report and the *Star*'s publicity were needed to jar councils into recognizing that "the era of suburban and metropolitan innocence is over." Task forces were set up to develop stronger community services, including group homes for the alienated and dispossessed, and to push the TTC to improve service for captive riders without cars.[41]

In the early 1980s the city departments of Housing and of Planning and Development and the Metro Planning Department still pointed to a "crisis" in housing. In the early 1970s when the vacancy rate rose to the unusually high level of 3 per cent, it seemed that private and public sector housing production was finally alleviating the problem. But shortages and high rents led to rent review by 1975, the year the Ontario Housing Corporation stopped produc-

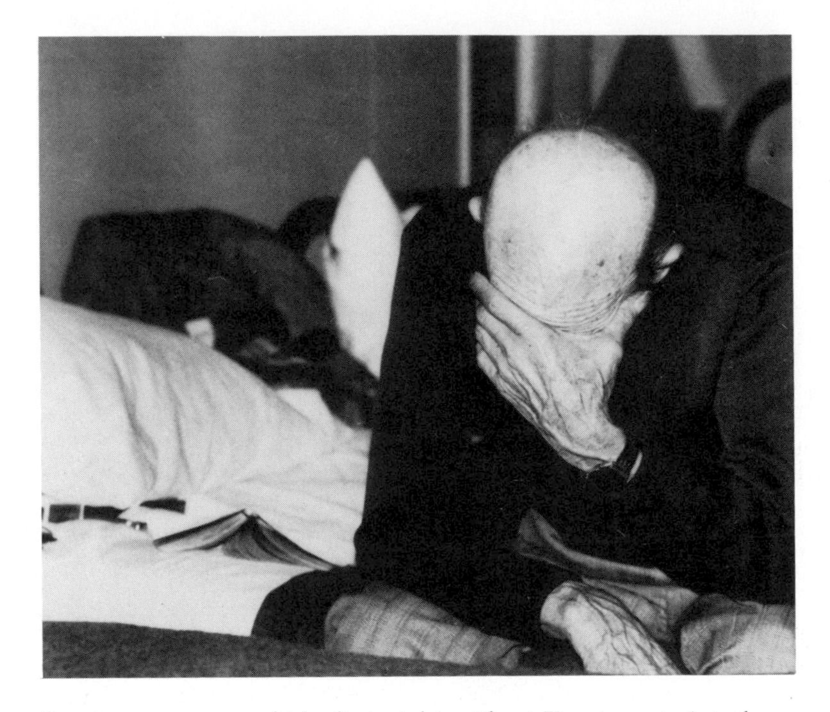

Poverty was never completely eliminated in affluent Toronto — in fact, the problem has worsened since cutbacks began in 1975. Additional emergency hostels appeared in the early 1980s as the recession swelled the numbers of homeless citizens. Many of the down-and-out found shelter in overcrowded prisons.

ing public units. The crisis as always was a shortage of rental shelter for low-income families, especially those supported by single mothers, and for senior citizens. At the end of 1982, 10,000 names were on the city's public-housing waiting list. The filtering-down notion — the older the housing the more it passes on to the poor — was finally recognized as a largely irrelevant solution, however, particularly as older housing actually appreciated in value.[42]

Establishing social housing solidly as a concept, if more fragilely as a reality, was a significant achievement of the reform movement. In contrast to the earlier goal of providing public housing as a privilege, the principle of decent housing as a right was adopted by Toronto. Housing as a right led Toronto's reform council to the mixing of incomes in public housing and into supporting group homes. By 1982 Cityhome provided about 3 per cent of Toronto's housing stock in St. Lawrence and other projects. In Metro as a whole, about 5 per cent was public, compared to only 2 per cent in 1965, through the efforts of the Ontario Housing Corporation and two Metro agencies. If co-operatives and limited dividend and rent-geared-to-income housing were added, nearly 10 per cent of Metro's stock could be described as "social." If all housing subsidized by government were included, possibly half the housing could be called "social." In fact, in 1976 a developer observed: "If subsidies stopped today, the level of housing starts would probably drop by more than 50 per cent." While the City of Toronto took the lead in mixing incomes, at least half of the old-style public housing was in the postwar suburbs. The suburbs, however, were reluctant to accept group homes for the handicapped, for ex-psychiatric patients and especially for ex-criminals. The affluent northern corridor in Toronto and North York and central Etobicoke have yet to see much of either public housing or group homes.[43]

Meanwhile, the number of renters increased. In 1971 and again in 1981, about 45 per cent of households in the metropolitan area were occupied by tenants. Rent control helped after 1975, but weaknesses in the system were exposed: after 1980 owners who did not go before the rent review board raised rents well above the prescribed 6 per cent; owners renovated their buildings to earn higher rents; and the number of post-1975 buildings, excluded from review, increased.

As in other sectors of the economy, speculation has driven land costs so high that public presence is likely to increase as the private sector delivers fewer and fewer rental units but more and more expensive condominiums. A major question will be whether co-operatives and tenant organizations can bring a measure of collective democracy, of self-management, to a higher level than exists at present.[44] (Table XIV)

Reforms in school programs were extensive particularly in the wake of the 1968 Hall-Dennis Report, *Living and Learning*, "the most radical and bold document ever to originate from the bureaucratic labyrinth of the provincial department of education." The old progressive view of child-centred education came to the fore: young people needed help "to cope with the accelerated rate of social change." Even before the report appeared, Toronto had been moving in this direction, setting up public alternative schools at both elementary and secondary levels and developing special education programs. With Regent Park mothers arguing that their children were not learning to read and write, inner-city programs were set up to help low-income children. The controversial book, *Cries from the Corridor*, highlighted inner-city problems in Jane-Finch schools. These initiatives had to share formula-finance dollars with new language programs.[45]

Balancing funds for upper middle-class interest in special education and French-language programs with working-class, inner-city and third-language programs, and then all of these with enrolments in regular classes, was a challenge. Ironically, teaching specific skills in high schools never reached the promise of the early 1960s. Even the infatuation with electronic media that led Education Minister Bill Davis in 1968 to assert "that each student must be taught ... above all, to communicate with computers" did not strengthen technical education. Toronto and Ontario remained dependent on immigrants to supply skills. The problem was that everyone waited for private industry to train apprentices.[46]

Although the "service state" was apparently completed, after 1975 it began eroding. Implementing "living and learning" cost a lot. But as early as November 1969, restraint was imposed on education costs by the province. Improvements in other social services continued for a while as the federal government funded half the cost of family benefits and general welfare assistance and a large share of medical insurance. The 1975 audit of the province's books triggered further restraint. By 1979 Ontario had sunk to ninth place in social spending per capita and seventh in social assistance per capita. So Metro had to pick up more of the social costs. Further expansion — day care, for example — was largely left to private arrangements, including corporate sponsors. In the early 1980s, some public services were contracted out or privatized.[47]

THE POPULATION DIVERSIFIES AND AGES

In the late 1950s Toronto discovered that it was changing. Immigrants began overwhelming the city's British traditions, and the notion of multiculturalism developed gradually, as the term "New Canadian" was shed. Toronto was caught up in the youth culture in the 1960s and then, as the baby boomers began nudging forty, it turned its attention to the problems of an aging population.

The multiculturalism impetus arose partly from the civil rights movement in the U.S. and partly from the quiet revolution in Quebec. Bilingualism and biculturalism were the channels by which Pierre Trudeau especially sought to maintain Canadian unity, and this process triggered a reaction from other ethnic groups. Unlike Quebec, with its francophone population in an English-speaking continent, Ontario and Toronto could accept ethnic pluralism much more easily, even if before 1945 that could hardly have been predicted.[48]

In 1974 the Toronto School Board set up the Work Group on Multicultural Programs. As effort went into improving the education of immigrant, and particularly working-class, children, many Torontonians were ready to agree that being British was just like being Slovenian — except, of course, that everyone would speak English. Many ethnic groups taught language classes in schools. The provincial government finally agreed to finance heritage language programs across the province, a move that was at least justified by the belief that immigrant children would learn English more easily if they had facility in their native tongues. In Metro, where a third of the population did not have English as its mother language, thirty heritage languages were being offered by 1983, though the debate continued on how they could be fitted into the programs of schools.[49]

The heritage languages program recognized Metro's remarkable ethnic mix, with perhaps as many as 200 groups represented. By 1961 the number of immigrants from western and eastern Europe was already receding as the number of southern Europeans, particularly Italians, was increasing. By the mid-1960s people were coming from most other parts of the globe and bringing with them exotic customs and traditions. Only a few came as refugees, notably the "boat people" from Viet Nam and others from Chile. By 1981, while Italians and Jews still led Metro's ethnic list, Chinese, Portuguese, Greeks and blacks (predominantly from the Caribbean) were next, all exceeding the previously larger German, Polish, Ukrainian and French groups. The British share continued to fall to less than half. As another result, the religious mix became much more varied, even while Roman Catholics far outstripped the large Protestant groups. (Tables VII, VIII, IX)

Spatially, the "British" still dominated Rosedale and other areas to the north. The Jews were concentrated up Bathurst, though now spreading over to Bayview as well. Together, these groups were overrepresented in the northern high-income sector. The other "older" ethnic groups became more scattered. (Maps 8, 9, 10, 11, pp. 176-77). While still concentrated in the band to the northwest from St. Clair and Dufferin, Italians actually fell as a proportion of Metro's population as many moved into the fringe suburbs. Most concentrated still were the Portuguese in west-central Toronto. The next group was the Chinese but they were considerably less concentrated. Poles and Ukrainians still were anchored adjacent to High Park but were gradually moving. Greeks congregated along the Danforth, but concentrated neighbourhoods were less conspicuous than in High Park. The longstanding west-central reception area decreased in importance as immigrant reception areas were scattered throughout the postwar suburbs, most noticeably in high-rise projects. Toronto remains only slightly more segregated than Vancouver or Winnipeg.[50]

Among the latter-day immigrants, the Portuguese — many coming from the Azores and other Atlantic islands — composed the largest group. The 70,000 or so constituted the largest cluster in Canada and, like the Italians, probably the largest outside their homeland (Brazil excepted). It was after 1953 that they began coming in increasingly larger numbers and, like most poor immigrants with rural backgrounds and skills, they started off in humble occupations. But by scrimping and saving they bought homes and stores, and the few elite ran travel agencies and real estate offices. They set up their own churches, celebrations, credit unions and newspapers. Although Portuguese communities emerged in Brampton, Oakville and Mississauga, the largest by far was near Kensington Market, where families lived in brightly painted houses. In fact, that formerly Jewish cluster of small shops was

The multicultural impulse resulted in heritage language programs in public schools.

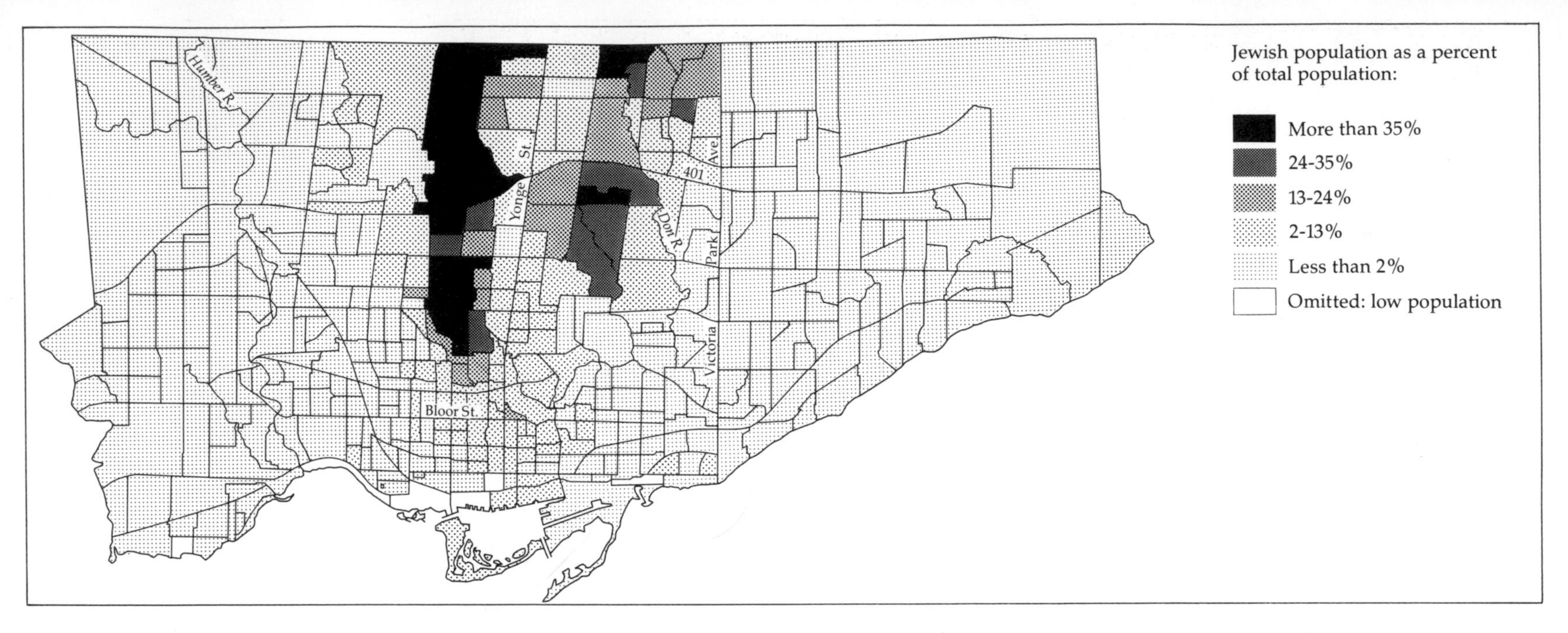

8 Distribution of Jewish Population in Metro Toronto, 1981: Jews were originally concentrated downtown. As this breakout by census tract shows, after 1945 they expanded up the Bathurst corridor and, more recently, along Bayview.

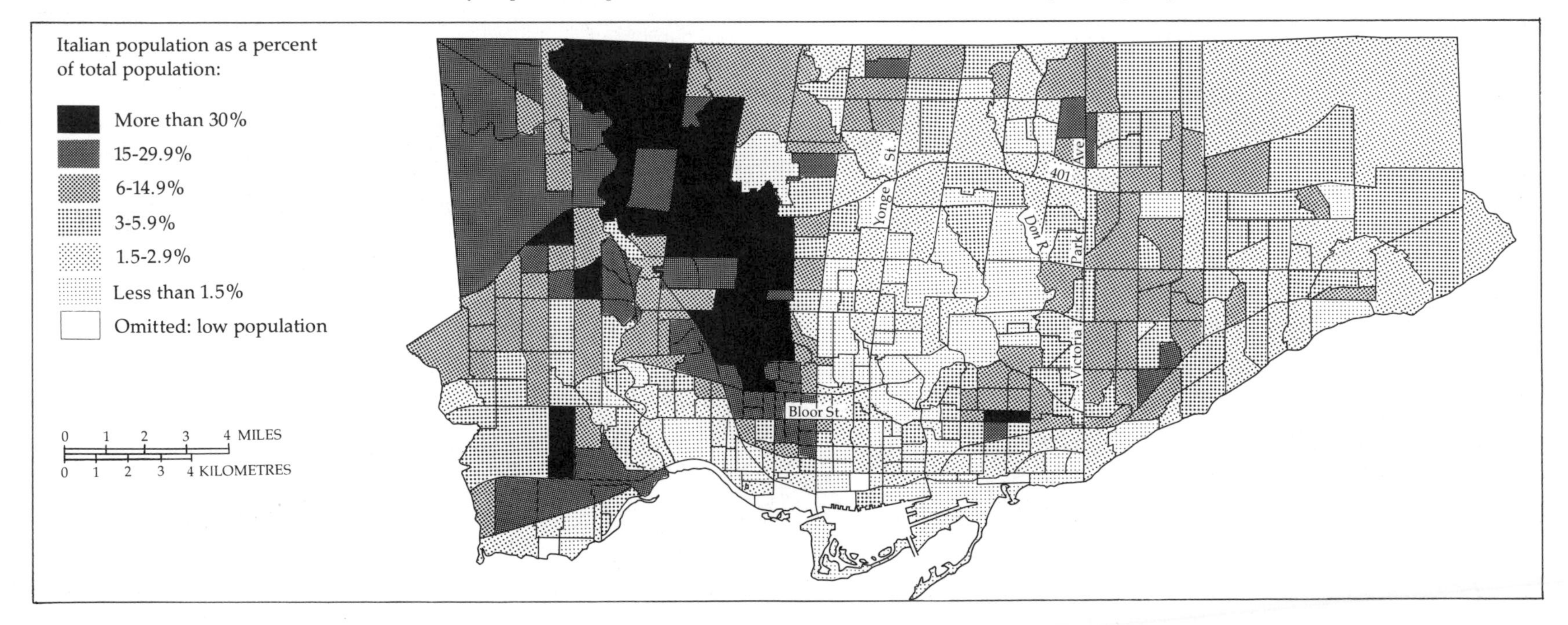

9 Distribution of Italian Population in Metro Toronto, 1981: Most Italians initially made their homes in Little Italy at Christie and Grace. They expanded north, founding a new Little Italy at Dufferin and St. Clair, and continued in that direction, even beyond Metro.

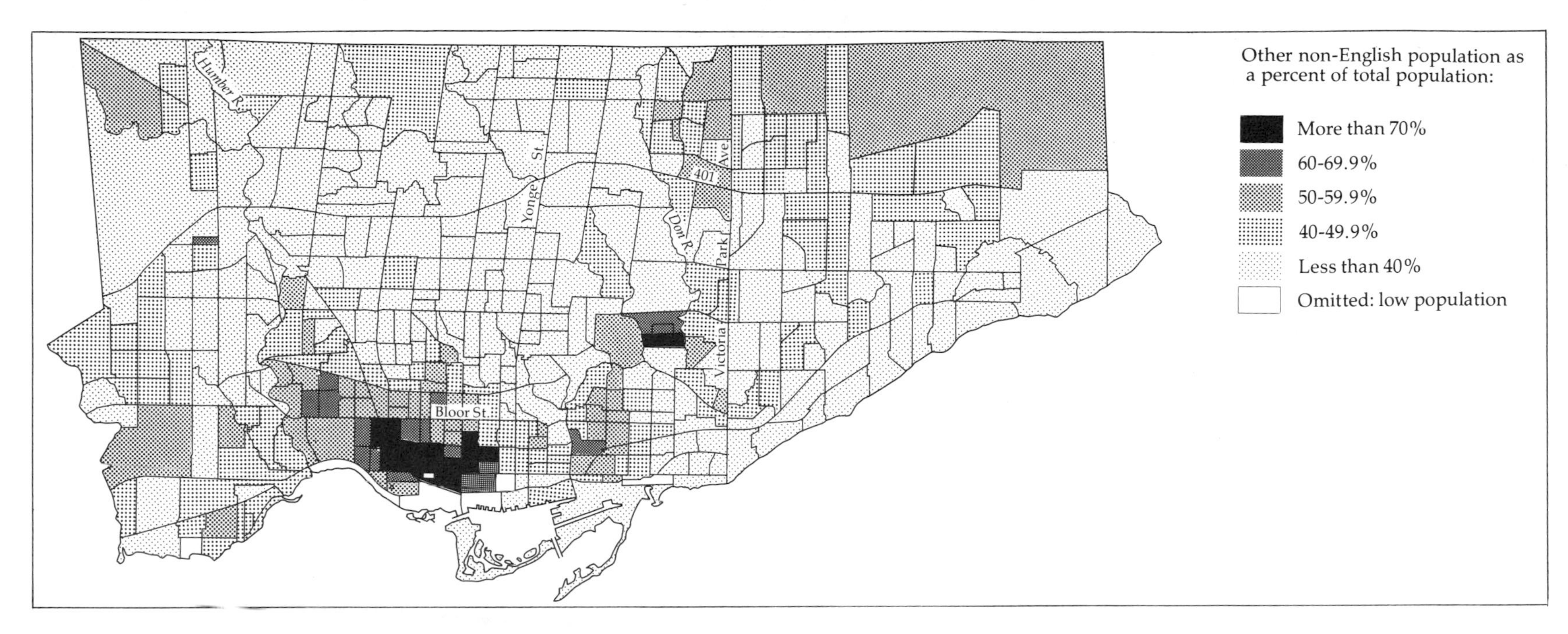

10 Distribution of Other Non-English Population in Metro Toronto, 1981: The swath of "ethnic" neighbourhoods from High Park to the Danforth includes concentrations (from west to east) of Ukrainians, Poles, Portuguese, Chinese and Greeks.

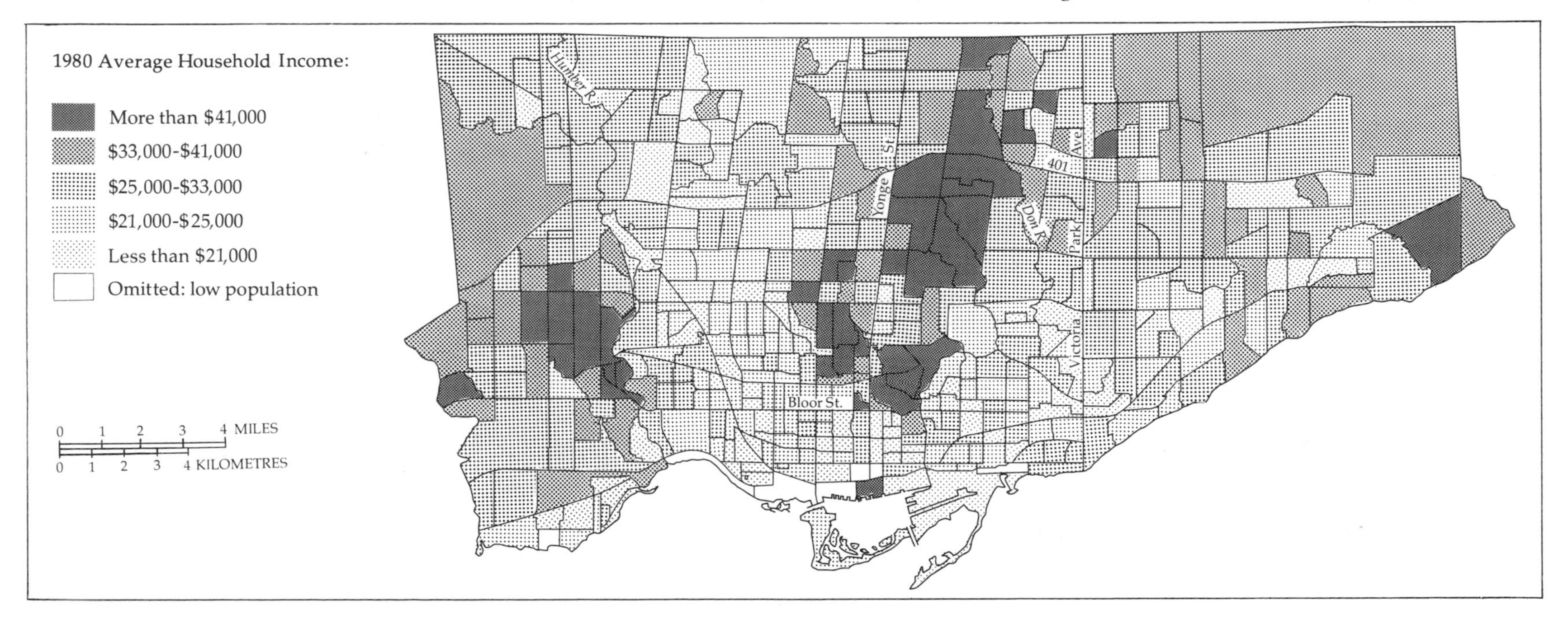

11 Average Household Income in Metro Toronto, 1980: The most British area, North Toronto, remains one of the most affluent. Notable poor areas are Regent Park, South Parkdale and Jane-Finch. Low average incomes in much of the prewar city reflect a persisting mix of people.

sometimes referred to as the Portuguese market, even though it shared the streets with West Indians, Spanish immigrants and even boutiques.[51]

New immigration regulations in the 1960s ended decades of official discrimination against the Chinese and other visible minorities. Urban, well-educated, well-financed, often English-speaking Chinese, mostly from Hong Kong but also from Singapore, Manila and elsewhere, arrived in such large numbers that Toronto's Chinese community reached the size of Vancouver's. In contrast with the older scene, there was no bar against women among the new immigrants, so the sex ratio became much more balanced. Institutionally, the community became more complex. Five daily newspapers provided news of China and Taiwan. Churches and celebrations continued, but the list of associations, according to one commentator, became "staggering." Old people's homes were built and day care, legal aid and other services provided. Young Chinese flocked to universities. The politics of the Chinese community became more diverse.[52]

Even though the Chinese were less concentrated than the Portuguese, their landscape was more conspicuous. Old Chinatown had expanded west on Dundas and up Spadina. A second Chinatown developed east of the Don River, and a third in Agincourt.[53]

The blacks in Toronto constituted a diverse group, but their numbers were unclear. While estimates suggested that there were 120,000, and perhaps as many as 200,000, West Indians in Metro, in the 1981 census various black groups seemed to add up to less than 60,000, or less than 3 per cent of the population. The relatively small number of blacks in Toronto shared some of the problems of urban American blacks: the frequency of households headed by single women working as domestics or in other personal services, major factors in contributing to low-income status; youth unemployment; and concentration in inner-city public housing such as Regent Park. In contrast to the U.S., many lived in suburban public housing projects, particularly in Scarborough and North York. They were generally more dispersed and better educated than American blacks. Many West Indian stores and professional offices were clustered on Bathurst at St. Clair and north of Bloor, but the ghettos were tiny. Like other ethnic groups, West Indian blacks developed their own institutions: two newspapers; Black Theatre Canada; the spectacularly colourful annual festival, Caribana; island associations and the Organization for Caribbean Initiatives, formed to articulate the needs of all West Indians.[54]

Multiculturalism and the exceptional ethnic mix undoubtedly helped minimize social tensions, but discrimination and occasional violence occurred. Fair housing and employment acts in the early 1950s may have prevented some exclusionary practices, and young blacks were not turned away from skating rinks as they had been in the 1940s. But blacks especially will likely remain at the end of the lineup for job opportunities. Neither their cause nor that of Toronto is served by the *Sun*, which published the following letter to the editor:

> The NDP's desperate pandering for visible minority voters drives them to advocate direct discrimination against whites. As a union member of 25 years, I am withholding that portion of my dues that goes to the NDP and donating it instead to the Canadian Cancer Society. It is to be hoped that thousands of other union members do likewise.

The editor's comment was: "And upset union bosses?"[55]

It was not only the ethnic mix of Metro's population that changed. The population also aged. The "baby boomers" grew up and the youth culture of the 1960s and early 1970s dissipated. But while it lasted, it drew hordes of young people to Toronto.

It was an era of protest, of challenging old ways of running society and of handling the environment. Toronto's young people marched to protest the Viet Nam war and Toronto emerged as the world's chief haven for draft dodgers. Students demonstrated against the maker of defoliants, Dow Chemical, and in May 1970 they demonstrated against the Cambodian bombings outside the American consulate, which led to nearly a hundred arrests.[56]

Yorkville and Rochdale College became the symbols of the sharp edge of the youth culture. By the summer of 1967 Yorkville had become "Canada's hippie capital." Ian and Sylvia and Gordon Lightfoot sang in the coffee houses, and police "busted" young people participating in "sit-ins" on Yorkville Avenue where they were attempting to liberate the street for pedestrians. For a few seasons, Torontonians and tourists came to gawk at the long-haired youth; then Yorkville was turned into an avenue of expensive shops and cafés. The urge for a libertine street was satisfied for a while with a pedestrian mall on Yonge Street; eventually a "village" developed on Queen Street West.[57]

West on Bloor, eighteen-storey Rochdale College was opened in

Kensington Market was "founded" by Jews before World War I. After 1950 it became predominantly Portuguese, but has recently become far more diversified.

Old World identities do not die: Toronto's Italians celebrate Italy's 1982 World Cup victory. The streets of Little Italy, around Dufferin and St. Clair, were filled for days with celebrants.

The Baby Boom generation displayed its concerns through alternative lifestyles and dissent. In 1968 Rochdale College at Bloor and Huron opened. The group posed around "the Unknown Student" above is about to leave on a fundraising tour in 1970. But finances, among other things, were not brought under control, and the experiment in alternative education failed. The Vietnam war provided a focus for dissatisfaction with the existing order, both for the young and for older peace advocates like the Reverend Dan Heap, seen picketing the Anglican Synod office in 1966.

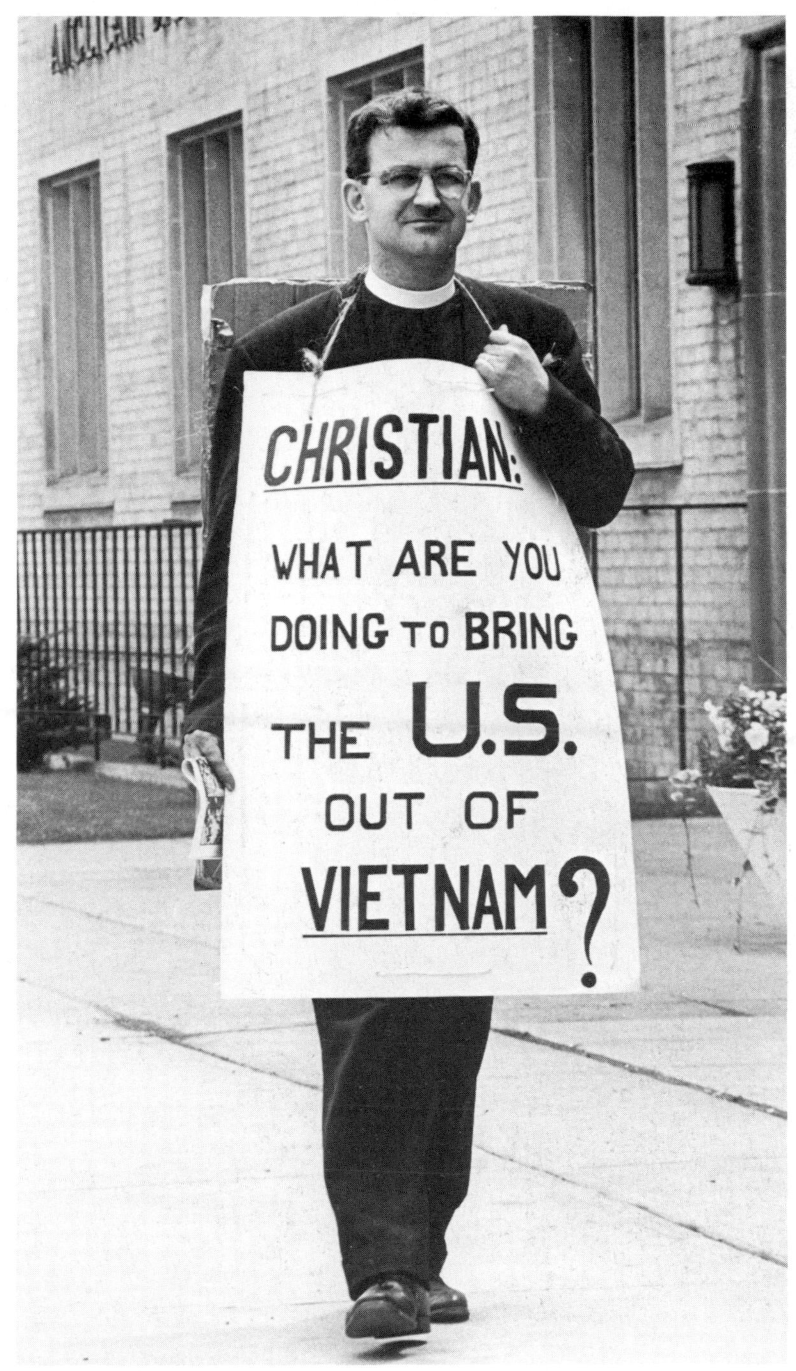

The youth culture found its niche on Yonge Street and, for a while, in Yorkville. For a few summers in the early 1970s, the Yonge Street mall (left) created a place for legitimate loitering — now a dying past-time, as private retail malls discourage it. Yorkville (right) first attracted long-haired youth; and then tourists to gawk at them. Eventually shops for the affluent crowded out the village culture, a process now underway in the latter-day village of Queen Street West.

1968, and was soon called the vertical Haight-Ashbury, after San Francisco's hotbed of the psychedelic movement. The college was intended to operate co-operatively, though the working-class pioneers of the movement in Rochdale, England, might well have wondered what was happening. The founders thought they could organize a democratic community, and apparently so did the CMHC which funded the project. For some it was an experiment in education, an attempt to free up the university system. Although some fairly ordinary people lived in the place, along with nearby Madison Avenue, Rochdale acquired the reputation of a drug-trafficking centre, and visits from the police were frequent. The experiment failed. One of the founders concluded that Rochdale was "really living out the fantasies of a liberal society," in which everyone was free to do "his own thing."[58]

Symptomatic of the change in Metro's population, Rochdale was eventually transformed into apartments for seniors and the handicapped. Faced with a rising proportion of senior citizens (11 per cent in 1981, up from 8 per cent after the war), Metro became more serious about housing them. It took over Rochdale after the CMHC foreclosed. More nursing homes were built, though some acquired poor reputations as profit-making dumping grounds for the elderly. New services appeared, such as Meals on Wheels; interest in the problems of aging increased and gerontology engaged more researchers.[59]

After spectacular postwar growth through natural increase and especially immigration, Toronto's growth slowed down. The heroic years, 1965 to 1975—heroic in firmly establishing a "new" Toronto—slipped into the conventionality of new ways. Households became smaller, more people lived on their own, couples cohabited rather than married, and the baby boom faded. Except on the urbanizing fringe mostly beyond Metro's boundaries, school enrollments fell. But Toronto's growth slowed down less than elsewhere. In Ontario, if Metro itself took a smaller share, the population of the metropolitan area reached 35 per cent of the province; the region, 40 per cent. The region contained nearly half the urban population of the province. Even while internally the population thinned out and continued to move proportionately outward overall, the centralization of Ontario's population was still taking place. Even more significant was Toronto's share of Canada's population. After 1966 the cities of the golden west—Calgary and Edmonton, Vancouver and Victoria—increased more quickly, from 1976 to 1981 Toronto absorbed a quarter of Canada's metropolitan growth. Significantly, Montreal's metropolitan area, let alone the city, did not grow at all. Toronto finally achieved first place in the dominant city sweepstakes.[60] (Tables I, III, IV, V)

CANADA'S FINANCIAL METROPOLIS?

Toronto's landscape is dominated by the towers of corporate barons. Less conspicuous than the towers but no less important are the headquarters of the Argus conglomerate on Toronto Street and clubs like the National where deals are concocted over lunch. A handful of companies and individuals control "about 80 per cent of the 300 Toronto Stock Exchange companies." Toronto appears to have become mainly a money-making machine for corporate power.

The city likes to boast of its newly achieved status as Canada's financial capital, which has tended to exacerbate regional tensions in the country. Though many believe Toronto has reached the status of holy see in Canadian corporate finance, is this really the case? Together with Queen's Park and other provincial capitals, Ottawa has become a major and direct actor in financing the country. But behind Ottawa and the provinces are New York and Washington and they constitute Canada's financial metropolis. Perhaps more than ever, Canada and Toronto are appendages to the greater sovereign power of the U.S.[61]

Toronto's employment structure changed radically after 1966. The manufacturing labour force declined relatively between 1961 and 1971, in Metro from 30 per cent to 24 per cent of the total work force. In the 1970s very few manufacturing jobs were added in the metropolitan area and by the early 1980s plant shutdowns were creating a downward trend. Many of the branch plants that rushed to the Toronto area in the 1950s and 1960s were packing up, as processing increasingly fell into the hands of efficient western European and Asian producers. Construction workers were, as always, subject to the vagaries of the field.[62] (Tables X, XI)

Among the corps of Toronto's manufacturers in trouble were Massey-Ferguson, CCM and Canada Packers, once proud, paternalistic employers of thousands of workers. In 1956 the holding company conglomerate Argus, under E.P. Taylor and Bud McDougald, took over Massey-Ferguson. Hired American executives revived the company through diversification and expansion overseas. Argus's "most profitable and best-known company" became overextended in 1965, recovered to a "banner" year in 1976, only to slide into an abyss of trouble. Despite retrenchment under Argus's Conrad Black — the *Globe and Mail's* businessman of the year in 1978 and *Fortune's* "boy wonder" — the company's poor record continued. After Black and Argus pulled out in 1980, domestic and foreign banks, particularly the Canadian Imperial Bank of Commerce, and Ottawa and Queen's Park had to solve the problem: Ottawa guaranteed $200 million, the banks stayed in, and then the Canadian Development Investment Corporation became directly involved. But things got worse, and in 1982 Massey-Ferguson lost $413 million, second only to Inco's record of $469 million. Many lost their jobs in the Toronto plant as world-wide employment was reduced to below 30,000, less than half the 1976 level. Despite a slight improvement in 1983 and 1984, Massey-Ferguson virtually became a possession of the banks and the federal government. There was bad news elsewhere as well. In the early 1980s, CCM went broke and Swift's Canadian and Canada Packers closed their Toronto plants.[63]

Meanwhile, an adaptive and efficient clothing manufacturing sector, seemingly running against the trend, continued to flourish on Spadina Avenue. De Havilland Aircraft, federal-government-owned since 1974, continued turning out airplanes the world could use, such as the Otter, Twin Otter, Dash 7 and Dash 8. De Havilland showed that research and development were possible in Canada, if the government took the risks. But Toronto has not been not a pacesetter in high technology.[64]

Social service employment saw a spectacular increase between 1960 and 1975 before falling off markedly, as governments — the chief supplier directly and indirectly — retrenched. Only municipal governments added staff. Metro increased its number of employees between 1973 and 1982, and the Metro police complement doubled. But the province remains Toronto's biggest employer. The number of teachers rose with the great expansion of universities and the introduction of community colleges and then fell despite the addition of new special programs. Workers in health and welfare fields followed the same pattern: up in the 1960s, down after 1975 under the cutback strategy of the provincial government. Environmental regulations and control measures were seriously undermined. The "distributive" sector, those engaged in retail and wholesale trade, communications, transportation and storage, grew substantially, continuing an earlier trend. But workers on the docks saw their jobs slip away.[65] (Table X)

Over the 1970s, business and personal services proliferated the most in Toronto's metropolitan area. Those relating to property and money — such as financial and legal services, insurance, real estate, engineering, architecture, accounting and advertising — expanded even more than earlier in the postwar period. Financial institutions added 68 per cent more workers in the 1970s, an indication of concentration in Toronto. The most dramatic increases, however, occurred in low-paid personal services, which included window cleaners, restaurant and hotel workers, repairmen, domestics, beauticians and employees in the recreational and entertainment fields. Since many firms employed temporary workers, the numbers were probably higher. With the weakening of the manufacturing sector, many laid-off workers took lower paying jobs. By 1981, 45 per cent of Toronto's metropolitan area work force were women, and most of them were employed in the personal services sector. And many young people were increasingly forced into this category. The social result of the regressively redistributed economy has been to create a greater gap between rich and poor, and to deprive many young people of opportunities. Toronto's work force has been less vulnerable than those of single-industry towns and cities and welfare has cushioned the problem of sheer survival, but this does not soften the ignominy of joblessness. Those with power shy away from supporting direct government job creation.[66]

The rapidly shifting employment base generated new tensions in Toronto's unions. The decline of manufacturing seriously undercut the power of industrial and, hence, of international unions. Whereas in 1965 three-quarters of the unionized work force of Canada belonged to the internationals, by 1975 the number had fallen to less than half, even while the number of persons working in Canadian unions rose from a third to two-fifths. Before 1975 the largest proportional gains in union membership were achieved in the public sector, which was the focus of a great deal of labour unrest after 1965. Postal workers were often on strike, or so it seemed to some taxpayers. Toronto's high school teachers marched in picket lines for two cold months in 1975. In 1976 unions organized a "day of protest" with a Queen's Park rally, but with little effect. After that, as social service cutbacks set in, public service unions had less power. Wage controls weakened free collective bargaining, a great achievement of the 1940s. Unresolved were the rights of public

In 1983 the Toronto Stock Exchange moved from its 1930s art deco building on Bay south of King to First Canadian Place to the northwest. While the TSE is established as the strongest exchange in Canada, New York's increasingly outstripped it for Canadian investments. As is obvious from the final-day fling at the old building, electronic impulses have not completely eliminated paper.

service employees who provided so many direct public services. A ray of light for unions was some success in organizing retail workers. Despite pressures in the workplace, the Labour Council had the energy to develop co-operative housing and to promote labour education.[67]

As Toronto's economic base became less diversified and more dependent on finance, it appropriated a far greater share of Canada's economic power, much of it at the expense of Montreal. There were immense changes. Measured by assets of corporations that moved to Toronto, between 1970 and 1981 Toronto gained $31.4 billion and Montreal lost $20.5 billion. Vancouver and Calgary gained and then lost far less. By 1983, of 278 Canadian-owned "industrials" in the *Financial Post's 500*, 197 operated out of headquarters in the Toronto area. Toronto's expansion at Montreal's expense began long before the Parti Quebecois victory in 1976: that only speeded up the process. Sadly noticed in Hamilton was Stelco's head office move to the Toronto-Dominion Centre. In economic terms, Hamilton became nothing more than a weakened industrial suburb of Toronto.[68] (Table XII)

The spectacular gains of Toronto's financial sector were obvious in other ways. In 1982 forty-four of the fifty-seven foreign banks which were allowed to set up branches in Canada chose Toronto. Even more telling were the *de facto* headquarter moves of the Royal Bank, Canada's largest corporation (by assets) and the Bank of Montreal, which holds third spot after Toronto's Canadian Imperial Bank of Commerce. As for bank clearances, Toronto shot away ahead of Montreal. The coming of Sun Life consolidated Toronto's power in insurance. The largest firms in accounting, investment dealing, management consulting, advertising, law and real estate were located in Toronto.[69]

Concentration in real estate and the development industry continued. Between 1967 and 1970 A.E. LePage set up branches across Ontario and then Canada, but moved less successfully into the U.S. After succeeding in office development in Toronto, Olympia and York and Cadillac-Fairview, a subsidiary of the Bronfman conglomerate and of Olympia and York, moved into rebuilding downtown Houston, Los Angeles and New York. Cadillac divested itself of 11,000 apartments in Toronto. As important as the subsequent dealings to drive up prices was the sheer magnitude of ownership. Not all developers flourished after 1974. Among those that floundered was one of the earlier "buccaneers," Bruce McLaughlin, head of Mascan and developer of Mississauga's Square One. Construction workers too did not fare well, even though Toronto led the country in building.[70]

A greatly expandedanglophone media concentrated more and more in Toronto, and hence more and more of what Canadians thought and imagined was of Toronto's making or filtering. All the regional complaints against the centre only underlined how much control it had. A revived belief in free enterprise promoted by the corporate media surfaced. Baton Broadcasting controlled CTV, which brought as many less expensive and hence profitable American programs as it could against all efforts to maintain Canadian content. While taking the edge off the urge to individualism, most of the CBC's original anglophone fare was produced, as before, in Toronto.[71]

Publishing too became far more centralized then earlier. In the magazine field, nearly half of the firms publishing two or more journals were located in Toronto. Maclean-Hunter and Southam dominated even more than they did before 1966. Despite the proliferation of publishers, paralleling the rapid increase of writing and the arts, more than half of the publishers and distributors gave Toronto metropolitan area addresses. Many of the lesser bookmen who set up shop elsewhere relied on larger Toronto firms to distribute their wares. As before, virtually all foreign companies, many concentrated by mergers and owned by multinational conglomerates, operated their Canadian branches from Toronto. Subsidized without strings in 1984, McClelland and Stewart, Canada's largest indigenous book publisher, enticed the public to "The World's Biggest Book Sale," while a handful of small bookstores hung on at the margins of a field increasingly falling under corporate control. American media influence continued to expand.[72]

The Kent Royal Commission on Newspapers did not result in controlling concentration any more than did the Bryce Royal Commission on the Concentration of Economic Power in 1978. According to one recent analysis, the newspaper chains with head offices in Toronto gobbled up nearly all small city dailies and many weeklies, relied for revenue more and more on advertising, cut back drastically on investigative reporting, and enjoyed high profits even in 1982. Like American conglomerates, they took to "paper entrepreneuralism," investing in fields extraneous to their traditional role. The Thomson empire owned most of the Hudson's Bay Company which, in turn, owned Simpsons. Torstar took over the Harlequin novels and Southam Coles books. The centralized control of media raised the spectre of a one-party — conservative — state. The *Sun* represented populist toryism; the *Globe and Mail*, business toryism; and even the *Star*, social conscience toryism (at least provincially). In the so-called "information society," it is control not over information but over finance that has become so overwhelming.[73]

Sovereign power in Ottawa and Queen's Park tried to keep the barons happy, or at least at bay, through subsidies and tax write-offs. But there was a price: to protect wage earners as well as a wisp of Canadian nationalism, Ottawa, Queen's Park and every other provincial government became direct actors in the economy. According to the *Financial Post*, Canada was the "land of the Big Bank, long on mortgages and life insurance" and short on "dash and daring." As in the U.S., "hundreds of millions are available for takeovers, while far too much innovation goes begging." So the Canada Development Corporation, the Canada Development Investment Corporation and more than 300 federal crown corporations, with head offices scattered across the country, took the risks and countered centralization in Toronto. Queen's Park did its part through several crown companies and especially through the Ontario Energy Corporation, which bought 25 per cent of Suncor (a subsidiary of the American Sun Oil Company). A stone's throw away, Ontario Hydro was second only to Quebec Hydro in assets among top "industrial" companies in Canada. The lethargic big banks still topped the list.[74]

From an urban system perspective, among cities controlling revenue flows in Canada, Toronto far outranked other Canadian cities. In 1977 Toronto's corporate and government flows totalled $92.6 billion compared to Montreal's $44.5 billion. But owing to federal social transfer payments and its direct economic involvement, Ottawa ranked third with $40.5 billion. While a minor actor in the "private" sector, Quebec City rose too at the expense of Montreal.[75]

In the above ranking of cities in the Canadian system, New York is fourth. Several other American cities, London and Tokyo make the top twenty-five. Because its role has not been so direct, Washington has been missed. Although American banking and manufacturing head offices are not nearly as centralized as in Canada, New York financiers have long been dominant. Since 1940 Washington has shared the spotlight with New York as a financier of U.S. corporate enterprise, particularly in defence and space which add up to an enormous presence, spilling over into Canada. As even the mainstream press in the U.S. has noted, the Pentagon has a "stranglehold" on the central lever of economic power. New York has been significant not only in financing Canada (though less directly than before) but also in controlling spending. Since the rise of state enterprises, the impact of credit ratings by Moody's Investment Services and Standard and Poor has increased. The over-extended and overly optimistic Ontario Hydro has brought Ontario close to losing its triple A rating. The experience of British Columbia testifies to the problems that follow lowered rating: massive cutbacks and firings in the public sector to compensate for speculative bullishness. Thereafter, Standard and Poor removed its "creditwatch." Washington and New York indeed control the central levers. Up to now, even though the provinces have laid more costs on the municipalities, Metro has managed to keep a triple A rating.[76]

The World Bank and the International Monetary Fund (IMF) met in Toronto in 1982, which helped create the impression, at least for the mayor, that Toronto is a "major business centre of the world." While Canada is not being run by the IMF, like some African and Latin American countries, the combination of cuts in public social spending, devaluation and wage (but not price) controls has followed IMF prescriptions. Mergers continued leading to a "new feudalism" in the Canadian economy. From the south, Merrill Lynch's invasion of the securities domain by the recent purchase of Royal Securities in Toronto may signal a new stage of American corporate intrusion. All the ink spilled in the name of Canadian nationalism over the past twenty years by the Committee for an Independent Canada and a variety of leftist groups, mostly focussed in Toronto, has not ensured the Federal Investment Review Agency's slowing down of foreign takeovers. At the grassroots level and behind the scenes, co-operatives, credit unions and some small businesses comprise a limited countervailing current of economic democracy.[77]

East meets West. Early in the century nearly nine out of of ten Torontonians were British; now more than half are of other origins.

Conclusion

Toronto Past and Future

Toronto of 1984 was not the Toronto of 1918. Yet much of its built environment and many of its institutions remain recognizable. In sorting through the changes of the last sixty-six years, restraint and stability must be given a great deal of weight. In fact, one of Toronto's cardinal qualities — the one that has enhanced, at least in American eyes, its image as an alternative civilization — is stability resulting from a consensus that has emerged in dealing with the urban environment. Changes have been absorbed with less difficulty than in American cities, but Torontonians still face ambiguities and problems.

The introduction mentioned several transformations experienced by Torontonians since 1918; here they will be reviewed with an eye to the future.

Toronto's metropolitan role in Canada has increased since 1918. As the economy shifted from manufacturing and resource extraction to finance and service in the late 1920s and 1930s, Toronto gained on Montreal. Again this became even more marked after 1965, when manufacturing once again faltered. Significantly, concentration accelerated when "paper entrepreneuralism" (that is, buying out other companies instead of investing in improvements to increase productivity) dominated economic activity. Anyone reading the business pages can recognize that this tendency has been continuing apace. As farming has fallen into fewer and fewer hands, so has manufacturing, as actual production increasingly moves across the Pacific. What is left is finance, retailing, urban development and media, all largely under corporate dominance and now focussed in Toronto. The number of self-employed has dropped enormously over the period. Western Canada has more reason to complain about Hogtown's dominance.

But this concentration is not without irony: the federal and provincial governments, after 1945 especially, gradually increased their economic power in the country through social programs and through crown corporations. The dismantling of the welfare net and public enterprises, advocated by believers in nineteenth-century free enterprise, will have to be constrained if Canada is to retain any sovereignty. Bay Street will continue to share the economy with Ottawa, Queen's Park and other provincial capitals. Even more, Bay Street must respond not only to Wall Street but also to Washington. American military spending has become the ominous centrepiece of economic life, and the nuclear blanket is hardly as comforting as the mantle of the Union Jack once was.

Democratization of the workplace through unions has been halting. After decades of insistence, it was industrial workers in Toronto and elsewhere who first achieved rights in the 1930s and 1940s. In the 1950s, during the postwar heyday of manufacturing, industrial corporations reached a *modus vivendi* with unions. With the dramatic rise of public employment, strong public sector unions emerged, to a much greater degree than in the U.S. They came to vie with international unions, many of them with their Canadian headquarters in Toronto, for control of the labour movement. Ottawa and the provincial capitals became more pivotal in union life as in the economy generally. As a capital, Toronto could not lose as these shifts took place. Big corporations and big governments induced big unions. The corner drug store run by the friendly neighbourhood owner has virtually disappeared — and with it the nineteenth century. Torontonians seeking a democratic world will have to pursue this impulse within this reality of bigness, not by hankering for a world that is lost.

Since 1918 the population of urban Toronto has quintupled to three million. Not surprisingly, projections before 1950 underestimated area expansion while more accurately predicting population growth. Because of expectations following the baby boom, later projections, even up to 1978, overestimated recent and future population growth. Fluctuating numbers of children strained

Renovated homes in the Annex, with the counterpoint of a high-rise apartment in the background. The last twenty years have seen some success in balancing development — though the need for affordable housing remains.

For leisure, celebration and public demonstration, Nathan Phillips Square has provided a focus for the heart of the city for the past two decades.

school planning: overcrowding in the 1920s, 1930s and 1950s was followed by falling enrollments. What will become more important are social measures for the young and, as the population ages, for the old.

As Toronto's population grew, its character changed. Most conspicuous was the transformation from a predominantly British and Protestant population to a mosaic of virtually every nationality and religious affiliation. The racism expressed in the 1920s, particularly against Jews, began to fade in the 1950s as immigrants with a full range of traditions and languages poured into the city. More recently, the reality of multiculturalism was expressed institutionally and most clearly through heritage language programs. But racism has not been eradicated, and sustaining a social mix will continue to demand the energy of Torontonians.

Greater ethnic diversity and more wealth have improved Toronto's social life. Free of the constraints of Sabbatarianism which hindered the generation of the 1920s, Torontonians flock to the city's playgrounds. Signs of sophistication are everywhere: an explosion of theatres after 1965 which left Toronto second only to New York City as a theatre centre; major league baseball; sidewalk cafés; an international film festival; a new music hall. A fairer taxation system, instead of Wintario and other lotteries, seems a more sensible way of meeting an increasing demand for more sports and cultural facilities to serve everyone.

The creation of the social service network in the late nineteenth and early twentieth centuries put Toronto in the forefront of public health, education and other human services. But it took the Great Depression, or more precisely the fear of lapsing back into it, to persuade Torontonians and other Canadians to press for security, which they did primarily through the CCF. While American society did not continue to add comprehensive social measures, Canada and Ontario did, undoubtedly enhancing the well-being of Torontonians. Social housing gradually, and often grudgingly, came to be accepted. At first it was experimental; in the 1940s it became a privilege conferred on the poor; and finally in the 1970s it came to be regarded as a social right, with mixed tenures, including co-operatives, varied incomes and more sensitive design. Mixing people since 1973 has contributed greatly to strengthening the fabric of Toronto life. But far more money has been going to expensive condominiums and to the suburban edge as higher levels of government try to evade their responsibility for social housing. The central role of Torontonians in the pursuit of greater equality in Canada, not least in social housing, will remain crucial.

The spreading of the city into adjacent rural Ontario continued in the 1920s, if less dynamically than before 1914. It accelerated again in the 1950s and 1960s, only to gradually slow down once again. Houses and garages on large lots, wide arterials and expressways, shopping malls and industrial parks with low-slung buildings characterize much of the post-1945 suburban environment. But unlike the U.S. scene, in the 1960s and 1970s high-rise apartments dotted the low-density suburbs. Only in recent years have developers constructed medium-density townhouses, copies of central semi-detached housing before 1930. This is a more sensible strategy that allows everyone sufficient ground space but that prevents waste in the use of services, materials and gasoline. Likewise, the belated focussing of office development in the city centres of Scarborough and North York is somewhat energy-conserving. Restraining mobility by holding back expressways and promoting public transportation has been a notable achievement, at least by North American standards. The struggle between advocates of expressways and those who favour more public transit will no doubt continue.

The landscape of the old inner city was altered, but not without considerable controversy. The central business district expanded outward but more noticeably upward in the speculative late 1920s and since 1965. The towers of commerce now dominate an almost entirely new downtown. In the 1950s and 1960s developers switched from constructing apartments to constructing office buildings, which were often forced on unwilling neighbourhoods. But then neighbourhoods with older housing became more attractive when protected from development and as smoke from trains and manufacturing left the inner city. On the bay front, recreation and housing have been replacing old industry built on landfill following the 1912 waterfront plan. Maintaining a social mix of population not only in old Toronto but throughout Metro will be an increasing challenge.

Planning as a central concept in urban life appeared in the 1940s; before then it had been largely an esoteric notion. By 1918, controlling the form of subdivisions on the margins had been legislated, if weakly, and zoning bylaws protected better-off neighbourhoods. Improving traffic flows was a preoccupation of the 1920s and 1930s. But comprehensiveness appeared in the development of a zoning system and then in the 1943 plan for the metropolitan area, arguably the most important one of the century. Businessmen, through the Board of Trade, became as anxious to manage growth as the social democrats were, though the latter sought to inject more social and housing content into the plans.

With the creation of Metropolitan Toronto as the culmination of a time of municipal stress, Metro Chairman Frederick Gardiner became the central planner, primarily of sewers, watermains, arterials and expressways. In the 1960s social objectives were reasserted, including a concern to preserve neighbourhoods at a time when growth through redevelopment appeared to be getting out of hand. After 1965 the reform effort resulted in closer attention to the urban fabric, and many of the initiatives were eventually pursued by the postwar suburban municipalities as social problems appeared. Today planning is well entrenched but, as private developers still initiate most projects, the rules can be breached. Were development to get too far out of hand, citizen groups would once again rise to impose limits. More serious, if still less obvious than the water pollution of the turn of the century, is the problem of toxic wastes. Planning will be increasingly challenged on this issue.

Electoral politics reflected times of reform and of relative quiescence. Reform impulses reappeared briefly after the First World War, particularly through the new involvement of women on City Council. But in the 1920s conservatism and the Conservative Party dominated Toronto at all government levels. In the Depression many workers felt the Tories had failed them, so their reign was broken provincially and the Liberals under the volatile Hepburn held power for nearly a decade. Municipally, more left-leaning politicians were elected. The turmoil of the early 1940s led to a sudden rise of the CCF. Red Toryism which advocated social welfare was not enough to prevent Toronto from switching strongly and fairly consistently to the federal Liberals, nor did the permanent presence of labour and other leftist representatives on city and some suburban councils. After the quiet 1950s when Conservatives regained strength, Toronto became more clearly divided. The federal Liberals continued to attract supporters, most conspicuously among immigrants. But provincially and even municipally, Liberals became far less obvious as New Democrats vied with Conservatives. The decline of self-employment and the rise of big business and big government have been the basis for these changes. In municipal politics, parties will likely become more prominent.

Stability in Toronto's urban environment has been partly the result of a close interrelationship (including many tugs-of-war) between the municipalities and the province. Unlike in the U.S., where the federal government had to intervene directly to hold up declining cities, Ottawa most often operated on the sidelines, except indirectly through welfare transfer payments and in housing, an area in which the province generally reflected a private-sector bias. Ironically, in the U.S. the cities' cries for "home rule" after 1850 cut the connections with states, creating a serious vacuum. This was not the case in Canada: the major change since the province increased its taxing power in the 1940s was its increased involvement in financing cities and education. Cutbacks since 1975 did not diminish the need, though more of the costs were passed back to local taxes. Whatever the government at Queen's Park, the connections will remain close.

Despite enormous growth and change through much of the twentieth century, Toronto remains an orderly and stable city. This is partly the good fortune of greater affluence, partly a consequence of avoiding the American preoccupation with defence which siphons off dollars and energy, and partly the result of the long struggle to establish and maintain a Canadian identity. A large part of the credit, however, belongs to Torontonians themselves who have, individually and collectively, participated in the affairs of their city, especially in local public issues that required a restraining hand. They have created a consensus on how Toronto's public environment should be managed, and have become major contributors in making Toronto work.

Appendix

Statistical Tables

TABLE I
Population Growth in Toronto and Region, 1911 - 1981

Year	Toronto	Per Cent Change	Metropolitan Toronto[1]	Per Cent Change	Census Metropolitan Area[2]	Per Cent Change	Toronto Region[3]	Per Cent Change
1911	376,471	—	409,925	—				
1916	460,526	22.3	—	—				
1921	521,893	13.3	611,443	49.2				
1926	556,691	6.7	—	—				
1931	631,207	13.4	818,348	33.8				
1936	645,462	2.3	—	—				
1941	667,457	3.4	909,928	11.2				
1946	696,555	4.4	—	—				
1951	675,754	-3.0	1,117,470	22.8				
1956	667,706	-1.2	1,358,028	21.5				
1961	672,407	0.7	1,618,787	19.2	1,824,481	—	2,118,250	—
1966	664,584	-1.2	1,881,691	16.2	2,158,496	18.3	2,536,577	19.7
1971	712,786	7.3	2,086,017	10.9	2,628,045	21.8	2,923,082	15.2
1976	633,318	-11.1	2,124,291	1.8	2,803,101	6.7	3,180,136	8.8
1981	599,217	-5.4	2,137,395	0.6	2,998,947	7.0	3,417,701	7.5

[1] Municipalities forming Municipality of Metropolitan Toronto in 1953.
[2] Area enlarged in 1971 and 1976.
[3] Metro Toronto and the Regional Municipalities of Durham, Halton, Peel and York created by 1974.

Sources: *Census of Canada*, 1911 - 1981. *City Assessment Department Reports*, 1916, 1926, 1936, 1946.

TABLE II
Population Growth in Toronto and Suburbs, 1911 - 1981

Metropolitan Toronto	1911	1921	1931	1941	1951	1961	1971	1976	1981
East York[1]	—	—	36,080	41,821	64,616	72,409	104,784	106,950	101,974
Etobicoke	5,507	10,445	13,769	18,973	53,779	156,035	282,686	297,109	298,713
Forest Hill[2]	—	—	5,207	11,757	15,305	20,489	—	—	—
Leaside[3]	—	325	938	6,183	16,223	18,579	—	—	—
Long Branch[4]	—	—	3,962	5,172	8,727	11,039	—	—	—
Mimico	1,373	3,751	6,800	8,070	11,342	18,212	—	—	—
New Toronto	686	2,669	7,146	9,504	11,194	13,384	—	—	—
North Toronto[5]	5,362	—	—	—	—	—	—	—	—
North York[6]	—	—	13,210	22,908	85,897	269,959	504,150	558,398	559,521
Scarborough	4,713	11,746	20,682	24,303	56,292	139,744	217,286	387,149	443,353
Swansea[7]	—	—	5,031	6,988	8,072	8,595	—	—	—
Toronto	376,471	521,893	631,207	667,457	675,754	672,407	712,786	633,318	599,217
Weston[8]	1,875	3,116	4,723	5,740	8,677	9,715	—	—	—
York	13,978	57,448	69,593	81,052	101,582	129,645	147,301	141,367	134,617
CMA[9] — Some places									
Brampton								103,441	149,030
Markham								56,206	77,037
Mississauga						74,875[11]	165,512[12]	250,035	315,056
Oakville								68,980	75,773
Pickering								27,879	37,754
Richmond Hill								34,716	37,778
Vaughan								17,782	29,674

[1] Separated from York Township, incorporated 1924.
[2] Separated from York Township, incorporated 1924, annexed to Toronto 1967.
[3] Incorporated 1913, amalgamated with East York Borough 1967.
[4] Incorporated 1930, amalgamated with Etobicoke Borough 1967.
[5] Annexed to Toronto 1912.
[6] Separated from York Township, incorporated 1923.
[7] Separated from York Township 1925, amalgamated with Toronto 1967.
[8] Amalgamated with York Borough 1967.
[9] Census Metropolitan Area
[10] 1981 boundaries. Earlier years not easily compared.
[11] Toronto Township, Streetsville, Port Credit.
[12] Incorporated 1966 from Toronto Township and Streetsville. Port Credit added 1974.

Source: *Census of Canada*, 1911 - 1981

TABLE III
Urban Population Growth and Distribution in Ontario, 1911 - 1981

Year	Metropolitan Toronto[1]	Ontario	Metropolitan Toronto as % of Total Population	Urban Population of Ontario	Metropolitan Toronto as % of Total Urban Population
1911	409,925	2,527,292	16.2	1,328,489	30.9
1921	611,443	2,933,662	20.8	1,706,632	35.8
1931	818,348	3,431,683	23.8	2,095,992	39.0
1941	909,928	3,787,655	24.0	2,338,633	38.9
1951	1,117,470	4,597,542	24.3	3,375,825	33.1
1956	1,358,028	5,404,933	25.1	4,102,919	33.1
1961	1,618,787	6,236,092	26.0	4,823,529	33.6
1966	1,881,691	6,960,870	27.0	5,593,440	33.6
1971	2,089,017	7,703,106	27.1	6,343,630	32.9
1976	2,124,291	8,264,465	25.7	6,708,520	31.7
1981	2,137,395	8,625,107	24.8	7,047,032	30.3
1981[2]	2,998,947	8,625,107	34.8	7,047,032	42.6
1981[3]	3,417,701	8,625,107	39.6	7,047,032	48.5

[1] All municipalities in Metropolitan Toronto in 1953.
[2] Census Metropolitan Area.
[3] Metro Toronto and the Regional Municipalities of Durham, Peel and York.

Source: *Census of Canada*, 1911 - 1981.

TABLE VI
Birthplace of Toronto's Canadian-born Population, 1911 - 61 (%)

	1911	1921	1931	1941	1951	1961	Metro 1961	CMA[1] 1981
Maritimes[2]	0.4	0.6	0.8	1.0	3.9	4.7	3.9	3.8
Quebec	1.1	1.2	1.3	1.6	2.2	2.0	2.0	3.1
Ontario	59.6	59.4	59.0	63.6	59.1	48.4	55.9	52.2
Manitoba	0.1	0.2	0.4	1.1	1.5	1.1	1.2	1.0
Saskatchewan	0.0[3]	0.1	0.2	0.7	1.2	0.9	1.0	0.7
Alberta	0.0	0.1	0.2	0.3	0.4	0.4	0.4	0.5
B.C.	0.0	0.1	0.1	0.2	0.7	0.6	0.6	0.6
Yukon and N.W.T.	0.0	0.0	0.0	0.0	0.0	0.0	0.0	0.0
Not Given	0.3	0.5	0.2	0.0	—	—	—	—
Total Canadian-born (%)	61.5	62.2	62.2	68.5	69.0	58.1	65.1	61.9
Total Population[4]	376,538	521,893	631,207	667,457	675,754	672,407	1,517,741	2,975,495

[1] Census Metropolitan Area.
[2] Includes Newfoundland in 1951, 1961 and 1981.
[3] Less than 0.05 per cent.
[4] Some vary from totals in Table I.

Source: *Census of Canada*, 1911 - 1981.

TABLE IV
Age Composition of Toronto's Population, 1921 - 1981 (%)

Year	0-14	15-24	25-44	45-64	65+	Population[1]
1921	26.8	17.0	35.7	16.6	3.9	520,987[2]
1931	23.1	18.5	33.2	19.8	5.4	630,952[2]
1941	19.0	17.3	32.1	23.9	7.7	667,457
1951	18.1	15.5	31.7	24.2	10.5	675,754
1956	24.9	12.6	33.7	20.4	8.4	1,358,028
1961	27.9	12.5	31.6	19.8	8.1	1,618,787
1966	28.2	15.1	29.6	19.2	7.9	1,881,691
1971	25.3	18.0	28.6	20.0	8.2	2,086,025
1976	21.9	18.4	29.3	21.1	9.2	2,124,295
1981	18.5	18.5	30.4	22.0	10.6	2,137,395

[1] City of Toronto, 1921 - 51; Metropolitan Toronto, 1956 - 81. Percentages may not add to 100 due to rounding.
[2] Some "no submissions."

Source: *Census of Canada*, 1921 - 1981.

TABLE V
School Enrollments in City of Toronto, Selected Years[1]

Year	Public Elementary Number	Public Elementary Ratio to Population	Year	Public Secondary Number	Public Secondary Ratio to Population
1900	26,770	13.4	1900	842	0.4
1918	63,338	12.9	1918	5,544	1.1
1924	77,732	14.3	1933	23,641	3.8
1935	82,118	12.9	1939	24,954	3.8
			1943	19,694[2]	2.9
1951	59,402	9.1	1953	16,896	2.5
1966	77,212	11.6	1970	36,308[3]	5.3
1983	42,136	7.1	1983	34,765	5.9
Metropolitan Toronto (excluding City of Toronto)[4]					
1970	196,512		1977	102,337	
Separate School Board (Elementary only)[5]					
1919	7,811	1947	11,860	1978	81,942
1934	13,581	1975	82,642	1983	82,222

[1] Except for 1900, 1918 and 1983, the years selected are peaks and troughs in total numbers.
[2] Reflects wartime. Slight recovery after war.
[3] Virtually constant, 1970 to 1976.
[4] Peak years.
[5] Except for 1919, the years selected are peaks and troughs. Figures have been virtually constant since 1973. Mimico and Etobicoke figures are not included before 1969.

Source: Toronto Board of Educaton; Metropolitan Board of Education; Metropolitan Toronto Separate School Board.

TABLE VII
Birthplace of Toronto's Foreign-born Population, 1911 – 81 (%)

	1911	1921	1931	1941	1951	1961	Metro 1961	1971	Metro 1971	CMA[1] 1981
Great Britain	28.7	27.7	25.3	19.9	15.5	11.6	12.5	7.9	9.3	7.6[4]
United States	3.1	2.9	2.3	2.0	1.6	1.2	1.3	1.5	1.3	1.3
Russia	2.7	2.1	1.5	1.4	3.3	3.6	2.4	2.4	1.7	1.2[5]
Italy	0.8	0.7	0.8	0.7	1.1	8.6	5.7	8.3	7.4	5.6
Germany	0.3	0.1	0.2	0.2	0.5	2.8	2.3	1.6	1.7	1.3
China	0.3	0.4	0.4	0.3	—	—	—	1.3	0.6	1.8[6]
Latin America[2]	0.1	0.2	0.2	0.2	—	—	—	2.9	2.2	4.7
India, Pakistan, S. Asia	0.1[3]	0.1[3]	0.1[3]	0.1[3]	—	—	—	0.7	0.5	1.5
Poland	—	1.4	3.3	3.3	4.1	3.0	2.4	2.4	1.8	1.3
Other	2.2	2.2	3.6	3.3	4.8	11.1	8.0	14.5	10.1	11.8[7]
Total Foreign-born (%)	38.3	37.8	37.7	31.4	30.9	41.9	34.7	43.5	36.7	38.1
Total Population[8]	376,460	521,893	631,207	667,457	675,754	672,407	1,599,444	713,315	2,086,205	2,975,495

[1] Census Metropolitan Area.
[2] West Indies only in 1911 and 1921; 1931–1981 figures include South America and West Indies.
[3] India.
[4] United Kingdom.
[5] U.S.S.R.
[6] Includes Hong Kong, Taiwan.
[7] Portugal, 2.2%; Greece, 1.4%; Yugoslavia, 1.1%.
[8] Some vary from totals in Table I.

Source: *Census of Canada*, 1911 – 1981.

TABLE VIII
Ethnic Origins of Toronto's Population, 1911 – 81 (%)[1]

	1911	1921	1931	1941	1951	Metro 1951	1961	Metro 1961	1971	Metro 1971	Metro 1981
British Isles	86.5	85.3	80.9	78.4	68.9	72.7	51.8	59.2	45.8	53.3	46.0
English	49.3	55.7	58.6	55.4	—	—	—	—	—	—	28.4
Irish	32.2	25.2	21.8	22.4	—	—	—	—	—	—	5.4
Scottish	18.1	18.5	18.8	21.1	—	—	—	—	—	—	6.8
Others	0.4	0.6	0.8	1.1	—	—	—	—	—	—	5.4
Jewish	4.9	6.6	7.2	7.3	6.0	5.3	1.7	3.3	3.5	5.1	4.9
Italian	1.2	1.6	2.1	2.1	2.7	2.5	11.6	8.3	12.6	12.0	11.7
French	1.3	1.6	1.7	2.3	3.2	2.9	4.1	3.4	3.7	3.4	2.5
German	2.6	0.9	1.5	1.3	1.7	1.7	4.6	4.4	3.3	4.1	2.6
Ukrainian	—	0.2	0.7	1.6	3.5	2.6	3.9	2.7	3.2	2.5	1.9
Polish	0.2	0.5	1.3	1.7	3.1	2.4	4.0	3.4	3.1	2.1	1.9
Hungarian	0.1	—	0.2	0.3	0.5	—	1.6	1.1	1.1	1.0	0.9
Dutch	0.4	0.8	0.8	1.0	1.0	1.1	1.0	1.5	0.8	1.2	0.8
Chinese	0.3	0.4	0.4	0.3	0.4	—	1.0	0.5	2.5	1.2	3.9
Japanese	0.0	0.4	0.4	—	0.7	—	0.7	0.5	0.5	0.5	0.5
African	0.1	0.2	—	—	—	—	0.5	0.3	0.7	0.6	2.9[2]
Native Peoples	—	—	—	0.1	0.1	—	0.2	0.1	0.4	0.3	0.5
Other	2.4	1.9	3.2	3.6	8.2	8.8	13.3	11.3	18.8	12.7	19.0[3]
Total	376,009	521,893	631,207	667,457	675,754	1,117,470	672,407	1,618,787	713,130	2,086,015	1,982,540[4]

[1] Those reaching 1.0% are specified (except Native Peoples and those in note 3).
[2] Mainly Caribbean. Calculations vary.
[3] Portuguese, 3.5% (City of Toronto, 8.9%); Greek, 3.0%; Indo-Pakistani, 2.6%; Balkan, 1.8%; Spanish and Latin American, 1.1%; Philippino, 1.1%; Baltic, 0.9%; other central European, 0.8%; Japanese, 0.5%; Korean, 0.5%; Arab, 0.5%; Scandinavian, 0.4%; Maltese, 0.4%; Armenian, 0.3% Russian, 0.2%; Vietnamese, 0.2%; all others, 1.1%.
[4] Single origins only. Compare totals to Table I.

Source: *Census of Canada*, 1911 – 1981.

TABLE IX
Religious Affiliations of Toronto's Population, 1911–81 (%)[1]

	1911	1921	1931	1941	1951	Metro 1951	1961	Metro 1961	1971	Metro 1971	CMA[2] 1981
Anglican	32.0	33.2	31.5	30.0	25.3	27.6	18.3	21.2	14.4	16.5	13.6
Baptist	5.5	5.0	5.1	5.1	4.3	4.6	3.2	3.6	2.9	3.0	3.0
Congregational	1.0	0.5	—	—	—	—	—	—	—	—	—
Greek Orthodox	—	—	0.7	1.2	2.2	1.6	4.0	2.6	5.9	3.8	3.1
Jehovah's Witness	—	—	—	—	—	—	0.3	0.3	1.2	1.0	0.5
Jewish	4.8	6.6	7.2	7.3	6.7	6.0	2.8	5.4	3.1	4.9	4.2
Lutheran	0.7	0.3	1.0	0.9	1.8	1.6	4.1	3.5	2.6	2.8	2.2
Methodist	19.5	16.3	—	—	—	—	—	—	—	—	—
Pentecostal	—	—	0.1	0.3	0.4	—	0.5	0.4	0.6	0.6	5.6
Presbyterian	20.1	21.7	15.3	13.5	10.4	10.5	7.2	8.0	5.3	6.5	1.9
Roman Catholic	12.3	12.4	14.3	14.6	19.3	16.8	34.7	27.3	38.6	34.0	35.3
Ukrainian[3]	0.4	0.7	[4]	0.9	1.8	1.3	2.1	1.2	1.7	1.1	1.4
United[5]	—	—	21.8	23.0	24.2	26.3	18.9	22.7	12.7	16.2	14.4
Other	3.7	3.3	3.0	3.2	3.6	3.7	3.9	3.8	11.0	9.6	15.5[6]
Total	376,538	521,893	631,207	667,457	675,754	1,117,470	672,407	1,618,787	713,135	2,086,020	2,975,495

[1] Those figures reaching 1.0% are specified.
[2] Census Metropolitan Area.
[3] Titles vary; 1981 figures combine Eastern Orthodox and Ukrainian Catholics.
[4] Included with Roman Catholics in census.
[5] 1925: all Methodists and Congregationalists and some Presbyterians.
[6] No religious preference, 9.2%; Eastern non-Christian, 3.2%; others, 3.1%.

Source: *Census of Canada*, 1911–1981.

TABLE X
Toronto's Labour Force, 1911–1981 (%)

Industry	1911[1]	1921[1]	1931	1941	Metro 1951	CMA[2] 1961	CMA 1971	CMA 1981
Extractive	1.1	0.7	0.7	0.7	0.8	1.1	1.0	0.8
Manufacturing	35.0	29.9	28.4	34.7	35.2	29.7	25.3	23.2
Construction	11.7	7.5	8.1	5.6	7.0	6.5	6.1	5.3
Transportation, Communication, Utilities	7.5	10.2	9.7	7.8	9.9	8.7	7.5	7.8
Wholesale, Retail Trade	19.7	18.6	17.8	19.4	19.2	18.5	16.7	17.6
Finance, Business Services[3]	4.3	5.8	7.4	7.0	8.6	10.0	11.0	15.5
Personal Services	11.0	10.9	14.8	13.4	7.7	9.6	8.3	10.1
Social Services, Public Administration[4]	9.7	10.6	10.5	10.5	10.6	13.7	17.0	16.7
Unspecified	—	5.8	2.6	0.9	1.0	2.2	7.1	3.0
Total (n)	169,520	223,399	280,383	285,778	526,828	789,651	1,244,855	1,667,800
Women in Labour Force (%)	25.2	26.8	28.2	32.0	30.2	33.0	38.1	44.0

[1] Some categories are occupational.
[2] Census Metropolitan Area.
[3] Primarily related to property and capital.
[4] Postal and utility workers are classified under Transportation, Communications and Utilities.

Source: *Census of Canada*, 1911–1981. See also Chapter 1, footnote 45.

TABLE XI
Growth and Decline of Manufacturing in Toronto, Metro and CMA, Selected Years[1]

Toronto	Establish-ments	Employees	Salaries & Wages ($000)	Value of Products ($000)
1916	1,200	78,000	42,000	180,000
1921	1,706	66,708	84,147	371,090
1929	2,236	102,406	133,723	593,254
1933	2,604	75,645	80,856	308,984
1939	2,885	98,702	122,533	482,532
1943	3,238	156,459	259,308	961,924
1950	4,011	160,063	392,754	1,686,923
1961	2,765	116,043	498,275	1,873,845
1975	1,791	79,747	824,956	4,303,389
1980	1,996	86,713	1,428,460	7,837,437
Metro				
1946	3,869	165,306	284,590	1,188,751
1956	4,704	207,860	743,830	2,924,421
1961	4,982	224,343	981,787	4,118,709
1971	4,883	237,833	1,787,617	6,804,051
1980	4,992	252,940	4,255,641	22,149,190
CMA				
1961	5,011	235,387	1,027,604	2,075,969
1966	5,629	293,301	1,600,346	7,848,654
1974	6,058	338,980	3,364,043	17,468,879
1976	5,688	322,452	3,928,623	20,270,095
1980	7,010	349,591	5,952,993	34,847,582

[1] CMA: Census Metropolitan Area. Selected years: partially peaks and troughs defined by number of employees.

Sources: *Postal Census*, 1916; *Canada Yearbook*, 1921–1980; *Manufacturing Industries of Canada*, 1941–1980.

TABLE XII
Economic Comparisons: Toronto vs Other Cities, Selected Years

Cheques Cashed (%)

Year	Toronto	Montreal	Vancouver[1]	Winnipeg	Others	Total ($000)
1901	32.0	47.5	2.5	7.2	10.8	1,871
1921	29.3	32.8	4.2	15.4	18.3	17,443
1931	30.5	34.3	4.9	13.4	16.9	16,828
1936	33.7	28.0	5.1	15.2	18.0	19,203
1946	28.7	27.2	6.6	9.2	28.3	69,248
1966	36.2	28.6	6.4	6.4	22.4	521,598
1980	57.3	13.5	5.7	2.9	20.6[2]	5,375,338

Head Offices[3]

Year	Toronto	Montreal	Vancouver	Calgary	Winnipeg	Others
1931	25	49	1	1	4	20
1961	32	32	7	3	4	22
1971	39	29	7	3	3	19
1977	40	25	11	6	2	16

Stocks Traded ($000)

Year	Toronto	Montreal	New York[4]
1936	699,262	—	20,386,624
1963	2,143,888	873,600	54,888,000
1980	29,514,530	3,856,700	374,911,000

[1] Includes New Westminster.
[2] Calgary 1979, 4.5%.
[3] Of top 100 Canadian corporations by assets. Those more than 50% foreign-owned are not included.
[4] New York Stock Exchange only.

Sources: *Canada Yearbook*, 1901–1980; *Survey of Industrials*, 1931–1977; *Report of the Superintendent of Insurance for Canada*, 1931–1977; Toronto Stock Exchange; *Canadian Statistical Review*, 1941–1981; *Bank of Canada Review*, 1968–1981; *Survey of Current Business*, 1916–1967; *Financial Post 500*.

TABLE XIII
Value of Buildings Erected and Assessment, Selected Years ($ million)

	Value of Buildings Erected[1]		Assessment	
Year	Toronto	Metro (CMA)[2]	Toronto	Metro
1918	8.5		605.7	
1922	35.2		775.6	
1928	51.6		922.7	
1933	4.3		1,048.3	
1937	11.2		971.3	
1943	6.2		956.3	
1950	55.2		1,372.0[3]	
1957	121.1	344.2	1,639.2	3,183.1
1960	107.4	358.2	1,795.2	3,977.6
1965	212.7	737.0	1,905.7	4,890.0
1975	554.6	1,835.4(CMA)	2,454.2	7,447.4[4]
1982	546.9	2,118.9(CMA)	3,017.7	8,535.2

[1] Mostly peak and trough years for building permits.
[2] Census Metropolitan Area.
[3] Reassessment upwards 1948 to 1949.
[4] 1976.

Sources: *Municipal Handbook*, 1918–1978; *Annual Report of Commissioner of Finance: Metropolitan Toronto*, 1954–1979; *Canada Yearbook*, 1918–1982.

TABLE XIV
Housing in Toronto and Montreal, 1921-1981

Year	Toronto Occupied Dwellings	Toronto Persons per Dwelling	Toronto Apartment Units (%)	Units Owned (%) Toronto	Units Owned (%) Montreal
1921	48,595	5.3	2.2	46.9[1]	14.8[1]
1931	120,419[2]	5.2	17.3[3]	46.4[4]	14.9[4]
1941	147, 180	4.5	24.8[3]	42.3	11.5
1951	157,175	4.3	29.7	62.2	17.5
1961	172, 809	3.9	36.5	56.4	20.2
1961 Metro	398,585	4.1	27.8	66.6	—
1971	224,440	3.2	45.9	41.8	19.2
1971 Metro	629,271	3.3	53.4	51.0	—
1976	230,395	2.7	59.2	41.4	19.5
1976 Metro	712,955	3.0	49.6	51.1	—
1976 CMA[5]	909,530	3.1	43.9	—	—
1981	243,713	2.4	—	39.0	21.9
1981 Metro	779,695	2.7	45.3[6]	50.1	—
1981 CMA	1,043,624	2.9	—	56.5	41.6

[1] Families.
[2] 149,966 households. (Data problematic, see Chapters 1, 2.)
[3] City Assessment data: 1931, 24.8%; 1941, 29.6% (data problematic).
[4] Households.
[5] Census Metropolitan Area.
[6] Over five storeys, 33.5%.

Sources: *Census of Canada*, 1921-1981; *Report of City Assessment Commissioner.*

TABLE XV
Public Transportation in Toronto, Selected Years

Year	Number of Passengers (000,000)	Passengers per Population	Streetcars, Trolley Buses	Buses	Subway Cars
1922	187	354	1,079	—	—
1928	194	331	1,039	161	—
1933	148	237	953	197	—
1939	154	237	918	257	—
1946	310	446	972	432	—
1952	273	410	1,141	594	64
1954	320[1]	256[2]	1,078	683	104
1961	268	170	981	574	140
1967	314[3]	167	828	939	334
1975	358	165	539	1,217	490
1983	407	194	456	1,470	630

[1] Yonge subway opened.
[2] Metro: TTC extended into suburbs.
[3] Bloor-Danforth subway opened in 1966.

Sources: *Municipal Handbook*, 1922-1976; J.F. Bromley and J. May, *Fifty Years of Progressive Transit* (1975); *TTC Annual Reports*; Metropolitan Toronto's *Annual Financial Report*, 1955-1980.

TABLE XVI
Municipal Expenditure, Toronto and Metro, Selected Years
($ million)

Year	City of Toronto[1]	Metro[2]
1919	22.5	
1920	27.4	
1926	30.4	
1931	41.6	
1933	38.0	
1939	39.3	
1945	36.2	
1953	74.3	
1954	76.6	58.6
1957	94.1	113.3[3]
1966	205.6	319.6
1967	230.8	487.1[4]
1978	650.1	1,462.2
1983	999.4	2,437.9

[1] Current, including debt payments and education costs, raised from property taxes.
[2] Metropolitan Corporation only, including property taxes transferred to Metro School Board. Expenditures by area municipalities, Metro and local school boards are not included.
[3] Police transferred to Metro.
[4] Social services (welfare especially) to Metro; most education revenues and expenditures channelled through Metro School Board.

Sources: City Commissioner of Finance, *Annual Report*, 1919-1978; Municipality of Metropolitan Toronto, *Annual Financial Report*, 1954-1983.

Notes

Abbreviations

BMR	Bureau of Municipal Research
CAC	Civic Advisory Council of the City of Toronto
CC	City Council *Minutes*
CT	City of Toronto
CTA	City of Toronto Archives
CTHD	City of Toronto Housing Department
CTPDD	City of Toronto Planning and Development Department
CUCS	Centre for Urban & Community Studies (University of Toronto)
FC	City Finance Commissioner *Report*
GM	*The Globe and Mail*
JTPIC	*Journal of the Town Planning Institute of Canada*
LCMT	Labour Council of Metropolitan Toronto
MT	Metropolitan Toronto
MTPD	Metropolitan Toronto Planning Department
OMB	Ontario Municipal Board
PBP	Planning Board Papers, City of Toronto Archives
SPC	Social Planning Council
TBE	Toronto Board of Education
TTC	Toronto Transportation (Transit after 1954) Commission
TTLC	Toronto Trades and Labour Council
TRC	Toronto Reconstruction Council
UHR	*Urban History Review*
UT	University of Toronto
UTA	University of Toronto Archives (student papers)
YU	York University

INTRODUCTION

[1] Anthony A. Strachan, "A City that Works," *Harpers* 249 (Dec. 1974), 14-19. Arthur Herschman, "Foreign Travel," *Science* 210 (14 Nov. 1980), 763. *Star*, 18 June 1982. Issues developed in James Lemon, "Toronto among North American Cities," in Victor L. Russell, ed., *Forging a Consensus: Historical Essays on Toronto* (Toronto, 1984), 323-51.

[2] U.S. literature, for example: Katharine Bradbury, Anthony Downs and Kenneth A. Small, *Urban Decline and the Future of American Cities* (Washington, 1982). William K. Tabb, *The Long Default: New York City and the Urban Fiscal Crisis* (New York, 1982).

[3] J.M.S. Careless, *Toronto to 1918: An Illustrated History* (Toronto, 1984), chapter 5. H.V. Nelles, *The Politics of Development: Forestry, Mines and Hydro-electric Power in Ontario, 1849-1941* (Toronto, 1974), 118. Jacob Spelt, *Urban Development in South-Central Ontario* (Toronto, 1955, 1972), chapter 5. William Stephenson, *The Store that Timothy Built* (Toronto, 1969). William L. Marr and Donald G. Paterson, *Canada: An Economic History* (Toronto, 1980), chapters 7-9.

[4] *Globe*, 31 May 1906. E.P. Neufeld, *The Financial System of Canada: Its Growth and Development* (Toronto, 1972), 99, 247.

[5] Spelt, *Urban Development*, chapter 5. John C. Weaver, *Shaping the Canadian City: Essays on Urban Politics and Policy, 1890-1920* (Toronto, 1977), chapter 1. Michael J. Piva, *The Condition of the Working Class in Toronto, 1900-1921* (Ottawa, 1979), chapter 2.

[6] Rupert Brooke, *Letters from America* (New York, 1916), 80. Anthony R. Kilgallin, "Toronto in Fiction, Poetry and Occasional Prose," MA thesis, UT, 1966. Robert M. Stamp, *The Schools of Ontario, 1876-1976* (Toronto, 1982), 92-96. Cecil J. Houston and William J. Smyth, *The Sash Canadians Wore: A Historical Geography of the Orange Order in Canada* (Toronto, 1980), 144-46, 156-59. Robert F. Harney and Harold Troper, *Immigrants: A Portrait of the Urban Experience* (Toronto, 1975).

[7] Plans: Kenneth Greenberg, "Toronto: The Unknown Grand Tradition," in *Trace: A Canadian Magazine about Architecture* 1 (May-June 1981), 37-46. Gunter Gad and Deryck Holdsworth, "Building for City, Region and Nation," in Russell, ed., *Forging a Consensus*, 272-319.

[8] John David Hulschanski, The Origins of Urban Land Use Planning in Ontario, 1900-1946," PhD thesis, UT, 1981, chapter 4. Peter W. Moore, "Zoning and Planning: The Toronto Experience, 1904-1970," in Alan F.J. Artibise and Gilbert A. Stelter, eds., *The Usable Urban Past: Planning and Politics in the Modern Canadian City* (Toronto, 1979), chapter 13. John Dakin, "Toronto Planning: A Planning Review of the Legal and Jurisdictional Contexts from

1912 to 1970," UT Department of Urban and Regional Papers on Planning and Design, 1974. Meena Dhar, "Emergence of Land Use Planning in Ontario: with Special Emphasis on Planning in the City of Toronto," MA thesis, University of Waterloo, 1980, chapter 4.

[9] Michael Doucet, "Politics, Space, and Trolleys: Mass Transit in Early Twentieth-Century Toronto," in Gilbert A. Stelter and Alan F.J. Artibise, eds., *Shaping the Urban Landscape: Aspects of the Canadian City-Building Process* (Ottawa, 1982), chapter 13.

[10] See annexation map in CTA, reproduced in J. Lemon and J. Simmons, "A Guide to Data on Nineteenth Century Toronto," UT Geography Department Discussion Paper, 1971, revised 1977. See also student papers on annexations in 1880s and from 1904 to 1912, 1983, UTA.

[11] Horatio C. Hocken, "The New Spirit in Municipal Government," in Canadian Club of Ottawa, *Addresses*, 19 Dec. 1914 (Ottawa, 1914), 85-97; partly reprinted in Paul Rutherford, ed., *Saving the Canadian City: The First Phase 1880-1920* (Toronto, 1974), 195-208. Richard Allen, *The Social Passion: Religion and Social Reform in Canada, 1914-1928* (Toronto, 1971), chapter 22. Weaver, *Shaping the Canadian City*, chapters 2-4. H.V. Nelles and Christopher Armstrong, "The Great Fight for Clean Government," *UHR* 2-76 (1976), 50-66. Armstrong and Nelles, "The Rise of Civic Populism in Toronto, 1870-1920" in Russell, ed., *Forging a Consensus*, 192-237. Shirley Spragge, "A Confluence of Interests: Housing Reform in Toronto, 1900-1920," in Artibise and Stelter, eds., *The Usable Urban Past*, chapter 10.

[12] Roger E. Riendeau, "Servicing the Modern City: 1900-1930," in Russell, ed., *Forging a Consensus*, 157-80.

[13] Brooke, *Letters from America*, 83-84. Gene H. Homel, "Toronto's Tobogganing Controversy of 1912," *UHR* 10 (Oct. 1981), 25-34. Joseph Schull, *Ontario Since 1867* (Toronto, 1978), 219-22.

CHAPTER ONE, 1918-1929

[1] FC, 1927, 52; FC, 1926, 43.

[2] Terry Copp, *The Anatomy of Poverty: The Condition of the Working Class in Montreal, 1897-1929* (Toronto, 1974).

[3] This narrative is based on newspaper clippings in Scrapbook 1, TBE Archives.

[4] Data: FC, 1929, 45-46. "Opportunity Classes," *Telegram*, 26 Aug. 1920. See also TBE, Minutes, 1918-1929; and *Handbooks*, 1918-1929. E.A. Hardy and Honora M. Cochrane, *Centennial Story: The Board of Education for the City of Toronto* (Toronto, 1950). Stamp, *Schools of Ontario*, chapters 5, 6. Reindeau, "Servicing the Modern City," in Russell, ed., *Forging a Consensus*, 157-80.

[5] Evening classes: FC, 1929, 45.

[6] CC, Appendix C, 1924, 133. Piva, *Condition of the Working Class*, chapter 5. "The City Improvement By-Law," *Saturday Night*, 7 Dec. 1929. Paul A. Bator, "'Saving Lives on the Wholesale Plan': Public Health Reform in the City of Toronto, 1900-1930," PhD thesis, UT, 1979. Bator, "Public Health Reform in Canada and Urban History: A Critical Survey", *UHR* 9 (Oct. 1980), 87-102. Robert Wilson, *A Retrospect: A Short Review of Steps Taken in Sanitation to Transform the Town of Muddy York into the Queen City of the West* (Toronto, 1934), pamphlet, CTA. Robert N. Woadden, "A Short Resume of Contributions of Past Medical Officers of Health," 1962, CTA. Michael Bliss, *The Discovery of Insulin* (Toronto, 1982).

[7] Piva, *Condition*, 39. Given nearly intractable data, Piva makes some ingenious calculations.

[8] On Toronto: CT, *Social Service Commission Report Dealing with the Origin, Duties, Growth and Work since 1912* (Toronto, 1921). Susan Friedman, "The Abolition of the Social Service Commission," 1978, UTA. James M. Pitsula, "The Relief of Poverty in Toronto, 1880-1930," PhD thesis, YU, 1979, chapter 6. Piva, *Condition*, 76. Data: FC, 1930, 27. James Struthers, *No Fault of Their Own: Unemployment and the Canadian Welfare State, 1914-1941* (Toronto, 1983), chapter 1. Gail Bauman, "Public Welfare: The Role of the Municipality in Toronto, 1912-1934," 1984, UTA.

[9] [Florence Philpott], "History and Background of the Welfare Council," ca. 1954, SPC and CTA. Pitsula, "Relief of Poverty." Benjamin Lappin, "Stages in the Development of Community Work as a Social Work Method," DSW thesis, UT, 1965, chapter 6. BMR, *Toronto Gives...* (Toronto, 1918). F.N. Stapleford, *After Twenty Years: A Short History of the Neighbourhood Workers Association, 1918-1938* (Toronto, 1938). H.C.F. Wasteneys, "A History of the University Settlement of Toronto, 1910-1958," DSW thesis, UT, 1975. *Star*, 9 Dec. 1920, 15 Jan. 1921. On NWA: *Johnny Canuck* 12 (3 Feb. 1923), 6, 7, 22. Stephen A. Speisman, *The Jews of Toronto: A History to 1937* (Toronto, 1979), chapters 13, 14.

[10] Piva, *Condition*, chapter 5. Shirley Spragge, "A Confluence of Interests: Housing Reform in Toronto, 1900-1920," in Artibise and Stelter, eds., *The Usable Urban Past*, 247-67. Hannah Shostack, "Business and Reform: The Lost History of the Toronto Housing Company," *City Magazine* 3 (Sept. 1978), 24-31. BMR, *What is "The Ward" Going to do with Toronto? A Report on Undesirable Living Conditions...* (Toronto, 1918).

[11] Piva, *Condition*, 135-38. "Why Toronto Housing Was Held Up," *JTPIC* 9 (Apr. 1930), 34-36. *Star Weekly*, 18 Mar. 1922. *Globe*, 29 Mar. 1922. A.G. Dalzell, *Housing in Canada*, 2 vols. (Toronto, 1927, 1928).

[12] John T. Saywell," Housing Canadians: Essays on the History of Residential Construction in Canada," Economic Council of Canada, Discussion

Paper 24 (Ottawa, 1975), 150-69. Peter W. Moore, "Zoning and Planning: The Toronto Experience," in Artibise and Stelter, *The Usable Urban Past*, 322. *Saturdy Night*, 29 Nov. 1924. Graph of vacancies, 1905-1942: PBP 19, 3, CTA. FC, 1926, 43.

[13] Copp, *Anatomy of Poverty*, 145-46. FC, 1929, 49, 39, 43.

[14] Mike Filey, *I Remember Sunnyside: The Rise and Fall of a Magical Era* (Toronto, 1981), chapters 1-4. Greenberg, "Toronto: The Unknown Grand Tradition," 38-39, 42-44. Neil Semple, "Toronto Park Development, 1920-1930," 1970, UTA.

[15] James Lorimer, *The Ex: A Picture History of the Canadian National Exhibition* (Toronto, 1973). Riendeau, "Servicing the Modern City," in Russell, ed., *Forging a Consensus*, 160-61.

[16] Conn Smythe with Scott Young, *Conn Smythe: If You Can't Beat 'Em in the Alley* (Toronto, 1981), 74-86, 108, 223. Toivo Kiil *et al.*, eds., *The Crazy Twenties 1920/1930: Canada's Illustrated Heritage* (Toronto, 1978), 73.

[17] Jack Sullivan, *The Grey Cup Story: The Dramatic History of Football's Most Coveted Award* (Toronto, 1974), 27-37, 223-24.

[18] Louis Cauz, *Baseball's Back in Town: From the Don to the Blue Jays: A History of Baseball in Toronto* (Toronto, [1977]), 51, 59-75.

[19] Robert Barry Scott, "A Study of Amateur Theatre in Toronto, 1900-1930," 2 vols., MA thesis, University of New Brunswick, 1966, chapters 6-8, 451-53. Raymond Card, "Drama in Toronto: The Forgotten Years," *English Quarterly* 6 (1973), 67-81. *Globe*, 25 Nov. 1929. Ross Harkness, *J.E. Atkinson and the Star* (Toronto, 1963), chapter 12. Frank W. Peers, *The Politics of Canadian Broadcasting, 1920-1957* (Toronto, 1969), 17-21. Donald Jack, *Sinc, Betty, and the Morning Man: The Story of CFRB* (Toronto, 1977), 18-23.

[20] FC, 1929, 8.

[21] FC, 1918, 47; FC, 1922, 35; FC, 1925, 52; FC, 1928, 70, 58, 61, 18, 24; FC, 1930, 27. Copp, *Anatomy of Poverty*, 146.

[22] FC, 1922, 19; FC, 1924, 18. *Star*, 27 Aug. 1921; noted in Pam Scott, "The Toronto Transportation Commission's Take-Over of 1921," 1978, UTA. BMR, *White Papers*, nos. 102-105, 107-108, 22 Sept. 1926-17 Jan. 1927. Arthur J. Langley, "The Leverage of Commitment: The Bureau of Municipal Research, 1914-1974," 1975. CC, 1926, Appendix C, 25-26.

[23] *Telegram*, 18 Jan. 1901.

[24] Linda Price, "Women Aldermen in the City of Toronto, 1920-1976," term paper, YU, 1981, CTA. Terry Crowley, "Ada May Brown Courtice: Pacifist, Feminist and Educational Reformer in Twentieth-Century Canada," *Studies in History and Politics*, 1980, 76-114.

[25] Careless, *Toronto to 1918*, 190, 193. See his sources. David R. Goldfield and Blaine A. Brownell, *Urban America: From Downtown to No Town* (Boston, 1979), 285-91, 355-59. TTLC, Minutes, 20 July 1922, LCMT offices. CT, *Report of the Civic Survey Commission* (Toronto, 1927), CTA. City Clerk's Department Employees' Salaries, 1917-1934, CTA.

[26] Harkness, *Atkinson of the Star*, chapters 9-14, *passim*. W.H. Kesterton, *A History of Journalism in Canada* (Toronto, 1967), 70, 84-89. I am grateful to Paul Rutherford for discussing the role of the press before 1918.

[27] *Globe*, 5 Mar. 1925. *Telegram*, 5 Mar. 1925. Thomas Suddon, "The Trinity College Park Stadium Question, 1925," 1978, UTA. Ratepayers groups: CC, Appendix A.

[28] J. Larkin, *Toronto Trades Assembly—Labour Council of Metropolitan Toronto* (Toronto, 1971); also in LCMT *Year Book*, 1971 (Toronto, 1971). G.H. Stanford, *To Serve the Community: The Story of Toronto's Board of Trade* (Toronto, 1974).

[29] Mary E. James, *Toronto Home and School Council: The First Fifty Years, 1916-1966* (Toronto, 1966), TBE. Susan W. Friedman, "Public Schools and Residential Areas in Toronto, 1871 to 1921," MA thesis, UT, 1980, chapter 5.

[30] Jesse E. Middleton, *Municipality of Toronto, Canada: A History*, 3 vols. (Toronto and New York, 1923), vol. 1, 371. R.V. Harrison Papers, 17, 46, CTA. FC, 1925, 43. On speculation: *Telegram*, 30 Dec. 1922. Timothy J. Colton, *Big Daddy: Frederick G. Gardiner and the Building of Metropolitan Toronto* (Toronto, 1980), 21, 53. Charles Clay, *The Leaside Story* (Leaside, 1958). J.I. Hempel, *The Town of Leaside: A Brief History* (Toronto, 1982).

[31] Borough of North York, *Historical Outline of the Administration of the Borough of North York* (North York, 1973), part 3. J.C. Boylen, *York Township, 1850-1954* (Toronto, 1954), 47-61.

[32] Ibid., 49, 53, 59. On Forest Hill: William French, *A Most Unlikely Village* (Toronto, 1964). True Davidson *et al.*, *The Golden Years of East York* (Toronto, 1976), chapter 1. Robert J. Wallace, "A Decade as a Village," Village of Swansea, Souvenir Brochure 1936, CTA. Esther Heyes, *Etobicoke From Furrow to Borough* (Etobicoke, 1974). Robert Bonis, *History of Scarborough* (Scarborough, 1965).

[33] Colton, *Big Daddy*, 21, 55. Weaver, *Shaping the Canadian City*, 66, 60. G.H. Ferguson, "Decentralizatin of Industry and Metropolitan Control," *JTPIC* 2 (1923), no. 2, 13-14; no. 3, 5-12.

[34] Michael J. Piva, "Workers and Tories: The Collapse of the Conservative Party in Urban Ontario, 1908-1919," *UHR* 3-76 (1977), 23-29. Schull, *Ontario Since 1867*, chapters 11, 12; quotation, 280. Peter Oliver, *G. Howard*

Ferguson: Ontario Tory (Toronto, 1977).

[35] TTLC, Minutes, 31 Aug. 1925; report of 41st convention of the Trades and Labour Congress.

[36] Harkness, *Atkinson*, 264. Victor Ross and A. St.L. Trigge, *A History of the Canadian Bank of Commerce*, 3 vols. (Toronto, 1920-1935), vol. 3, 190. John Kenneth Galbraith, *The Great Crash, 1929* (Harmondsworth, England, 1961).

[37] *Financial Post*, 14 Nov. 1929. Toronto Stock Exchange listing of shares and values. Shares: *Houston's Annual Financial Review*; data assembled by Donald Kerr, for which I am grateful.

[38] *Financial Post*, 7 Nov. 1929

[39] Neufeld, *Financial System of Canada*, 76-81, 97-101, 573-74. Michael Bliss, *A Canadian Millionaire: The Life and Business Times of Sir Joseph Flavelle, Bart., 1858-1939* (Toronto, 1978), 470. Donald Kerr, "The Emergence of the Industrial Heartland, c. 1750-1950," in L.D. McCann ed., *Heartland and Hinterland: A Geography of Canada* (Scarborough, 1982), 96. *Saturday Night*, 15 Sept. 1923. On mergers: Ross and Trigge, *Bank of Commerce*, vol. 3, esp. 191, 204. Graph of mergers: William R. Code, "The Spatial Dynamics of Financial Intermediaries in Canada," PhD thesis, University of California, Berkeley, 1974.

[40] Carlie Oreskovich, *Sir Henry Pellatt: The King of Casa Loma* (Toronto, 1982), 190-204. Joseph Schull, *100 Years of Banking in Canada: A History of the Toronto-Dominion Bank* (Toronto, 1958), 132-33.

[41] Comparisons: Neufeld, *Financial System of Canada*, tables. Kerr, "Emergence of the Industrial Heartland," in McCann, ed., *Heartland and Hinterland*, 94-96. Branches: R.G. Dun & Co., *The Mercantile Agency Reference Book* (Calgary, etc., 1929), 529-30, 750-51. FC, 1929, 49. On bank investment: Neil Quigley personal communication, 1983.

[42] *1917 Lydiatt's Book: What's What in Canadian Advertising* (Toronto, 1917), 89, 93, Thomas Fisher Rare Book Library. *Canadian Advertising* 2 (Apr. 1929), 69. Canada, Royal Commission on Publications, *Report* (Ottawa, 1961), 233-34. Stanley Psutka, "Equalization of Retail Prices in Canada: The Case of the T. Eaton Company, 1869-1976," 1976, UTA.

[43] FC, 1930, 69; 1929, 64, 39. E.M. Ashworth, *Toronto Hydro Recollections* (Toronto, 1955), 99. Tourist and Convention Bureau, *Annual Report*, 1927-1930; quotation, 1927 (courtesy of Metropolitan Toronto Tourist and Convention Bureau).

[44] FC, 1921, 19; FC, 1923, 10. G.H. Ferguson, "Decentralization of Industry." Data prior to 1921 were inflated guesses, it seems. Richard Pomfret, *The Economic Development of Canada* (Toronto, 1981), 184.

[45] Table X drawn from the *Census of Canada* is categorized by *sector* not by *occupation* because the latter are less manageable where given. Besides, categories change: to provide continuity the subcategories have been rearranged into the general categories, in large part following Loren Simerl and Howard Goldfinger, "Job Growth by Industry in the Toronto Area, 1941-1980," SPC, Working Papers for Full Employment 6, 1982, who in turn use Joachim Singlemann, *From Agriculture to Services: The Transformation of Industrial Employment* (Beverly Hills, 1978). I wish to thank Loren Simerl for discussing these matters.

[46] Veronica Strong-Boag, "The Girl of the New Day: Canadian Working Women in the 1920s," *Labour/le Travailleur* 4 (1979), 131-64. Mary Vipond, "The Image of Women in Mass Circulation Magazines in the 1920s," in Susan M. Trofimenkoff and Alison Prentice, eds., *The Neglected Majority: Essays in Canadian Women's History* (Toronto, 1977), 116-24. Graham S. Lowe, "Class, Job and Gender in the Canadian Office," *Labour/le Travaileur* 10 (1982), 11-37.

[47] Calculations from Table XI. Wage, consumer price and cost of living indices for Canada: M.C. Urquhart and K.A.H. Buckley, *Historical Statistics of Canada* (Cambridge, Toronto, 1965), 84, 304. Unfortunately, precise comparisons over time between series are not possible using indices. Piva, *Condition*, chapter 2. Strong-Boag, "Girl of the New Day," 147. Calculations on cost of living and arguments for raising wages: *Star*, 16 Mar. 1920.

[48] TTLC, Minutes, LCMT offices. Desmond Morton and Terry Copp, *Working People* (Ottawa, 1980), chapter 13. M. Biderman, "Father and Friends Organize a Union," in Irving Abella and David Millar , eds., *The Canadian Worker in the Twentieth Century* (Toronto, 1978), 240-45. James Struthers, "Prelude to Depression: The Federal Government and Unemployment, 1918-1929," *Canadian Historical Review* 58 (1977), 292.

[49] Bruce Scott, "'A Place in the Sun': The Industrial Council at Massey Harris, 1919-1929," *Labour/le Travailleur* I (1976), 158-92. Merrill Denison, *Harvest Triumphant: The Story of Massey-Harris* (Toronto, 1948). E.P. Neufeld, *A Global Corporation: A History of the Industrial Development of Massey-Ferguson Limited* (Toronto, 1969). Peter Cook, *Massey at the Brink: The Story of Canada's Greatest Multinational and its Struggle to Survive* (Toronto, 1982).

[50] Sally F Zerker, *The Rise and Fall of the Toronto Typographical Union, 1832-1972: A Case Study of Foreign Domination* (Toronto, 1982), chapter 9.

[51] FC, 1929, 44. Charles Dickens, *American Notes and Pictures from Italy* (London, 1908), 202-3. *Star*, 21 Feb. 1920. Town Planning Committee 1924: Norman Wilson to R.C. Harris, 3 Mar. 1927; Tracy leMay to Wilson, 27 Oct. 1928, in Norman Wilson Papers, Toronto General Box I, PAC.

[52] R.C. Harris, F.H. Gaby, and E.L. Cousins, *Report of the Civic Transportation Committee on Radial Entrances and Rapid Transit for the City of Toronto*, 2 vols. (Toronto, 1915). Doucet, "Politics, Space, and Trolleys." Donald F. Davis, "Mass Transit and Private Ownership: An Alternative Perspective in the

Case of Toronto," *UHR* 3-78 (1979), 60-98. Toronto Transit Commission, *Transit in Toronto* (Toronto, 1967). Louis H. Pursley, *Street Railways of Toronto, 1861-1921, Interurbans*, Special Volume 25 (Los Angeles, 1958). John F. Bromley and Jack May, *Fifty Years of Progressive Transit: A History of the Toronto Transit Commission* (n.p,1975). Frances Frisken, "A Triumph for Public Ownership: The TTC, 1921-1953," in Russell, ed., *Forging a Consensus*, 238-71.

[53] *Star*, 29 Jan. 1921. CC, Appendix C, 1917-1921.

[54] Frisken, "Triumph for Public Ownership," in Russell, ed., *Forging a Consensus*. Davis, "Mass Transit," 62-63.

[55] TTC, *Ten Years of Progressive Public Service, 1921-1931* (Toronto, 1931). TTC, *Wheels of Progress: A Story of the Developent of Toronto and its Public Transportaton Services* (Toronto, n.d.) 37-53. Davis, "Mass Transit," 78, 94, 67.

[56] Ibid., 97.

[57] *Star*, 4 Aug. 1921. Davis, "Mass Transit," 82.

[58] Ibid., 77-79. Number of vehicles: Provincial Department of Highways, PBP 13, File on Traffic Study, 28 Mar. 1929, CTA. Traffic flows: CT, *Report of the Advisory City Planning Commission with Recommendations for the Improvement of the Central Business Section, City of Toronto* (Toronto, 1929), 6, CTA.

[59] *Star Weekly*, 15 Dec. 1923.

[60] F.H. Marani, "Sky-scrapers," *JTPIC* 2 (May 1923), 12-13. "Skyscrapers and Traffic Congestion," *Saturday Night*, Jan. 1927. Tracy leMay, "Sky-scraper Problem in Town Planning," *Canadian Engineer* 58 (4 Feb. 1930), 189. On buildings constructed: *Report . . . Central Business Section*, 16; and FC, 1930, 9; and Gad and Holdsworth," Building for City," in Russell, ed., *Forging a Consensus*, 303.

[61] Norman Wilson Papers, City Planning Correspondence, 1924-1926, Town Planning Committee 1924, PAC. University Avenue Extension Act, 1928, provided permission: see Bylaw 13409, CC, 2 Nov. 1931. For accusations: *Telegram*, 23 Mar. 1929. Bliss, *A Canadian Millionaire*, 540, n. 54. William A. Deacon, "Toronto," *Canadian Geographical Journal* 2 (1931), 343.

[62] *Report . . . Central Business Section*. Greenberg, "Toronto: The Unknown Grand Tradition," 44-46.

[63] CC, 1929, Appendix C.

[64] Greenberg, "Toronto: The Unknown Grand Tradition," 42-44. James O'Mara, "Shaping Urban Waterfronts: The Role of Toronto's Harbour Commissioners, 1911-1960," YU Geography Department Discussion Paper 13, 1976. O'Mara, "The Toronto Harbour Commissioners' Financial Arrangements and City Waterfront Development, 1910 to 1950," YU Geography Department Discussion Paper 30, 1984. "Cyclone Helps Shape Harbour," *Port of Toronto News* 23 (Dec. 1976), 6. FC, 1929, 62-64; FC, 1930, 68-69.

[65] Richard Bébout, ed., *The Open Gate: Toronto Union Station* (Toronto, 1972), especially Ron Haggart, 15-19, and Robert McMann, 20-51. John F. Due, *The Intercity Electric Railway Industry in Canada* (Toronto, 1966), 82-87, 109. R.C. Harris, F.H. Gaby, and E.L. Cousins, *Report on Radial Entrances*, conclusion. Ontario, Commission on Hydro-Electric Railways Report (Toronto, 1921). John Buchanan, "The Sutherland Report and Provincial Involvement in Inter-urban Railways," 1970; Wendy Kell, or Report No. 19 of the Board of Control: "The Hydro Radial Entrance and the Subway Agreement, or the Waterfront 'Grab,' 1922," 1970; and Tony Usher, "Toronto, 1922: The Radial Entrance Issue," 1970, among others, UTA. *Telegram*, 23 Dec. 1922. *Star*, 1 Dec. 1922. W.R. Plewman, *Adam Beck and the Ontario Hydro* (Toronto, 1947).

[66] Middleton, *Municipality of Toronto*, vol. I, 402. Harney and Troper, *Immigrants*. Henry Radecki, *Ethnic Organizational Dynamics: The Polish Group in Canada* (Waterloo, 1979), chapter 1. Vladimir J. Kaye (Kysilewsky) and Frances Swyripa, "Settlement and Colonization," in Manoly R. Lupul, ed., *A Heritage in Transition: Essays in the History of Ukrainians in Canada* (Toronto, 1982), 50-52. N.F. Dreisziger, "Years of Growth and Change, 1918-1929," in Dreisziger *et al.*, eds., *Struggle and Hope: The Hungarian-Canadian Experience* (Toronto, 1982), chapter 5. Anthony W. Raspovich, *For a Better Life: A History of the Croatians in Canada* (Toronto, 1982), chapter 5. Special issue on immigrants, *UHR* 2-78 (1978). Warren E. Kalbach, "Historical and Generational Perspectives of Ethnic Residential Segregation in Toronto, Canada, 1851-1971," CUCS, Research Paper 118, 1980. CTPB, "A Report on the Ethnic Origins of the Population of Toronto 1960," 1961.

[67] *Star Weekly*, 11 Nov. 1916 to 15 June 1918.

[68] BMR, *What is "The Ward."* Harney and Troper, *Immigrants*, chapter 2. Speisman, *The Jews of Toronto*, chapters 6, 14, 15. S. Paul Bain, "Jewish Residential Segregation in the City of Toronto 1840-1971," BA thesis, YU, 1974, chapter 4. Edgar Wickberg *et al.*, *From China to Canada: A History of the Chinese Community in Canada* (Toronto, 1982), 93-98, 263.

[69] For an analysis of the Chicago School of Sociology: Peter G. Goheen, *Victorian Toronto*, University of Chicago, Department of Geography Research Paper 127 (Chicago 1970), chapter 2.

[70] Lillian Petroff, "Macedonians in Toronto: From Encampment to Settlement," *UHR* 2-78 (1978), 58-73.

[71] Bain, "Jewish Residential Segregation," 32-35. Cf. Louis Rosenberg, *A Study of the Changes in the Geographic Distribution of the Jewish Population in the*

Metropolitan Area of Toronto 1851 - 1951, Canadian Jewish Congress, Jewish Community Studies I (Montreal, 1954). Vicki W. Graff, "A Quantitative Historical Study of the Social Geography of an Urban Community: Kensington Market, 1901 - 1950," 1972, UTA. Daniel Hiebert, verbal communication on garment district, Jan. 1983.

[72] Papers by Stephen Speisman, James Lemon and Speisman, C.A. Russell, and Bev Stager in Lydia Burton and David Morley, eds., "The Annex Book," unpublished manuscript, 1978, Sections 1, 2, CTA and several libraries. John Punter *et al.* "The Annex Study: An Independent Input into the Part II Planning Process," YU Urban Studies Program, 1973, chapter 1. Karina A.C. Bordessa, "A Corporate Suburb of Toronto: Lawrence Park, 1905 - 1930," MA thesis, YU, 1980. Ross Hunter Paterson, "Kingsway Park, Etobicoke: An Analysis of the Development of an Early Twentieth Century Suburb," MA thesis, YU, 1982. Katherine Hale, pseudo, A.B. Garvin, *Toronto: Romance of a Great City* (Toronto, 1956), 208, 210. Moore, "Zoning and Planning," 322 - 23.

[73] Barbara M. Wilson, ed., *Ontario and the First World War, 1914 - 1918: A Collection of Documents* (Toronto, 1077), lxvii-lxviii. Wickberg, *From China to Canada*, chapter 10.

[74] Speisman, *Jews of Toronto*, 318 - 23. Bain, "Jewish Residential Segregation," chapter 5. *Mail and Empire*, 12 Mar. 1920. *Telegram*, 29 Apr. 1920. *Saturday Night*, 13 Aug. 1921, 1; 8 Oct. 1921, 1; 29 Sept. 1923, 1.

[75] Michiel Horn, "Keeping Canada 'Canadian': Anti-Communism and Canadianism in Toronto, 1928 - 29," *Canada* 3 (Sept. 1975), 35 - 47. Lita-Rose Betcherman, *The Little Band: The Clashes Between the Communists and the Political Establishment in Canada, 1928 - 1932* (Ottawa, 1982), chapters 1 - 7. Speisman, *Jews of Toronto*, 316 - 17. Erna Paris, *Jews: An Account of their Experience in Toronto* (Toronto, 1980).

[76] Horn, "Keeping Canada 'Canadian'," 45. Smyth and Houston, *The Sash Canada Wore*, chapter 8. Nathan Phillips, *Mayor of All the People* (Toronto, 1967), 58. Leslie Saunders, *An Orangeman in Public Life* (Toronto, 1980).

[77] John Webster Grant, *The Canadian Experience of Church Union* (London, 1967), chapters 2 - 6. Grant, *The Church in the Canadian Era: The First Century of Confederation* (Toronto, 1972), chapter 6. Donald Jones, "Young Presbyterian Minister Fought Hard Against Union," *Star*, 25 June 1983.

[78] Grant, *Church in the Canadian Era*, 130, 123 - 24.

[79] Peter Mellen, *The Group of Seven* (Toronto, 1970), 26, 200. J. Russell Harper, *Painting in Canada: A History*, 2nd ed. (Toronto, 1977), chapter 22. Barker Fairley, "What is Wrong with Canadian Art?" *Canadian Art* 6 (Autumn 1948), reprinted in *Arts Canada* 244 - 247 (Mar. 1982), 37. Sarah Milroy, "A Contract with Nature," *Canadian Forum* 64 (May 1984), 27 - 29.

[80] Ernest Hemingway, *Selected Letters, 1917 - 1961*, ed. Carlos Baker (New York), 84, 88, 95. Robert Fulford, "Emma Goldman Saw Toronto Harshly," *Star*, 19 Feb. 1983.

CHAPTER TWO, 1930s

[1] CC, 1934, Appendix C.

[2] Morton and Copp, *Working People*, 140. Pomfret, *Economic Development*, 185 - 87. Patricia V. Schulz, *The East York Workers' Association: A Response to the Great Depression* (Toronto, 1975), 1 - 13. Roger E. Riendeau, "A Clash of Interests: Dependency and the Municipal Problem in the Great Depression," *Journal of Canadian Studies* 14 (1979), 50 - 58. Hugh Garner, "Toronto's Cabbagetown," *Canadian Forum* 14 (July 1936), reprinted in J.L. Granatstein and Peter Stevens, eds., *Forum: Canadian Life and Letters, 1920 - 1970: Selections from the Canadian Forum* (Toronto, 1972), 146 - 47. Bernice T. Hunter, *That Scatterbrain Booky* (Richmond Hill, 1981); more recently, *With Love from Booky* (Richmond Hill, 1983). I also thank Ms Hunter for discussing the issues, notably the politics of the time. FC, 1933, 12; FC, 1937, 8; FC, 1939, 7. George H. Rust D'Eye, *Cabbagetown Remembered* (Erin, Ont., 1984).

[3] Saywell, "Housing Canadians," 169 - 89. Toronto Real Estate Board memo on office vacancies, PBP 1, 4.

[4] FC, 1938, 55. Toronto Industrial Commission, *Toronto and the Toronto Area* (Toronto, ca.1931), 41, 45, and *Fourth Annual Report*, 1932, CTA.

[5] Urquhart and Buckley, *Historical Statistics*, 88. Rental index, PBP 2, 2. Stamp, *Schools of Ontario*, 146 - 47.

[6] Michiel Horn, ed., *The Dirty Thirties: Canadians in the Great Depression* (Toronto, 1972), 122 - 29. Irving Abella and David Millar, eds., *The Canadian Worker in the Twentieth Century* (Toronto, 1978), 185 - 94. Morton and Copp, *Working People*, 138. Barry Broadfoot, *Ten Lost Years, 1929 - 1939: Memories of Canadians Who Survived the Depression* (Don Mills, 1973).

[7] Michiel Horn, *The League for Social Reconstruction: Intellectual Origins of the Democratic Left in Canada, 1930 - 1942* (Toronto, 1980). Grant, *Church in the Canadian Era*, 141. Betcherman, *The Little Band*, chapter 6.

[8] Stanford, *To Serve the Community*, 183. Riendeau, "Clash of Interests," 53. [Philpott], "History and Background of the Welfare Council," 2 - 3. Lappin, "Stages in the Development of Community Organization Work," 285 - 309.

[9] Riendeau, "Clash of Interests." Struthers, *No Fault of Their Own*, chapters 2 - 6. Alvin Finkel, *Business and Social Reform in the Thirties* (Toronto, 1979).

[10] H.M. Cassidy, *Unemployment and Relief in Ontario, 1929 - 1932* (Toronto, 1933).

[11] Riendeau, "Clash of Interests," 54, 52. Schulz, *East York Workers' Association*, 8.

[12] FC, 1938, 16–17; FC, 1939, 9.

[13] Stanford, *To Serve the Community*, 189. Horn, *The Dirty Thirties*, 600–01.

[14] Federation Council, Minutes, 27 Nov. 1933; including Joint Meeting of Board of Directors and Social Policy Committee, 14 Nov. 1933; and "Steps Taken Towards Retrenchment after the 1933 Campaign," 8 Nov. 1933, CTA.

[15] Ibid.

[16] Paris, *Jews*, 140–41. Betcherman, *The Little Band*, chapter 9. Schulz, *East York Workers' Association*, 26–32. Reginald A. McQuay, "Strikes in Toronto During the Depression," 1974, UTA.

[17] J. Larkin, *Toronto Trades Assembly*, 25–29. Neil McKenty, *Mitch Hepburn* (Toronto, 1967), chapter 8. Deborah Nowski, "Labour in Toronto: The Needle Trade, 1930–1938," 1974, UTA.

[18] FC, 1929, 64; FC, 1939, 35; FC, 1932, 55; FC, 1938, 55. Ashworth, *Toronto Hydro Recollections*, 99. Convention Bureau, *Annual Reports*, esp. 1940.

[19] *Financial Post*, 7 Jan. 1939; quoted by Kerr "Emergence of the Industrial Heartland," in McCann, ed., *Heartland and Hinterland*, 95–96. *Globe*, 31 May 1906. Neufeld, *Financial System of Canada*, 412, 419.

[20] Neufeld, *Financial System of Canada*, 495–97, 52, 99–101, 246, 252, 280. Nelles, *Politics of Development*, 434–37. Marr and Paterson, *Canada*, 266.

[21] Canada, Royal Commission on Publications, *Report*, 234. *Canadian Advertising* 12 (April-June 1939), 85–97. "Statistics of the Press," *Canada Year Book*, 1939 (Ottawa, 1939), 758–73. Peers, *Politics of Canadian Broadcasting*, 21. Max Braithwaite, *The Hungry Thirties 1930/1940: Canada's Illustrated Heritage* (Toronto, 1977), 84.

[22] Ontario, *Report of the Lieutentant-Governor's Committee on Housing Conditions in Toronto* (Toronto, 1934), esp. 15–18, 24, 31–32 (hereafter, *Bruce Report*). *Star*, 13 Nov. 1934. Garner, "Toronto's Cabbagetown," 145–48. Christopher Thompson, "The Great Depression and the Beginning of Social Housing . . . ," 1983, UTA.

[23] Bylaws: Moore "Zoning and Planning", 320–24.

[24] Bev Stager, "The Founding of an Association: The Early Annex Ratepayers, 1928–1940," in Burton and Morley, eds., "The Annex Book." Annex Ratepayers' Association, Minutes and Correspondence, 1931–1940, Metropolitan Public Library, Baldwin Room, especially George Gooderham to Ross Taylor, 8 Oct. 1932.

[25] Ibid. South Parkdale flyer; Lumsden Cummings, President, Citizens League of Toronto, to Ross Taylor, 24 Sept. 1935—3 Jan. 1936.

[26] Saywell, "Housing Canadians," 171. Data: PBP 1,2; 2,2; 3,3. City assessment data presented a somewhat more optimistic picture than the census. On roomers: Robert Thomas Allen, *When Toronto was for Kids* (Toronto, 1961), chapter 7.

[27] Humphrey Carver, *Compassionate Landscape: Places and People in a Man's Life* (Toronto, 1975), chapter 4. League for Social Reconstruction, "A Housing Programme," in *Social Planning for Canada* (Toronto, 1935). Saywell, "Housing Canadians," 171.

[28] *Bruce Report*, 117–20. Joint Committee, *A Low Cost Housing Project for the City of Toronto* (Toronto, 1934), presented to Board of Control, 17 Jan. 1934, in PBP 2,5. James H. Craig, "What Can Be Learned from State Housing in Great Britain and the United States?" *Journal of the Royal Architectural Institute of Canada* 11 (1935), 79–81.

[29] CC, 1934, Appendix C. A.E. LePage to CC, 29 Jan. 1934; PBP 2,5. Garner, "Toronto's Cabbagetown," 147. Ratepayers: *Star*, 8 Nov. 1934. LeMay to K.S. Gillies, Commissioner of Buildings, 25 Jan. 1934; leMay to Wadsworth [fall 1934], PBP 2,5; 1,2.

[30] Albert Rose, *Canadian Housing Policies, 1935–1980* (Toronto, 1980), 3, 166. John Bacher, "The Federal Government's Entry into Housing: The Origins and Implementation of the Dominion Housing Act of 1935," paper, Canadian Historical Association, 1982. Lending institutions: PBP 2,2.

[31] Development and Recovery Committee, Interim Report, June 1936, 4–6. PBP 4,5. CC, Special Committee on Housing, PBP 1,2. H.M.S. Carver, "The Housing Centre," *Saturday Night* 3 Oct. 1936. FC, 1936, 11–12; FC, 1937, 11–12; FC, 1938, 9–10. Tracy leMay memo on housing in Toronto (Aug. 1937), PBP 2,2. Canadian figures: Saywell, "Housing Canadians," 182. CC, 1937, Appendix C, 28.

[32] Urwick to leMay, 1 June and 5 June 1939, PBP 2,4.

[33] Hunter, *Scatterbrain Booky*. Frank E. Heard, "Summer Dance Hall was Utopia," *G & M*, 30 July 1983.

[34] Smythe and Young, *Conn Smythe*, 102–38. Stan Obodiac, *Maple Leaf Gardens: Fifty Years of History* (Toronto, 1981), 15. Sullivan, *Grey Cup Story*, 38–46. Cauz, *Baseball's Back*, 77–81.

[35] Emigration: Roderic Beaujot and Kevin McQuillan, *Growth and Dualism: The Demographic Development of Canadian Society* (Toronto, 1982), 83.

[36] Pierre Berton, *The Dionne Years: A Thirties Melodrama* (Toronto, 1977), esp. chapter 8; quotation, on title page. On *Star*: Kesterton, *History of Journalism*, 86.

[37] Mark M. Orkin, *The Great Stork Derby* (Don Mills, 1981). Braithwaite, *Hungry Thirties*, 49–50. Foster: *Star*, 4 June 1983.

[38] Frank Jones, "Death and Injustice in East Toronto," *Star*, 1 Nov. 1981. Morley Callaghan, *More Joy in Heaven* (Toronto, 1937, 1970).

[39] Speisman, *Jews of Toronto*, 332–35. Paris, *Jews*, 166, 145, 142. Sandra Souchotte, "Canada's Workers' Theatre II," *Canadian Theatre Review* 10 (Spring 1976), 92–93.

[40] Boylen, *York Township*, 63–79. Davidson, *East York*, 68, 73. Shultz, *The*

East York Workers' Association, 3 - 4.

[41] Report Submitted by Heads of Department on Proposed Annexation of the Townships of York and East York, 31 Mar. 1931; Report on Suggested Annexation of York and East York, 31 Oct. 1931; *Star*, 17 Apr. and 18 May 1939 and other clippings; R.V. Harrison Papers, 17, 46, 47, CTA.

[42] Colton, *Big Daddy*, 56. A.F.W. Plumptre, Report on the Government of Metropolitan Toronto to the Hon. D. Croll, Minister of Municipal Affairs of the Province of Ontario, 20 June 1935, UT Department of Political Science and Economics, manuscript, Fisher Rare Book Library.

[43] *Telegram*, 1 Aug. 1935; quoted in Smylie, "Toronto Civic Affairs in 1935," 1981, UTA. Harkness, *Atkinson*, 252. William Dennison, "Jimmie Simpson: Toronto's Militant Mayor," LCMT *Year Book*, 1971 (Toronto, 1971), 48 - 49.

[44] Newspapers, *Canada Year Book*, 1939, 761.

[45] Theresa G. Falkner, *The Early History of the Association of Women Electors of Metropolitan Toronto* (Toronto, 1977). Results: CC, Appendix C.

[46] Braithwaite, *The Hungry Thirties*, 38 - 39, 42. Betcherman, *The Little Band*, chapters 9 - 18. Paris, *Jews*, 169 - 70. "The Intellectual Capital of Canada," in Granatstein and Stevens, *Forum*, 77 - 84. Arrest data: Frederick I. Hill, "Crime in Toronto: An Historical-Geographical Overview," 1970, UTA.

[47] Schull, *Ontario Since 1867*, chapters 13, 14. McKenty, *Mitch Hepburn*, chapters 5 - 12.

[48] CT, Advisory City Planning Committee, *Report on Street Extensions, Widenings and Improvements in the City of Toronto* (Toronto, 1930), CTA. Map: *Telegram*, 15 May 1930. LeMay to mayor, 8 June 1931. Los Angeles: R.C. Harris to mayor and council, 12 May 1930, PBP 8, 4. Plans reviewed with further proposals: Development and Recovery Committee, subcommittee on Highways, PBP 4,5. Bylaw 13409: CC, 1931, Appendix B. Map of changes: R.V. Burgess, Clerk (Leaside) to leMay, 31 June 1940, PBP 14,5. LeMay to Albert Rose, Civic Advisory Council, 7 Dec. 1948, PBP 12,6. Nadine A. Hooper, "Toronto: A Study in Urban Geography," MA thesis, UT, 1941.

[49] A.E.K. Bunnell, Memo on Don River Boulevards, 12 Oct. 1931; Don Valley Association proposals, 27 Oct. 1932, PBP 4,5. Wilson to leMay, 19 June 1939, PBP 4,6. Maps for 1939 proposals: *Star*, 26 Dec. 1939. Norman D. Wilson, "Some Problems of Urban Transportation," in Harold A. Innis, ed., *Essays in Transportation in Honour of W.T. Jackman* (Toronto, 1941), 85 - 118.

[50] Figures in *Municipal Handbook*; also Bromley and May, *Fifty Years of Progressive Transit*, 47, 59, 61. Albert S. Richey, "The Local Service of the Toronto Transportation Commission," 1934, Municipal Reference Library. Frisken, "A Triumph for Public Ownership," in Russell, ed., *Forging a Consensus*, 255 - 59.

[51] Debt: FC, 1939, 36. Wilson and Bunnell, Memo on Proposed Subway for Street Cars, 17 Mar. 1937, PBP 4,5.

[52] FC, 1937, 11; FC, 1938, 55. Sally Gibson, *More Than an Island: A History of the Toronto Island* (Toronto, 1984), 195 - 98.

[53] LeMay to A.J. Bowring, 20 Oct. 1933, PBP 8,4. Plumptre, Report on the Government of Metropolitan Toronto, 1935, 106. BMR, *White Paper*, no. 226, 23 Nov. 1937. Minutes of Public Meeting at the Housing Centre, 19 May 1937, PBP 1,4.

[54] LeMay, Memo Respecting the Report of the Lieut.-Governor's Committee on Housing, Fall 1934 (draft); and leMay to Wadsworth [fall 1934], PBP 1,2.

[55] LeMay, Memo on housing in Toronto, Aug. 1937. BMR, *White Paper*, no. 226, 23 Nov. 1937. Moore, "Zoning and Planning," in Artibise and Stelter, *The Usable Urban Past*, 326 - 27. Minutes of Public Meeting at Housing Centre, 19 May 1937, PBP 1,4.

[56] "The Manly Bosom," *Saturday Night*, 11 July 1936. Jesse E. Middleton, for the Centennial Committee, *Toronto's 100 Years* (Toronto, 1934), 149. *G&M*, 7 Sept. 1937. Kilgallin, "Toronto in Fiction," 114 - 53. Braithwaite, *Hungry Thirties*, 69.

CHAPTER THREE, 1940 - 1953

[1] Oriole Park Neighbourhood Association, flyer for mass meeting, Harold Clark Papers, Box 1, CTA.

[2] OPNA, brief, 1 Apr. 1947; S.J. Allin to leMay, 16 June 1947; Mayor to leMay, 13 Sept. 1948, and other items, PBP 6, 1. Frank Tumpane, "The Press and Local News," CAC, *News Bulletin* (Apr. 1951), 21. Kathleen D. Allin letter, *G&M*, 11 Mar. 1947. *Star*, 17 April. 1947. *The Herald* (North Toronto), 11 Apr. 1947. *G&M*, 14 Apr. 1947. Harold Clark letter, *Star*, *Telegram*, 4 Apr. 1947; and "The Neighbourhood Movement," speech, Clark Papers, Box 1, CTA.

[3] Gerald L. Caplan, *The Dilemma of Canadian Socialism: The CCF in Ontario* (Toronto, 1973), 88 - 92. J.T. Morley, *Secular Socialists: The CCF/NDP in Ontario: A Biography* (Kingston and Montreal, 1984). J.L. Granatstein, *Canada's War: The Politics of the Mackenzie King Government, 1939 - 1945* (Toronto, 1975), 220 - 21, 264 - 65. Schull, *Ontario Since 1867*, chapter 15. Gad Horowitz, *Canadian Labour in Politics* (Toronto, 1968), chapters 3, 4. Finkel, *Social and Business Reforms*.

[4] Caplan, *Dilemma*, chapters 10 - 12. David Lewis, *The Good Fight: Political*

Memoirs, 1909–1958 (Toronto, 1981), chapter 12. Jonathan Manthorpe, *The Power and the Tories* (Toronto, 1974), 34–38. Schull, *Ontario Since 1867*, 330, 334. Larkin, *Toronto Trades Assembly*, 29–32.

[5] Granatstein, *Canada's War*, chapter 10.

[6] *Telegram*, 23 Dec. 1940, 24 Dec. 1941. *G&M*, 26 Dec. 1941.

[7] Caplan, *Dilemma*, 118–20. Stanford, *To Serve the Community*, 203.

[8] Leslie H. Saunders, *An Orangeman in Public Life: The Memories of Leslie Howard Saunders* (Toronto, ca. 1980), 107.

[9] *G&M*, quoted in Patricia Hibben, "An Examination of the Candidates and the Voting Trends of the Civic Elections of 1952 to 1954," 1976, UTA.

[10] John H. Mollenkopf, *The Contested City* (Princeton, 1983).

[11] Granatstein, *Canada's War*. Robert Bothwell and William Kilbourn, *C.D. Howe: a Biography* (Toronto, 1979), 188–89. Robert Bothwell, "'Who's Paying for Anything These Days?': War Production in Canada, 1939–45," in N.F. Dreisiger, ed., *Mobilization for Total War: The Canadian, American and British Experience, 1914–1918, 1939–1945* (Waterloo, 1981), 57–69.

[12] PBP 13, 6. Bothwell and Kilbourn, *Howe*, 161, 165, 190, 155, 168, 189, 206. Stephen Franklin, *A Time of Heroes 1940/1950: Canada's Illustrated Heritage* (Toronto, 1977), 13. Denison, *Harvest Triumphant*, chapter 17. Neufeld, *A Global Corporation*, chapter 3.

[13] Gulbrand Loken, *From Fjord to Frontier: A History of the Norwegians in Canada* (Toronto, 1980), 121–23.

[14] Granatstein, *Canada's War*, 277–78. Bothwell and Kilbourn, *Howe*, 194–96, 189–90, 205, 212. Schull, *Ontario Since 1867*, 312.

[15] TRC, "Report 4, 1944," 27. G.F. Davies, "Planning Post-War Jobs," speech to Empire Club, 30 Nov. 1944, TRC, "Annual Report, 1944," Appendix. TRC, "Annual Report, 1945," 33, CTA. R.D. Cuff and J.L. Granatstein, *American Dollars—Canadian Prosperity: Canadian-American Economic Relations, 1945–1950* (Toronto, 1978), 230.

[16] Unemployment: *Census of Canada*, 1941, vol. 6, Table 15; *Census*, 1951, vol. 5, Table 3. B.G. Sullivan, "Labour," in CAC, "Working and Living in Toronto: Prospects and Problems: Research Conference," December 1948, 13–14, CTA.

[17] Jacob Spelt, *Urban Development in South-Central Ontario* (Assen, Netherlands, 1955; Toronto, 1972), 204–05. N.C. Field and D.P. Kerr, "Geographical Aspects of Industrial Growth in the Metropolitan Toronto Region," Department of Treasury and Economics, Regional Development Branch, Research Paper 1 (1968), chapter 2. A.E.K. Bunnell to leMay, 13 May 1944, PBP 12, 2. Memo, leMay to City Planning Board, 16 Aug. 1945, PBP 8, 5. T.H. Bartley, "Industrial Development," in CAC, "Working and Living in Toronto," 6, CTA.

[18] Field and Kerr, "Geographic Aspects of Industrial Growth," chapter 2. Bartley, "Industrial Development," 5.

[19] J.A. Rhind, "Prospects and Problems of Commerce and Finance in Toronto," in CAC, "Working and Living in Toronto," 8, CTA. J.B. McGeachy, "Toronto? E-r, u-h," *Maclean's*, 15 Nov. 1947; Marshall McLuhan, *The Mechanical Bride: Folklore of Industrial Man* (New York, 1951; Boston, 1967). John P. Seeley *et al.*, *Crestwood Heights: A North American Suburb* (Toronto, 1956).

[20] Wages and cost of living: Urquhart and Buckley, *Historical Statistics of Canada*, 84, 304. Retail sales: *Census of Canada*, 1941, vol. 10, Table 8; *Census*, 1951, vol. 7, Table 3–54, Table 2–21.

[21] CAC, *Report on Auditorium and Convention Hall Facilities for Toronto* (Toronto, 1950).

[22] Ashworth, *Toronto Hydro Recollections*, 99.

[23] On vacancies: Lewis Duncan, *Report of the Advisory Committee Studying on Housing in the City of Toronto* (Toronto, 1942). Community Planning Association of Canada, Greater Toronto Branch, *Housing and Planning Digest*, vol. 3, bulletin 10, 1 Oct, 1948; bulletin 11, 1 Nov. 1948. Toronto Labour Council (CCL), Minutes, 12 Jan. 1948; LCMT offices. Canada, Dominion Bureau of Statistics, *Greater Toronto Housing Atlas* (Ottawa, 1946).

[24] Humphrey Carver and Robert Adamson, *How Much Housing Does Greater Toronto Need?* (Toronto, 1946), 38; and *Who Can Pay for Housing?* (Toronto, 1946), 4–5. See Carver's *Compassionate Landscape: Places and People in a Man's Life* (Toronto, 1975). Table assembled by leMay from Dominion Bureau of Statistics data 1945–1949, PBP 14, 13. CAC, Committee on Metropolitan Problems, *First Report* (Toronto, 1949–50), Section One, 21, 23, CTA. P.S. Secord of CMHC, CAC, "Working and Living in Toronto," 34–35, 39, CTA.

[25] Carver, *Houses for Canadians* (Toronto, 1948), 40.

[26] Ownership: George Farley to mayor and Board of Control, 25 Nov. 1946, PBP 3, 6.

[27] Stuart M. Jamieson, *Times of Trouble: Labour Unrest and Industrial Conflict in Canada, 1900–66* (Ottawa, 1968), chapter 6. Morton and Copp, *Working People*, chapters 16–19.

[28] Jeff Abrams, "T.T.C. on Strike," 1979, UTA. Morton and Copp, *Working People*, 215. Eileen Sufrin, *The Eaton Drive: The Campaign to Organize Canada's Largest Department Store, 1948 to 1952* (Toronto, 1982).

[29] Larkin, *Toronto Trades Assembly*, 29–32.

[30] Jean Bruce, *After the War* (Toronto, 1982), 14–18, chapter 3. John M. Gibbon, *New Colour for the Canadian Mosaic: The Displaced Persons* (Toronto, 1951). Alan G. Green, *Immigration and the Postwar Canadian Economy* (Toronto, 1976), 16–30. Irving Abella and Harold Troper, *None is More than Enough:*

Canadians and the Jews of Europe, 1933–1948 (Toronto, 1982). Recent volumes of the Multiculturalism Directorate, Department of the Secretary of State, some of which are cited below.

[31] Jean Bruce, *After the War*, chapter 32.

[32] Hortense C.F. Wasteneys, "The Adequacy of the Social Services Made Available to Displaced Families in Toronto," MSW thesis, UT, 1950, 48.

[33] Edgar Wickberg *et al.*, *From China to Canada: A History of the Chinese Communities in Canada* (Toronto, 1982), 205–08. Gordon Milling, "Five Years toward Fair Practices," in Toronto and District Trades and Labour Council, *Year Book*, 1952 (Toronto, 1952), 33.

[34] Wasteneys, "Adequacy of Social Services;" and Wasteneys, "A History of the University Settlement of Toronto, 1910–1958," PhD thesis, UT, 1975, chapters 4–5.

[35] Guest, *Emergence of Social Security*, chapters 8–9, 141. Richard M. Bird, *The Growth of Government Spending in Canada*, Canadian Tax Papers 51 (Toronto, 1970), Table 12.

[36] FC, 1950, 18; FC, 1953, 10,38.

[37] Welfare Council, "Annual Report, 1946," SPC offices. [Philpott], "History and Background of the Welfare Council," 6–7.

[38] Albert Rose, *Regent Park: a Study of Slum Clearance* (Toronto, 1958). J.B. Conacher, "A Canadian Social Scandal," *Canadian Forum* 33 (Aug. 1953), also in Granatstein and Stevens, *Forum*, 288–89. Duncan, *Report on Housing*, 13–23.

[39] Clark Papers, Box 1, CTA.

[40] Rose, *Regent Park*.

[41] CAC, "Report of Community Council Committee, 1948"; Joint Committee on the Future of the Position of Community Counsellor, Minutes, 6, 22 June 1949, CTA.

[42] Hugo W. Wolter, "Living in our Community," in CAC, "Working and Living in Toronto," 28–30.

[43] Schull, *Ontario Since 1867*, 277. Bruce West, *Toronto* (Toronto, 1967), 293–94. *G&M*, *Star* and *Telegram*, 1 April 1947.

[44] Ontario Law Reform Commission, *Report on Sunday Observance* (Toronto, 1970), 63–66. CC, 1949, Appendix C, 15. *G&M*, 25 Feb. 1941; 4 Oct. 1949; 23 Dec. 1949. *Star*, 2 Jan. 1950; 20 Mar. 1950. Ron Haggart, "Situation Comedy in City Hall," in William Kilbourn, ed., *The Toronto Book: An Anthology of Writings Past and Present* (Toronto, 1976), 255. John Robert Colombo, comp., "A Lampy Sampler," *City Magazine* 2 (9 Apr. 1978), 11–13, 29.

[45] Sullivan, *Grey Cup Story*, 63–64, 73–107.

[46] Obodiac, *Maple Leaf Gardens*, 30–33.

[47] Cauz, *Baseball's Back*, 91–102.

[48] Filey, *I Remember Sunnyside*, chapters 4, 5.

[49] Ontario Council for the Arts, *The Awkward Stage* (Toronto, 1969), 181–82. Wayne E. Edmonston, *Nathan Cohen, The Making of a Critic* (Toronto, 1977).

[50] Moore, "Zoning and Planning," 326–35. Transcripts of ICZ, PBP 10, 1. Quotations, Jarvis Collegiate meeting, 16 Sept. 1941. Table of Percentage Use of Developed Areas in Cities, PBP 10, 2.

[51] Transcripts, Jarvis meetings, 16 Sept. 1941, 19; 23 Sept. 1941, 3–30; Harbord meeting, 7 Oct. 1941, 13–15, 23; Parkdale meeting, 10 Oct. 1941, 29–30, PBP 10, 1.

[52] Northern Vocational School meeting, 19 Sept. 1941, PBP 10, 1. *Star*, 19 Sept. 1942.

[53] CTPB, Minutes, 15 Apr. 1942 onward, PBP 12, 1. The plan appears in the "Second Annual Report" of the board and in special brochure for the public, *The Master Plan for the City of Toronto and Environs* (Toronto, 1943).

[54] *Master Plan*, 15. Displayed and explained to public in Simpsons.

[55] TRC, "Interim Report to the City Council of the Corporation of Toronto," 30 May 1944, 36; and Appendix 2, 2–3, Box 1, CTA.

[56] CTPB, "Third Annual Report of the City Planning Board," 30 Dec. 1944, CTA.

[57] CAC, "Report of One Day Conference on Community Research, 16 Oct. 1947," PBP 12, 6. Committee on Statistical Areas, Minutes, 1948–50, PBP 13, 3.

[58] "Report No. 1 of the Committee Surveying the Declining Areas of the City," 2 Dec. 1946; quoting letter of Miss Jean Boyes, 20 Nov. 1946, PBP 3, 6. Annex Ratepayers' Association, Minutes, 19 Sept. 1948, Metro Library, Baldwin Room. Burton and Morley, eds. "The Annex Book." Draft of leMay speech to American Society of Planning Officials, 28 July 1950, PBP 8,7. Also leMay on Jack McCabe Show, CJBC, 24 Nov. 1947, PBP 8, 7.

[59] Hulchanski, "Origins of Urban Land Use Planning," chapters 7–9. Dhar, "Emergence of Land Use Planning," chapter 5.

[60] LeMay correspondence with officials, 1949; leMay to Clark, 16 May 1947, PBP, 8, 5. CTPB, "Third Report and Official Plan," June 21, 1949. CAC, Committee on Metropolitan Problems *First Report*, Section Two, 95. *G&M*, quoted in Community Planning Association, Toronto Branch, *Housing and Planning Digest*, bulletin 10 (1 Oct. 1947). FC, 1946, 30; FC, 1949, 9, 18, 32; FC, 1950, 49; FC, 1951, 18. CT, *Municipal Finance: A Report Prepared by the Civic Advisory Council* (Toronto, 1950).

[61] A.E.K. Bunnell, Community Planning Branch, Ontario Department of Planning and Development, to leMay, 20 June 1948. Bunnell, to secretaries of all planning boards and clerks of all municipalities in the County of York,

19 Apr. 1949. LeMay, list of subdivisions, 1950, PBP 9, 1. Carver, *Houses for Canadians*, 40. John Sewell, "Where the suburbs came from," *City Magazine* 2 (Jan. 1977), 20-27. E.G. Faludi, *Land Development in the Metropolitan Area of Toronto* (Toronto, 1952).

[62] Colton, *Big Daddy*, chapters 2, 3; 61-63, 64.

[63] Major analyses of Metro: Harold Kaplan, *Urban Political Systems: A Functional Analysis of Metro Toronto* (New York, 1967). Albert Rose, *Governing Metropolitan Toronto: A Social and Political Analysis, 1953-71* (Berkeley, 1972). Frank Smallwood, *Metro Toronto: A Decade Later* (Toronto, 1963). On steps leading to Metro: leMay, memo on planning, ca. 1951, PBP 6,2. LeMay to mayor, 20 Mar. 1946, PBP 9, 6. LeMay to Lawrence M. Orton, 15 July 1946. Orton to leMay, 24 July 1946, PBP 12, 3. TRC, "Annual Report 1946", 14, CTA. *G&M*, 8 July, 1948, and other clippings, PBP 6, 6.

[64] CAC, Committee on Metropolitan Problems, *First Report*, Section One, iv-v, 14-30. FC, 1950, 18.

[65] CAC, Committee on Metropolitan Problems, *First Report*, Section One, 33-53. McKenty, *Mitch Hepburn*, 175-77, 249-50, 257. Norman D. Wilson, "A Transportation Plan for Metropolitan Toronto Area and the Suburban Area Adjacent," Apr. 1948, CTA. Metro Toronto Transportation Plan Review, *A Catalogue of Transportation Concepts* (Toronto, 1973). D.S. Wilson to N.D. Wilson, 12 and 29 Aug. 1948, Norman D. Wilson Papers, Box 3, PAC. William Storrie and Norman G. McDonald, "Report on Water Supply and Sewage Disposal for the City of Toronto and Related Areas," 15 Sept. 1949.

[66] CAC, Committee on Metropolitan Problems, *First Report*, Section One, 55-64.

[67] CAC, Committee on Metropolitan Problems, *First Report*, Section One, 65-85; *Final Report* (Toronto, 1951), iv, 90-49.

[68] Colton, *Big Daddy*, 63-73.

[69] Rose, *Governing Metropolitan Toronto*, 25-27.

[70] LeMay, "Tour of Inspection," 30 Apr. 1953; "Tour of City, 1948," PBP 13, 7. On Humber Valley Village: *Telegram*, 3 Mar. 1954.

[71] Murray Jones, "Metropolitan Man: Some Economic and Social Aspects," *Plan Canada* 4 (June 1963), 21; reprinted in Leonard O. Gertler, ed., *Planning the Canadian Environment* (Montreal, 1968), 235-49.

CHAPTER FOUR, 1954-1966

[1] Henri Rossier and Pierre Berton, *The New City: A Prejudiced View of Toronto* (Toronto, 1961), 26, 30. Pierre Berton, *The Comfortable Pew: A Critical Look at the Religious Establishment in a New Age* (Toronto, 1965). William Kilbourn, ed., *The Restless Church: A Response to the Comfortable Pew* (Toronto, 1966).

[2] Jones, "Metropolitan Man," 21.

[3] Phillips, *Mayor of All the People*, 188.

[4] SPC, Immigration Section, "Immigration Issues Today: Reports and Papers Presented at the 1962 Conference on Immigration," 38, 64. Warren E. Kalbach, *The Effect of Immigration on Population* (Ottawa, 1974), 7. Anthony H. Richmond, *Immigrants and Ethnic Groups in Metropolitan Toronto* (Downsview, 1967).

[5] Compared to other cities, Jeffrey G. Reitz, *The Survival of Ethnic Groups* (Toronto, 1980), 250.

[6] N.F. Dreisziger *et al.*, *Struggle and Hope: The Hungarian-Canadian Experience* (Toronto, 1982), chapter 7.

[7] Green, *Immigration and the Postwar Canadian Economy*, 35, 140. Robert Winters, SPC, "Highlights of Second Immigration Conference and Annual Meeting of Immigration Section," 1960, 26.

[8] Henry G. MacLeod, "The Transformation of the United Church of Canada, 1946-1977: a Study in the Sociology of the Denomination," PhD thesis, UT, 1980, 13, 16, 20, 60, 98.

[9] Compiled from census tracts by Susan Nimchick, "Ethnic Distributions in Metropolitan Toronto, 1951-1971," 6, Fig, 2, UTA. Maps 8-11 redrawn from those provided by Geoffrey Dobilas, Stephen Dynes and Thomas Ostler, CTPDD (Stephen McLaughlin, Commissioner), for which I am grateful. Originally derived from Statistics Canada, *Metropolitan Atlas Series: Toronto* (Ottawa, 1984) 112-13.

[10] Kalbach, "Historical and Generational Perspectives of Ethnic Residential Segregation," 14, 18-23. Albert Rose, ed., *A People and its Faith* (Toronto, 1959). Bain, "Jewish Residential Segregation in the City of Toronto," chapters 6, 7. The measures widely used, for example, in Kalbach, are the Index of Dissimilarity and the Index of Segregation.

[11] On institutions: Reitz, *Survival of Ethnic Groups*, 218-19. Metropolitan Toronto, *Ten Years of Progress: Metropolitan Toronto, 1953-1963* (Toronto, 1963), 36. Kalbach, "Historical and Generational Perspectives of Ethnic Residential Segregation," 19, 26. Samuel Sidlofsky, "Post-War Immigrants in the Changing Metropolis with Special Reference to Toronto's Italian Population," PhD thesis, UT, 1969.

[12] Nimchick, "Ethnic Distributions," 21-26, Figs. 18-25. On variations within national groupings, especially Yugoslavian, David F. Stermole and H.A. Gleason, Jr., "Residential Patterns of Ethnic Subgroups in Toronto," in E.W. Hanten and J.J. Utano, eds., *The Urban Environment in a Spatial Perspective* (Akron, 1979), 63-67.

[13] Laurier F.J. Therrien, "A Structural Analysis of the Residential Space of 'French Toronto' 1951-1971," YU Geography Research Paper 1975, 94, 96, 103, 105. Nimchick, "Ethnic Distributions," 19-21, 26-27, Figs. 14-16,

26–28. Kalbach, "Historical and Generational Perspectives of Ethnic Residential Segregation," 26.

[14] Rossier and Berton, *The New City*, 39.

[15] SPC, Immigration Section, "Conference Highlights," 1959. "Glass curtain", Roman Olynyk phrase.

[16] SPC, Immigration Section, "Highlights of Second Immigration Conference and Annual Meeting of Immigration Section," 1960, 26–27, 18–21, 11–12. SPC, "Community Planning for Immigration: Reports and Papers Presented at the Immigration Conference and Annual Meeting," 1961, 45. SPC, "Immigration Issues Today," 1962, 50, 52. On Toronto's volunteer groups and government, see Freda Hawkins, *Canada and Immigration: Public Policy and Public Concern* (Montreal, 1972), 314–19; and Edith Ferguson, *Newcomers in Toronto* (Toronto, 1964).

[17] Phillips, *Mayor of All the People*, 91–129. Saunders, *Orangeman*, 117.

[18] Braithwaite, *Star*, 18 June 1959. Vizinczey, *In Praise of Older Women* (Toronto, 1965, 1977), 169–70. Jeann Beattie, *Behold the Hour* (Toronto, 1959), 73. Phyllis B. Young, *The Torontonians* (Toronto, 1960), 240. All quoted in Kilgallin, *Toronto in Fiction*, 270, 237–39, 262–67.

[19] FC, 1960, 7. R.J. Needham, *Boom Town Metro: a Toronto Daily Star Report* (Toronto, 1964).

[20] Burton, "The Redevelopment of Downtown Toronto," speech to Downtown Business Men's Association, 1 Mar. 1961, 6, in Redevelopment Advisory Council File, CTA. Neufeld, *Financial System of Canada*, 99, 246.

[21] Ibid., 508. Donald P. Kerr, "Some Aspects of the Geography of Finance in Canada", *Canadian Geographer*, 9 (1965), 175–92, esp. Tables 2, 3.

[22] Neufeld, *Financial System of Canada*, 498–500, 22. Frederick G. Gardiner, "What Metropolitan Government during the Past Seven Years has Accomplished for Toronto," Address to Economic Club of Detroit, 10 Apr. 1961, in Cornish Papers, CTA.

[23] John Porter, *The Vertical Mosaic: An Analysis of Social Class and Power in Canada* (Toronto, 1965), 461. W.A. Craick, "Words in Print," CT, *Toronto '59: One Hundred and Twenty Fifth Anniversary* (Toronto, 1959), 31. Circulation: Kesterton, *History of Journalism*, 72, 175. Russell Braddon, *Roy Thomson of Fleet Street—and How He Got There* (London, Toronto, 1965).

[24] Craick, "Words in Print," 31–32. Kesterton, *History of Journalism*, 171–74. Canada, *Royal Commission on Publications: Background Papers* (Ottawa, 1961), esp. 15, 99. *Canadian Advertising* 27 (Mar.-Apr. 1954), 125–26. Ibid., 38 (Mar.-Apr. 1965), 95–96, 124–25.

[25] Frank W. Peers, *The Public Eye: Televison and Politics of Canadian Broadcasting, 1952–1968* (Toronto, 1979), esp. 17, 31, 46, 59, 65, 152, 229–31, 239–42. Maggie Siggins, *Bassett* (Toronto, 1979), 206–22.

[26] Porter, *Vertical Mosaic*, esp. chapter 8.

[27] Field and Kerr, "Geographic Aspects of Industrial Growth," 11–40. Needham et al., *Boom Town Metro*, 11. Donald Kerr and Jacob Spelt, "Manufacturing in Downtown Toronto," *Geographical Bulletin*, No. 10 (1957), 5–20; and "Manufacturing in Suburban Toronto," *Canadian Geographer*, No. 12 (1958), 12–19.

[28] Ibid. Field and Kerr, "Geographical Aspects of Industrial Growth," 23–27. D. Michael Ray, "The Location of United States Subsidiaries in Southern Ontario" in R. Louis Gentilcore, ed., *Canada's Changing Geography* (Scarborough, 1967), 149–62; reprinted in Gentilcore, ed., *Geographical Approaches to Canadian Problems* (Scarborough, 1971), 69–82.

[29] Richard Organ *et al.*, *Avro Arrow: The Story of the Avro Arrow from its Evolution to its Execution* (Cheltenham, Ont., 1981). Bothwell, Drummond and English, *Canada since 1945*, 243–44.

[30] Ibid., 243, 207, 326–33. Canada, Privy Council, *Foreign Ownership and the Structure of Canadian Industry* (Ottawa, 1968). A.E. Safarian, *Foreign Ownership of Canadian Industry* (Toronto, 1973). Robert M. Dunn, *The Canada–U.S. Capital Market: Intermediation, Integration, and Policy Independence*, Canada–U.S. Prospects Series of C.D. Howe Institute and National Planning Association (Montreal and Washington, 1978), 42–44.

[31] Lex Schrag, "Metropolitan Toronto: Services for Subdivisions," *G&M*, 19 Oct. 1955. James Lorimer, *The Developers* (Toronto, 1978), part one, esp. 43–44. Catherine Wismer, *Sweethearts: The Builders, the Mob and the Men* (Toronto, 1980), chapter 4 and 69–71. Jeremy Rudin, "The Changing Structure of the Land Development Industry," CUCS Major Report 13, 1978. Colton, *Big Daddy*, 163.

[32] Neufeld, *Financial System of Canada*, 434–36. Lorimer, *Developers*, 71–77. High housing costs compared to other government services: SPC, "Focus: the Impact on Community Services of our Changing Population," Sept. 1959, 12–13.

[33] CTPB, "Changes in Housing Stock, 1951–1971," Research Bulletin 4, 1974, 19–22, compiled from CMHC data.

[34] Ibid. Rose, *Canadian Housing Policies*, 35. MT, *Metropolitan Toronto 1967* (Toronto, 1967), 22–23. Larry S. Bourne, "Market, Location, and Site Selection," *Canadian Geographer*, 12 (1968), 211–26. Bourne, *The Geography of Housing* (London, 1981), 46–47.

[35] Morton and Copp, *Working People*, chapters 20, 21. Larkin, *Toronto Trades Assembly*, 32–35. LCMT, *Yearbook*, 1962 (Toronto, 1962), 22.

[36] Jamieson, *Times of Trouble*, 359, 367, 373, 396, 408–10, 414–17. Morton and Copp, *Working People*, 240. Wismer, *Sweethearts*, chapter 5.

[37] Ibid., chapters 7–9. On finer distinctions regarding areas of origin and

types of work, Sidlofsky, "Post-War Immigrants . . . Toronto's Italian Population," 73-76, 269.

[38] Zerker, *Rise and Fall of the Toronto Typographical Union*, chapters 12, 13. Morton and Copp, *Working People*, 240.

[39] On public service unions, Morton and Copp, *Working People*, chapter 23.

[40] Merrijoy S. Kelner, "The Elite Structure of Toronto: Ethnic Composition and Paths of Recruitment," PhD thesis, UT, 1969, esp. 219-44. Also Kelner, "Changes in Toronto's Elite Structure," in W.E. Mann, ed., *The Underside of Toronto* (Toronto, 1970), 197-204.

[41] SPC, *Annual Report*, 1958-66. Campaign history, United Way of Greater Toronto, *1980 Annual Report: 25th Anniversary* (Toronto, 1980). SPC, "The Development of Area Social Planning Councils, 1957-1959," 1959. Lappin, "Stages in the Development of Community Organization Work," chapter 7.

[42] CT, Consultative Committee on Housing Policies for the City of Toronto, *Final Report* (Toronto, 1966), CTA.

[43] Max Rosenfeld and Earle Beattie, *A Blot on the Face of the City: The Story of "Inglewood," Toronto's Notorious Slum Empire* (Toronto, 1955), reprinted from *Telegram*, 11-24 Oct. 1955. CT, Advisory Committee on the Urban Renewal Study, "Urban Renewal: a Study of the City of Toronto", 10 Aug. 1956; and *Urban Renewal: a Study of the City of Toronto 1956: Short Statement* (Ottawa, 1956), 4. W.E. Mann, "The Social System of the Slum: the Lower Ward, Toronto" in S.D. Clark, ed., *Urbanism and the Changing Canadian Society* (Toronto, 1961), 39-69.

[44] MT, *Metropolitan Toronto 1965* (Toronto, 1965), 36. Albert Rose, "Slum Clearance will Continue in Toronto," *Community Planning Review* 5, no. 3 (1955).

[45] CTPB, *The Changing City: a Forecast of Planning Issues for the City of Toronto 1956-1980* (Toronto, 1959), 27-28. CTPB, "Improvement Programme for Residential Areas," Jan. 1965. MTPB, *Metropolitan Toronto Urban Renewal Study* (Toronto, 1966), chapter 5. On 1956-1966, Graham Fraser, *Fighting Back: Urban Renewal in Trefann Court* (Toronto, 1972), chapter 4.

[46] Colton, *Big Daddy*, 133, 143-44, 160-63.

[47] Frances Friskin and Dale Hauser, "Local Autonomy vs Fair Share: Intergovernmental Housing Issues in the Toronto Region, 1950-1980," Paper presented to Canadian Political Science Association, 1983. MT, *Metropolitan Toronto 1967*, 22-23.

[48] CC, 1956, Appendix A, 2848-51. Papers on 1950s, Burton and Morley, eds., "The Annex Book."

[49] Guest, *Emergence of Social Security*, chapters 9, 10. Kenneth Bryden, "How Public Medicare Came to Ontario" in Donald C. MacDonald, ed., *Government and Politics in Ontario* (Toronto, 1975), 34-47.

[50] Vernon Lang, *The Service State Emerges in Ontario* (Toronto, 1974), 20-38. D.R. Richmond, *The Economic Tranformation of Ontario: 1945-1973* (Toronto, 1974), 42, 44, 45. Lionel D. Feldman, *Ontario 1945-1973: The Municipal Dynamic* (Toronto, 1974), 10-12. The above in the Ontario Economic Council, The Evolution of Policy in Contemporary Ontario Series, nos. 4, 1 and 5. See also, J.S. Dupré, *Intergovernmental Finance in Ontario: a Provincial-Local Perspective* (Toronto, 1968). Guest, *Emergence of Social Security*, 174.

[51] Stamp, *Schools of Ontario*, chapter 9, esp. 188-89, 196-97, 198-99.

[52] Ibid., 202 and chapter 10, esp. 203-12. Marshall McLuhan, *Understanding Media: The Extensions of Man* (New York, 1964). Robert J. Ferguson, "What's New in Educaton?" *Board of Trade Journal* 54 (Sept. 1964), 4-8.

[53] Northrop Frye, ed., *Design for Learning: Reports Submitted to the Joint Committee of the Toronto Board of Education and the University of Toronto* (Toronto, 1962), esp. 16.

[54] Ibid., 16. Paul Axelrod, *Scholars and Dollars: Politics, Economics, and the Universities of Ontario* (Toronto, 1982), 25, 58.

[55] Ibid., chapters 3-5. Stamp, *Schools of Ontario*, 209-10.

[56] Jack Batten, *Honest Ed's Story: the Crazy Rags to Riches Story of Ed Mirvish* (Toronto, 1972), 175-77. Ontario Council for the Arts, *The Awkward Stage*, 94-96, 185.

[57] Obodiac, *Maple Leaf Gardens*, 33.

[58] Cauz, *Baseball's Back*, 101-26. Speculation about churches, conversation with Bruce Kidd, 6 July 1983.

[59] Kesterton, *History of Journalism*, 90. Nancy Howell and Maxwell L. Howell, *Sports and Games in Canadian Life 1700 to the Present* (Toronto, 1969), 231-32, 273. Alexander Ross, *The Booming Fifties 1950-1960: Canada's Illustrated Heritage* (Toronto, 1977), 105, 107, 109. Henry Roxborough, *Canada at the Olympics* (Toronto, 1969), 173.

[60] Jones, "Metropolitan Man," 14, 21. Frederick Hill, "Spatio-Temporal Trends in Population Density: Toronto, 1932-1966", CUCS Research Paper 34, 1970. Spelt, *Toronto*, chapters 6 and 7. MT, *Metropolitan Toronto 1967*, 10-12.

[61] BMR, "The Toronto Region's Privately Developed New Communities," *Civic Affairs* 2 (1972), 13, 16. John Sewell, "Don Mills: E.P. Taylor and Canada's First Corporate Suburb," *City Magazine* 2 (Jan. 1977), 28-38. Macklin L. Hancock, "Policies, Problems, and Prospects in Legislation, Design and Administration," in American Society of Planning Officials, *Planning 1965: Selected Papers from the Joint Planning Conference . . . 1965* (Chicago, 1965), 260-70.

[62] BMR, "Toronto Region's New Communities," 16-17. S.D. Clark, *The*

Suburban Society (Toronto, 1966) on a variety of subdivisions in Metro and to the north.

[63] Macklin L. Hancock, "Flemingdon Park, a New Urban Community" in Gertler, ed., *Planning the Canadian Environment*, 205-28.

[64] MT, *Metropolitan Toronto 1967*, 20-21. Churches: Ross, *The Booming Fifties*, 29.

[65] James W. Simmons, *Metro's Changing Retail Complex: a Study in Growth and Blight*, University of Chicago Geography Research Paper 104 (Chicago, 1966). Spelt, *Toronto*, 137-39. MTPB, "Shopping Centres and Strip Retail Areas, 1971," August 1972.

[66] Lorimer, *Developers*, 36, 191. Laurie Newton, The Shopping Centre Boom: Planning for Yorkdale, 1979, UTA.

[67] David and Nadine Nowlan, *The Bad Trip: the Untold Story of the Spadina Expressway* (Toronto, 1970), 66, 71-74. Colton, *Big Daddy*, 171-73. Harry Bruce, *The Short Happy Walks of Max MacPherson* (Toronto, 1968), 78.

[68] Spelt, *Toronto*, 135-36. Field and Kerr,"Geographical Aspects of Industrial Growth," 30-37. MTPB, *Draft Official Plan of the Metropolitan Toronto Planning Area* (Toronto, 1959), 86-94.

[69] Ibid., 87. MTPB, *Proposed Official Plan of the Metropolitan Toronto Planning Area* (Toronto, 1965). Space extravagance noted by CTPB, "Preliminary Report on the Proposed Official Plan of the Metropolitan Toronto Planning Area," 1965, 5, 24.

[70] Field and Kerr, "Geographical Aspects of Industrial Growth," 32, 36.

[71] MT, *Metropolitan Toronto 1967*, 18-19.

[72] Ibid., 19. Betty Kennedy, *Hurricane Hazel* (Toronto, 1979), esp. 140, 150-54.

[73] MT, *Metropolitan Toronto, 1965*, 22-25.

[74] Ibid., 14, and *1963*, 16-17. Colton, *Big Daddy*, 62, 164.

[75] MTPB, *Draft Official Plan* (1959), 152-54, Plate 42. MT, *Metropolitan Toronto 1967*, 15. MTPB, *Report on the Metropolitan Toronto Transportation Plan* (Toronto, 1964).

[76] Bromley and May, *Fifty Years of Progressive Transit*, chapter 9. Colton, *Big Daddy*, 166. Frederick Gardiner, "What Metropolitan Government during the Past Seven Years has Accomplished for Toronto," Cornish Papers, CTA.

[77] Bromley and May, *Fifty Years of Progressive Transit*, chapters 10, 11. Jones, "Metropolitan Man," 14.

[78] MTPB, *Metropolitan Toronto Urban Renewal Study*, 1966, ii. MTPB, "The Study of Apartment Distribution and Apartment Densities in the Metropolitan Toronto Planning Area," draft, 3rd edition. 1967, 13-18. Larry S. Bourne, *Private Redevelopment of the Central City: Spatial Processes of Structural Change in the City of Toronto*, University of Chicago Geography Research Paper 112 (Chicago, 1967). On sectors: Robert A. Murdie, *Factorial Ecology of Metropolitan Toronto, 1951-1961: an Essay on the Social Geography of the City*, University of Chicago Geography Research Paper 116 (Chicago, 1969). Projects in the corridor and elsewhere found in *Daily Commercial News*. Interview with Matthew Lawson, Sept. 1982.

[79] *Urban Renewal: Short Statement*, 6. Area considered for private redevelopment as early as 1 Feb. 1951: *Daily Commercial News*. Arthur Lowe, "Arthur Lowe's Page," *Apartment Owner and Builder* 2 (Feb. 1957), 5, 26 and much of issue regarding failed predecessor of St. James Town. Assessment, *Telegram*, 4 June 1956.

[80] From Census, CMHC and City Building Department, CTPB, "Changes in Housing Stock, 1951-1971," 4, 11. Data for 1971, Philip S. Morrison, "Mortgage Lending in Canadian Cities", CUCS Research Paper 111, 1979. More recently, see Robert S. Murdie, "The Demand for Institutional Mortgage Financing in Metropolitan Toronto," YU Urban Studies Working Paper 6, 1982. M.B.M. Lawson, "Neighbourhood Planning in Toronto," *Plan Canada* 3 (1962), 36-40, reprinted in Gertler, ed., *Planning the Canadian Environment*, 229-34. Norah Johnson, "It's Smart to Live in the Annex," *Habitat* 5 (Jan.-Feb. 1962), 1-7. Margaret Fullerton, "New Life for Old Houses," *Ontario Housing* 8 (Dec. 1962), 9-11. Even earlier, see Lex Schrag, "Practice Conservation in City, Too: West Annex Spruced Up," *G&M*, 26 Apr. 1954. Burton and Morley, eds., "The Annex Book."

[81] *Urban Renewal: Short Statement*, 6. *Daily Commercial News*, 7 Aug. 1951. CTPB, "Core Area Task Force: Technical Appendix," 1974, 67, 264, Table 7. Gunter H.K. Gad, "Toronto's Central Office Complex: Growth, Structure and Linkages," PhD thesis, UT, 1975, esp. 132-47. Data from Metropolitan Planning Department and A.E. LePage. Bourne, *Private Redevelopment*, 100-18.

[82] Pearl McCarthy, "Design has Beauty, Zestful Verve" and Stanley Westall, "City Hall Cost Seen $30,000,000," *G&M*, 27 Sept. 1958. Phillips, *Mayor of All the People*, 141-49.

[83] Ibid., 153-56, 198-99. Allan Burton, "The Redevelopment of Downtown Toronto," 6, 9-11, CTA. Interview with Matthew Lawson, Sept. 1982. Stanford, *To Serve the Community*.

[84] Macy Dubois *et al.*, "A Plan for Central Toronto," *Canadian Architect* 7 (Aug. 1962), 41-72. CTPB, *Plan for Downtown Toronto* (Toronto, 1963), esp. 9-10, 18, 26-27. Downtown in the early 1960s, see Spelt, *Toronto*, 141-52, in part based on G.H. Zieber, "Toronto's Central Business District," MA thesis, UT, 1961.

[85] "Toronto becoming MAJOR WORLD PORT," MT, *Metropolitan*

Toronto ... Seaway Year 1959 (Toronto, 1959), 21. Ibid., *1967*, 20. Roderick D. Ramlalsingh, "A Study of the Decline of Trade at the Port of Toronto," YU, Department of Geography Discussion Paper 12, 1975, 21. Macy Dubois *et al.*, "A Plan for Central Toronto," 68-69.

[86] Colton, *Big Daddy*, ix, 80; and my review, *American Review of Canadian Studies* 11 (Autumn 1981), 107-09. Robert Caro, *The Power Broker: Robert Moses and the Fall of New York* (New York, 1974); and my review "Of Power and Contemptuousness," *Canadian Review of American Studies* 7 (1976), 88-92. Robert Fitch, "Planning New York" in Roger E. Alcaly and David Mermelstein, eds., *The Fiscal Crisis of American Cities: Essays on the Political Economy of Urban America with Special Reference to New York* (New York, 1977), 264-84. Also compared with Fiorello La Guardia, New York mayor in the 1930s, Rose, *Governing Metropolitan Toronto*, 97.

[87] Colton, *Big Daddy*, 99-100, 106. On Manthorpe, see Fraser, *Fighting Back*, 96-103. Fraser, "Planning vs. Development: Placing Bets on Toronto's Future," in Alan Powell, ed., *The City: Attacking Modern Myths* (Toronto, 1972), 101-13. The city administration was restructured somewhat after a J.D. Woods & Gordon survey, *G&M*, 16 Feb. 1957.

[88] Rose, *Governing Metropolitan Toronto*, chapters 6, 7; esp. 87. Ontario, *Report of the Royal Commission on Metropolitan Toronto* (Toronto, 1965).

[89] Ontario, Bill 81, "An Act to Amend the Municipality of Metropolitan Toronto Act," 18 May 1966. H.C. Campbell, *Public Libraries in the Urban Metropolitan Setting* (London, 1973), 145-64.

[90] MT, *Metropolitan Toronto 1967*, 12-13; *1964*, 11; *1968*, 13. Regarding vote, see CT, *Handbook*, 1968, 35. In contrast to the pre-Metro era, finances became a complex thicket. Don Richmond and P.S. Ross Partners, *The Financial Structure of Metropolitan Toronto*, Background Studies in the Metropolitan Plan Preparation Programme (Toronto, 1975); and Harry M. Kitchen, "Public Finance in Metropolitan Toronto: A Study for the Royal Commission on Metropolitan Toronto" (Toronto, 1977). Major changes occurred in 1967 with restructuring.

[91] MT, *Metropolitan Toronto 1967*, 13. Richmond, *Economic Transformation of Ontario*. Manthorpe, *The Power and the Tories*, esp. 177.

[92] Ross, *The Booming Fifties*, 18, 20. Edmonds, *The Years of Protest*, 13 , 10. Ralph Greenhill, *The Face of Toronto* (Toronto, 1960), 16.

[93] Peers, *The Public Eye*, 327. Gardiner, *Star*, 5 Aug. 1969.

CHAPTER FIVE, 1966-1984

[1] William Davis, Ontario Legislature, 3 June 1971. Jane Jacobs, "A City Getting Hooked on the Expressway Drug," *G&M*, 1 Nov. 1969. James Mackenzie, "How the 20-year Political Nightmare of the Spadina Expressway Happened," *G&M*, 26 Jan. 1970. Nowlan and Nowlan, *The Bad Trip*, chapter 4. Christopher Leo, *The Politics of Urban Development in Canadian Urban Expressway Disputes*, Institute of Public Administration of Canada, Monograph 3 (Toronto, 1977), chapter 4. *Star*, 4 June 1971.

[2] Fraser, *Fighting Back*, chapters 4-9. Donald R. Keating, *The Power to Make It Happen: Mass-Based Community Organizing: What It Is and How It Works* (Toronto, 1975). CTPB, "Public Meeting to Obtain Views and Opinions on the Proposals for the Sussex Area," 28 Nov. 1966. *Telegram*, 29 Nov. 1966.

[3] Fraser, *Fighting Back*, 161-66. James Lorimer, *The Real World of City Politics* (Toronto, 1970), chapter 2. CT, "Report of the Special Committee on Ward Boundaries 1959," and clippings, CTA. OMB, "Decision of the board," delivered by J.A. Kennedy, 3 July 1969.

[4] Michael Goldrick, "The Anatomy of Urban Reform in Toronto," *City Magazine* 3 (May-June 1978), 29-39. J.T. Lemon, "Toronto: Is It a Model of Urban Life and Citizen Participation?" in David Ley, ed., *Community Participation and the Spatial Order of the City*, B.C. Geographical Series 19 (Vancouver, 1974). Michael S. Cross, "In Search of Indentity: Opposition Politics in Toronto," *Canadian Forum* 52 (May 1972), 48-50. Jack K. Masson and James D. Anderson, eds., *Emerging Party Politics in Urban Canada* (Toronto, 1972), 60-67. Stephen Clarkson, *City Lib* (Toronto, 1972). James Draper, ed., *Citizen Participation: Canada* (Toronto 1971). J.L. Granatstein, *Marlborough Marathon: One Street Against a Developer* (Toronto, 1971). James Lorimer, *The Real World of City Politics*. Lorimer and Myfawny Phillips, *Working People: Life in a Downtown City Neighbourhood* (Toronto, 1971). Lorimer, *A Citizen's Guide to City Politics* (Toronto, 1972). Alan Powell, ed., *The City*. John Sewell, *Up Against City Hall* (Toronto, 1972). David Lewis Stein, *Toronto for Sale: The Destruction of a City* (Toronto, 1972). David Clark *et al.*, *Rules of the Game: A Handbook for Tenants and Homeowners* (Toronto, 1972). Maps of community groups: Ontario, Royal Commission on Metropolitan Toronto, *Report* (*Robarts Report*), 2 vols. (Toronto, 1977), vol. 2, 144-53.

[5] Jon Caulfield, *The Tiny Perfect Mayor: David Crombie and Toronto's Reform Aldermen* (Toronto, 1974). Goldrick, "Anatomy of Reform." Lemon, "Toronto: Is It a Model?"

[6] Lemon, Ibid. Janice Dineen, "The Rise and Fall of Ratepayer Groups," *Star*, 14 Oct. 1978. Ross Laver, "Battles Seem All in the Past for Toronto's Citizen Activists," *G&M*, 14 Aug. 1982. On Association of Women Electors: Salem Alaton, "Ladies Eye the Polls' Progress," *G&M*, 24 Apr. 1983.

[7] Loren Jay Lind, *The Learning Machine: A Hard Look at Toronto Schools* (Toronto, 1974), chapter 8. Though not the whole story, see Howard Buchbinder, "Social Planning and Social Control: An Account of a Confron-

tation with the Social Welfare Establishment," and John McCready, "Lucky Who? The Unity Community Fund of Greater Toronto," in Alan Powell, ed., *The City*, chapters 12, 14. Loren Lind, "Council in Agonizing Review," *G&M*, 23 Mar. 1970. SPC, Annual Report, 1969, 1970. Claude Bissell, *Halfway Up Parnassus: A Personal Account of the University of Toronto, 1932–1971* (Toronto, 1974), chapters 7, 8, 9. Axelrod, *Scholars and Dollars*, 156–57.

[8] Alden Baker, "Metro at 30: Cracks in Government are Widening," *G&M*, 14 Apr. 1983. Frances Frisken, "Factors Contributing to Public Service Equalization in a Restructured Metropolis: The Case of Toronto," paper, Canadian Political Science Association Annual Meeting, 1981. *Robarts Report*, vol. 2, 249, 156, 138–39. W.J. McCordic, "Urban Educaton: An Experiment in Two-tiered Administration," in Lionel D. Feldman and Michael D. Goldrick, eds., *Politics and Government of Urban Canada: Selected Readings*, 1st ed. (Toronto, 1969), 108–20. T.R. Williams, "Some Facts and Fantasies Concerning Local Autonomy in the Metropolitan Toronto School System" in Feldman and Goldrick, *Politics and Government*, 3rd ed. (Toronto, 1976), 296–309.

[9] *Robarts Report*, vol. 2, 84–89. Dominic Del Guidice and Stephen M. Sacks, *The 101 Governments of Metro Toronto* (Toronto, 1968). Meyer Brownstone, quoted in Baker, "Metro at 30," *G&M*, 14 Apr. 1983.

[10] Richard M. Bird and N. Enid Slack, *Urban Public Finance in Canada* (Toronto, 1983), 56–58, 61.

[11] *Robarts Report*, vol. 2, 189; D. Richmond and P.S. Ross Partners, *Metroplan: The Financial Structure of Metropolitan Toronto*, 92. Kitchen, "Public Finance in Metropolitan Toronto," 88.

[12] Rose, *Governing Metropolitan Toronto*, 144–54, 162–66. John Robarts, "Opening Remarks: Presentation of a Design for Development: Toronto-Centre Region," 5 May 1970, 7. Process reviewed by Norman Pearson, "Regional Government and Development," in Donald C. MacDonald, ed., *Government and Politics of Ontario*, 172–94.

[13] Colin Vaughan, "Mayor Bill," *Quest* 11 (Summer 1982), 42a–42d.

[14] To 1974: Manthorpe, *The Power and the Tories*, chapters 5–21. Part 3 papers in Donald C. MacDonald, ed., *Government and Politics of Ontario*. Rosemary Speirs, "Staying Power," *G&M*, 23 July 1983.

[15] Gunter H.K. Gad for CTPB, "Toronto's Central Offices: Observations on Location Patterns and Linkages," 1975. CTPDD, *1981 Quinquennial Review* (Toronto, 1981), 16, 82. A.E. LePage, *Toronto Office Leasing Directory, Incorporating the Toronto Space Market Survey* (Toronto, 1983), 6; calculations on buildings with more than 20,000 square feet. Robert W. Collier, *Contemporary Cathedrals: Large Scale Development in Canadian Cities* (Montreal, 1974), chapter 4.

[16] Stein, *Toronto for Sale*, chapter 7. Bébout, *Open Gate*.

[17] Stein, *Toronto for Sale*, chapter 8. Bronwyn Lewis, "Negotiating Urban Development: the Eaton Centre," MA research paper, UT, 1983.

[18] On decentralization: J.T. Lemon and L.S. Bourne, "On the Form of the City and the Wronski Report," Brief to Metro Transportation Committee, 1 Apr. 1970. CT, Core Area Task Force, *Report and Recommendations* and *Technical Appendix* (Toronto, 1974). William R. Code, *Controlling the Physical Growth of the Urban Core: A Study on the Implications of Restrictive Zoning in the Central Business District of Toronto* (Toronto, 1975). CT, "Central Area Plan," 1976, amendments to Official Plan, 1976. CTPDD, *1981 Quinquennial Review*, 2–3. MTPD, *Metroplan: Concept & Objectives: A Summary* (Toronto, 1976), 11.

[19] CTPDD, *1981 Quinquennial Review*, 16. A.E. LePage, *Toronto Office Leasing Directory*, 11. David Miller, "Boomtown Metro," *Star*, 29 Aug. 1982. Miller, "$2 Billion Plan for Waterfront," *Star*, 26 Sept. 1982. CTPDD, *Office Monitor '84* (Toronto, 1984).

[20] Fraser, *Fighting Back*, chapters 13, 14. Maggie Siggins, "Death of a Dream," *Macleans*, 4 Oct. 1982, T1–3.

[21] Data: George A. Nader, *Cities of Canada*, 2 vols. (Toronto, 1975, 1976), vol. 1, 72. CTHD, *Shifting Foundations: Addressing Shelter Needs and Responsibilities in Toronto* (Toronto, 1983), 24–34. CT, *Official Plan for City of Toronto Planning Area: Part I* (Toronto, 1969), 17, 22–23. Sussex: note 2 above. Stein, *Toronto for Sale*, chapters 1–6. Sewell, *Up Against City Hall*, chapters, 6–8. Lemon, "Toronto: Is It a Model?" Lorimer, *Real World*, chapter 6. On York: Leon R. Kentridge and Peter F. Oliphant, "High-Rise vs. No Rise: the Municipal Cost-Benefit Equation," in Powell, eds., *The City*, chapter 1.

[22] J. Hanson for CT, Development Department, *St. James Town* (Toronto, 1970), esp. 3, 9. Data on units: John Gladke, personal communication, 1983, CTPDD.

[23] Lemon, "Toronto: Is It a Model?"

[24] On preference for ground level, see William Michaelson, *Man and his Urban Environment: A Sociological Approach* (Reading, Mass., 1970), 96, 105. Julia Weston, "Gentrification and Displacement," *Habitat* 25, no. 1. (1982), 10–19. Stephen Dynes, "Housing Deconversion," CTPDD Research Bulletin 16 (Toronto, 1980). Bourne, *Geography of Housing*, 165–67. Murdie, "Demand for Institutional Mortgage Financing." David Morley and Lydia Burton, "Reflecting on Neighbourhood Futures: A Toronto Example," *Urban Resources* 1 (Winter 1984), 7–14. On East York families and neighbours: Barry Wellman and Robert Hiscott, "From Social Support to Social Network," CUCS Research Paper 146, 1983.

[25] Students of Toronto Island Public School, *A History of the Toronto Islands* (Toronto, 1972). Robert Sward, *The Toronto Islands* (Toronto, 1983). Sally

Gibson, *More Than an Island*, chapters 11, 12.

[26] John Robarts, Opening Remarks, and Charles MacNaughton, Address, in "Presentation of Design for Development," 1970, 3. MTPB, *Draft Official Plan of the Metropolitan Toronto Planning Area*, 1959, 17–19. CTPDD, *Toronto in Transition: Demographic Trends in the Toronto Region* (Toronto, 1980), 39. Janice Dineen, "Our Planning is Years Behind the Realities," *Star*, 10 June 1979. Larry Bourne *et al.* eds., *Urban Futures for Central Canada: Perspectives on Forecasting Urban Growth and Form* (Toronto, 1974).

[27] A.E. LePage, *Toronto Office Leasing Directory*, 6.

[28] MacNaughton, Address, in "Design for Development." W. Darcy McKeogh, *A Status Report on the Toronto-Centred Region* (Toronto, 1971). Warren Gerard, "Critics Don't Think the Toronto-Centred Growth Concept Will Work," *G&M*, 30 Dec. 1970.

[29] BMR, *Toronto Region's New Communities*, 16–21. Lorimer, *Developers*, chapter 4.

[30] Ontario, Ministry of Housing, *North Pickering Project: Summary of Recommended Plan* (Toronto, 1975). Sandra Budden and Joseph Ernest, *The Movable Airport: The Politics of Government Planning* (Toronto, 1973). Margaret D. Gane, "Children Still Weep for 'Stolen' Homes," *Star*, 10 Feb. 1979. Dineen, "Our Planning is Years Behind the Realities."

[31] Leo, *Politics of Urban Development*, chapter 4. Nowlan and Nowlan, *The Bad Trip*, chapters 2, 3. Crosstown: *G&M*, 20 Sept. 1966. MT Transportation Plan Review, *A Catalogue of Transportation Concepts*, C64–6. MTPD and Metropolitan Advisory Committee, *Draft Plan for the Urban Structure: Metropolitan Toronto* (Toronto, 1978), 48. Eudora Pendergrast, "Suburbanizing the Central City: An Analysis of the Shift in Transportation Policies Governing the Development of Metropolitan Toronto, 1950–1978," MSc(PI) thesis, UT, 1979. Alden Baker, "Metro's Traffic Trauma: A Crunch is Coming," *G&M*, 15 Feb. 1982.

[32] *Star*, 10 Mar. 1982. BMR, *Understanding Metro's Transit Problems* (Toronto, 1979), 15–19. Alden Baker, 'Finch Transit is Favoured by Planner," *G&M*, 13 Mar. 1982. TTC, *Transit in Toronto: The Story of Public Transportation in Metropolitan Toronto* (Toronto, 1982).

[33] *G&M*, 10 Nov. 1983. Toronto Hydro-Electric System, *Annual Report, 1980* (Toronto, 1981); *Annual Report, 1982* (Toronto, 1983). Alex Telegdi, CTPDD, personal communication, June 1982.

[34] Arlene Gemmil, "Ontario Place: The Origins and Planning of an Urban Waterfront Park," YU Geography Department Discussion Paper 75, 1981.

[35] Howard Cohen, "Harbourfront 'Will Belong to Everyone'," letter to *Star*, 30 Aug. 1981. CTPDD, *The Central Waterfront: Proposals* (Toronto, 1982).

[36] Leon Whiteson and S.R. Gage, *The Liveable City: The Architecture and Neighbourhoods of Toronto* (Oakville, 1982), 63–68.

[37] Cauz, *Baseball's Back*. Paul Palango, "U.S. College Sports Pay a Heavy Price," *G&M*, 1 Mar. 1983. Bruce Kidd, *The Political Economy of Sport*, CAHPER Sociology of Sport Monograph Series (Calgary, 1980).

[38] Nalini Stewart, ed., *The Toronto Art Guide* (Toronto, 1976). Marq de Villiers, "The Culture Brokers: Measuring the Power of an Arts Establishment," *Toronto Life*, Mar. 1980, 31–35, 46–50.

[39] Ontario Arts Council, *Awkward Stage*, 94–96, 186. Paul Walsh and Marg Wilson, eds., *Canadian Theatre Checklist: 1982–83 Edition* (Toronto, 1982). Tom Hendry, "Theatre in Canada: A Reluctant Citizen," in Abraham Rotstein and Gary Lax, eds., *Getting it Back: A Program for Canadian Independence* (Toronto, 1974), 266–84. Mira Friedlander, "Risk before Security on the Alternative State," *Performing Arts* 17 (Winter 1981), 39–42. Paul Milliken, "Leaving Home: The Glassco Decade Ends at Tarragon," *Performing Arts* 17 (Winter 1981), 22–24. Rick Salutin, "The Meaning of it All," *Canadian Theatre Review*, no. 34 (Spring 1982), 190, 91. Association for Canadian Theatre History, *Newsletter*, 1977.

[40] SPC, "... And the Poor Get Poorer: A Study of Social Welfare Problems in Ontario," 1983. Ian Adams *et al.*, *The Real Poverty Report* (Edmonton, 1971). Michael Dennis and Susan Fish, *Programs in Search of a Policy: Low Income Housing in Canada* (Toronto, 1982). Various papers in W.E. Mann, ed., *Underside of Toronto*.

[41] Marvyn Novick, *Metro's Suburbs in Transition*, 2 vols. (Toronto, 1979, 1980). Whiteson and Gage, *The Liveable City*, 125–28. Peter McLaren, *Cries from the Corridor: The New Suburban Ghettos* (Toronto, 1980).

[42] CTHD, *Confronting the Crisis: A Review of City Housing Policy, 1976–1981* (Toronto, 1982), 41. MTPD, *Metropolitan Toronto Annual Housing Report 1981* (Toronto, 1982). George B. Fallis, *Housing Programs and Income Distribution in Ontario* (Toronto, 1980). CTHD, *Shifting Foundations*, 16–17, 22. Toronto Home Builders' Association, *Housing Demand and Constraints on Residential Construction in Toronto in the 1980s* (Toronto, 1981). C.A. Maher, "Spatial Patterns in Urban Housing Markets: Filtering in Toronto, 1953–71," *Canadian Geographer* 78 (1974), 108–24.

[43] CTHD, *Shifting Foundations*, chapter 3. MTPD, *Metropolitan Toronto Annual Housing Report 1981*, 8. Lorimer, *The Developers*, 19. Peel, "1980 Housing Study," *Regional Reflections* 4 (First Quarter 1981), 20–21. Frances Frisken and Dale Hauser, "Local Autonomy Vs Fair Share."

[44] CTHD, *Shifting Foundations*, 21. David Stein, "The Breakdown of Metro's Rent Control System," *Star*, 14 Nov. 1982. Ross Howard, "Families Flee Assisted Housing Projects," *Star*, 16–17 Nov. 1981.

[45] Stamp, *Schools of Ontario*, 217–20, 225–33. Lorimer, *Real World*, chapter

4. Lind, *Learning Machine*, chapter 1. McLaren, *Cries from the Corridor*.

[46] Lind, *Learning Machine*, 204.

[47] Stamp, *Schools of Ontario*, 239–41. Novick, *Metro's Suburbs*, vol. 2, 56. Axelrod, *Scholars and Dollars*, 181.

[48] Allan Smith, "Metaphor and Nationality in North America," *Canadian Historical Review* 51 (1970), 242–69.

[49] TBE, *We Are All Immigrants to this Place* (Toronto, 1976). Stamp, *Schools of Ontario*, 234–36. Muriel Anderson, "President's Newsletter on Heritage Language," Toronto Teachers' Federation, June 1983.

[50] 1971: Anthony H. Richmond and Warren E. Kalbach, *Factors in the Adjustment of Immigrants and their Descendants* (Ottawa, 1980), 188–91, 280–82, 308.

[51] Grace M. Anderson and David Higgs, *A Future to Inherit: Portuguese Communities in Canada* (Toronto, 1976), 69–78, chapters 6–11.

[52] Edgar Wickberg, ed., *From China to Canada: A History of the Chinese Communities in Canada* (Toronto, 1982), chapters 17, 18; esp. 257.

[53] Ibid., 264–65.

[54] Oakland Ross, "In Search of a Better Life" and "Some Success Stories, Others not so Lucky," *G&M*, 10 Jan. 1981. Elaine Carey, "Islanders Remain Islands Apart," *Star*, 14 July 1983.

[55] Winks, *Blacks in Canada*, 420. *Sun*, 14 Feb. 1983. Frances Henry, "The Dynamics of Racism in Toronto," research paper, YU Department of Anthropology, 1978.

[56] On the contradictions of the times, see paintings of William Kurelek, *O Toronto* (Toronto, 1973).

[57] Reginald G. Smart and David Jackson, "Yorkville Subculture," and June Callwood, "Digger House," in Mann, ed., *Underside of Toronto*, 109–28. William Cameron, "Portrait of a Super-Hippie," *Star Weekly*, 23 Sept. 1967, 1–6.

[58] Barrie Zwicker, "Rochdale: The Ultimate Freedom," in Mann, *Underside of Toronto*, 207–17. Edmonds, *Years of Protest*, 86–88.

[59] Among recent numerous discussions, see Albert Rose, "Retirement: Golden Days or the Worst of Times'," *Star*, 13 June. 1982.

[60] John R. Miron, "Changing Patterns of Household Formation in the Toronto CMA: 1951 to 1976," CUCS Research Paper 106, 1979. CTPDD, *Toronto in Transition*, 17–23.

[61] Diane Francis, "Where Will It all End," *Star*, 11 Nov. 1984 (series on coporations, Sept. 23–Nov. 11). Alan Toulin, "City's Role as Finance Hub is Enhanced," *Star*, 7 Sept. 1982.

[62] Matthew B.M. Lawson, *Metroplan: Jobs and the Economy: a Study of Employment and Employment Generating Activities* (Toronto, 1975). Simerl and Goldfinger, "Job Growth by Industry in the Toronto Area." Municipality of Metropolitan Toronto, *Analysis of Industrial Activity Patterns in the Toronto C.M.A.* (Toronto, 1980).

[63] Peter Cook, *Massey at the Brink*, esp. 17, 192, 218–20, 228, 246, 258. "Massey and its Friends," *Economist* 287 (26 Mar. 1983), 10, 15–16. Robert L. Perry, "The CDIC: Jobs for the Boys or Jobs for the Country?" in *The Financial Post 500: the 1983 Ranking of Canada's Largest Companies in Industry and Finance* (Toronto, 1983), 54. Peter C. Newman, *The Establishment Man: A Portrait of Power* (Toronto, 1982), chapter 6. Jack Willoughby, "CCM, Industrial Pioneer, Finds Quality not Enough," *G&M*, 28 Feb. 1983. Oliver Bertin, "Canada's Meat Packers Cut to the Bone," *G&M*, 28 May 1983. Robert B. Reich, *America's New Frontier* (New York, 1983), and Barry Bluestone and Bennett Harrison, *The Deindustrialization of America* (New York, 1982).

[64] Perry, "The CDIC," 51.

[65] David Lewis Stein, "No Recession in the Metro Civil Service," *Star*, 20 June 1982. Novick, *Metro Suburbs*, vol. 2, 76–77. D.B. Freeman *et al.*, "The Decline of General Cargo Trade at the Port of Toronto: Patterns and Impacts of Change in Transport Technology and Industrial Economics," UT/YU Joint Program in Transportation Research Paper 78 (Toronto, 1981). Pat McNenly, "Seaway Dream Fades on Idle Toronto Docks," *Star*, 7 Aug. 1980.

[66] Leon Muszynski, "Unemployment in Toronto: Hidden and Real," SPC Working Paper for Full Employment 1, 1980, and others in series.

[67] Morton and Copp, *Working People*, esp. 261, 274, 310.

[68] R. Keith Sample and W.R. Smith, "Metropolitan Dominance and Foreign Ownership in the Canadian Urban System," *Canadian Geographer* 25 (1981), 4–26. Semple and Milford R. Green, "Interurban Corporate Headquarters Relocation in Canada," paper, International Geographical Union Commission on National Settlement Systems, Toronto, 1982. J. Tait Davis, "Government and Directed Money Flows and the Discordance between Production and Consumption in Provincial Economics," *Canadian Geographer* 26 (1982), 1–20. James W. Simmons, "The Impact of the Public Sector on the Canadian Urban System," in A.F. Artibise and Gilbert Stelter, eds., *The North American City* (Vancouver, 1985). *Financial Post 500*, 1983, 67. John C. Weaver, *Hamilton: An Illustrated History* (Toronto, 1982), 164, 166.

[69] *Financial Post 500*, 1983, 119–65.

[70] Paul Delaney, "LePage", *Saturday Night*, Feb. 1983, 46–54. Lorimer, *The Developers*, 261–62, 9–15. Patricia Lush, "Mascan Default Triggers Demand for Repayment," *G&M*, 13 Aug. 1983.

[71] Siggins, *Bassett*, 220–23.

[72] *Canadian Advertising Rates and Data* 56 (Apr. 1983). "Canadian Publishers

Directory," *Quill and Quire*, Supplement, May 1982, 48, 1–14. Judy Steed, "Down but not Out," *G&M*, 28 May 1983.

[73] Nick Filmore, "The Illusion of Poverty: Media Profits in the Eighties," *This Magazine* 17 (June 1983), 25–28. Term "paper entrepreneuralism" widely used now: Reich, *America's New Frontier*. Cf. Harry J. Boyle, "Dreams, Money and Culture," *G&M*, 7 May 1983, a review of Paul Audley, *Canada's Cultural Industries* (Toronto, 1983.)

[74] Robert L. Perry, "The CDIC," 49. Perry, "Special Companies: the Hows and Whys of Government-Directed Enterprises," in *Financial Post 500*, 58, 61–62.

[75] J.T. Davis, "Government-Directed Money Flows," 18. Stanley V. Psutka, "The Spatial Behaviour, Structure and Impacts of Labour Unions in Canada," PhD thesis, UT, 1983, chapter 3.

[76] Ibid. "B.C. Debts Downgraded by S and P," *G&M*, 4 Aug. 1983.

[77] Toulin, "City's Role as Financial Hub Enhanced." Catherine Hawkins, "Members Only Please," *G&M*, 14 July 1979. Peter C. Newman, *The Canadian Establishment*, 2 vols. (Toronto, 1975, 1981). Wallace Clement, *Continental Corporate Power: Economic Linkages between Canada and the United States* (Toronto, 1977). Mel Hurtig, "Canadians Finance Own Sellout," *G&M*, 21 Apr. 1983. Rone Tempest, "Pentagon's Stranglehold on U.S.," *Star*, 10 July 1983 (from *Los Angeles Times*).

A Note on Sources

There are few general scholarly works on Toronto, though the number of popular books and articles has mounted in recent years. G.P. de T. Glazebrook's *The Story of Toronto* (Toronto, 1971) is the standard overall history, and E.C. Guillet, *Toronto from Trading Post to Great City* (Toronto, 1934), covers events to the Centennial year. Donald Kerr and Jacob Spelt's *The Changing Face of Toronto—a Study in Urban Georgaphy* (Ottawa, 1965) and Professor Spelt's revision and expansion, *Toronto* (Toronto, 1973), complement the above with stronger spatial and environment concerns. Frederick H. Armstrong's *Toronto, A Place of Meeting: An Illustrated History* (np, 1983) provides a brief historical overview. Edith Firth's *Toronto in Art* (Toronto, 1983) is a masterly presentation of paintings with splendid captions. Richard P. Baine and A. Lynn McMurray's *Toronto: An Urban Study* (Toronto, 1970; revised 1977) offers useful recent maps and photos. Maurice Careless's insightful *Toronto to 1918: An Illustrated History* (Toronto, 1984), the companion to this volume, is the most comprehensive for the period. The City of Toronto's sesquicentennial volume, *Forging a Consensus: Historical Essays on Toronto*, edited by Victor L. Russell (Toronto, 1984), is a collection of recent groundbreaking research by several scholars specializing in Toronto issues. Fifteen years ago hardly anyone considered the pursuit worthwhile.

An extensive bibliography on Toronto is found in Alan F.J. Artibise and Gilbert A. Stelter, *Canada's Urban Past: A Bibliography to 1980 and Guide to Canadian Urban Studies* (Vancouver, 1981). The Toronto Planning and Development Department's *Bibliography of Major Planning Publications, May 1942–August 1981* (Toronto, 1981) is an obvious starting point. Roy Merrens, "A Selected Bibliography on Toronto's Port and Waterfront" (York University, 1983), is one of a number of new specialized bibliographies. A selected bibliography prepared for my students in my course "Historical Toronto" is available on request.

As readers will see in the footnotes, this study has relied heavily on secondary sources. Although general works are few, many recent journal articles, such as those in *Urban History Review*, and many popular works have proved useful. Manuscript primary material in the City of Toronto Archives especially, but also in the Public Archives of Canada and the Ontario Archives have been used, though in the latter much provincial material on municipalities, including Toronto, awaits further research. Reports of municipal departments, of university urban studies groups and of quasi-public bodies have been used extensively, especially for the years since 1946. Newspapers are obviously important sources. The most helpful source of newspaper references for this volume has been research papers written by students at the University of Toronto, and deposited in the university archives. Some have been cited above where secondary sources are not available. York University student papers, placed in its archives, are also valuable. Volumes of earlier newspaper clippings are found in the Municipal Reference Library at City Hall (generally the place to look for books and reports), at the Board of Education and in the Baldwin Room of the Metropolitan Library. Many corporate archives and those of the Harbour Commissioners are available for specialized topics. The Toronto Area Archivists Group's *Guide to Archives in the Toronto Area* (Toronto, 1975) is helpful in pointing one in the right direction. Neighbourhood libraries have in recent years been collecting local material. In some areas of Metro local historical societies have been formed, but a city or Metro-wide historical and geographical society has yet to be created. Finally, in designating buildings, the work of the Toronto Historical Board should not be underestimated in creating interest in Toronto's development.

Index

Adamson, Robert, 90
Adolescent Attendance Act, 21
Alexandra Park, 126, 152
Allan, William, 147, 157
American Federation of Labour (AFL), 31, 92
American Motors, 121
Ames (A.E.) Co, 14, 118
Anglicans, 13, 50, 114, 197
Annex, 51, 65, 143
Annex Ratepayers' Association (ARA), 65, 106, 124
Anti-Communism, 53, 75, 82, 99
Argonauts (football club), 26, 99, 130, 170
Argus Corporation, 120, 122, 183, 184
Arthur, Eric, 65
Art Gallery of Ontario, 168, 170
Arts and Letters Club, 26
Association for a Better City (ABC), 82
Association of Women Electors, 75, 128
Atkinson, Joseph, 33
Atlas Building, 45
Atwood, Margaret, 120
Automobiles, 12, 13, 14, 41, 45, 100, 104, 138, 166
AVRO Arrow (plane), 121

B.C. Forest Products, 120
Baby boom, 94, 113
Ballard, Harold, 170
Balmy Beach Football Club, 26, 68, 99
Bank of Commerce Tower, 45
Banks, 11, 37, 118, 186, 197, 198
Banting, F.G., 25
Barrie, 166
Bassett, John, 120
Bathurst Street, 136, 142
Baton Broadcasting, 176
Beare Road disposal site, 164
Bell, Marilyn, 134
Belmont Corporation, 122, 164
Bennett, R.B., 35, 59, 62
Berton, Pierre, 113, 115, 116, 149
Best, C.H., 23
Bird life, 170
Black, Conrad, 184, 186
Black Creek Drive, 166
Black Creek Pioneer Village, 138
Blacks, 70, 178
Bland, Salem, 53
Blatz, Dr. William, 70
Bloor-Danforth Subway, 166, 199
Bloor Street, 17, 41, 45, 160
Blue Book, 51, 53
Blue Jay baseball team, 170
Bradshaw, Thomas, 19, 21
Bramalea, 136, 166
Brampton, 166 174, 194
Brand, Ford, 84
Brandon Hall Union Group, 125
British, 12, 13, 19, 50, 92, 103, 174, 196
Bronfman, Sam, 122, 186
Brooke, Rupert, 14, 17
Brown, Dr. Alan, 70
Brown, Les, 100
Brittain, Horace, 31
Bruce, Harry, 136
Bruce, Herbert, 59, 65, 67, 74, 124
Bruce Report, 65, 67, 76, 77, 79
Bryce Royal Commission, 186
Buck, Tim, 75
Burrell, Arthur, 77
Bureau of Municipal Research, 21, 25, 35, 51, 65, 102, 108, 126
Burton, Alan C., 118
Burton, Allan G., 145
Burton, Edgar, 126

CBL (radio), 65
CFCA (radio), 31
CFRB (radio), 31, 120
CFTO (television station), 120
CKEY (radio), 120
CN Hotel, 160
CN Tower, 160
CTV network, 120
Cabbagetown, 51, 59, 60, 65, 67, 152
Cadillac-Fairview, 186
Calgary, 186, 198
Callaghan, Morley, *More Joy in Heaven*, 70
Cameron, Robert, 21
Campbell, Albert, 157
Campbell, Margaret, 158
Canada Development Corporation, 187
Canada Development Investment Corporation, 107
Canada Life, 13
  Building, 45
Canada Mortgage and Housing Corporation (CMHC), 158, 183
Canada Packers, 92, 183, 184
Canada Pension Plan, 128
Canada Permanent Building, 45
Canadair, 121
Canada's Wonderland, 168
Canadian Bank of Commerce, 37, 184
Canadian Breweries, 120
Canadian Broadcasting Corporation (CBC), 65, 120
Canadian Congress of Labour, 122
Canadian Cycle and Motor (CCM), 13, 183, 184
Canadian Drama League, 31
Canadian Forum, 56, 57
Canadian General Electric (CGE), 15
Canadian Home Journal, 38
Canadian Imperial Bank of Commerce, 126
Canadian Labour Congress, 122
Canadian Manufacturers' Association, 21
Canadian National Exhibition (CNE), 26, 31, 68, 170
Canadian Union of Public Employees (CUPE), 125
Caribana Festival, 170, 178

Carruthers, Bill, 139
Carver, Humphrey, 90, 106, 122, 134
Casa Loma, 17, 37, 53
Cass, Sam, 158
Cassidy, Harry, 62, 65
Catholic Women's League, 94
Cayuga, 68
Cemp Investment Limited, 122
Central Council of Ratepayers' Associations, 33, 65, 67
Central Mortgage and Housing Corporation (CMHC), 85, 98, 122, 158
Central Tenants Association, 90
Chatelaine, 100
Cherry Beach, 50
Chester Players, 26
Child Welfare Council, 25
Children's Aid Society, 62
Chinatown, 51, 178
Chinese, 114, 178, 196
Chinese Immigration Act, 53, 94
Christie Pits Riot, 70
Church, Tommy, 17, 21, 35
Cinesphere, 168
Cities, American, 11, 12, 43, 90, 126, 142, 166
City Park Apartments, 142
Cityhome, 178
CIVIC (Civic Action), 152
Civic Advisory Council (CAC), 90, 98, 108, 110
Clair, Frank, 99
Cobourg, 166
Cohen, Nathan, 100
College of Education, 128
Colleges of Applied Arts and Technology, 130
Collip, J.B., 23
Colonnade Theatre, 130
Commerce Court, 160
Commission on the Government of the Metropolitan Area of Toronto, 78
Communists, 75, 81, 82, 92, 113
Conacher, Lionel, 26
Conboy, Fred, 82
Confederation Bridge, 43
Confederation of Resident and Ratepayer Associations (CORRA), 152
Conservative Party, 74, 75, 82, 84, 158, 193
Consumerism, 38, 90
Cooke, Jack Kent, 100, 134
Cooperative Commonwealth Federation (CCF), 13, 60, 75, 76, 81, 90, 94, 102, 108, 192
Council of Social Agencies, 25
Council of Women, 21
Courtice, Ada, 31
Cowan, John, 53
Craick, W.A., 50, 51
Crang Estate, 111
Crest Theatre, 100
Cries from the Corridor, 173
Crombie, David, 152
Comming, Lorne, 110
Curtis Report on housing, 96
Customs Building, 76
Cyclone, 50

Dalhousie City, 68
Danforth Avenue, 174
Davidson, Trump, 68, 100
Davis, William ("Bill"), 128, 151, 158, 162, 173
Day, Ralph, 73
de Havilland Aircraft, 121, 184
Dennison, William, 82, 128, 164
Depression, 35, 37, 38, 59, 60, 62, 64
"Design for Development: Toronto-Centred Region," 157, 158, 166
Design for Learning, 130
Diamond, A.E., 122
Diamond, Jack, 162
Dionne Quintuplets, 70
Domestic Service Programme, 94
Dominion Housing Act, 68
Dominion Stores, 120
Domtar, 120
Don Mills, 122, 134, 166
Don Mills Development Corporation, 134
Don Mount, 126, 151
Don Valley Parkway, 138, 143
Douglas Aircraft, 121
Downtown Businessmen's Association, 145
Draper, Denis C., 53, 75
Drea, Frank, 125
Drew, George, 81, 82
Drury, E.C., 33, 35
Duncan, Lewis, 82, 85, 96
Dunlop, W.J., 128, 130

Earle Grey Players, 100
East York, 35, 43, 62, 74, 150, 164, 194
Easter Parade, 26, 100
Eaton Centre, 160
Eaton's, 13, 14, 38, 51, 136
College Street Store, 76
garment factory, 14, 51, 60
Eggleton, Arthur, 152
Employment Service of Canada, 41
Erin Mills, 136, 166
Etobicoke, 35, 113, 138, 194
Etobicoke Creek, 104, 164
Everywoman's World, 39
Exhibition Stadium, 168, 170
Expo 67, 149, 168

Fair Accommodation Act, 94
Fair Employment Practices Act, 94
Fairley, Barker, 57
Family Herald and Weekly Star, 38, 64
Family Service Association of Metropolitan Toronto, 126
Farmers' Advocate, 38
Federal-provincial partnership, 126
Federated Charities, 25
Federation for Community Services, 62
Fellowship of Reconciliation, 75
Ferguson, Howard, 25, 35
Financial Post, 37, 62, 64, 186, 187
First Canadian Place, 160
Flavelle, Joseph, 14, 37
Fleming, R.J., 43
Flemingdon Park, 136
Ford Co., 121
Forest Hill, 35, 43, 53, 70, 194
Fort York, 138
Forty-five foot holding bylaw, 160
Foster, Thomas, 31, 70
Freed, Norman, 82
French-speaking Canadians, 115, 174, 196
Frost, Leslie, 82, 110, 113, 147
Frye, Northrop, 130

Galbraith, J.S., 102
Gardiner, Fred, 82, 84, 108, 110, 112, 118, 122, 126, 142, 145, 147, 149, 168, 193
Gardiner Expressway, 111, 138
Garner, Hugh, 59, 67
George, Henry, 35, 75
Germans, 92, 94, 115, 174, 196
Gerrard Village, 79, 113
Glendon College, 130
Globe, 13, 19, 33, 53, 75, 76, 82
Globe and Mail, 76, 79, 83, 96, 111, 118, 187
Godfrey, Paul, 157

Golden Mile, 111, 134
Goldenberg, H. Carl, 47
Goldman, Emma, 57
Gooderham, George, 65
Goodhead, Norman, 147
Gordon, Walter, 122
Gore and Storrie Report, 108
Gould, Glenn, 134
Government involvement
  Canada, 62, 84, 96, 126, 187
  Ontario, 62, 68, 74, 84, 110, 126, 147, 157, 158, 181, 193
Gray Coach Lines, 43, 50
Greenwin Corporation, 122
Group of Seven, 56, 57, 170
Guild of Civic Art, 17, 26

Hall-Dennis Report, 173
Hamilton, 13, 186
Hamilton, Constance, 31
Hanlan's Point, 17, 126
Happy Gang, 65
Harbour Square, 145
Harbourfront, 168, 170
Harris, Lawren, 57
Hart House, 26, 53, 100
Hastings, Dr. Charles, 19, 21, 23
Hearst, William H., 35
Hees, George, 98
Hemingway, Ernest, 57
Henry, George S., 35, 74, 75
Hepburn, Mitchell, 64, 74, 75, 81, 108, 192
Hester How School, 51
Hewitt, Foster, 26, 99
High Park, 51, 53, 174
Hillier, Bunty, 70
Hiltz, William, 31
Hippies, 178
Hocken, Horatio, 14, 17, 19, 26
"Hockey Night in Canada," 26
Hoffman, Abby, 134
Hogg's Hollow, 35
Highway 400, 111
Holland Marsh, 41
Holy Trinity Church, 14
Home and School Associations, 33
Home Bank failure, 30
Hope Report, 128
Howe, C.D., 84, 85
Hudson's Bay Company, 186, 187
Hughes, J.L., 17
Humber Sewage Disposal Plant, 138
Humber Valley Estates, 33
Hungarians, 114, 116, 196
Hunter, Bernice, 57
Hurricane Hazel, 138
Hurricanes (football club) (RCAF), 99

IBM, 136
Ian and Sylvia, 178
Imlach, Punch, 130
Inco, 184
Independent Committee on Zoning, 78, 102
Industrial Council, 41
Industrial Development Bank, 85
Influenza, 23
Insulin, 23
Interchurch Committee, 94
International Refugee Organization, 92
International Typographical Union, 125
Irish, 14, 50, 196
Italians, 51, 113, 125, 174, 176, 196

Jarvis Street Extension, 77
Jews, 50, 51, 53, 70, 92, 94, 96, 113, 115, 125, 176, 192, 196, 197
Joint Traffic Committee, 45
Jolliffe, E.B., 82
Jones, Murray, 111, 134, 172
Jupiter Theatre, 100

Kennedy, J.A., 152
Kensington Market, 51, 174
Kent Commission, 186
Kidd, Bruce, 134
King, Mackenzie, 25, 32, 59, 62, 76
Kingsway Park, 53
Knox College, 56
Korean War, 85, 90, 92

Ladies' Home Journal, 38
Lakeshore Boulevard, 26, 50
Lamport, Allan, 84, 99, 116
Lawrence Heights, 126
Lawrence Park, 53
Lawson, Matthew, 145
League for Social Reconstruction, 60
Leaside, 33, 38, 70, 194
leMay, Tracy, 67, 68, 76, 77, 102, 111
LePage (A.E.), 162, 186
Leslie Street Extension, 158
Liberal Party, 13, 74, 75, 82, 92, 152, 158, 192
Lightfoot, Gordon, 178
Lionstar Corporation, 164
Liquor Control Board, 99
Little Italy, 51, 115
Little Norway, 84
Living and Learning, 173
Long Branch, 35, 194
Los Angeles, 168
Lumsden, Cliff, 134

McBride, Sam, 23, 31, 33, 37, 45, 53, 74
McCallum, Hiram, 82, 84
McClelland and Stewart, 186
McClure Crescent radioactive site, 168
McCullagh, George, 76
McCutcheon, Wallace M., 120, 126
McDougald, J.A., 120, 183
McGuigan, Cardinal, 99
Macintosh, W.A., 85
Mackenzie-Mann utilities, 41, 45
McLaughlin, Bruce, 186
Maclean-Hunter, 136, 186
Maclean's, 38, 64, 116, 120
McLeod, Alexander, 116
Macleod, J.J.R., 23
McLuhan, Marshall, 90, 130, 149, 168
McMichael Art Collection, 170
Macpherson, Duncan, 116
Magyar Élet (Hungarian Life), 114
Mail and Empire, 19, 33, 45, 53, 76
Malton Airport, 77
Malvern project, 166
Manthorpe, Walter, 147
Manufacturing, 13, 38, 60, 120, 125, 197, 198
Maple Leaf Gardens, 26, 68, 75, 76, 170
Maple Leafs (baseball team), 26, 68
Maple Leafs (hockey team), 26, 68, 130
Mariposa Festival, 170
Market gardening, 41
Markham, 166, 194
Markham Side Road, 104
Marsh Report, 94, 96
Marshall, Lois, 134
Massey, Raymond, 26
Massey Commission on the Arts in Canada, 100, 120
Massey-Ferguson, 120, 183, 184
Massey Foundation, 26

Massey Hall, 170
Massey Harris, 14, 41, 84
Mayfair, 38
Meadowvale, 166
Meals on Wheels, 183
Medical Arts Building, 45
Mendelssohn Choir, 31, 170
Meridian Corporation, 122, 164
Merrill Lynch, 187
Metro Housing Company, 126
Metropolitan and Region Conservation Authority, 138, 157
Metropolitan Area Committee, 74
Metropolitan Toronto, 82, 108, 110, 111
Middleton, Jesse, 50, 79
Millar, Charles Vance, 70
Mimico, 35, 73, 110, 194
Mirvish, Ed, 130
Mississauga, 166, 168, 174
Montreal, 13, 19, 26, 37, 38, 60, 64, 85, 118, 128, 151, 166, 183, 186, 189, 198, 199
Moody's Investment Services, 187
Moore, Dora Mavor, 100
Moore, Henry, 170
Moore Park, 14, 33, 53
Moore Park Avenue, 45
Moriyama, Raymond, 170
Moses, Robert, 145, 147
Moss Park, 126
Municipality of Metropolitan Toronto Act, 110
Mutual Street Arena, 68
Myers, Barton, 162

National Housing Act, 68
National Policy, 13
National Steel Car, 84
"The Neighbourhood Plan of Toronto," 104
Neighbourhood Workers Association (NWA), 25, 62, 126
New Democratic Party (NDP), 13, 125, 149, 152, 193
New Outlook, 53
New Play Society, 100
New Toronto, 38, 194
New York, 11, 43, 90, 142, 198
Newmarket, 138
Niosi, Bert, 68
Nordheimer Ravine Streetcar Route, 77
North Toronto, 14, 33, 194
North York, 108, 113, 138, 164, 194
Northern Miner, 64
Northern Ontario Building, 45
Northumberland, 68

Oakville, 138, 174, 194
O'Keefe Centre, 99, 130, 145
Old Age Pension Act, 96
O'Leary, Grattan, 112, 120
Olympia and York Development Corporation, 186
Ontario
  Politics, 35, 75, 76, 81, 82
Ontario Association of Architects, 102
Ontario College of Art, 170
Ontario Department of Planning and Development, 106
Ontario Energy Corporation, 187
Ontario Housing and Planning Commission, 79
Ontario Housing Corporation, 126, 128, 172, 173
Ontario Hydro, 187
  Building, 45, 160
Ontario Institute for Studies in Education, (OISE), 130
Ontario Municipal Board, 74, 110, 152, 160
Ontario Place, 168, 170
Ontario Railway and Municipal Board, 43
Ontario Rugby Football Union, 99
Ontario Science Centre, 168, 170
Ontario Securities Board, 64
Orange Order, 33, 56, 116
Oriole Park, 81, 106
Oriole Park Neighbourhood Association (OPNA), 81
Oshawa, 138

Park Plaza Building, 45
Parkdale, 51, 142
Parti Québécois, 186
Peanut vendors, 170
Pellatt, Henry, 17, 37
"People or Planes," 166
Phillips, Nathan, 56, 84, 116, 145, 147
Phillips, W.E., 120
Pickering, 166, 194
Planning Act, 106
Players Club, 26
Plumptre, A.F.W., 74, 77
Plumptre, Adelaide, 73
Poor Alex Theatre, 130
Port Hope, 166
Portuguese, 174
Power Corporation, 120
Presbyterians, 13, 50, 114, 197
Prince Edward Viaduct, 41

Quebec City, 187
Quebec-Gothic Corporation, 164
Queen Elizabeth Docks, 145
Queensway, 138

Railways, 13, 50, 145
Redevelopment Advisory Council (RAC), 145
Redpath Sugar Refinery, 145
Regent Park, 51, 82, 126
  Rental housing project, 96, 98
Rent control, 173
Research Enterprises, 84, 85
Revell, Viljo, 143
Rexdale, 111
Riverdale Court, 25
Robarts, John, 147, 157
Robbins, William, 74
Robertson, John Ross, 31, 84
Rochdale College, 178, 183
Roe (A.V.), 85, 111, 121
Roebuck, Arthur, 76
Rogers, Ted, 31
Roman Catholics, 23, 37, 50, 94, 114, 136, 174, 197
Rose, Albert, 108, 126
Rosedale, 33, 65, 77
Rosenfeld, Bobbie, 26
Ross, George, 19, 25, 37, 41, 50
Rotary Club, 25
Roy Thomson Hall, 160, 168, 170
Royal Alexandra Theatre, 130
Royal Bank, 13, 14, 186
Royal Commission on Price Spreads, 60
Royal Ontario Museum, 170
Royal Securities, 187
Royal Winter Fair, 26, 170
Royal York Hotel, 45, 76, 125, 145
Ryan, Red, 70
Ryerson Polytechnic Institute, 130
Ryerson Press, 56

St. Christopher Settlement Houses, 94
St. Clair Avenue, 53
St. James Town, 142, 151, 164
St.. Lawrence Corporation, 120

St. Lawrence project, 162
Salsberg, Joseph, 74, 82
Saltzman, Percy, 149
San Francisco, 43
Sanderson, M.A., 82
Saturday Night, 25, 37, 38, 53
Saunders, Leslie, 82, 96, 116
Saunders, Robert, 152
Scarborough, 108, 113, 138, 168, 194
Scarborough Beach Park, 17, 26
Scarborough Expressway, 158
Scouting, 26
Sears, 187
Seaton, 166
Seeley, John, 90
Sewell, John, 151, 152
Shakespeare Society of Toronto, 26
Sharp, Mitchell, 122
Shields, T.T., 57
Shiner, Esther, 158
Shopping centres, 136
Shulman, Morton, 152
Simpson, James ("Jimmie"), 17, 33, 38, 51, 74
Simpson's, 13, 14, 38, 136, 187
Sims, Charles, 82
Sinclair, Lister, 90
Small, Ethel, 31
Smith, Robert Home, 33, 136
Smith, Stewart, 82
Smythe, Conn, 26, 99
Social Gospel, 14, 51, 57
Sommerville, David, 147
Southam newspaper chain, 118, 186
Spadina Avenue, 51
Spadina Expressway, 136, 142, 151, 158, 166
Spadina Heights, 35
Spring Thaw, 100
Spruce Court, 25
Sputnik, 114
Standard and Poor, 157
Star, 21, 25, 31, 33, 43, 53, 70, 74, 82, 96, 100, 118, 172, 187
Star Building, 45, 160
Star Weekly, 45, 51, 64, 120
Sterling Tower Building, 45
Stewart, William, 67, 74
Student Christian Movement, 56
Sudbury, 13
Sun, 174, 187
Sun Life, 37, 64, 160, 186
Suncor, 187
Sunday observance, 17, 192
Sunnyside, 26, 100
Swansea, 35, 194
Swift's Canadian, 92, 184

Taylor, E.P., 120, 122, 134
Telegram, 21, 33, 45, 50, 53, 56, 70, 82, 96, 116, 118, 120, 125, 126
Temple, Bill, 82
Theatre, 26, 31, 100, 130, 170
Theatre-in-the-Dell, 130
"This Hour has Seven Days," 149
Thomson newspaper chain, 118, 186
Tornado, 50
Toronto
- airports, 77
- American influence, 19, 25, 26, 35, 56, 176
- annexation, 17, 35, 38, 74
- apartments, 199
- arts, 11, 170
- beach pollution, 168
- Board of Control, 17, 21, 65, 67, 79, 96
- Board of Education, 17, 21, 130, 147, 157
- Board of Trade, 21, 62, 102, 193
- building, 12, 41, 42, 45, 50, 51, 111, 192, 197, 198
- buildings and landmarks, 12, 13, 45, 160
- Central Library Theatre, 130
- City Hall, 14, 145
- Civic Unemployment Relief, 60
- convention centre, 160
- cultural life, 12, 26, 31, 116, 170, 192
- Department of Housing, 172
- Department of Planning, 172
- domed stadium, 158
- education, 11, 12, 19, 21, 23, 26, 33, 70, 108, 110, 111, 128, 130, 134, 136, 157, 168, 173
- employment, 41, 183, 184, 197
- finances, 17, 19, 21, 23, 31, 35, 38, 147, 199
- financial base, 11, 13, 38, 85, 118, 183, 187, 193
- Harbour Commissioners, 14, 31, 60
- Health Department, 23
- housing, 12, 14, 17, 19, 25, 59, 60, 65, 67, 68, 90, 104, 105, 106, 111, 122, 125, 128, 142, 162, 164, 168, 170, 172, 173, 186, 192, 199
- immigration, 14, 19, 70, 92, 94, 113, 114, 196
- industries, 14, 38, 60, 197, 198
- Labour Council, 122, 186
- Metropolitan Zoo, 168, 170

Toronto (continued)
- multiculturalism, 11, 12, 14, 50, 94, 96, 174
- New City Hall, 143, 145
- newspapers, 33. *See also* names of individual papers
- occupations, 13, 38, 60, 85, 98, 125, 183, 197
- Parks Commission, 19
- Planetarium, 168
- planning and development, 41, 79, 81, 102, 104, 106, 108, 110, 111, 135, 138, 140, 151, 152, 157, 167, 172, 192
- Planning Board, 104, 126, 172
- Police Commission, 75
- politics and government, 12, 31, 74, 75
- population, 11, 12, 14, 50, 70, 92, 94, 104, 113, 164, 176-77, 189, 194-97,
- poverty, 11, 23, 51, 68, 128, 172
- public housing, 96, 98, 152, 173, 192
- Public Welfare Department, 60, 62
- regional centre, 13, 64
- religious composition and differences, 13, 17, 50, 98, 197
- renewal, 11
- expressways, 102, 138
- schools, 51, 195
- Separate School Board, 108
- separate schools, 23, 108, 136, 195
- social conditions, 11, 12, 26, 38, 59, 60, 62, 98, 116
- Social Planning Council (SPC), 12, 25, 114, 115, 126, 157, 172
- Social Service Commission, 17, 23
- social services, 14, 17, 19, 23, 25, 26, 86, 93, 125, 128, 147, 168, 172-174, 184
- sporting life, 26, 68, 99, 100, 130, 134, 170, 192
- streetcars, 11, 41, 43, 45, 77, 166, 199
- subways, 77, 81, 82, 104, 111, 134, 138, 142, 199
- taxation, 17, 21, 38, 106, 154
- Tourist and Convention Bureau, 38
- Trades and Labour Council, 33, 53, 64, 82
- transportation and traffic, 12, 13, 19, 41, 77, 142, 166, 168, 192, 197
- wards, 17, 35, 152, 154
- Welfare Council, 62, 96, 115
- Welfare Department, 23
- Works Commission, 19
- World War 1, 13
- World War II, 84, 85
- xenophobia, 53, 56, 57, 92, 113

Toronto and Suburban Planning Board, 106, 108

Toronto and York Planning Board, 108
Toronto and York Roads Commission, 108
Toronto Area Operating Authority, 168
Toronto Children's Players, 31, 100
Toronto Citizens' Committee, 99
Toronto Civic Advisory Council, 104
Toronto-Dominion Centre, 145, 186
"Toronto Gives," 25
Toronto Housing Association, 96
Toronto Housing Authority, 96
Toronto Housing Commission, 25
Toronto Hydro, 31, 45
Toronto Industrial Commission, 60
Toronto Island, 77, 164
Toronto Railway Company, 14, 41
Toronto Reconstruction Council, 85, 98, 104, 108
Toronto Stock Exchange, 37, 198
Toronto Symphony, 170
Toronto Transportation (Transit) Commission (TTC), 14, 31, 41, 43, 100, 106, 110, 142, 157, 172, 199
Town, Harold, 134
Trades and Labour Congress, 64, 122
Trans-Canada Airlines, 77
Trefann Court, 151, 162
Trinity College, 35
Trizec Corporation, 122, 136
Trudeau, Pierre, 151, 174

Ukrainians, 94, 114, 115, 196, 197,
Union Station, 50, 160
Unions, 62, 64, 92, 122, 125, 189
United Church, 50, 56, 99, 114, 136, 197
United Farmers of Ontario, 33, 35
United Way, 126
United Women Voters, 21, 23
University Alumnae, 31, 100, 160
University Avenue, 45, 160
University of Toronto, 56, 75, 94, 130, 170
Urban Development Institute, 160
Urwick, E.J., 68

Vancouver, 118, 186, 198
Varley, Fred, 57
Victoria College, 56
Victorian Order of Nurses, 62
Victory Aircraft, 84, 85
Viet Nam war, 151, 178
Vizinczey, Stephen, 116

Wadsworth, William, 68
Wages, 13, 25, 38, 60, 85
The Ward, 45, 51, 126
Wartime Prices and Trade Board, 90
Waste disposal, 168
Waterfront Transit line, 168
Watkins, Mel, 122
Welland Canal, 64
Wemp, Bert, 45, 74, 76
West Toronto, 99
Weston, 38, 194
Whitney Block, 45
Wickett, Morley, 35
Wilson, Norman, 77
Windlass Corporation, 164
Wolter, Hugo, 98, 99
Women
  work force, 38, 41, 85, 197
  politics, 31, 192
Women's suffrage, 17, 31
Wood, Gundy & Co., 118
Workers' Experimental Theatre, 74
World, 33
World Bank, 187
Wychwood District, 53

YMCA, 26, 164
YWCA, 26, 94
Yonge Street, 35, 50, 142
Yonge Subway, 142
York (borough, city), 157, 164, 194
York Township, 35, 43, 74
York University, 130
Yorkdale Shopping Centre, 134, 136
Yorkville, 77, 116, 178